GV
863
.A1
F53
2010

Final innings.

$29.95

DATE			

BAKER & TAYLOR

Final Innings

A DOCUMENTARY HISTORY

OF BASEBALL, 1972–2008

COMPILED AND EDITED

BY DEAN A. SULLIVAN

UNIVERSITY OF NEBRASKA PRESS

LINCOLN AND LONDON

Library of Congress
Cataloging-in-Publication Data
Final innings : a documentary history of
baseball, 1972–2008 / compiled and edited by
Dean A. Sullivan.
    p. cm.
Includes bibliographical references and index.
ISBN 978-0-8032-5965-2 (pbk. : alk. paper)
1. Baseball—United States—History—20th
century—Sources. 2. Baseball—United
States—History—21st century—Sources.
I. Sullivan, Dean A., 1963–
GV863.A1F53   2010
796.3570973'09045—dc22
2009047698

Set in Minion by Kim Essman.

Contents

CHAPTER 5. ROSE, GIAMATTI, AND COLLUSION

CHAPTER 6. SELIG, FEHR, AND THE STRIKE

CHAPTER 7. BASEBALL STARTS TO HEAL

CHAPTER 8. BASEBALL ENTERS THE TWENTY-FIRST CENTURY

Illustrations

Preface

Since completing my previous book, *Late Innings: A Documentary History of Baseball, 1945–1972* (2002), it has become easier than ever to research and collect baseball documents, thanks to the Internet. Every newspaper has its own Web site, where recent articles (and occasionally primary-source documents) can readily be downloaded. Thanks to my membership in the Society for American Baseball Research (SABR), I have access to countless older articles published in prominent newspapers like the *New York Times*, *Los Angeles Times*, *Chicago Tribune*, and *Washington Post*. I can visit a plethora of Web sites run by major entities like ESPN, the U.S. Congress, or dedicated individuals, to obtain or verify information.

However, I collected the vast majority of the documents in *Final Innings* the old-fashioned way—by visiting research libraries and archives, scanning microfilm, reading books, and donning gloves to handle original documents. The latter task was made easier by the helpful staffs administering the Harold and Dorothy Seymour Papers at Cornell University; the Peter Seitz Papers at the Kheel Center, Martin P. Catherwood Library, Cornell University; and the Marvin Miller Papers at the Robert F. Wagner Labor Archives, Tamiment Library, New York University. In addition, the staff of the National Baseball Hall of Fame Library was extremely patient with my numerous requests for files. I also owe several individuals special thanks for helping me to complete this book. The late Doug Pappas not only gave me permission to use his powerful editorial on baseball's decision to contract two teams following the 2001 season, but also inspired me through his vast knowledge of the business of baseball and the invaluable Web site he created to disseminate his research on this subject, and through his generosity of spirit. Bruce Markusen helped me identify documents on the Oakland A's of the 1970s. Alan Schwarz, a prominent writer for *Baseball America* and the *New York Times*, took the time to correct several mistakes and offer me much-needed encouragement. Of course my greatest debt is to my family, which has never lost faith that I would complete this book, even when I thought that day would never come. My greatest regret is that my father, Donald Sullivan, did not survive to see the publication of this book.

Introduction

A recurrent theme in the recent history of major league baseball is the tendency of its leaders to proclaim the sport's doom if circumstances did not change, or were changed in a different manner than they desired. The emergence of Marvin Miller and his Major League Baseball Players Association (MLBPA) as a formidable opponent generated such fear and loathing among baseball owners that statements declaring "the end of baseball as we knew it" (uttered in 1967 by Paul Richards upon the signing of the first Basic Agreement with the MLBPA) became commonplace. The perpetual state of tension between the union and both the owners and their commissioner, though occasionally interrupted by triumphal accomplishments on the field, has cast a shadow over baseball for most of the past three decades.

The tension reached a high in the spring of 1972, when Miller led the players on their first strike, over a dispute regarding pension contributions by the owners. The owners, establishing a pattern they repeated for decades thereafter, refused to negotiate initially, only to settle for terms available to them earlier. They received a victory of sorts when the Supreme Court preserved the reserve clause by ruling against Curt Flood, but the victory proved to be short-lived, and Flood came to be regarded as an inspirational figure by the players.

Another star, Roberto Clemente, demonstrated his courage in a more tragic fashion. Following the 1972 season, which he concluded by slashing his 3,000th hit, Clemente insisted on accompanying a plane overstuffed with relief supplies for victims of a devastating earthquake in Nicaragua. The plane crashed into the ocean immediately after takeoff, killing all aboard. Clemente was swiftly enshrined in the Baseball Hall of Fame—becoming only the second player for whom the five-year waiting period was waived. More importantly, Clemente was recognized by white Americans as an icon for the rapidly growing number of Hispanic players.

In the early 1970s baseball was emerging from the offensive depression of the previous decade, but not quickly enough. Runs, home runs, and batting averages were still below historic norms, and attendance levels remained static—even World Series games often did not sell out. The greatest batting stars of the era, including Clemente, Willie Mays, Hank Aaron, and Frank Robinson, all of whom started their careers in the 1950s, were clearly past their primes. The institution of the designated hitter rule in 1973 by the American League was designed to increase attendance both by stimulating offense and by offering aging but popular veterans the opportunity to extend their careers. Aaron concluded his career as a DH, but achieved his greatest accomplishment by passing Babe Ruth's career home run record in 1974 while manning left field. The implementation of the DH did improve the AL offensively, but it had at best a negligible impact on attendance. Robinson achieved another important first the following season by being hired as the first black manager in major league history by the Cleveland Indians.

The stars who emerged in the 1960s, such as Pete Rose and Carl Yastrzemski, had strong local appeal but did not yet have the same national status as their predecessors. Both men won three batting titles, but they achieved their greatest audience while opposing each other in the 1975 World Series, considered by many to be among the most exciting ever. Rose was the lead-off man for the Cincinnati Reds, known as the "Big Red Machine," who along with the Oakland A's (winners of three consecutive World Series) were the dominant teams of the era. Oakland was led by pitcher Jim "Catfish" Hunter and "superduperstar" Reggie Jackson, each of whom would play even greater roles in baseball history as the decade progressed.

The most visible representative of the A's, even aside from Jackson and Hunter, was flamboyant owner Charlie Finley, who made his fortune in the insurance industry. When he realized that Hunter's contract required him to pay Hunter $50,000 in deferred compensation throughout the 1974 season into an annuity specified by Hunter, which Finley could not deduct, he refused to make the payments. Hunter objected, eventually filing a grievance that, under the terms of the Basic Agreement, was to be settled by an impartial arbitrator. When Peter Seitz announced that as a result of the breach of contract Hunter was a free agent, the wall separating players from learning their true worth on the open market was forever shattered.

Almost exactly one year later Seitz gave the same opportunity to all other players who allowed their contracts to expire. Previously, the owners interpreted the reserve clause in the standard player contract as giving them the right to indefinitely renew the contract, rather than just once, which effectively bound players to their teams for as long as the teams desired. When pitchers Andy Messersmith and Dave McNally played the entire 1975 seasons under renewed 1974 contracts and claimed free-agent status, Seitz granted it—only after warning owners of his impending decision and urging them to come to an agreement with the MLBPA.

Predictably, many owners (and some columnists, such as Dick Young, who called Seitz a "terrorist") expressed their belief that baseball would be destroyed, but younger owners like George Steinbrenner and Ted Turner eagerly took advantage of the new landscape to reconfigure their teams. Among Steinbrenner's acquisitions were Hunter and Jackson, who together helped the New York Yankees stage a brief revival of their former greatness by making the World Series four times between 1976 and 1981, winning twice. During that period the average salary increased from $51,501 in 1976 to $185,651 in 1981, an improvement of nearly 30 percent per season, with no end in sight.

Many of the first generation of free agents were mediocre players who took advantage of desperate owners and their statistical ignorance to earn undeservedly large contracts. Some owners responded by abstaining from the free-agent market;

others, like Finley, responded by attempting to sell his best players for millions of dollars so he could reinvest the profits in younger, cheaper players. Although Finley, for all his eccentricities, clearly had an eye for talent, Commissioner Bowie Kuhn used his "best interests of baseball" power and invalidated the sales on the basis that such actions could destroy the competitive balance of baseball. Finley filed a federal lawsuit against Kuhn, whose victory validated his activist philosophy.

Finley, though hated by the other owners, was not the only owner opposed to Kuhn. In the aftermath of the 1976 Messersmith decision, the owners locked the players out of spring training, only to have Kuhn unilaterally reopen the camps. The commissioner saw himself as an impartial chief executive empowered to balance the needs of the players and the owners, which made him suspect in the eyes of those who elected him into office. Marvin Miller and the MLBPA never had any illusions that Kuhn was not acting on behalf of the owners, even if Kuhn often did.

In the midst of these controversies, the union and the owners agreed on a new Basic Agreement, which included a provision allowing a player free agency after he had six years of major league service, with provisions for compensation to teams losing free agents through additional picks in the amateur draft. Hidden in the legalese was a clause added at the insistence of the owners forbidding collusive action on the part of both players and owners. Baseball officials had in mind the 1966 dual holdout staged by Dodgers stars Sandy Koufax and Don Drysdale. They did not envision a scenario in which they would not only commit acts of collusion against players but also be caught and punished for their arrogance.

Baseball flourished on the field during the four years of peace ensured by the signing of the Basic Agreement. The "Big Red Machine" dismantled many of its key components but remained a top-level team. Cincinnati was replaced as baseball's dominant franchise by the resurgent New York Yankees, who rebounded from being swept by the Reds in the 1976 World Series to winning the next two over their old foes, the Los Angeles Dodgers. The Bronx Bombers were led by volatile manager Billy Martin and Reggie Jackson, whose five-home-run performance in the 1977 Series ensured his reputation as "Mr. October." New York won the 1978 pennant only after an epic comeback during the season over the Boston Red Sox, who not only blew a fourteen-game lead but also lost the one-game playoff in hallowed Fenway Park, in part by surrendering a home run to weak-hitting Bucky Dent. The other highlight of this season was Pete Rose's pursuit of baseball's foremost single-season record, Joe DiMaggio's fifty-six-game consecutive hitting streak. Rose, even in the midst of a mediocre .302 season, flourished in the intense media spotlight and tied the NL record with a forty-four-game streak.

Another streak unprecedented in major league history also commenced in 1978. Starting with the Yankees' second straight Series triumph, the next fourteen Series featured fourteen different champions. Only the Dodgers (who won in 1981 and 1988) and the Minnesota Twins (1987 and 1991) won multiple Series during this period. Most of the Series winners represented smaller market cities like Kansas City, Pittsburgh, and Baltimore. Baseball officials and fans alike became accustomed to this a historical pattern and came to expect that such competitive balance would remain the norm.

Whatever peaceful feelings might have accrued during the term of the Basic Agreement quickly dissipated in 1980, when the owners' Player Relations Committee (PRC) and the union failed to reach a new agreement after the previous one expired at the end of 1979. The feelings between the groups' respective leaders, Ray Grebey and Marvin Miller, were especially bitter. Throughout the spring both sides swapped accusations, threats, and misinformation through the press. The MLBPA selected a strike date of May 23 but at the last minute came to terms with the owners. The key issue in dispute, compensation for the loss of free agents, was postponed for future study.

To no one's surprise, the issue was not resolved during the off-season. When the owners announced the unilateral imposition of a system of compensation, the players set a new strike date, and in June they initiated the longest strike in baseball history. Marvin Miller initially announced that he would sit out the negotiations to avoid the problems he experienced with Grebey the previous year, but in time the owners demoted Grebey and negotiated a truce with the union. A consequence of the strike was the imposition of a controversial split-season format, in which the year was divided into prestrike and poststrike halves, with the divisional winners of each half to meet in a playoff series prior to the League Championship Series. The two NL teams with the best overall records, the Cincinnati Reds and the St. Louis Cardinals, both missed the postseason because their wins were not optimally distributed.

The settlement of the latest labor dispute ended the last major confrontation between Miller and Bowie Kuhn, whose careers would soon end. Miller voluntarily stepped down, but when replacement Ken Moffett proved inadequate to the task, Miller (who was instrumental in Moffett's removal) filled in until Donald Fehr was elected the new MLBPA executive director in 1983. Kuhn's departure resulted from the owners' dissatisfaction with his meddling in the name of "the best interests of baseball," particularly during labor negotiations. The new commissioner, Peter Ueberroth, demonstrated his authority early on by reinstating Willie Mays and Mickey Mantle, who had been barred from representing major league teams due to their employment by casinos, and by pressuring the Chicago Cubs to become the final team to install lights and play night games. Unfortunately for baseball, Ueberroth's legacy will forever be the leading role he played in instructing the owners to collude against giving free agents large salaries. In the late 1980s arbitrators found the owners guilty in three collusion cases, costing them nearly $300 million in fines and even further embittering the players.

The mid-1980s featured some of the most exciting postseason action in baseball history. The 1986 LCS in each league was especially dramatic. The California Angels were one pitch away from clinching their first pennant, but Dave Henderson's ninth-inning home run sent the sixth game into extra innings, when the Boston Red Sox triumphed, propelling them to win the following day and return to the

World Series. The NLCS also hinged on the sixth game. The New York Mets, desperate to avoid facing invincible Houston Astros ace Mike Scott in a seventh game, rallied in the ninth inning to tie the game and survived a furious rally to take the pennant-clinching game in sixteen thrilling innings. The World Series was nearly as exciting, but it is remembered more for a stunning error by Red Sox first baseman Bill Buckner, the last of a series of misplays in the tenth inning of Game 6 that allowed the Mets to overcome what appeared to be a safe lead and the first Series win for Boston since 1918.

In addition to the three collusion decisions, baseball also suffered from several other embarrassing episodes. In April 1987 Dodgers executive Al Campanis, during a live nationally televised interview intended to commemorate the fortieth anniversary of Jackie Robinson's major league debut, declared that African Americans were severely underrepresented in baseball's executive ranks because they "lacked the necessities" to advance in baseball's hierarchy. Campanis was fired and Commissioner Ueberroth vowed to improve minority hiring, but progress was slow at best.

In the late 1980s Pete Rose, the manager of the Cincinnati Reds, was still basking in the glory of breaking the career hits record of Ty Cobb in 1985. When new commissioner A. Bartlett Giamatti announced that baseball was investigating charges that Rose had violated baseball's cardinal rule of betting on baseball, including on his own team, Rose and his legions of fans (including local judges and politicians, who temporarily derailed the investigation) vociferously declared his innocence. Even after John Dowd, Giamatti's chief investigator, released his findings and Rose subsequently accepted a lifetime ban from baseball, Rose refused to admit his guilt. The pressure of the investigation weighed heavily on Giamatti, who died of a heart attack only days after his ruling was announced.

Giamatti's replacement and close friend, Fay Vincent, was tested almost immediately, as a devastating earthquake struck the San Francisco Bay area during the 1989 World Series between the Giants and the Oakland Athletics. Vincent was praised for his actions, but he did not have the opportunity to rest on his laurels. The following year Vincent presided over the suspension of Yankees owner George Steinbrenner, whose participation in a bizarre relationship with con artist Howard Spira to discredit Yankees outfielder Dave Winfield tarnished baseball further. When Vincent later acted under the "best interests" clause to compel the NL to realign, the owners rebelled and forced him from office in what was termed a "resignation." Milwaukee Brewers owner and longtime power broker Bud Selig was named acting commissioner while a search for a permanent commissioner was initiated.

The promotion of Selig—even on a temporary basis—signaled a shift in the public perception of the commissioner's office. Traditionally, the commissioner positioned himself as an intermediary between the fans and the owners, although the MLBPA always saw the commissioner as a representative of the owners. With Selig, still the owner of the Brewers, in charge of baseball as another labor showdown approached, the tension level was especially high.

When owners voted in January 1992—just four months after the owners revolted against Vincent—to unilaterally reopen negotiations for a new Basic Agreement, few were surprised. Two years later the owners and Selig increased the stakes further by agreeing (after years of contention between owners) on a revenue-sharing plan and radically redefining the powers of the commissioner's office in a manner nearly all critics felt significantly weakened the position. Selig attempted to defend baseball's actions before a Senate committee without success. He was even less persuasive when, on September 12, Selig canceled the remainder of the season, including the World Series, after the players' strike had been in effect for a month. Although the players had timed their strike to allow for this possibility, the open hostility and inflexibility of the owners caused public opinion to blame Selig and the owners for this unprecedented calamity. Even the fortuitous airing of Ken Burns's eighteen-hour documentary *Baseball* just days after Selig's announcement did not salve the wounds of the nation's baseball fans.

The 1994 season had featured a number of players seemingly en route to record seasons, including Tony Gwynn's quest to hit .400 and Matt Williams's assault on Roger Maris's home run mark of 61. In addition, the Montreal Expos had the best record in the major leagues and were seeking the first pennant in the history of the franchise. None of these dreams were fulfilled.

Prospects for a settlement in the off-season seemed dim after President Bill Clinton's mandate to reach an agreement by February 6, 1995, was not achieved. The owners announced that they would unilaterally reinstate the previous agreement and hire replacement players to fill their rosters, even after the owners of the Baltimore Orioles (Peter Angelos, a noted labor lawyer) and the Toronto Blue Jays refused to comply. On March 27 the MLBPA filed an unfair labor practices complaint with the National Labor Relations Board. Four days later the strike was ended when federal judge Sonia Sotomayor issued a preliminary injunction against the owners, which was upheld on appeal. The 1995 season started on April 25 and was shortened to 144 games. A new Basic Agreement was not signed until 1996.

During the strike many angry fans declared they had finally had enough and would not return to the ballparks, and reduced attendance figures reflected their resolve. In search of saviors, baseball first claimed Cal Ripken Jr., who in 1995 finally surpassed Lou Gehrig's 2,130 consecutive-games-played streak, as the player who would revive baseball's popularity. Three years later Mark McGwire and Sammy Sosa staged a thrilling race to surpass Maris, enthralling the nation and generating a number of books by veteran baseball writers who declared baseball healed. Also contributing to the perceived revival of baseball in 1998 were memorable performances by rookies Kerry Wood and Cuban refugee Orlando "El Duque" Hernandez, and Hernandez's New York Yankees, who won an incredible 114 games in the regular season and easily won their second World Series in three years, to be followed by two more successive titles.

Hernandez's triumphant arrival in the majors (which mirrored the previous success of his half brother, Livan, who led the Florida Marlins to a stunning victory in the 1997 Series) was merely the latest indication of the surge in the significance of foreign talent in baseball. Baseball cleverly tried to capitalize on the importance of the Hispanic market by arranging for the Baltimore Orioles to play a Cuban All-Star team in a home-and-away series in 1999. When the Orioles, one of the better major league teams, had trouble splitting the series, few were surprised. The following year, when eleven Hispanic players and many coaches and other baseball personnel boycotted a game to protest the actions of the federal government in forcibly seizing Cuban child Elian Gonzalez to return him to his father in Cuba, they were not punished. Baseball has stepped up its efforts to promote the game across the globe, even playing regular-season games in Mexico, Puerto Rico, and Japan (which contributed its own superstar, Ichiro Suzuki, to the majors in 2001). The only unfortunate consequence was that Americans demonstrated their lack of world dominance by failing to win the Olympic gold medal in 2004 or the inaugural World Baseball Classic two years later.

As baseball entered the twenty-first century, it still could not help but shoot itself in the foot. Commissioner Selig appointed a "blue-ribbon commission," comprised solely of prominent figures with ties to ownership, which to no one's surprise concluded that baseball suffered from competitive imbalance that threatened to destroy baseball and could only be cured by imposing severe revenue-sharing measures and salary caps, all measures rejected previously by the union. The commission members ignored baseball history, which was replete with examples of teams that remained dominant for decades, and of teams with few resources that succeeded through intelligent management and cost-effective talent acquisition.

This debate was overshadowed by the horrors of the September 11, 2001, terrorist attacks, which interrupted the season for one week. When the games resumed, fans were thrilled to see the New York teams play well before their shell-shocked fans. The Mets fell short of the playoffs, but the Yankees advanced to their fourth consecutive World Series, thanks in large part to an incredible play by shortstop Derek Jeter in the ALDS. They lost to the Arizona Diamondbacks, led by pitchers Randy Johnson and Curt Schilling, in seven compelling games, but still succeeded in helping to uplift a nation in need of relief.

Just days after the Series's conclusion, Selig announced that due to problems detailed in the blue-ribbon report, two teams would be contracted. Fans of the Florida Marlins and Minnesota Twins soon learned that their clubs, if baseball had its way, had played their last games. Somehow Selig and the owners failed to anticipate the furious reaction of appalled baseball fans across the nation. Once again sportswriters reveled in baseball's astonishing capacity for self-destruction. They were given additional ammunition with the postseason success of small-market teams like the Marlins (who won the 2003 World Series over the Yankees), Twins, and Athletics (whose management strategies were celebrated in a best-selling book, *Moneyball*). However, in the new Basic Agreement signed soon afterward, baseball maintained the right to contract teams at the conclusion of the 2006 season.

The early 2000s were characterized by the triumph of not only small-market clubs but also long-suffering franchises. Clubs like the Arizona Diamondbacks and the Anaheim Angels (later renamed the Los Angeles Angels of Anaheim in a unique marketing strategy) won their first World Series, and the Boston Red Sox and Chicago White Sox won their first Series since World War I. Boston's triumph in 2004 was particularly dramatic, not only because they became the first club in baseball history to rebound from a three-games-to-none deficit in a playoff series, but because they did it against their detested rivals, the Yankees. The previous season the Chicago Cubs seemed certain of reaching their first Series since 1945, but a sixth-game NLCS collapse blamed unfairly on an overzealous fan led to their crushing defeat. Not all curses were overcome in baseball, as would soon become apparent.

Since at least the 1970 publication of Jim Bouton's *Ball Four*, baseball fans had been aware that players had consumed performance-enhancing drugs (PEDs) of various kinds. Neither baseball officials nor players had any serious interest in regulating or outlawing these drugs. Fans were distracted by several cocaine scandals in the 1980s and 1990s involving noted players like Keith Hernandez, Willie Wilson, and Steve Howe, who was suspended numerous times but was always reinstated after protests by MLBPA officials. When extraordinarily muscled stars such as Jose Canseco, Mark McGwire, Sammy Sosa, and Barry Bonds started hitting home runs in record-setting fashion, fans and owners alike were thrilled.

Not until *San Francisco Chronicle* reporters Lance Williams and Mark Fainaru-Wada started reporting on a federal investigation on the production and sale of custom-made steroids to elite athletes at a small company called BALCO did outrage over PEDs in baseball emerge. Their 2005 book *Game of Shadows* convincingly argued that Bonds, one of the greatest players of all time, had knowingly used various substances, including human growth hormone and concoctions known as "the cream" and "the clear," to increase his muscle mass and endurance and thereby lift his performance to unprecedented levels. The U.S. Congress reacted by holding nationally televised hearings that excluded Bonds but exposed Sosa and especially McGwire as pathetic figures unable or unwilling to admit their usage of PEDs. Star first baseman Rafael Palmeiro, who would soon hit his 500th home run, emerged from the hearings as a hero for his emphatic denial that he had ever taken steroids, but was soon revealed as a liar and hypocrite when his positive test result for a steroid was revealed.

After the congressional hearings, the recent accomplishments of many of the game's stars were assumed to be tainted. Certain players whose bodies had not changed appreciably over their careers (and who were well-liked by the media) such as Ken Griffey Jr., Jeff Bagwell, and more recent stars such as David Ortiz and Ryan Howard, were usually given a pass by the media, but many others were considered guilty simply by virtue of having performed during the "steroid era." The existence of a testing program—agreed to by the union only after intense pressure from the owners, baseball fans, and especially Congress—has by no means ended the usage of PEDs, particularly those currently undetectable by urine tests. A public conditioned by baseball administrators to believe the worst about their sport has become skeptical about the achievements of the game's greatest players.

Final Innings

1

The Players Discover Their Freedom

In the early 1970s baseball was still recovering from the doldrums of the previous decade. Attendance continued to lag, which spurred the owners to start playing World Series games at night and to introduce the designated hitter—the most fundamental change in baseball rules in the twentieth century. Both innovations proved popular with fans, but empty seats remained, even with great teams like the Cincinnati Reds and the outrageous Oakland A's making regular appearances in the postseason. The owners' confidence was further undermined by the continuing gains of the MLBPA—which to its own surprise held firm during its first strike and gained the right to salary arbitration—and by the antics of owners like Charlie Finley and new Yankees owner George Steinbrenner.

Baseball did enjoy several historic moments, most notably Hank Aaron's triumphant assault on the home run record of Babe Ruth and the signing of the first African American manager, Frank Robinson, by the Cleveland Indians. Both events, unfortunately, were marred by racist hate mail reflecting the relative lack of progress of race relations in the immediate aftermath of the civil rights era. This attitude was revealed in a different way after the tragic death of Roberto Clemente in a plane crash following the 1972 season, which he concluded by making his 3,000th hit. Only then did many fans realize the extent to which he was idolized by Hispanics throughout the Americas, and how much Clemente resented and fought against the treatment he and other Latino players routinely received.

Marvin Miller Comments on Strike (1972)

SOURCE: Speech at Harvard University, April 27, 1972, Marvin Miller Papers, Series II, Box 6, Folder 6, Robert F. Wagner Labor Archives, Tamiment Library

The first organized players' strike in American sports history (except for a one-day strike by the Detroit Tigers in 1912) was initiated on April Fool's Day, a date that seems appropriate given the trivial issues responsible for the conflict between the Player Relations Committee (PRC) and the Major League Baseball Players Association (MLBPA). Union executive director Marvin Miller had requested that baseball owners increase contributions to the players' pension fund by $500,000 per year, and include an annual cost-of-living adjustment. He argued that since the fund generated a greater profit than the amount requested, the owners would lose nothing. The PRC and its director, John Gaherin, refused to consider the pension supplement, perhaps calculating that Miller and the union would back down—a mistake the owners have since repeated many times.

To the shock of the PRC (and Miller himself), the players voted 663–10, with two abstentions, to authorize a strike. The strike lasted thirteen days and resulted in teams missing between seven and nine games each, costing the Boston Red Sox a chance at the American League East pennant since they played one game less than the Detroit Tigers and finished a half game behind them. The strike ended when the owners agreed to Miller's original proposal.

Marvin J. Miller, Lawyer for Association of Professional Ball Players of America at Littnaur Center, Harvard University, April 27, 1972

In considering the recent baseball strike as a labor relations problem, deep down I don't consider it a momentous problem in the whole labor relations field. But the amount of newsprint dumped on that strike I believe exceeded the coverage given to the 116-day steel strike which shut down half the country.

To realize the people who are interested in baseball, consider that 140 million people, two-thirds of the population of the United States, watched or listened to the last year's World Series.

Besides the fans' interest in baseball, the off-the-field aspects of the game are of growing interest. Baseball is being discussed in the Halls of Congress and the Courts as well. The Curt Flood case is now before the Supreme Court. . . .

There's a gap, a lag in knowledge on the part of the owners. That plus a lot of stupidity and incompetence, too. Owners are always surprised at everything that happens. Surprised at any trade union movement. Surprised at the Curt Flood case. After four months of refusing to bargain this spring, then they were surprised when the strike vote was being taken.

The Curt Flood case is somewhat a matter of dollars and cents. It is also a matter of personal dignity. The Reserve Clause is not a clause, but a way of talking about a combination of rules that are collusive to restraint of trade.

This is a property question. Players are property in the legal sense of the word. Under the tax law they are property. They are the only human beings that are depreciated under the IRS Code. When a conservative court deals with a property question, I don't know whether the fact that they are human beings will come through.

I think the owners in forcing the players into a strike have put the Players Association into a much stronger position and made that organization able to deal with the reserve clause problem better than they could have dealt with it before.

I have seen bad press coverage of strikes, but I think I have never seen a more shameful coverage of a strike than in these past few weeks.

American Broadcasting System and parts of the New York press and a few others were exceptions, but the overwhelming majority were a mass of inflammatory remarks. I am surprised that there was not more fan reprisal, considering the press.

Most people are not even aware of the conflict of interest that gets in the way of press coverage. CBS owns the New York Yankees. Now I think there is reason to feel it is unconscionable for them to have editorials blasting the hell out of the players without mentioning that they are a party to the dispute.

NBC is the holder of the television contract for televising the game of the week, all-star game, others. I say to them they have a right to their views, but their viewers have a right to know they are losing money because of the strike because of commercials cancelled. Their response indicates that no, they don't think they have such an obligation to their public.

During the strike a player said, "Don't you think we should have a public relations staff?" We were in Cincinnati and I said, "[I] don't think that would cure your ills." We had a copy of the *Cincinnati Enquirer*, the largest and the [most] influential newspaper there. [The] owner and publisher is Francis L. Dale. Now Francis L. Dale also owns the Cincinnati Reds. All the public relations would not help you in that situation.

A fan is not like other people. In his relationship with and to the players it is a complex love/hate relationship. I don't pretend to understand the psychology of the relationship.

Brooks Robinson in Baltimore is a household word. He can do no wrong. He's a fine, warm fellow. He deserves that kind of name. When he batted the first time after the strike the Baltimore fans booed the hell out of him, the first time he batted. What they didn't like was Brooks Robinson as a strike leader. Several of the fans were interviewed afterwards and we asked them why they booed him.

What they didn't like was Brooks Robinson as a strike leader, because he was depriving them of the right to see Brooks Robinson play. How dare you deprive me of watching you and enjoying your performance was the fans' position.

I don't want to indict all sports writers. That would be untrue and unfair. But there's an amazing proportion who do things you and I would consider scandalous, but they consider normal. The Los Angeles press collects at Vero Beach. They have been there for six weeks, housed, liquored, fed by the Dodger management. Then they write those objective stories for the Dodgers.

I don't know of a parallel in industry-press relations. Suppose the reporter assigned to City Hall arrived there to find a large office assigned to him, a limo at his service, his golf fees paid. In any other department of the newspaper this would be scandalous.

In the course of the strike the issues became terribly confused. Pensions and money were not the issue. It became a pure challenge. The owners miscalculated. They live on myths and fantasies. They operate on them. One myth is that baseball players don't strike. Thirty days in a row we had the strike vote in the news. Where else do you get that kind of coverage? But it didn't shake their myth.

Another myth is that even if they should strike—they won't—it'll end as soon as spring training period is over. Then as that time elapsed and the strike was still on, they said, "The ballplayers are hypnotized. Miller is Svengali." The duration of the strike was an issue of hypnosis.

We are a union, and bargain as one. But we are a young union, with two paid employees, and no strike fund. Up against 24 organizations with multimillionaire backing. The players were magnificent. Some of them have no other jobs and were not paid since the previous September. They chartered buses, kept the ballplayers together, found out-of-the-way practice fields. There were cases I heard of only afterwards of established players taking younger players into their homes to save money. All of this on a spontaneous basis. These are men with no trade union background. They surprised everybody.

I think now we have got—to use an old cliche—a whole new ball game. The strike has answered questions in the affirmative. It will make a tremendous difference not just in baseball, but in all sports.

2

Marvin Miller Responds to Critic (1972)

SOURCE: Letter from Marvin J. Miller to E. J. "Buzzie" Bavasi, June 22, 1972, Marvin Miller Papers, Series II, Box 2, Folder 29, Robert F. Wagner Labor Archives, Tamiment Library

Not only did Marvin Miller not suffer fools, he made every effort to expose their ignorance and correct their mistakes. He frequently wrote baseball officials, journalists, and fans who dared to question his tactics in sharp, unforgiving—yet often humorous—language. In the following letter Miller used the pretext of a reported $100 bet that Miller had been paid during the just-ended strike to scold San Diego Padres President Buzzie Bavasi for reportedly lying about Miller's conduct during the recently concluded strike. Such letters made clear to all Miller's passion (fanaticism to some) for his cause, and help explain the personal animosity of the baseball establishment toward him.

Dear Buzzie:

It is *alleged* that you have been trying to get out of paying a $100 bet which you lost, by falsely claiming that you won.

I have been advised that, following the strike, you incorrectly told the players on your club that I had been paid for the strike period; that you "knew" I had been paid because dues were deducted by the clubs for the 9-day period of the strike, and therefore you "won" your bet.

If your remarks have been reported accurately, and if you are a man of integrity, you will feel obliged to inform the players that you were wrong in misinforming them as to the facts, pay the $100 bet which you lost to Bob Barton, and explain why you did what you did.

The facts are as follows:

1. Dues deductions have nothing to do with the matter.

2. *No* dues were deducted for the 9-day period of the strike. Dues are paid only for days for which salaries are paid. Accordingly, your alleged statement is flat wrong.

3. *No* salary was paid either to me or to Dick Moss for the 9-day period from April 6 through April 14, inclusive. Accordingly, your alleged statement to the contrary was untrue. (It may interest you to know that the players did not request this. The decision to forego salary was made voluntarily by Dick and me based on our conviction that it is never proper to be paid when those we are representing are not paid.

Fact number 1 is self-evident.

Fact number 2 you know to be true. (See the Dues Report of your own club, and of all the other 23 clubs, showing dues deductions starting April 15, the day salaries began to be paid.)

Fact number 3 is easily verifiable. The Financial Reports of the Major League Baseball Players Association are audited by the nationally-known firm of J. K. Lasser and Company. Copies of the Audited Reports are sent annually to each member of the Players Association. Furthermore, financial reports are filed with the Government under the law and are a matter of public record.

Although I know that you have spent a tremendous amount of your time and that of other people to try to improperly save trifling amounts such as $.75 a day in spring training rooming allowances, still I cannot believe you would deliberately tell untruths to the players in order to avoid paying a $100 bet which you lost. If that is so, you must have had a different motive. I will not guess why you made up such a story out of whole cloth.

Sincerely,

Marvin J. Miller

Pirates Lose NLCS in Dramatic Fashion

in Clemente's Final Game (1972)

SOURCE: *Pittsburgh Press*, October 12, 1972

Roberto Clemente ended the 1972 season on a high note. He slashed a double against the Mets' rookie Jon Matlack on September 30 to earn his 3,000th hit, becoming only the eleventh player to reach that milestone. Clemente played a major role, in spite of injuries that limited him to 102 games, in leading his Pittsburgh Pirates to the National League East pennant. In the National League Championship Series (NLCS), the Pirates were ahead in the ninth inning of the fifth and final game, only to fall victim to a two-out wild pitch by Bob Moose that allowed the winning run to score for the Cincinnati Reds. Understandably, the Pirates were devastated.

As the following article makes clear, Clemente asserted himself as the unquestioned leader of the Pirates and urged them to be proud and stand tall, despite the defeat. His leadership qualities, unnoticed by most of the country prior to Clemente's tremendous performance in the 1971 World Series, would soon be revealed to a nation that for too long had been unwilling to attribute characteristics such as nobility or heroism to Hispanic players.

The Scoreboard

Pirates Go Out with Their Heads High

By Pat Livingston, Sports Editor

CINCINNATI—For the first time this year, the inky gloom of defeat hung over the Pirate clubhouse. The Pirates had lost before—in April they dropped six in a row—but not once did this ball club concede anything. There was always tomorrow.

But now, with Bob Moose's uncontrolled pitch bouncing into the dirt, there was no tomorrow.

Men in a trance, the disrobed Pirates stared sullenly in front of them. Half-dressed and lounging atop a table, Moose quietly muttered expletives to himself before bracing for the questions from the press. Dave Giusti sat on the floor, his chin slumped against his chest, contemplating his knee.

The reporters were slow to arrive. They had gone to Cincinnati's clubhouse first, and when they started straggling in to dissect the game with the losers, it was Willie Stargell, easy to talk to, whom they sought out first.

But Stargell had difficulty finding words.

"It's tough right now," said Willie softly. "Six months of planning and preparation and everything and it comes to this. Just like that, it's over."

Sadly, Willie shook his head. "This is a bad time for an interview," he begged off. "Any other time but today. There's just nothing I can say. I can't even concentrate on your questions. I can do better, maybe tomorrow or the next day."

Suddenly, there was a commotion in the center of the room. Roberto Clemente, climbing to his feet, had something to say.

"Okay, can you help it? Can you help it?" shrieked Roberto, his Latin voice rising. "Don't worry about it. What we need is a sense of humor. There's nothing you can do about it.

"Giusti! Damn you, Giusti," Clemente screamed at the crestfallen pitcher on the floor. "Look straight ahead. Pick up your head. We don't quit now. We go home and come back in February. Luke Walker, we'll have an oxygen tank for you when you run the bases."

"Wait a minute," protested Walker. "You're the old man around here. I'm not."

Dave Giusti began to laugh at that.

"Long as you mope, they're going to have something to write about," continued Clemente, motioning to the press. "I don't want anybody writing about the Pirates moping.

"You win and you lose. Win or lose, that's all you can do. We don't think we throw the game away. We're Pirates and we lose."

Clemente's remarks chased off some of the gloom. Across the way, a few pitchers started to move. Lifting his shaggy head, Bob Johnson shouted to all in the room:

"Anybody in here who wants to, come to my house for a party. I'm buying all the drinks."

"Where do you live at?" asked Clemente brightly, the leader taking charge. "Miller, get a map. Get me a map. Let me write it down. He might back out."

"I won't back out," promised Johnson. Johnson didn't back out. Later, waiting for the plane, Johnson's wife, Geraldine, was instructing the Davalillos on how to get to their house. Clemente took it upon himself to invite his teammates to the party, checking off names, one by one, as they agreed to be there.

Dock Ellis finally conceded victory to the Reds.

"They can represent me in the World Series," said Dock, "long as they don't lose. I don't want them representing us if they lose, like they did two years ago. I don't want anybody fouling up my share."

In his office, Bill Virdon bore up remarkably well under the strain. He declined to attribute the Reds' victory to the bad bounces—the run-scoring double by Pete Rose which ricocheted over Willie Stargell after hitting an Astroturf seam, or Moose's wild pitch which bounced over Manny Sanguillen's glove. "Bounces are part of the game," said Virdon.

Virdon should know that. It was Virdon's double play grounder which bounced against Tony Kubek's Adam's apple, a key play in the Pirates' World Series triumph in 1960.

"I guess the bounces were evening out," a writer suggested to Virdon.

"They may have evened out for me," Virdon replied, motioning to the other room. "They weren't evening out for 25 guys in there."

Spectacular Catch Saves Series Win

for Oakland (1972)

SOURCE: *San Francisco Examiner*, October 16, 1972

The garish Oakland A's, led by their outlandish and visionary owner Charles O. Finley, were matched against baseball's most conservative franchise, the Cincinnati Reds, in the 1972 World Series. Many commentators, including the Reds' Pete Rose, openly dismissed the A's and the rest of the American League as viable opponents for the Big Red Machine or any other top NL club. Oakland's chances were further diminished by the absence of star outfielder Reggie Jackson, who broke his leg in the final game of the ALCS against the Detroit Tigers.

The A's further shocked baseball fans by winning the first two games of the Series by one run each. The hero of the first game was platoon catcher Gene Tenace, who set a record by hitting home runs in his first two World Series at bats. In Game 2 Oakland was led to victory by left fielder Joe Rudi, who not only hit a home run but also made an incredible catch against the wall to help stop a ninth-inning rally. The A's won the Series in seven exciting games, and then became the first team in more than twenty years to win three consecutive World Series by beating the New York Mets and Los Angeles Dodgers, respectively, in the following two seasons.

Wells Twombly, whose column is reprinted here, was one of the most popular sportswriters in the country. He wrote 200 Years of Sport in America: A Pageant of a Nation at Play *(New York: McGraw-Hill, 1976), which was published shortly before his death in 1977. A brief biographical sketch of Twombly is in Richard Orodenker, ed.,* American Sportswriters and Writers on Sport, *Dictionary of Literary Biography vol. 241 (Detroit: Bruccoli, Clark and Layman, 2001), 303–8.*

Joe Rudi's Moment in the Sun
Wells Twombly

Utterly impervious to the men at play on the plastic carpet down by Cincinnati's riverside, the immortal sun transcribed an arc through the northern sky, pushing a gigantic shadow across the field. By mid-afternoon there was a fiercesome [*sic*] glow burning in Joe Rudi's eyes. For the next hour or so playing left field would be an adventure comparable to watching for bombs during the blitz. A man knows there's a missile up there someplace, only he's not quite sure where.

It is possible to follow a batted baseball upward in its flight, despite the harlequin pattern of shirts and jackets and dresses. It is easy to follow it as it breaks loose momentarily from the earth's grasp and soars above the roof of the stadium, outlined against the blue-gray October sky. It is damned near impossible to see it as it comes rocketing out of the sun on its return trip. At this precise moment it is man against nature. Sometimes man is frail.

There stood Joe Rudi in the ninth inning of the second game of the World Series, his gaudy green tunic flashing in the bright daylight. The implausible Oakland A's had the Cincinnati Reds down on the ground for the second straight day, leading the champions of the National League by a 2–0 score that grew more impressive with every pitch thrown by James Augustus (Catfish) Hunter, the greatest man ever to come out of Bear Swamp, N.C.

On base was Tony Perez, the most amiable of super heroes and, possibly, the least known. Up stepped Denis Menke, who sent a high fly ball sailing off into the sun. The crowd gurgled happily. Then it cheered madly as Rudi began what looked like a hopeless pursuit. In the television booth next to the press, a voice was beginning the familiar countdown . . . "going, going, going."

For an instant, Rudi thought about flipping his sunglasses down over his eyes. Earlier in the game yesterday he had been playing Cincinnati's Ted Uhlaender close to the foul line and when he had to sprint toward center field after a ball that turned into a double, he lost the drive in the sun. This time, he at least had the notion rolling around in his mind.

"I don't recall if I did or I didn't get the glasses down," he said. "The ball was straight over my head. I went up against the wall, running as hard as I could. I could feel it when I made contact. My glove never hit the wall, though. Another four inches in altitude and that ball was gone. I came down and the ball was stuck in the webbing. Now, my glove has what they call an 'M-webbing.' It's not very big. That's how close that ball was to being gone."

As he turned to follow the ball, Rudi misplaced it briefly. When he looked back it seemed to be hanging there, right on the edge of the sun. Another hour, another 45 minutes maybe, and the ball might have been blocked out entirely. Of such small scraps are great moments constructed. This was the most exotic moment in Joe Rudi's life. Cincinnati scored one run and then lost for the second straight day.

In the interview room, with the flower and chivalry of American letters looking on, Rudi's manager immediately canonized him. This was a catch to rank with the one Al Gionfriddo made in 1947, filching a home run off the sainted Joe DiMaggio, and the one Willie Mays made in 1954, stealing one from Vic Wertz. There is something about a magnificent catch by an outfielder in the World Series that makes it imperishable.

"That catch was as spectacular as either of those two," said the A's Dick Williams, whose drooping mustache makes him look like a middle-aged gunfighter. "What I liked about this one was that it was made for a team I manage."

Already the side effects of instant immortality were swirling around Rudi. The press surrounded him, asking him just when he ceased to be a mediocre first baseman and became a brilliant left fielder. Rudi wasn't sure the metamorphosis had actually taken place. He still considered himself merely adequate. Someday, when he was older, he said, he'd like to try first base again.

"He's a complete ball player, that Rudi," said Cincinnati's permanent speaker of the House, Pete Rose. "He really cut two important parts of our anatomy off today with that home run and that catch."

It is possible to feel deep sorrow for the Reds. They had been told that the National League was far superior to the American League. Therefore, the really important series was the one between Cincinnati and Pittsburgh, not the one between Cincinnati and Oakland. They even went so far as to demean the A's with cheap praise, calling them the only "National League-type team in the American League." That was similar to calling them a credit to their race.

So, in the first match, a catcher whose name the Reds never got—it was either Fury Gene Tenace or Fiori Gino Tenacchi—singed them with two home runs, good for a 3–2 victory. Then it was Rudi, his home run and his magic glove. The Oakland pitching has been superb, to the point where Rose, Joe Morgan and Bobby Tolan, their three advance men, have hardly been on base. Catcher John Bench was the leadoff man in every inning but the first.

No one should forget that this is Charles O. Finley's World Series. He bought and paid for it. He's a self-made man, so it's okay. He has been scattering coins among his troops like a Roman emperor home from Gaul. He gave Dick Williams a new contract. He raised Tenace's pay $5,000 on Saturday and then dropped $5,000 on Rudi yesterday. Then while a private Dixieland band played Charlie's theme song, "Sugar In The Morning!", he headed off to the airport with his party of 154. On the nose of the chartered jet were gigantic pictures of the mule and Charlie. Whatever happened to Bill Veeck?

5

George Steinbrenner–Led Group Buys New York Yankees (1973)

SOURCE: *New York Daily News*, January 4, 1973

The baseball world was introduced to George Steinbrenner when he led a group of eleven owners who purchased the New York Yankees for $10 million. Even though he was the primary investor in the owners' group, the focus of the article below is Mike Burke, who was the Yankees' chief executive as a representative of CBS and was leaving the network to continue his service with the Yankees. It would not take the people of New York long to learn that Steinbrenner was an outspoken, often controversial owner whose words and actions would all too often cast the franchise in a poor light. Nevertheless, Steinbrenner's willingness to plunge into the new free-agent market and his frequent hiring of equally controversial manager Billy Martin was largely responsible for propelling the Yankees to four World Series appearances in the first nine years of his ownership.

CBS Sells Yanks to Burke, 11 Others

Group Pays $10 Million—MacPhail, Houk Stay
By Phil Pepe

The Yankees have been sold to Mike Burke and George Steinbrenner III and 10 owners to be named later.

At a press conference yesterday in Yankee Stadium, Michael Burke presiding, it was announced that the CBS eye has had it. After nine years, the network is bowing out of the baseball business for $10 million, or $3.2 million less than CBS paid for the club.

Burke pointed out, however, that the loss was no loss at all to the network. Because of its corporate structure, tax losses, and the like, CBS "substantially recouped its investment," according to Burke.

TO STAY AT TOP

In making the announcement, Burke, looking affluent in a navy blue, double-breasted suit (pin-striped, naturally), said: "CBS has agreed to sell the New York Yankees to a group of individuals headed by George Steinbrenner . . . for $10 million in cash." Burke added that he will carry on as chief executive of the Yankees and that the Yankee organization will remain intact from top to bottom—including Lee MacPhail as general manager and Ralph Houk as field manager.

Burke also said, "The club will remain in the city," an announcement Mayor Lindsay endorsed in a separate statement of his own and through the presence at the press conference of Deputy Mayor Edward Hamilton.

As a result of the new deal, Burke will disassociate himself from CBS, for which he has worked since 1956 and where he became a vice president in 1962.

From his vantage point as vice president of CBS in charge of the Yankees, a wholly-owned subsidiary of the network, and as a potential purchaser of the club, Burke was in an advantageous position to learn that CBS was ready to unload the team and what it would take to buy it.

"NO LONGER FIT IN"

Trying to speak for the network, Burke said he believed "The New York Yankees no longer fit comfortably in the plans of CBS." He said his group's offer of $10 million "in cash, not a dollar down and a dollar a week" was made on December 19 and accepted on December 22, to the surprise (because of the swiftness of the decision) of Burke and his group. A memo of understanding outlining the transaction was drawn up only last Friday, the last business day of the old year.

The Yankee president applauded CBS as "a good owner" because of its "patience and strength." While he would not say his group got the club for a bargain price, he said, "The Yankees would always be a desirable purchase. Having an American League team in New York is desirable, particularly at this time, with the team having fought its way back into contention."

Only Burke and Steinbrenner of the new owners attended the conference. The names of the other 10 owners, in fact, have been withheld temporarily. They will be revealed, and the men introduced to the press, at a future press conference.

COLLEAGUES, FRIENDS

The common denominator between Burke, Steinbrenner and [the] other 10 is "business relationship and personal friendship." One of the other 10 may be Lamar Hunt, owner of the Kansas City Chiefs, whose relation to Steinbrenner is that both are members of the board of directors of the Chicago Bulls of the NBA.

The 12 new owners will be equal partners. Steinbrenner took center stage because, presumably, he is the man who put together the group.

Until only a few months ago, Steinbrenner and Burke did not know each other. But Burke's search for money men who might enter into a deal to buy the Yankees, eventually led, through a mutual friend, to Steinbrenner.

It was obvious, from his background, that Steinbrenner was the perfect man for Burke. For one thing, he had the money. For another, he had the interest. For a third, he could afford to have the Yankees as a toy. Steinbrenner has other toys. Boars [sic; Boats]. Real ones. He is Chairman and chief executive officer of The American Ship Building Company of Cleveland. That's not all. He is owner of Kinsman Stud Farm in Ocala, Fla., part owner of the Chicago Bulls, [and] partner in production of the Broadway musical "Applause" and the national companies of "Funny Girl," "George M.," and "On a Clear Day."

Although he was born and brought up in Cleveland, Steinbrenner says he was always a Yankee fan, sort of. "The Yankees are important to the nation," he said. "I couldn't root for them against the Indians, but I admired them. There's a wave of nostalgia sweeping the country. Take the success of 'No, No, Nanette.' I even watched Guy Lombardo on New Year's Eve. I think the Yankees can be part of that nostalgia."

6

"Explanation of Designated Hitter Rule" (1973)

Source: "Explanation of Designated Hitter Rule As Adopted by the American League for the 1973 Championship Season," "Designated Hitter" file, undated, National Baseball Hall of Fame Library

After enduring nearly a decade of declining offense, American League owners voted to permit teams to substitute a "designated pinch-hitter" for pitchers on a three-year trial basis. The designated hitter (DH) had first been suggested by National League president John Heydler in 1928. In 1969 the AL approved an experiment to allow several minor leagues to use variations of the DH rule, but the NL declined to participate (see Sullivan, Late Innings, 238–40). By 1973 the AL was ready to institute the DH on the major league level in the hope that by adding offense, attendance would also increase, and formally approved the landmark change in mid-January 1973. League officials may also have been influenced by a computer study by Stanford graduate student Art Peterson, who determined that replacing the pitcher with an average batter significantly increased scoring. Offense improved immediately, but attendance was not affected by the DH. The AL also hoped to start playing interleague games with the NL (which in exchange wanted six games added to the schedule), but when the issue was formally raised following the signing of the new Basic Agreement, the NL voted unanimously against it.

In the twenty seasons prior to 1973 the AL only beat the NL in OPS (on-base percentage plus slugging average) five times. For the remainder of the twentieth century the AL beat the NL in OPS every season, although the difference between the leagues remained small until around 1980. This may help to explain why the AL lost nineteen of twenty All-Star Games between 1963 and 1982.

The following document was undated but attached to another document on the DH dated January 25, 1973. It includes a description of how AL managers could use a double-switch with the DH—ironically, a strategy now used almost exclusively by the NL because of its refusal to adopt the DH.

EXPLANATION OF DESIGNATED HITTER RULE AS ADOPTED BY THE AMERICAN LEAGUE FOR THE 1973 CHAMPIONSHIP SEASON

A Designated Hitter must be named prior to the game and his name included on the lineup card presented to the Umpire-in-Chief.

It is not mandatory to use a Designated Hitter.

If nominated prior to the game, the Designated Hitter must bat only for the pitcher.

A manager may pinch hit for the Designated Hitter and the substitute batter becomes the Designated Hitter.

The game pitcher may bat for the Designated Hitter, which ends the Designated Hitter for the remainder of the game, and regular Playing Rules prevail.

A Designated Hitter is "locked" into the batting order. No multiple substitutions may be made that will alter the batting rotation of the Designated Hitter.

Example: Norman Cash is Detroit's Designated Hitter. Manager Billy Martin, in the eighth inning, decides he wants to make a change that will enable him to get his pitcher up in the ninth inning in order to pinch hit for him.

How can Martin work it?

He removes Ed Brinkman, the shortstop, who is scheduled to bat in the ninth and replaces him with Tony Taylor. Taylor moves into the Designated Hitter's spot in the batting order. The pitcher is then placed in the lineup in Brinkman's spot, thus bringing the pitcher to bat in the ninth inning instead of Brinkman.

Example: Red Sox pitcher Sonny Siebert pinch hits for second baseman Doug Griffin. Siebert then enters the game to pitch. John Kennedy comes in to take Griffin's defensive position at second base.

How does the substitution sequence work?

Siebert must occupy Griffin's position in the batting order while Kennedy assumes that of the Designated Hitter.

Example: Fritz Peterson is pitching for the Yankees who are using Ron Blomberg as the Designated Hitter. Manager Ralph Houk decides he will place Peterson at first base so that a new pitcher can come in to pitch to one hitter and then send Peterson back to the mound.

In moving Peterson to first base, Houk is automatically forfeiting his right to a Designated Hitter. So that Peterson, now at first base, enters the batting order in the first baseman's spot and the new pitcher bats in place of the Designated Hitter.

A Designated Hitter may enter the game defensively. When he does, this terminates the Designated Hitter role for the remainder of the game. The pitcher then must bat in the spot in the batting order the Designated Hitter substituted for, unless more than one substitution is made and the manager must designate spots in batting order.

A runner may be substituted for the Designated Hitter, and the runner assumes the role of Designated Hitter.

A Designated Hitter will be eligible for all American League batting titles provided he has a sufficient number of plate appearances in one season.

7

Salary Arbitration Permitted in New Basic Agreement (1973)

SOURCE: Basic Agreement, Peter Seitz Papers, #5733, Box 22, Folder 3, Kheel Center for Labor-Management Documentation and Archives, Cornell University Library

The new Basic Agreement, signed February 25, 1973, included another substantial advance for the players—salary arbitration. Previously, the owners held all the power in salary negotiations. Players had little option but to accept their club's offer since they could not leave and accept a higher offer elsewhere. With arbitration, the player and the club each submitted a figure to an arbitrator approved by both the owners and the MLBPA. The arbitrator—who might know little about baseball—would listen to arguments on both sides and select one of the proposed salaries, with no compromise permitted. In theory salary arbitration would force both players and clubs to make fair, realistic salary proposals, but some critics (and many owners) complained that the effect of arbitration was to force the clubs to pay salaries based on the decisions of the least capable owners and arbitrators.

Presented below are the rules governing salary arbitration from the Basic Agreement.

ARTICLE V—SALARIES
D. Salary Arbitration

Effective with the 1974 championship season, the following salary arbitration procedure shall be applicable:

(1) *Eligibility.* Any Club, or any Player with both a total of two years of Major League experience and Major League service in at least three different championship seasons, may submit the issue of the Player's salary to final and binding arbitration.

(2) *Notice of submission.* Notice of submission to arbitration shall be given in writing by the party electing arbitration to the other party, the Association and the designated representative of the Player Relations Committee.

(3) *Form of submission.* The Player and the Club shall each submit to the arbitrator and exchange with each other in advance of the hearing single salary figures for the coming season (which need not be figures offered during the prior negotiations). At the hearing, the Player and Club shall deliver to the arbitrator a Uniform Player's Contract executed in duplicate, complete except for the salary figure to be inserted in Paragraph 2. Upon submission of a salary issue to arbitration by either Player or Club, the Player shall be regarded as a signed Player (unless the Player withdraws from arbitration as provided in subparagraph 4 below).

(4) *Timetable and decision.* Submission may be made at any time between February 1 and February 10. In the event the offer of the Club is reduced on or subsequent to February 10, the Player's right to submit to arbitration shall be reinstated for a period of 7 days. Arbitration hearings shall be held as soon as possible after submission, but, in any event, shall be scheduled to be held before February 20. The decision shall be rendered by the arbitrator within 72 hours after the hearing. The arbitrator shall be limited to awarding only one or the other of the two figures submitted. There shall be no opinion and no release of the arbitration award by the arbitrator except to the Club and the Player concerned. The arbitrator shall insert the figure awarded in Paragraph 2 of the duplicate Uniform Player's Contracts delivered to him at the hearing and shall forward both copies to the League office of the Player concerned.

(5) *Withdrawal from arbitration.* In the event the Club submits the matter to arbitration, the Player may within 7 days after receipt of the Club's salary arbitration figure notify the Club that he does not wish to arbitrate and the matter shall be deemed withdrawn from arbitration. In such event, or in the event that neither the Club nor the Player submit to arbitration, the rights and obligations of the Club and Player shall be unchanged from those which existed prior to the adoption of this salary arbitration procedure. In the event the Club and Player reach agreement on salary before the arbitrator reaches his decision, the matter shall be deemed withdrawn from arbitration.

(6) *Selection of arbitrator.* The Players Association and the Player Relations

Committee shall annually select the arbitrators. In the event they are unable to agree by January 1 in any year, they jointly shall request that the American Arbitration Association furnish them lists of prominent, professional arbitrators convenient to the hearing sites. Upon receipt of such lists, the arbitrators shall be selected by alternately striking names from the lists.

(7) *Location of hearings.* The hearing sites will be located in Los Angeles, Chicago, New York and such other Major League cities as the parties may agree upon, with a single arbitrator at each site. The hearings shall be held at the site closest to the home city of the Club involved.

(8) *Conduct of hearing.* The hearings shall be conducted on a private and confidential basis. There shall be no continuances or adjournments of a hearing, but the commencement of a hearing may be postponed by the arbitrator upon the application of either the Player or Club based upon a showing of substantial cause.

(9) *Hearing costs.* The Player and Club shall divide equally the costs of the hearing, and each shall be responsible for his own expenses and those of his counsel or other representatives; provided, however, that the Club and Player shall divide equally the total of (a) the round trip air fare for one Club representative from the Club's home city to the arbitration site plus (b) the round trip air fare for the Player or one representative from the Player's residence to the arbitration site.

(10) *Criteria.* The criteria will be the quality of the Player's contribution to his Club during the past season (including but not limited to his overall performance, special qualities of leadership and public appeal), the length and consistency of his career contribution, the record of the Player's past compensation, comparative baseball salaries (see subparagraph (11) below for confidential salary data), the existence of any physical or mental defects on the part of the Player, and the recent performance record of the Club including but not limited to its League standing and attendance as an indication of public acceptance (subject to the exclusion stated in (a) below). Any evidence may be submitted which is relevant to the above criteria, and the arbitrator shall assign such weight to the evidence as shall to him appear appropriate under the circumstances. The following items, however, shall be excluded:

> (a) The financial position of the Player and the Club.
> (b) Press comments, testimonials or similar material bearing on the performance of either the Player or the Club, except that recognized annual Player awards for playing excellence shall not be excluded.
> (c) Offers made by either Player or Club prior to arbitration.
> (d) The cost to the parties of their representatives, attorneys, etc.
> (e) Salaries in other sports or occupations.

(11) *Confidential Major League salary data.** For his own confidential use, as

*According to Marvin Miller, baseball officials avoided fulfilling their obligation to provide salary data until they realized that the union's data was virtually identical to their own.

background information, the arbitrator will be given a tabulation showing the minimum salary in the Major Leagues and salaries for the preceding season of all Players on Major League rosters as of August 31, broken down by years of Major League service. The names and Clubs of the Players concerned will appear on the tabulation.

8

Poll Reveals Support for New DH Rule (1973)

SOURCE: Louis Harris Poll, unidentified clipping in "Designated Hitter" file, May 31, 1973, National Baseball Hall of Fame Library

The following article on a survey conducted by Louis Harris in April 1973 reveals strong support for the American League's experiment with the designated hitter. The DH was especially popular with well-educated, higher-income fans, who according to Harris had been losing interest in baseball in recent years. However, a plurality of less affluent fans also favored the DH in the belief that it would make AL games more exciting. The complete poll results can be found in The Harris Survey Yearbook of Public Opinion 1973: A Compendium of Current American Attitudes *(New York: Louis Harris and Associates Inc., 1976), 425–26.*

An excellent contemporary analysis of the designated hitter can be found in Leonard Koppett, All About Baseball *(New York: Quadrangle/New York Times Book Co., 1974), 149–55. This is a revised version of an earlier, classic book, recently revised again and released under its original title,* The Thinking Fan's Guide to Baseball *(Toronto: Sport Classic Books, 2004).*

HARRIS SURVEY

3 Strikes but Still in Game
By Louis Harris

By 50–31 per cent, baseball fans give their endorsement to the new designated hitter rule being tried out in the American League for the first time this season. Easily the most appealing part of the DH innovation is that it allows "older or slower players who can still hit to be useful to the game," a view endorsed by 74–10 per cent among diamond fans.

Although the aggregate batting average of designated hitters is well below the .300 mark since the new rule went into effect, DH run production, including home runs and runs batted in, has been well above the averages compiled by pitchers still taking their turn at bat in the National League. Basically, of course, the rule allowing a proven hitter to bat for the pitcher without requiring the latter to be removed from the game was instituted to build up interest at the gate.

Recently, a nationwide cross section of 1271 sports fans was asked:

"This year the American League has changed its rules so that each team can put a designated hitter up to bat instead of the pitcher, but the pitcher doesn't have to leave the game. Do you approve or disapprove of the new designated hitter rule in the American League?"

NEW DH RULE IN AMERICAN LEAGUE

	APPROVE (PERCENTAGE)	DISAPPROVE (PERCENTAGE)	NOT SURE (PERCENTAGE)
Total baseball fans	50	31	19
By age			
18–29	53	32	15
30–49	52	36	12
50 and over	45	30	25
By education			
Eighth grade or less	38	28	34
High school	49	31	20
College	57	31	12
By income			
Under $5,000	43	32	25
$5,000–$9,999	47	29	24
$10,000–$14,999	55	31	14
$15,000 and over	55	32	13

The DH experiment is most popular with better educated, and higher income fans, all of whom have been least attracted by baseball in recent years. Older and lower income fans are more conservative about preserving the traditional rules of the game.

A series of three criticisms volunteered by some against the DH were tested by the Harris Sports Survey, and only one appears to have garnered much following.

— By 42–40 per cent, baseball fans worry that the new rule could be "unfair to pitchers who are also good hitters." While most pitchers are dismal hitters, baseball history has been studded with pitchers, such as Red Ruffing of the New York Yankees and Bob Gibson of the St. Louis Cardinals, who could hold their own with other members of the line-up with the bat. Many fans feel that under the DH rule, pitchers will be reduced to pampered specialists.

— But by 51–34 per cent, a majority of fans reject the complaint of some oldtimers that "they shouldn't tinker around with the rules in baseball because they will ruin the game." In fact, a number of fans feel that one of the troubles with baseball is that it has been reluctant to change as modern tastes and styles have taken over in other areas of sports and leisure time activities.

—By a narrower 40–31 per cent, the fans also turn down the criticism that "the designated hitter rule will mean offense will take over from defense and that is bad." Implicitly, the fans are saying that they are willing to take the risk of higher scoring games instead of more pitchers' duels which result in low-scoring contests.

In fact, an eagerness to see more runs scored is the chief source of support of the DH experiment.

—By a substantial 62–24 per cent, a majority of fans agree that "by allowing a real hitter up at bat instead of the pitcher, it means more runs and more action, and that's good." In recent years, baseball has fallen off in popularity primarily because fans feel the pace of the game is too slow and there is simply not enough action, compared with football, basketball, or hockey. Action in baseball to most fans means more hits, more running, and higher scores. Some traditionalists might take their pleasure in the fine and subtle arts of defensive play and low hit and run games, filled with managerial maneuvering, but today's fans appear to crave less subtle excitement. And that means stressing the offensive part of the game.

—However, fans also see pitchers benefitting from the new DH rule. By 65–19 per cent, a solid majority also believe that "good pitchers will win more games because they won't be lifted for a pinch hitter late in a close game, and that's good." Some students of the game have viewed taking out a pitcher locked in a 2–1 duel in the seventh or eighth inning as a waste of first-line talent. Yet, when a team needed a run to tie late in the game, a manager was usually forced to yank a weak-hitting pitcher. The DH rule, most fans feel, allows baseball to have the best of both worlds: the manager can put in hitting strength and at the same time not lose his best pitching talent.

All in all, judging from these results, the DH rule is off to a positive start with baseball fans themselves. This may be a signal to the holdouts against the idea in the National League. It seems clear that the fans are ready for even more innovations that will liven up the onetime national pastime.

9

Finley Punishes Player Whose Errors Cost A's Series Game (1973)

SOURCE: *San Jose Mercury*, October 15, 1973

The second game of the 1973 World Series was tied 6–6 entering the twelfth inning. After the New York Mets' aging star Willie Mays had driven in the go-ahead run in the top of the inning, Oakland A's second baseman Mike Andrews committed errors on consecutive plays, permitting an additional three runs to cross the plate. Those unearned runs prevented the A's, who scored only once in the bottom of the twelfth, from tying the game again and from possibly taking a 2–0 lead in the Series before flying cross-country to New York.

Oakland owner Charles Finley acted swiftly. Immediately following the game Finley summoned Andrews to meet with team doctor Harry Walker and then talk with Finley and manager Dick Williams. Nearly an hour later Finley emerged with a statement signed by Walker and Andrews stating that "Mike Andrews is unable to play his position because of a bicep groove tencosynotitis of the right shoulder. It is my opinion that he is disabled for the rest of the year."

The statement convinced no one, least of all Andrews' teammates, who rallied behind him. Commissioner Bowie Kuhn ruled that since Andrews' "injury" was a recurrence of a preexisting condition, that he could not be placed on the disabled list and replaced on the roster by Manny Trillo, an excellent second baseman. The incident, according to some, helped persuade Williams to offer his resignation at the conclusion of the Series, won by Oakland. It also reaffirmed Finley's image as an unstable despot to the baseball public, and deepened the rift between Finley and Kuhn that ultimately would lead to a federal lawsuit against the commissioner by Finley.

Perhaps the best of the many histories of the colorful A's is Bruce Markusen, Baseball's Last Dynasty: Charlie Finley's Oakland A's *(Indianapolis: Masters Press, 1998).*

"Andrews On (Finley's) Disabled List"

OAKLAND—Utilityman Mike Andrews, showing no signs of an injury, apparently is to be placed on the disabled list by the Oakland Athletics, The Mercury learned Sunday.

It is believed A's owner Charles O. Finley ordered the action after Andrews, playing second base, committed two errors in the 12th inning which allowed the decisive runs to score during the New York Mets' 10–7 victory over Oakland in the second game of the World Series.

Finley kept the press waiting outside the A's clubhouse for 10 minutes while he reprimanded his team before taking an elevator to his office.

When Finley reboarded the elevator, he had an angry look on his face. "This is an emergency," Finley said while asking the elevator to return to the Athletics' locker room. "Is Mike Andrews on this elevator?"

Then Finley entered manager Dick Williams' office and locked the door for 15 minutes.

"You know what this is all about?" Vida Blue asked a reporter—both of whom had been on the elevator. "The man (Finley) is going in there to put Mike Andrews on the disabled list."

"I plain kicked things around," said Andrews.

"Sure, I'd like to have them back," he said, "but I can't and that's it. I'm the goat and I'm sorry as hell about it. I'm too old to cry and I don't want to quit but those are my only options right now."

The Mets had scored the go-ahead run on a single by Willie Mays in the 12th. Then, with the bases loaded and two out, John Milner sent a routine roller to second.

Andrews, who has played only 20 innings in the field this year, put his glove down but the ball went through him into center. Two runs scored on the bobble, similar to the one Felix Millan booted in the first game Saturday to help the A's to their only runs in a 2–1 victory.

"I honestly thought I had the ball," said the 30-year-old veteran of seven big league seasons, "but when I brought my glove up, I saw the ball wasn't there. If there was a hole big enough out there I would have buried myself."

That one error was enough to ruin any man's day, but on the very next batter—Jerry Grote—Andrews came up with a second miscue.

Grote hit a chopper behind the mound near second and Andrews speared it with little trouble, but throwing off balance, he pulled first baseman Gene Tenace off the bag and Grote was safe at first. That allowed the fourth run of the inning to score and the Mets made three of them stand up for the victory.

"If we'd been able to add Manny Trillo to the roster, he would have been there instead of Andrews," manager Dick Williams said, referring to the infielder whose proposed addition to the roster was vetoed by the Mets.

10

Peter Seitz on Salary Arbitration (1974)

SOURCE: *Arbitration Journal* 29, no. 2 (June 1974): 98–103

Peter Seitz was not yet the celebrated figure (or to owners, the reviled villain) he would later become as a result of his decisions in December 1974 and December 1975 to grant free agency to three players. The latter decision permanently established free agency in major league baseball and got Seitz fired by the owners. In the article below Seitz explains to his fellow arbitrators the unique factors involved in "high-low arbitration," in which the arbitrator must decide the salary of a player based on proposals by the player and his club. He notes the complicated nature of the statistics used by both sides to bolster their position, and that at this stage the players often did not have competent representation to argue their case. Seitz describes the difficulty involved in putting baseball statistics in their proper context (especially for arbitrators unfamiliar with baseball) and the frustration in not being allowed, according to the rules spelled out in the Basic Agreement, to attach an explanation of the decision.

FOOTNOTES TO BASEBALL SALARY ARBITRATION
By Peter Seitz

Practitioners and academics in the field of dispute-settlement methods have evinced curiosity and interest in the recent round of arbitration of salaries of Major League baseball players. As one of the cadre of arbitrators retained by the club and the player associations for this imaginative exercise, I have received many telephone calls and letters of inquiry in respect of various aspects of the process. The extent of interest persuades me that the desperate thirst for information may be slaked by a few observations of a participant. This is not written as a submission for a doctor-ate, nor does it purport to constitute an exhaustive evaluation of the procedure. It is in the nature of a footnote to whatever may be written by those who will subject the procedure to more intensive and deliberate scrutiny.

First, it should be observed that the idea of what I prefer to call "High-Low Ar-bitration" (a term suggested by a more sedentary and, frequently, a less profitable game than baseball) is not new. The idea was bruited about in the late 1940's and 1950's as one of the alternatives to the national emergency dispute procedures in the Taft-Hartley Act. Probably it never caught on because, in industrial controver-sies arising out of the inability of the parties to bring their negotiations for a con-tract to fruition, in addition to wages, there are commonly a number of other issues to be resolved. The usual impasse in bargaining does not lead itself, conveniently, to resolution of the dispute by the choice of an arbitrator of the employer's offer or the employee's demand. So far as the writer is informed (and he may be imperfect-ly informed), High-Low Arbitration has not been utilized, previously, in any major industry in any significant way. The club and player associations cannot be cred-ited with having invented the procedure that was used; but they are deserving of an accolade for the imagination that prompted them to recognize the fact that the procedure is well designed for coping with a persistent problem in Baseball: unre-alistic salary bargaining which frequently continued into the training season and, indeed, into the playing season. They were able to apply the procedure to the solu-tion of this problem because all of the terms and conditions applicable to the ser-vices of baseball players are contained in the uniform player contract. Accordingly, at the beginning of each baseball salary arbitration hearing, the club and the play-ers signed copies of the uniform player contract and handed them to the arbitrator, who, following the hearing, after appropriate study, incantation and prayer, would write in the salary numbers in the appropriate blank space. This act of the Arbitra-tor constituted the "Award." Nothing but salary was involved.

The writer can testify only as to the five hearings at which he presided. At those hearings it seemed to him that the clubs, on the whole (with exceptions), were bet-ter prepared and made a more professional presentation than the players. Some of the players were represented by agents or attorneys who, although knowledge-able in the baseball field, exhibited no high degree of professional expertise in the art of advocacy in arbitration. Other players, to be sure, especially where the play-ers' association provided them with counsel, were skillfully represented. However, it was obvious to this Arbitrator that the clubs, on the whole, had spent much more time and effort in the preparation of what they considered to be meaningful statis-tical data bearing on the case than the players' representatives. I mention this, not because the statistical exhibits necessarily decided any particular case, but only to observe that if the "high-low" procedure should be utilized in the future, it is im-portant that there be a parity of professional skill in advocacy on both sides of the arbitration table.

The hearings were noteworthy in the respect that the hearings at which I presided were inundated by a torrent of statistical data. I had a feeling that I had more figures before me than exist in the files of the Census Bureau and the Bureau of Labor Statistics. To be sure, the mystique of statistics which makes its appearance in many sports has always been found in baseball. Everything, or almost everything, is appraised and evaluated in terms of numbers or averages. Although the associations took the trouble to agree upon and prescribe what criteria might or might not be used by the arbitrator, statistical data as to RBI's, ERA's, strike-outs, hitting and fielding averages, etc., etc., dominated the presentations.

Statistics are the normal food and drink of arbitrators with experience in industrial disputes—particularly in "contract arbitration." The Battle of Statistics, however, in baseball salary arbitration seemed to be of a special nature. The accuracy of the statistic was never challenged but its significance was almost always called into question. For example, a club asserts that in the past year, the earned run average of batters against a pitcher increased significantly and his win-lose figure was less impressive than in previous years. Accordingly, no increase in pay was offered by the club. The pitcher, however, argues, with a wealth of figures, that in the games he lost, the margin of defeat was mostly by one or two runs; and in most of those games, his team hit well below its season's batting average. What weight should be given to the raw yearly statistics presented by a club in the face of this kind of explanation? Are a pitcher's yearly statistics the result of his own efforts or failure exclusively, or are they the product of the mutual efforts and performance of his teammates? Are all accidentals and unfortuitous circumstances wiped out by the process of averaging?

Or, for example, consider the problem presented by a fielder who had an impressive batting average and RBI figure in the past, but who had a relatively poor batting average and RBI figure in 1973. The club offers him an increase, but he demands a much larger amount. He explains that he had sustained a baseball injury in the past year and resumed playing, perhaps earlier than he should have, because his participation was urgently needed by his team. For some weeks after his return, according to his argument his batting average declined; but in the closing weeks of the season it improved considerably. Thus, he contends, as does the pitcher in the previously mentioned example, that the yearly statistics are misleading and the arbitrator should give more weight to performance at the end of the season as evidence of what his value to the club will be in the ensuing year. Furthermore, he points out, his failure to maintain his customary level of performance in batting after return to playing after the injury, resulted in his being assigned to seventh or eighth in the batting order instead of second, third, or fifth. This, he contends, lowered his yearly RBI figure materially because, as he points out, the likelihood of a runner being on base to be batted in home is not great when one is at the foot of the batting order. Does this explain his comparatively poor showing last year? What weight should be given to these considerations in ascertaining his value to the club in the *next* year; which, after all, is the question to be answered by the Arbitrator.

It seems desirable to repeat that these illustrations are given, not to suggest that any decisions actually turned on the matters referred to, but to demonstrate that the battle of raw statistics did not furnish easy answers for the arbitrator. If the statistical averages were to be accepted at full face value as conclusively determining the issues, the parties would probably do better with a computer than with a more or less human arbitrator.

Of course, the statistical averages and figures placed in evidence in the records of the cases had much to do with the process of decision-making; but the ultimate decisions, inescapably, were affected by imponderables less objective and susceptible to measurement than statistics. Cardoza, Jerome Frank and Morris Raphael Cohen, among others, have written brilliantly on the role that subjective processes ("gut reactions") play in judicial decisions. Only the unsophisticated and naive entertain the view that quasi-judicial decision-makers such as arbitrators can decide wholly and exclusively on quantitative and objective phenomena. Practice in decision-making is not entirely consistent with theory. Every arbitrator should (and tries to) decide on the basis of the objective data in the record to the extent that such data furnish a sound guide to his decisions; but as arbitrators analyze their own performance, they come to realize that, frequently, there are considerations other than those susceptible of simple measurement that influence their conclusions. In the baseball salary arbitrations under consideration this realization was given emphasis.

Normally, in arbitration, the arbitrator's Opinion affords him an opportunity to explain how he reached the conclusion that may seem curious or even outrageous to a disappointed litigant. Not so, however, in salary baseball arbitration as it was practiced this year. The arbitrator's decisions were not to be accompanied by a description of his fascinating ratiocinations. Absent an *apologia* in the form of an Opinion he is sensitively aware that those who believe another decision should have been reached have *carte blanche* to accuse him of arbitrariness and capriciousness at best, or unjust discrimination at the worst. This places a heavy burden of pressure on the harassed arbitrator (who wonders why he ever subjected himself to this cruel and unusual punishment). Particularly is this the case when his viscera secretly but convincingly whisper to him that if "justice" should be served, the correct (or "best") figure is somewhere between what the player demanded and what the club offered.

That legendary super-Arbitrator, Solomon, was never in such a fix. The baseball salary arbitrator was required to pick one figure or the other, without explaining why, and with a conviction that neither was "right" but that some intermediate conclusion would be more just. Anyone who believes that this poses no special difficulty should try it! In fact, in several of the cases, if the clubs had offered an increase over the last year or a somewhat larger increase than was proposed, they *might* have prevailed; and, similarly, if the players had moderated their demands to a degree, they *might* have prevailed. However, the Arbitrator with the blindfold firmly tied on his eyes and the scales swinging in his palsied hand did not have this option. It was "either-or"; "high or low." Hard cases may or may not make bad law; but in the baseball arbitrations the arbitrators could only do their best, neither more nor less, in the circumstances under which they served. I believe that they all did this even if a Divine Board of Review, on celestial appeal for remand, should be appalled at the decision reached.

The worth of the procedure, however, should not be judged by the difficulties it may impose on arbitrators or by how "right" they were in their conclusions. After all, what the parties wanted most was an impartial and knowledgeable *decision* to resolve a dispute; and such a decision has its own value even if not ideally "right." Even more important than this consideration, however, is the effect of the arbitration procedure on the bargaining of the clubs and the players that took place before arbitration. The arbitrators have insufficient knowledge or insight to be able to speak authoritatively on this; but the impression garnered is that the procedures used have had an extraordinary success in encouraging the bargaining parties to submit realistic figures to each other and to eliminate the "out of this world" haggling of the past. Clubs that were too niggardly or tight-fisted in their offers ran the risk of having an arbitrator select the more reasonable players' figures; players who grossly overrated their value to the clubs ran the risk of ending up with the clubs' offers. This, I believe, led to moderation in positions and a salutory respect for the realities. It resulted in many settlements before arbitration.

In conclusion, as an arbitrator-participant, I should say that the experience was stimulating and challenging. I am grateful for the opportunity to participate in the effort; and I congratulate the officials of the club association and the players' association for their imagination and innovative courage and for the manner in which they administered the novel procedure. Employers and unions generally would do well to take note of and to emulate the creativity in procedures for dispute settlement demonstrated by the clubs' and the players' associations.

11

Ten-Cent "Beer Night" Leads to Riot, Forfeit in Cleveland (1974)

SOURCE: Cleveland *Plain Dealer*, June 5, 1974

The June 4 contest between the Texas Rangers and the Cleveland Indians, a meaningless contest between two poor clubs, became a bizarre footnote to baseball history due to a misguided promotion and the frightening response to it by Cleveland fans. The promotion was "Ten-Cent Beer Night," and the result of this was a full-scale riot during the bottom of the ninth inning (when the Indians were staging a dramatic comeback) and the first forfeit since the final game of the 1971 season by the Washington Senators. Reporter Russell Schneider makes clear that this was not simply a wild frolic on the part of the fans, but rather a dangerous mass assault on players and others on the field, and on those fans unfortunate enough to get in the way of the drunken rioters. He did not mention that the teams had fought with each other the previous month, yet another reason why the promotion was such a bad idea.

Stadium Beer Night Fans Riot; Ending Indians' Rally in Forfeit

By Russell Schneider

A flash "Beer Night" crowd of 25,134 fans erupted in a riot at the Stadium, last night, forcing a 9–0 forfeit of the Indians' baseball game with the Texas Rangers.

The riot broke out in the last of the ninth inning as the Indians fought back from a 5–3 deficit to tie the score.

They had two men on base with two out when a couple of spectators leaped onto the playing field and tried to steal the cap from the head of Jeff Burroughs, the Rangers' right fielder.

Burroughs fought back and, quickly, scores of youths jumped over the railing and onto the field—while players from both the Indians and Rangers raced to the defense of the outfielder.

This time the Indians and Rangers—who fought each other last Wednesday night in Arlington, Tex.—joined forces to protect themselves from the unruly mob.

Many of the players suffered bruises. The most serious injury among the Tribesmen was suffered by relief pitcher Tom Hilgendorf.

Hilgendorf was hit on the head and shoulders with a steel folding chair tossed out of the stands. Umpire Nestor Chylak was cut on the hand.

At least 11 persons were arrested for disorderly conduct at the Stadium and taken to Central Police Station last night. They were being charged early this morning and were expected to be released on personal bond.

First reports indicated injuries suffered in the melee were of a minor nature. Only two persons were taken to St. Vincent Charity Hospital. Because the emergency ward was already filled with more seriously injured persons, both refused to wait for treatment, a hospital spokesman said.

It was not immediately determined if anyone was treated at the Stadium's first aid clinic. When reporters went there it was closed.

When the trouble started, Cleveland Police Sgt. Hubert J. Forray, who was on the Stadium detail, called for help to beef up his force of one other off-duty Cleveland policeman and 50 Stadium police. He said 20 police cars from the tactical and impact units and the 3rd, 4th and 5th Districts responded.

After the players fought off the mob and reached their clubhouses, Ranger manager Billy Martin called his Cleveland counterpart, Ken Aspromonte, to express his appreciation.

"Billy called to thank us for helping him and his players," related Aspromonte, stunned and shaken.

"I've never seen anything like that in all my life and I have played baseball all over the world," said Aspromonte.

Indian players were angry because the riot probably cost them the game—although all of them were grateful to escape.

The last major league game to be forfeited was in September 1971, when the

Washington Senators played their final game in Washington. They were given permission to switch to Dallas a week earlier.

Indians' pitcher Dick Bosman, then a member of the Senators, was there, but this riot was "different," he said.

"The fans in Washington were not mean . . . they were only looking for mementos," said Bosman. "This was a mean, ugly, frightening crowd."

About 12,000 fans were expected, and 48 policemen were in attendance at the onset. That was 16 more than under ordinary circumstances.

The interruptions by fans racing across the outfield began about the fourth inning and increased in number as the game wore on—and as fans guzzled more beer.

In the sixth inning, one of the youths who raced across the outfield, stopped and disrobed—then streaked back and forth until he escaped over the right field fence and into the arms of a policeman.

Even a woman had to be apprehended by the police and she was wobbling, too.

Among the objects thrown onto the field were many firecrackers, including a string of them near the Rangers' bullpen in the seventh inning.

When that happened, the Rangers in the bullpen raced across the field to their dugout. The Indians' bullpenners did the same thing a half-inning later.

The Indians, who trailed until the ninth, were victimized by outfielder Tom Grieve, who blasted two solo homers and singled in four trips to the plate.

It was largely through Grieve's efforts that the Rangers were on top and Ferguson Jenkins seemed headed for his eighth victory with relative ease.

However, Jenkins was forced out of the game with a nonriot injury in the sixth. Jenkins, who was struck in the midsection by a line drive earlier in the game, was spiked in a play at third base.

Steve Foucault, who took over for Jenkins, blanked the Indians until the ninth when, with one out, George Hendrick doubled.

As the fans became more and more agitated, Ed Crosby, making his first appearance in a Cleveland uniform, batted for Ossie Blanco and singled to cut the Tribe deficit to 5–4.

Rusty Torres then went to the plate for Dave Duncan and also singled, sending Crosby to second.

Martin, obviously determined to stick with Foucault—he had nobody warming up because the bullpen was barren of players—visited the mound and this, too, set off another ear-breaking reaction by the spectators.

Martin returned to the dugout amid a shower of boos and beer while policemen were helpless to stop the offenders. Alan Ashby batted for Frank Duffy and beat out an infield single that loaded the bases.

That brought John Lowenstein to the plate to the accompaniment of feet-stomping spectators and the organist playing fight-song music.

Lowenstein went to a 3-and-2 count and lofted a sacrifice fly to Joe Lovitto that tied the score and moved the potential winning run to third base with two out.

At that moment, as the dust was clearing from Crosby's slide across the plate, the youths jumped out seeking Burroughs' cap.

Then people were coming from everywhere—including players from both teams racing to protect Burroughs. It was then that Hilgendorf was hit by the chair.

The brawl, fans vs. players, went on for nearly 10 minutes. It never totally stopped, but at least the Rangers and Indians were able to get away and head for their dugouts.

However, by the time the Rangers got as far as the pitching mound, another brawl broke out.

This time most of the Indians formed a wall in front of several Texas players grappling with fans, trying to hold off the rest of the youths trying to get into the fray.

As the Indians trooped into the clubhouse, many bleeding and bruised, they screamed frustration.

Aspromonte, choked with anger, disgust and frustration, couldn't talk for 10 minutes.

Finally, in a soft voice, Aspromonte shook his head and commented, "Those people were like animals. But it's not just baseball, it's the society we live in. Nobody seems to care about anything.

"We complained about their people in Arlington last week when they threw beer on us and taunted us to fight, but look at our people. They were worse.

"I don't know if it was just the beer . . . I don't know what it was, and I don't know who's to blame, but I'm scared."

The phone rang. It was Martin. The two managers spoke for a few minutes and Aspromonte thanked Martin at the end. He also apologized to Martin.

"Billy feels as badly as we do, but he was grateful we helped," said Aspromonte.

It was a bad day for baseball in Cleveland.

12

Frank Robinson Hired as First African American Manager (1974)

SOURCE: Cleveland *Plain Dealer*, October 3, 1974

On September 8, 1974, the New York Times *published a letter from former major leaguer Billy Werber, written in response to a statement by Bowie Kuhn that the hiring of an African American manager was overdue. Werber questioned the morality and literacy of several leading candidates and even cited the record of various African dictators in his attempt to counter Kuhn's comment. Kuhn characterized Werber's argument as "irrelevant" and added that "there are qualified men available and it is only simple justice for baseball to recognize that fact."*

Less than one month after the publication of Werber's letter, the Cleveland Indians repudiated his arguments and made history by hiring Frank Robinson as the game's first African American manager. Although Werber (who attacked Robinson in his letter) is never mentioned by Hal Leibovitz in his editorial, his accusations are addressed in Lebovitz's commentary on Robinson's sterling character. Lebovitz concluded his column with a word of caution: "I wish him the very best. I hope every Indians' fan does." Robinson's record in his two and a half years with the Indians, while admirable given Cleveland's mediocre talent, was an unspectacular 186-189. He later managed the San Francisco Giants, Baltimore Orioles, and Montreal Expos/Washington Nationals franchise. Interestingly, Robinson's managerial debut with the Indians occurred on April 8, 1975, exactly one year after Hank Aaron exposed racist attitudes by breaking Babe Ruth's home run record.

Hal Asks . . .

Robbie . . . His Time Has Come
By Hal Lebovitz
Sports Editor

Frank Robinson is a man whose time has come and who is entitled to the opportunity to which he has dedicated himself.

He didn't kick another man out to get it. He worked hard and waited and he dreamed and he prayed and he hoped.

Many men aspire and dream and hope and their time does come and it passes them by because those in power pass them by.

Frank Robinson's time has come and fate has not passed him by.

Today, in the national spotlight, while the cameras of all three major TV networks point at him, in front of a packed Stadium Club, Frank Robinson will be unveiled officially as manager of the Cleveland Indians—the first black manager in the history of the major leagues.

Because he is the first, there will be much made of the color of his skin in all the dispatches and tapes and films. As we wrote Sunday, he will be the first black manager at the start of the season—perhaps the first half—but after that, he'll no longer be unique. He'll simply become Frank Robinson, Manager. And he'll rise or fall, not on the color of his skin but on his ability, or lack of it, to handle pitchers; on his ability, or lack of it, to run a ball club. And a ball club is 25 men, not just a George Hendrick who perhaps cannot be handled by anybody.

Robinson is getting his chance because Indians' general manager Phil Seghi is willing to put himself on the spot. He has taken the risk. In his opinion, the Indians should have been a contender all season, not just the first half. He had made up his mind many weeks ago to dump Ken Aspromonte, concluding Ken wasn't getting the most out of the material with which he had been provided. Seghi decided Robinson could.

It's a monumental gamble only because it is impossible to make an advance evaluation of Robinson's ability to manage. Except for some experience in Puerto Rico, which most executives write off as inconsequential, he has no track record as a manager.

His appointment can be likened to that of Gabe Paul's decision to name Joe Adcock in 1967. Adcock had been a fine player. He appeared to have a strong personality. The California Angels' bosses had said they were grooming him for managership. Paul stepped in and signed him. Adcock was a flop. His time had come—but he was found wanting.

Robinson may prove out differently. Nobody knows. But personally, I'm glad to see he is getting the opportunity.

I would rather have a fresh, eager, deserving Robinson than some washed-out manager who has made the rounds. It's another exciting adventure in Cleveland baseball history and I'm glad to be aboard for the ride. I hope all the fans look at it this way.

I don't know Robinson personally. I interviewed him briefly when he was with other teams. I asked direct questions and he gave direct answers. He was not easy to approach, rather cold, in fact. But we look[ed] each other in the eye and in a few words he answered each question clearly and honestly. That's all I wanted or expected.

He is the same with most writers he doesn't know well. Yet with those who cover him daily, the rapport is excellent.

Richard Bilotti, who covers the local sports scene for the Associated Press, properly looks at all aspects of his beat in a questioning, almost skeptical manner. He buys nothing and nobody at first glance. He expressed his grave doubts about the acquisition of Robinson. He wondered if Robinson could handle the many problems woven into the Indians.

After he heard there had been a clubhouse squabble between Robinson and Gaylord Perry, he went to Robinson. It's never easy to approach a superstar and say, "Did you have a fight?" The reaction usually is, "It was nothing." Or, "What do you want to write about that for?" Or, "Why do you want to bring up that kind of garbage?"

Instead, Robinson said, "Yes, we did have words. I raised my voice. Gaylord didn't. We had it out and as far as I'm concerned, it's all over."

The candidness was refreshing and Robinson gained in stature with Bilotti. I'm told this is how it is with everyone who gets to know him. I called a close friend in New York, a successful author, who knows Robinson well and whose judgment I value.

"The more you're with Robinson the more you will appreciate him," said my friend. "He is highly intelligent, articulate and decent. He always has wanted to be a manager, like somebody might always want to be a doctor. It's not that he wanted to be the first black manager. He wanted to be a manager, period. He has groomed himself for the job. He watched other managers and players and he put all the data in his mind. I think he'll be a good one, yes, an outstanding one. Certainly he deserves the chance."

Nobody can argue that. He is a man whose time has come and who has been given the opportunity. I wish him the very best. I hope every Indians' fan does.

13

"Catfish" Hunter Granted Free Agency by Arbitrator (1974)

SOURCE: Statement from MLBPA, December 16, 1974, Peter Seitz Papers, #5733, Box 1, Folder 22, Kheel Center for Labor-Management and Archives, Cornell University Library

Oakland A's star pitcher Jim "Catfish" Hunter's 1974 contract stipulated that $50,000 of his salary for that season was to be paid into an annuity fund administered by Hunter's insurance company. When Oakland owner Charles Finley—who earned his fortune in the insurance industry—realized that this sum could not be deducted from his club's taxes, he refused to make the payment. Upon learning this, MLBPA executive director Marvin Miller persuaded Hunter to file a grievance. According to the Basic Agreement, the grievance hearing would be decided by representatives of the players (Miller), the owners (John Gaherin), and an independent arbitrator agreed to by both sides, Peter Seitz.

On December 13 Seitz ruled that Finley's violation of Hunter's contract invalidated the contract and made Hunter baseball's first free agent. The result of this momentous decision was a frenzied bidding war for Hunter's services, slowed only temporarily by Commissioner Kuhn's efforts to curtail the process. Before the end of the year Hunter signed a five-year, $3.75 million contract with the New York Yankees (which was exceeded by two other clubs), proving that the value of star players on the open market was far higher than they had even dared to dream. However, since this was a onetime exception, they would have to wait another year before free agency became a possibility for them.

Printed here is the official statement following Seitz's decision by the MLBPA.

For Immediate Release

DECEMBER 16, 1974

The Major League Baseball Players Association today issued the following statement:

"The action of Mr. James A. Hunter in terminating his contract with the Oakland Athletics because of a violation of that contract by the Club has been upheld by a final and binding decision of the Arbitration Panel in Major League baseball. The Panel sustained Mr. Hunter by awarding as follows:

'Mr. Hunter's Contract for services to be performed during the 1975 season no longer binds him and he is a free agent. The Club shall compensate Mr. Hunter in the amount deducted from his salary during the 1974 season, as deferred compensation, with interest from August 1, 1974 at 6% per annum.'

"The Arbitration Panel, established under the Basic Agreement between the 24 clubs and the Players Association to render final and binding decisions on grievances referred to it, held a Hearing on November 26, 1974. It heard the testimony of Mr. Charles O. Finley, part Owner of the Club, of Mr. Lee MacPhail, President of the American League, Mr. Hunter, Mr. J. Carlton Cherry, Mr. Hunter's attorney, and of an expert witness on deferred compensation. On the basis of all the testimony and examination of all the relevant documents, the Arbitration Panel found that the Oakland Club had breached its contract with Mr. Hunter and had refused to correct that breach.

"The Panel found that the contract between Mr. Hunter and the Oakland Club was clear and free from ambiguity. It provided that the Club agreed to 'pay to any person, firm or corporation designated by said Player (Hunter), the sum of Fifty Thousand ($50,000.00) Dollars per year, for the duration of this contract to be deferred compensation, same to be paid during the season as earned.'

"Despite Mr. Hunter's designation of an insurance company to which the funds were to be paid, the Oakland Club improperly retained the money and refused to carry out its contractual commitment. The Panel found this to be a breach of Mr. Hunter's contract by the Oakland Club and justified its termination by Mr. Hunter.

"As a result of the final and binding Decision of the Arbitration Panel, Mr. Hunter is a free agent and can enter into a contract with any of the 24 Major League Clubs.

"The Impartial Chairman of the Arbitration Panel, who wrote the 40-page Opinion in the case, is Mr. Peter Seitz of New York City. His Decision was concurred in by Marvin J. Miller, the Players Association's member of the Panel. Mr. John J. Gaherin, the Clubs' member, dissented. A majority decision of the Panel is binding on the Parties.

"Mr. Richard Moss, General Counsel of the Players Association, presented the Association's case at the hearing. Mr. Barry Rona presented the Clubs' case. Counsel for the American League and the National League also participated.

"Commenting upon the Decision, Mr. Miller stated that:

'The Decision represented forthright affirmation of the sanctity of contracts, the cornerstone of peaceful and constructive employer-employee relationships. Although, in this instance, the Decision affirmed the termination of a contract, it did so squarely on the basis of upholding and affirming the termination provisions of the contract between Players and Clubs. Each player's contract contains a number of provisions under which a Club may terminate a contract with a player. These provisions are used frequently by the Clubs; i.e., unconditional release of a player by a Club during the period of his contract. Each such contract also contains a provision under which a player may terminate his contract:

"The Player may terminate this contract upon written notice to the Club, if the Club shall default in the payments to the Player provided for in Paragraph 2 hereof or shall fail to perform any other obligation agreed to be performed by the Club hereunder and if the Club shall fail to remedy such a default within ten (10) days after the receipt by the Club of written notice of such default."

"In essence, the Panel found that Mr. Hunter properly terminated his contract and was a free agent because the Club defaulted in payments due and failed to remedy such default (to this date) long after its receipt of written notice of such default. The Panel's Decision, therefore, upholds the sanctity of a contract and nothing more."

2

The Seitz Era

The mid-1970s marked the first of what would be many periods during which the owners, like Chicken Little, cried that the sky was falling. The declaration by independent arbitrator Peter Seitz that Jim "Catfish" Hunter was a free agent due to the failure of A's owner Charlie Finley to carry out the terms of his contract was bad enough. But when Seitz decided the following year that the reserve clause, as traditionally enforced by teams, was invalid since it permitted the club to hold the rights to a player for only one season played without a contract, all hell broke loose. The owners conceded defeat only after firing Seitz and fighting his decision in federal court, and agreed to a form of free agency in a new Basic Agreement that, unknown to them, sowed the seeds for an even greater defeat in the late 1980s.

On a brighter note this period was highlighted by what many consider the greatest World Series ever played, the 1975 classic between the Cincinnati Reds and the Boston Red Sox, and arguably the first great league championship series between AL rivals New York and Kansas City in 1976. Baseball's prospects were good enough that Commissioner Kuhn nearly convinced the State Department to permit a series of games between American and Cuban all-stars (which would not take place until 1999) and bragged to Congress about rising attendance, but he and the owners feared the future under the specter of free agency and the continued reign of Marvin Miller.

14

State Department Considers Permitting Exhibition

Game with Cuba (1975)

SOURCE: Freedom of Information Act Request No. 199903253, Department of State telegram from Assistant Secretary of State William D. Rogers, February 15, 1975. Also see http://www.gwu .edu/~nsarchiv/NSAEBB/NSAEBB12/nsaebb12.htm, "Beisbol Diplomacy."

On January 17, 1999, Peter Kornbluh, a researcher with the National Security Archive, published an article in the Washington Post *in which he outlined efforts by Bowie Kuhn and several members of the Ford administration to organize a series of baseball games between Cuban and American all-star teams in the mid-1970s. The effort to stage the series was conducted at the top levels of the State Department and was supported by Assistant Secretary of State William Rogers, Senator George McGovern, and Lawrence Eagleburger, an aide to Secretary of State Henry Kissinger. Eventually Kissinger rejected Kuhn's efforts to practice "ping-pong diplomacy" with Cuba. The initiative was not entirely secret; occasional articles on the proposal appeared in the* New York Times *and the* Washington Post *between May 1975 (when McGovern discussed it with Fidel Castro on a well-publicized trip to Cuba) and January 1976, by which time all hopes for approval of the series had been dashed.*

Kornbluh uncovered eighteen documents from January to June 1975, which are posted on the National Security Archives Web site under the title "Beisbol Diplomacy." A Freedom of Information Act request by this author yielded thirty-four additional documents, one of which is printed here. In this letter William Rogers explains the positive aspects of a baseball series with Cuba from a diplomatic perspective.

1. THE ADVANTAGES TO THE BASEBALL VISIT ARE THESE:

A. The political center of gravity in the U.S. on the Cuban issue is shifting. As of now, a very large number of those in the Congress who speak to foreign policy issues are in favor of some movement on Cuba. We received more criticism for our failure to go all the way and vote yes in Quito than for moving to a neutral position. And since then, the sentiment in the new Congress is moving steadily in that direction. Even Gale McGee, who has been a good soldier, is now positioning himself in favor of some normalization. So we think that politically the step would be applauded domestically. Some Cuban exile groups and others are poised against any movement on Cuba. A baseball trip would disarm them. It is much more difficult for the angries to attack a baseball game than an OAS or third country sanctions move.

B. Baseball is close to non-political. The trip would give to the president, and to whatever congressman chose to comment, the opportunity to stress their interest in sports, and their perception that competitive athletics can contribute to world understanding. This would be an appealing posture for the president, both domestically and internationally.

C. To send a team to Cuba would of course attract publicity at this time and would be regarded as "ping-pong diplomacy" but with the additional advantage that baseball is our national sport, and our teams are far and away the best. Moving Cuba to the sports pages would be a refreshing relief from the tortured debates over Cuba in the OAS.

D. As to the effect in Cuba, although Castro has an interest in our trade and technology, it is clear that he must be concerned over the long haul with the contamination of his revolution by American values; to which Cubans were more addicted than any other Latin American nation in pre-Castro times. A baseball visit would nurture other pressures within Cuba toward a more open society, and it would say something to the Cuban people that we are not a hard, unchanging adversary.

E. In Latin America, the effect of the trip would on the whole be positive. We would emphasize, beforehand to Ambassador Araujo Castro and one or two others, that the trip is a response to the demands of American sports fans. It is not so much a departure, as it is an effort to make practice in the field of professional baseball—our national sport—consistent with the traditions of World Cup competition, where, we would recall, Brazil and other western national soccer teams competed against East Germany long before the nations had exchanged ambassadors. In such countries as Mexico, Colombia, and Venezuela the trip would give a bit of earnest to our representations that we are willing to consider ways to untie the Cuban knot. This may therefore give us some chips in the bargaining over U.S. subsidiary exports. We would also point out that it is not a radical change in our policy; we have permitted the travel of many athletes to Cuba, including baseball teams (though not of our top professionals). And we would add that there is nothing in the OAS sanctions, to which we continue to adhere, embargoing sports relationships.

F. The game would occur within a few hours of your stop in Chile, if you hold to the tentative schedule of an early-April visit.

G. Finally, the visit would compromise whatever pretensions Castro still has as a heroic figure opposed to everything American.

Ingersoll

15

Congress Recognizes Promotion of Baseball's One Millionth Run (1975)

SOURCE: *Congressional Record*, April 28, 1975, E 2022

Bob Watson of the Houston Astros is credited with scoring major league baseball's one millionth run on May 4, 1975, in the second inning of a game against the San Francisco Giants. The only reason this information was known—and why Watson raced around the bases to ensure that he would score the "historic" run—is that the event had become a promotional vehicle for Tootsie Roll Industries and major league baseball, endorsed by Congress. It should be noted that Watson's achievement was one of public relations only—statistical totals for baseball's early years have changed with every new encyclopedia edition as additional research reveals more errors, and the significance of any run total is entirely arbitrary in any case.

COMMEMORATION PLANNED OF BASEBALL'S 1-MILLIONTH RUN

HON. HENRY J. HYDE of Illinois
IN THE HOUSE OF REPRESENTATIVES
Monday, April 28, 1975

Mr. HYDE. Mr. Speaker, baseball, America's national pastime, will reach an unusual milestone this spring, thanks to an enterprising young man with a flair for statistics—and a public-spirited company that brought his discovery to the public.

Mark Jay Sackler, a 24-year-old radio announcer from Westport, Conn., researched the Baseball Encyclopedia and determined that someone in baseball will score the 1,000,000th run in the history of the National—since 1876—and American—since 1901—Leagues sometime this spring. At the end of the 1974 season, a total of 997,869 runs had been scored in regular season play in both leagues; 2,131 shy of the magic number.

Mr. Sackler took his idea to Tootsie Roll Industries, whose national headquarters are in Chicago; and that company, like baseball an American institution, is sponsoring a nationwide consumer project centered around the recording of the 1,000,000th run.

The player who actually scores the landmark run will receive from Tootsie Roll among other awards the sum of $10,000, which he will, in turn, donate to the Association of Professional Ball Players, an organization dedicated to the needs of former major and minor league players. Fred Haney is president and Joe DiMaggio, first vice president, of this organization.

The 1,000,000th Run promotion is being directed by Hall of Famer Stan Musial, the former St. Louis Cardinal great; Ernie Banks, the all-time star Chicago Cubs shortstop; and ex–Brooklyn Dodger pitcher, Ralph Branca.

Baseball and the Tootsie Roll Co. are to be commended for fostering projects such as this, which prove that the youth of America, as exemplified by the scores of talented athletes and creative young men like Mr. Sackler, continues to be the most vital force in our country.

16

Rules for Joe Garagiola/Bazooka Big League Bubble Gum Blowing Championship (1975)

SOURCE: Pamphlet, August 8, 1975, "Tobacco" file, National Baseball Hall of Fame Library

Another promotional device for major league baseball was the Bazooka Big League Bubble Gum Blowing Championship, hosted by NBC baseball announcer Joe Garagiola. Early rounds in the competition were aired during NBC's Saturday Game of the Week broadcasts, with the final rounds staged during the playoffs and World Series, also on NBC. The first-place award in this contest—won by Milwaukee's Kurt Bevacqua—and for baseball's one millionth run promotion, and the apparent popularity of the events for players, reflect the scarcity of promotional opportunities and the significance of additional income in the pre–free agency era.

Joe Garagiola/Bazooka BIG LEAGUE BUBBLE GUM BLOWING CHAMPIONSHIP

PURPOSE

To establish, through a full-scale elimination tournament among major league baseball players, the one player capable of blowing the largest Bazooka bubble gum bubble. The tournament is to be conducted in a formal and serious manner.

ELIGIBILITY

To be eligible, each participant must be on the active roster of a major league baseball team and, at the time of participation, must have been on the roster for a minimum of 30 days during the 1975 season.

1. Active roster includes players on disabled list.

2. Suspended, voluntarily retired and restricted players are not eligible to participate.

PROCEDURE

Each major league baseball team will stage a bubble gum blowing championship to determine its individual team champion.

An elimination tournament among team champions will be conducted in both the American and National Leagues to determine the individual league champions.

The American and National League champions will compete at the World Series to determine the "Big League Bubble Gum Blowing Champion."

AWARDS

Each team champion will receive a Mounted Citation.

The American and National League champions will receive giant size baseball cards of themselves.

The major league champion will receive a cash award of $1,000, plus a full case of Bazooka Bubble Gum for himself and a full case of Bazooka Bubble Gum and $1,000 to his favorite charity serving youngsters.

RULES

All competitions at every stage of the tournament will be conducted under the following rules:

1. Each participant will be given five (5) packages of Bazooka Bubble Gum and may use any part—or all—of the gum for his participation.

2. The participant will be permitted 15 minutes to condition the bubble gum prior to the Bubble Gum Blowing Competition. No special ingredients may be added to the bubble gum. No mechanical devices may be used to soften the bubble gum.

3. Each contestant will be given three (3) tries at bubble blowing.

4. The bubble blown will be measured at its largest circumference upon a signal from the player, so that it can be measured at its widest point. The responsibility for maintaining the bubble long enough to be measured will be the player's.

5. In the event that winds are strong enough to distort the blown bubble, the competition will be held indoors or in a sheltered area.

JUDGING

The size of the blown bubbles will be measured by a specially-designed set of calipers supplied by Topps Chewing Gum.

In the competition for the Individual Team Champions, the bubbles will be measured by a responsible person, such as a team executive, a local dignitary, a local sports writer or editor, a local TV or radio broadcaster, or a local clergyman. It can be judged by a committee of the aforementioned.

In the contests between Individual Team Champions to determine the League Champion, the measuring and judging will be done by a committee consisting of a sports writer or sportscaster representing each competing team and a clergyman or Major League Umpire.

In the Championship contest, the judging will be done by one of the Major League Umpires assigned to officiate at the World Series.

17

Fisk Home Run Ends Classic World Series Game (1975)

SOURCE: *Cincinnati Enquirer*, October 22, 1975

The sixth game of the 1975 World Series has been described by many fans and experts as one of the most exciting baseball games of all time. The context in which the game was played is critical to understanding the game's significance. The Cincinnati Reds, winners of 108 games during the regular season, were considered one of the greatest teams ever. The Reds entered this game with a three-games-to-two lead over the Boston Red Sox, with the final two games of the Series to be played in Boston's Fenway Park. The pivotal sixth game was delayed for three days by rain, raising the anticipation level even higher. Players such as Bernie Carbo, George Foster, Dwight Evans, and especially Carlton Fisk rose to the occasion, as described below.

Gullett to Face Sox' Lee

Fisk's Homer Beats Reds in 12th; Finale Tonight
By Bob Hertzel
Enquirer Sports Reporter

BOSTON—A dramatic home run by Carlton Fisk in the bottom of the 12th inning lifted the Boston Red Sox to a 7–6 victory over the Cincinnati Reds Wednesday night and forced the 1975 World Series into a seventh game.

The seventh game will be played at 8:30 tonight, Don Gullett going against Bill Lee.

Fisk's homer, a tremendous drive that ripped into the foul pole high above "the Green Monster" wall, came at the expense of Pat Darcy, the eighth Cincinnati pitcher in the game, tying a World Series record.

"I didn't know if it was fair or foul but I knew it was gone," said Fisk, who half ran, half leaped around the bases four hours and one minute after the start of a game that had been postponed three days by rain.

And that the homer was meaningful goes back to Dwight Evans, who turned in what was perhaps the greatest defensive play ever in a World Series game.

With Ken Griffey on first base and one out in the 11th inning, Joe Morgan sent a tremendous drive into the right-field corner.

Evans, his back to the plate, raced toward the wall. At the last second, still heading toward the fence, Evans stuck out his glove and corralled the ball.

By this time Griffey was all the way around past second base. He was doubled off first base.

"The greatest catch I've ever seen," was Sparky Anderson's comment.

The game started in a swirl of controversy, Anderson going with Gary Nolan over Jack Billingham, drawing the ire of Billingham and a lot of second-guessing from his players.

It didn't take long until Anderson was proved wrong. Fred Lynn followed singles by Carl Yastrzemski and Fisk with a home run into the right-field bleachers to put Boston on top, 3–0, in the first inning.

Anderson's decision looked even more questionable in the third inning. With the bases loaded and two out and Fred Norman in the game in relief of Nolan, Anderson came on with Billingham.

The tall right-hander struck out Rico Petrocelli to end that Boston threat. An inning later Billingham worked out of a one-out, man-on-second-and-third situation.

That gave the Reds a chance to fight back into the game with three runs in the fifth off Luis Tiant, who had won twice in the Series.

The rally started with an Ed Armbrister walk. Followed by a Pete Rose single.

Ken Griffey then drove a line drive off the centerfield wall for a triple, Fred Lynn crashing into the concrete and tumbling into an immobile mass at the base of the fence.

There was total silence among the 35,205 in the stands, lasting for many moments until Lynn finally rose.

Tiant was losing it fast by the seventh inning. That inning started with singles by Griffey and Joe Morgan.

Then, with two out, George Foster slammed a double to center and the Reds were on top, 5–3. A home run by Cesar Geronimo off Tiant added a sixth run for the Reds in the top of the eighth.

When the first two Boston batters reached base against Pedro Borbon in the bottom of the eighth, Rawly Eastwick was called up to nail down the championship.

He retired two men, then former Red Bernie Carbo took care of a fast ball out over the plate, driving it deep into the centerfield seats for a tie.

But the action was just starting. In the bottom of the ninth the Red Sox loaded the bases with no one out. Will McEnaney now was the pitcher.

Lynn sent a fly ball into short left, Foster coming over to make the catch, then uncorking a perfect throw home. It went as a double play and, when Petrocelli grounded out, the game continued.

Evans' catch on Morgan was the next game-saving play.

"I was just hoping it would get to the seats before he got to it. I knew it was sinking fast," said Morgan. And Morgan had one other comment to make.

"Beer tonight," he said as he took a swallow. "Champagne tomorrow."

18

Massachusetts Congressman Complains to Kuhn about Series Umpiring (1975)

SOURCE: House of Representatives, Hearings Before the Subcommittee on Communications of the Committee on Interstate and Foreign Commerce, *Sports Broadcasting Act of 1975*, 94th Cong., 1st sess., October 31, 1975, 142–43

Disappointed in the outcome of the 1975 Series and in particular bothered by a controversial umpire's decision, Congressman Torbert MacDonald took advantage of a congressional hearing on baseball to complain to Commissioner Kuhn. Kuhn helps to explain the arrangement under which the American and National Leagues agreed to compromise their rules, especially the designated hitter rule, in order to stage the Series.

Mr. [Torbert H.] MACDONALD [D-Mass.]. Before I turn the floor over to the other two gentlemen, I have two nongermane questions. They are very germane, but not to this hearing, that is.

Question No. 1: Why is it that the American League always has to play under National League rules in the World Series, with no designated hitter and where their hitters have hit all year long? Even though Tiant got two hits, he looks like my Aunt Mame.

Mr. KUHN. Under the arrangement that was made between the two leagues at the time the designated hitter was adopted, it was agreed by both that the designated hitter would not be used in the World Series.

Mr. MACDONALD. The American League agreed to that?

Mr. KUHN. Yes; agreed to that, yes, and in All Star games. That, however desirable it might have been as a solution to an immediate problem, in my judgment does not promise to be a very satisfactory situation for the long term, and I have told the clubs that I think they are going to have to find some solution to this problem, and if they don't, maybe the Commissioner will have to find one for them.

Mr. MACDONALD. My second and last question of any sort, I repeat, is not germane to this hearing, but it is a great curiosity to me. Why, in the World Series, aren't there at least one or two officials, and I was going to say "umpires," plate umpires automatically, since it was the plate umpire that was at fault for blowing a game for the Red Sox? Why not have at least a couple that went through it before? Why have six or eight or however many you have in reserve as well as the ones on the field who have never been in a series before? Because, well, I am prejudiced, maybe, but I have seen the rerun about 20 times, and I have seen stills, and I have seen everything, and Armbrister—is that his name?

Mr. KUHN. Armbrister, yes.

Mr. MACDONALD. He was throwing a block on Fisk. Fisk couldn't get him away to throw the ball, and he said, "Well, he has a right to first base."

Nobody is disputing that, but he didn't have a right to stand in front of the catcher. I just think it was inexperience.

Mr. KUHN. The situation on the umpires is this. Under the collective bargaining agreement between the two leagues and their umpires' associations, there is a required rotation of the umpires into the World Series, and the staffing of the World Series this year was the fruit of that collective bargaining agreement.

I would say, though, that no umpire can appear in the World Series or is eligible for the rotation unless he has been an umpire in the major leagues for at least 6 years, so that all of the umpires in the World Series were very experienced professional umpires of ability, and I think overall did a very commendable job in the series, although I know that Boston fans do not in all regards agree with me.

Mr. MACDONALD. Well, there were two that were getting to be called the Cisco Kid from the National League, and Umpire Bernhart—is that his name?

Mr. KUHN. Barnett.

Mr. MACDONALD. Barnett, who is being called less polite things, but I couldn't understand why none of them had been, you know, through a series before, even a playoff series.

Mr. KUHN. I will tell you, Mr. Chairman, I asked our leagues to review that situation with the umpires association.

Mr. MACDONALD. That is good news. Thank you very much.

19

Arbitrator Decides Against Validity of Reserve Clause (1975)

SOURCE: Marvin Miller Papers, Series II, Box 3, Folder 16, Robert F. Wagner Labor Archives Tamiment Library; Peter Seitz Papers, #5733, Box 2, Folder 2, Kheel Center for Labor-Management and Archives, Cornell University Library

The documents presented here are among the most important baseball documents of the twentieth century. Andy Messersmith, a star pitcher for the Los Angeles Dodgers, and Dave McNally, a pitcher for the Montreal Expos contemplating retirement, played the entire 1975 season without contracts and claimed free-agent status in grievances filed by the union on October 7. Their clubs countered by asserting that the reserve clause in their previously signed contracts gave the clubs the right to indefinitely reserve their rights to the players. The MLBPA and Marvin Miller regarded the reserve clause, as traditionally interpreted, as illegal, while the owners believed it was absolutely essential to the economic health of baseball.

Arbitrator Seitz concluded that the law clearly supported the MLBPA's position, but felt that for the reserve clause to be overturned on an arbitrator's decision would initiate a war between players and owners. In his letter to both parties he made clear his intention to vote for the MLBPA but urged them to meet and agree to amend the reserve clause themselves. The owners, convinced of the validity of their position, failed to heed the warning and suffered the consequences.

NOTICE OF GRIEVANCE

TO: Player Relations Committee
FROM: Major League Baseball Players Association
DATE: October 7, 1975
SUBJECT: Grievance No. 75-27. Major League Baseball Players Association and the 24 Major League Clubs

On or about March 10, 1975, the Los Angeles Dodgers renewed the 1974 Uniform Player's Contract of John A. Messersmith, pursuant to paragraph 10 (a) thereof, for the period of one year.

Paragraph 10 (a) of the Contract provides, in relevant part, as follows:

" . . . If prior to the March 1 next succeeding said December 20, the Player and the Club have not agreed upon the terms of such contract, then on or before 10 days after said March 1, the Club shall have the right by written notice to the player . . . to renew this contract *for the period of one year* on the same terms . . . " (Emphasis supplied)

The Uniform Player's Contract defines "year," in paragraph 1, as:

" . . . including the Club's training season, the Club's exhibition games, the Club's playing season, the League Championship Series and the World Series (or any other official series in which the Club may participate and in any receipts of which the Player may be entitled to share)."

Mr. Messersmith performed for the Los Angeles Club in 1975 under the renewed Contract, and, since the Club was not eligible for any official post-season series, he completed the renewal year on September 28, 1975. As of September 29, 1975, the specified term of Mr. Messersmith's renewed Contract having expired, there was no longer any relation between the Los Angeles Club and the player, and Mr. Messersmith became free to negotiate with any of the 24 clubs with regard to his services for 1976. However, the clubs, acting through their agents and representatives, have conspired to deny Mr. Messersmith that right, and have maintained the position that the Los Angeles Club is still exclusively entitled to his services.

The clubs promptly should be ordered to treat Mr. Messersmith as a free agent, and should make Mr. Messersmith whole for any damages he may suffer due to the delay in doing so.

STATEMENT BY CHAIRMAN OF ARBITRATION PANEL

The parties having been fully heard in respect of the Messersmith and McNally grievances, the Panel has met in executive session. No definitive or final action on the grievances has been taken by the Arbitration Panel. No Award has been issued. I have informed my colleagues on the Panel, however, of the two decisions I have made:

1) After full consideration of the jurisdictional problem presented, at the proper time I intend to cast my vote to sustain the position of the Players Association that the Arbitration Panel has authority to act on the two grievances. A Panel decision on jurisdiction will issue in due course, accompanied by an Opinion expressing the Chairman's reasoning supporting the conclusions reached by him.

2) Briefly stated, the grievances raise the question whether a player, after the expiration of his "option year," on further renewal of his contract, can be "reserved" by his club to play for it, exclusively. The decision on the issue involves a complex of provisions (most of which appear in the Major League Rules) making up the Reserve System. These grievances present the first occasion since the advent of the Players Association in organized baseball on which this question is presented to the Arbitration Panel. The singularity of the circumstances is demonstrated by the

fact that only one other grievance had been filed, previously, during the period of the relationship; and that grievance had been rendered moot by subsequent action by the Player.

I have informed my colleagues on the Panel that I am not yet prepared to cast my vote with respect to the "merits" of the issue. I require additional time to study the voluminous transcript of the arbitration proceedings and the 97 documentary exhibits presented. There are other more important reasons than my own unreadiness to act, however, which persuade me that final action by the Panel should be delayed for a short time.

In the relatively brief period of nine years during which the Players Association has been in the picture in organized baseball, there has been conflict between the parties with respect to the Reserve System—the machinery by means of which the clubs reserve to their exclusive use the future services of players who had contracted to play for them. Excepting for its declared position in the *Flood Case* (expressed for the purposes of the anti-trust litigation) the Players Association has consistently recognized the need for *a* Reserve System, but regarded the present system as being too restrictive and requiring modification and relaxation. The leagues, on the infrequent occasions when the subject was under negotiation, have rejected, successfully, all Association demands (except for two provisions placed in the Basic Agreement now in force dealing with salary arbitration and veteran players). As a result of the discussions held, however, both parties are sufficiently conversant with each other's positions on the Reserve System to lead me to believe that if they were disposed to do so, they could mark out broad areas of agreement in very little time.

In the past, circumstances have militated against a full opportunity for collective bargaining by the parties to resolve their differences on the Reserve System. Their initial Basic Agreement (1968) provided for a joint study of the problem. Nothing seems to have come of this. Before negotiations started for the second Basic Agreement (1970) the parties were locked into impasse on the issue of the Reserve System by the *Flood Case* litigation. In that 1970 Basic Agreement, entered into before the end of litigation, they agreed that "there shall be no obligation to negotiate with respect to the reserve system" pending such litigation. Although two modifications of the Reserve System (in a sense) were made in the third and present Basic Agreement (1973) it appears to me that the scope and breadth of the System was not bargained out in such a way as to resolve the basic conflicts on the Reserve System. Since 1973 the parties have been at impasse on the resolution of these conflicts inasmuch as the 1973 Basic Agreement, like its predecessor, provided that during its term "there shall be no obligation to bargain with respect to the reserve system." In consequence, this Panel is called upon to make a final and binding decision as to a single facet of a system on the whole of which there has been insufficient bargaining.

It should be understood that these two grievances, important as they undoubtedly are, relate to only one small section of the territory embraced by the Reserve System. Both the clubs and the players have vital interests in the operation and scope of the Reserve System not brought into focus by the facts underpinning these two grievances.

It is my deep conviction that questions as to the scope and operation of a Reserve System—so critical to the interests of the clubs and the players—are much better answered by the parties affected, themselves, by pursuing the national policy of collective bargaining, than by a tribunal performing the quasi-judicial function of arbitration. As a witness before the Panel, the Commissioner of Baseball, Mr. Kuhn, expressed a like conviction. Referring to the problems raised by the differences between the parties on the Reserve System, he asserted that a "solution" alternative to the adjudication of such grievances as were before the Panel "is the one that I have fought for as long as we have had a collective bargaining relationship in this industry and that is to solve problems of this kind * * * through collective bargaining * * *." He observed, without the attribution of fault, that "both (parties) have shown a tendency to work very slowly in the process of collective bargaining"; but then he asserted, "*When I said that I felt collective bargaining can solve the problems that exist, I said that very seriously.*" (Emphasis supplied.)

I draw a great deal of encouragement from this constructive approach of the Commissioner.

I note a fortuitous circumstance: The Panel is supposed to issue its decision on these two grievances involving an important but relatively singular aspect of the Reserve System, and, coincidentally, the parties are engaged in negotiations for a new Basic Agreement to replace the 1973 Agreement. The entire scope and all aspects of the Reserve System are appropriate subjects for bargaining in those negotiations. Clearly, it would be vastly more desirable and profitable for the parties to take advantage of this coincidence of events, to endeavor to accommodate their objectives and interests in their bargaining than for this Panel to make a final Award on what has been an unusual state of facts affecting the Reserve System. Indeed, should the Panel decide these grievances today, it is not unlikely that its action would throw new obstacles and barriers in the path of collective bargaining to eliminate the conflicts—as the Commissioner and I envision it.

The Panel will not shrink from the performance of its duty; which is to make a decision *promptly* on the merits. This member of the Panel, however, believes that in terms of the interest of the sport, the clubs and the players, the business before the parties in their bargaining sessions on the Reserve System is infinitely more important than what is before the Panel—however important that business may be to two players and two clubs—and deserves priority ranking in consideration and action.

The relationship between these two parties is a relatively new one, as bargaining relationships in our industrial society go; and still requires much development. If the parties should be successful in bargaining to eliminate the conflicts relating to the Reserve System, they will have achieved a great deal for that relationship and those whom they represent. How can they fail to seize this unusual opportunity to demonstrate that collective bargaining is not merely something that the leagues and the

Players Association profess in speeches, as a matter of public relations, but, rather, a process in which they believe and which they are determined to make work?

Accordingly, as Chairman of the Arbitration Panel, I have made the following procedural decisions: The Panel's decision "on the merits" of the grievances will be delayed for a short period pending efforts of the leagues and the Players Association to accommodate their positions on the Reserve System, generally, through bargaining. Such bargaining should be given the first rank in priority in matters on their agenda. The parties shall report to the Chairman, not later than December 24, 1975 whether sufficient progress has been achieved to justify any further suspension of action by the Panel on the two grievances. If either the leagues or the Association, by such date, reports that the prospects in the bargaining described are unpromising, the Panel will issue its Award on the merits, forthwith, accompanied or unaccompanied, as the circumstances permit, by a Chairman's Opinion setting forth the reasons for his findings. If unaccompanied by such an Opinion, it will be issued as soon thereafter as possible. It is essential to the success of such bargaining that the two grievants and the two clubs, immediately, should put forth earnest and good faith efforts, in the interests of the sport, the clubs and all of the players, to resolve their particular disputes.

Both of the grievants and the two clubs, the leagues and the Players Association have a unique opportunity to demonstrate to the world of baseball and to our society, generally, that not only do they recognize their responsibilities, but that they have the competence to discharge them. I wish them success in their endeavors.

Peter Seitz, Chairman, Arbitration Panel
for the Major League Baseball Association
December 8, 1975

20

Seitz Fired by Major League Baseball; Columnist Attacks Seitz and His Decision (1975)

SOURCES: Letter from John J. Gaherin to Peter Seitz, December 23, 1975, Peter Seitz Papers, #5733, Box 2, Folder 2, Kheel Center; unlabelled copy, December 24, 1975, National Baseball Hall of Fame Library

Immediately after Seitz's decision in the Messersmith/McNally case was officially announced, the Player Relations Committee exercised its right under the Basic Agreement and fired Seitz. That decision pleased baseball columnist Dick Young, who attacked Seitz in an editorial the following day. Young's column no doubt pleased Bowie Kuhn, who in his autobiography referred to Seitz as "the fox in the henhouse."

December 23, 1975

Peter Seitz, Esq.
285 Central Park West
New York, NY 10024
Dear Mr. Seitz:

Article X—*Grievance Procedure* 10 (Arbitration Panel) provides in pertinent part as follows:

"At any time during the term of this Agreement either of the Party arbitrators may terminate the appointment of the impartial arbitrator by serving written notice upon him and the other Party arbitrator."

This is notice, served in accordance with the foregoing, that you are terminated as impartial arbitrator effective upon receipt of this notice.
Sincerely,
John J. Gaherin

DICK YOUNG'S REACTION:
"FREEING MESSERSMITH WORK OF BOMB-THROWER"

Peter Seitz reminds me of a terrorist, a little man to whom nothing very important has happened in his lifetime, who suddenly decides to create some excitement by tossing a bomb into things.

Seitz likes to do his thing during the holiday season. It was just about a year ago that he declared Catfish Hunter a free agent, creating an explosive bidding contest that went to the New York Yankees for $2.8 million on a three-year contract.

That was nothing compared to the dynamite Peter Seitz, labor arbitrator, tossed into the lobby of organized baseball yesterday. He has ruled that Andy Messersmith and Dave McNally are free agents by reason of the fact that they did not sign their 1975 contracts, therefore permitting the automatic renewal clause to lapse.

What Peter Seitz has ruled, in effect, is that there is no reserve clause. He has made it possible for a ballplayer to walk away from his team after one year. To trade himself, in actuality. Seitz has decided to override the Supreme Court of the United States. This is pretty much like a traffic court judge deciding that Standard Oil is in violation of the anti-trust laws.

It will be different this time. It won't be another Catfish Hunter case, with wild bidding by major league clubs for the services of Andy Messersmith, 19-game winner, and certainly not for Dave McNally, who walked away from his job last summer.

In the first place, Commissioner Bowie Kuhn has barred a bidding contest immediately. He has done it in a rather reverse way. He has not prohibited the 24 major league clubs from negotiating with Messersmith and-or McNally. He simply has failed to advise the clubs that the players are free agents. In the absence of such a declaration, the clubs cannot do business with either man. In the eyes of baseball, Peter Seitz notwithstanding, Messersmith and McNally are not free agents.

When Catfish Hunter was declared a free agent a year ago, Commissioner Kuhn announced shortly thereafter that, as of such-and-such a date, bids may be present-ed to Hunter by the ballclubs. This time, there has been no such starter's gun. This time there is the significant sentence at the conclusion of a joint statement issued by league presidents Lee MacPhail, AL, and Chub Feeney, NL:

" . . . At this time, our clubs have not been advised that players Messersmith and McNally are free to negotiate with other clubs."

The joint statement also contains the promise to take the Seitz decision to court. The lords of baseball had, in fact, taken this case to court even before it got to arbi-tration. On Oct. 28, in U.S. District Court, Western District of Missouri, the owner of the Kansas City Royals brought suit to block the arbitration action by Seitz. Ew-ing Kauffman, owner, claimed that the arbitor [sic] did not have the authority to consider such an important case.

Oddly, Kauffman did not own the contract of Andy Messersmith, a Los Angeles Dodger, nor Dave McNally, a Montreal Expo. Kauffman was acting as a clubowner who felt his investment in the Kansas City team jeopardized by the arbitration, so he filed the suit. Such are the wondrous ways of our jurisprudence.

Anyway, the judge in Kansas City told Kauffman to let the case go to arbitration and, if he didn't like the result, come back to court and fight it. This, Kauffman and the other lords intend to do. It will go quickly before Judge Oliver in Kansas City, and quite possibly be appealed by either side to the appellate court, and perhaps wind up in the U.S. Supreme Court, where it belongs.

While all this happens, winding through the time-taking corridors of the courts, what of Messersmith and McNally? Who owns them? For whom do they pitch, if at all?

The McNally case seems academic. Dave, disgusted with his performance, and obviously convinced his arm no longer had it, packed and went home on his own. He was making an enslaved $125,000. It is difficult to conceive of anyone bidding for him.

Messersmith, a quality pitcher, made a reported $90,000 in 1974 and held out for a three-year package totaling $770,000, it is said. The Dodgers, in panic as he played out the season without a contract, are believed to have offered him a package, esca-lating over three years, worth $540,000. They are said to have offered Messersmith $150,000 for this past season, $170,000 for next and $220,000 in 1977. Meanwhile, they were paying him on the basis of $115,000 for 1974, when they could legally have paid him $72,000.

Arbitration was set up, basically, for salary disputes, and such grievances as plane fare for a player's wife. The so-called nuts-and-bolts problems. Arbitration was not set up so that a man with a Napoleon complex could change the basic structure of the sport.

21

Kuhn Ends Lockout by Opening Spring Training Camps (1976)

SOURCE: *Sporting News*, April 3, 1976

Following the federal court decision supporting the ruling of Peter Seitz, angry owners responded by locking the players out of spring training until the two groups could agree on a modification of the Basic Agreement that would, for the first time, permit free agency under certain circumstances. After the MLBPA rejected what the owners called their "final offer" on March 17, Commissioner Kuhn unilaterally ended the lockout and reopened the camps effective the following day. The MLBPA and the PRC continued to discuss this critical issue, and finally drafted a new Basic Agreement during the All-Star break in mid-July.

Kuhn Opens Doors to Spring Training Camps
By Stan Isle
Associate Editor

ST. LOUIS—Sunshine broke through baseball's negotiating clouds March 18 when spring training started on major league fronts in Florida, Arizona and California.

That most welcome sound of spring—the crack of a bat on a ball—was heard in all 24 major league camps by March 20 and there were assurances from all sides the season would open April 8 as advertised.

A three-week delay in the start of training, caused by the impasse in tedious negotiations between owners and players over a new Basic Agreement, already had cut into the exhibition schedule. However, several clubs said they would be ready to begin exhibition play March 23 or 24.

Commissioner Bowie Kuhn ordered that all training camps be opened "at the earliest possible time" only a few hours after the Major League Players Association had, in effect, rejected what the owners termed their "best and final" offer March 17.

Kuhn interceded after the players, for the first time, indicated they might be ready to compromise on the key "one-and-one" issue in the reserve clause.

"Because I think it is now vital that spring training get under way without further delay, I have directed that all camps be opened at the earliest possible time," Kuhn said.

"While nobody is more disappointed than I that we do not have solid progress toward a final agreement, the fans are the most important people around and their interests now become paramount.

"Opening the camps and starting the season on time is what they want," the commissioner added.

Meanwhile, the war of words between management and players raged on and on.

Shocked at the players' refusal to accept their "best and final" offer, the Player Relations Committee met with other club executives for three hours in New York March 20, then announced their offer had been withdrawn.

"The offer has been withdrawn," said Lee MacPhail, American League president and spokesman for management. "We are going to negotiate further. We want to wait to hear their (the players') ideas."

Withdrawal of the offer came as no surprise to Marvin Miller, Players Association executive director and chief negotiator.

"When an offer is not acceptable to the other side, it's standard procedure to withdraw it," said Miller.

Ed Fitzgerald, Brewers' board chairman and head of the Player Relations Committee, said, "We had a very thorough and frank discussion of the current situation. Various opinions were expressed as to the wisdom of the offer made last week. There were very strong feelings on all sides concerning the wisdom of the offer."

Fitzgerald acknowledged that several owners felt the committee had gone too far in its offer, which accepted the "one-and-one" decision handed down last December by arbitrator Peter Seitz in the cases of pitchers Andy Messersmith and Dave McNally. The decision since has been upheld in two federal courts.

The owners came to two conclusions during their New York meeting, Fitzgerald said.

"Our committee is to press on in an attempt to gain resolution (of the issues) as quickly as possible," Fitzgerald said. "The owners also gave a unanimous vote of confidence to the committee's actions."

Earlier, Miller expressed puzzlement in describing what the owners termed their "final" offer.

"It contained at least a dozen points that have not been subject to negotiation," Miller said. "And it contained at least 20 items that were labeled 'to be discussed later.'"

Miller called the owners' proposal, a 10-page document submitted to the players at the 30th negotiating session, in St. Petersburg, March 15, a "public relations ploy."

"How can this be called a final offer?" he mused. "Look at Page 9. There's a list of 14 items headed 'Other Open Issues to Be Discussed.' How can we vote on such a paper? We have nothing to vote on."

Miller said the owners' proposal did not grant the players with current contracts their full rights under the Messersmith-McNally ruling and consequently they could sue for violation of their rights.

He also noted the proposal would permit the owners to reopen the negotiations on the Basic Agreement after two years although they supposedly have been negotiating on a four-year pact.

John Gaherin, who leads negotiations for management, expressed shock at the players' rejection of the March 15 package and warned, "We won't submit a better one."

Gaherin sluffed [sic] off the emphasis on liability and described it as "a smoke screen which the players have been employing." He said any player could always "initiate litigation but that the filing of a suit doesn't preclude that it has merit."

Was there still a ray of hope for a breakthrough in negotiations that have dragged on for nearly nine months?

One of the more outspoken player representatives, Bill Singer of the Rangers, revealed that the players were willing to come off their "total free agent" stance regarding the "one-and-one" issue.

"We're willing to go along with the guidelines the owners proposed (a player being eligible to negotiate with a maximum of eight clubs)," Singer said.

Then the players are willing to give up the bargaining power with all 24 clubs? "Yes," said Singer, "We're willing to compromise there."

Miller affirmed Singer's comment, with some reservation.

"That, I think is a significant step forward," said the players' chief negotiator.

While rejecting the owners' total package, the players proposed federal mediation to help break the logjam in negotiations.

The players also asked that the Basic Agreement, which expired December 31, be extended until a new agreement is signed and that a no-strike, no-lockout provision be reinstated.

Gaherin and the owners saw no merit in the proposal for federal mediation. "I don't think mediation is the answer," said Gaherin. "I don't feel a third party is needed."

There was almost unanimous agreement on one development.

Kuhn's decision to open the training camps was applauded by nearly everyone concerned.

Reaction ranged from the enthusiastic praise of Owner Brad Corbett of the Rangers to the less-than-enthusiastic compliance by August A. Busch, Jr., chief executive of the Cardinals.

"We were in a tenuous position," said Corbett. "Something had to be done and the commissioner did it. I've been an outspoken critic of his in the past, but I give him credit for what he did. It was a bold move and a good one," Corbett added.

Busch said Kuhn "believes this action is in the best interest of the fans and the game, plus assuring a more calm atmosphere for negotiations to continue.

"While the St. Louis Cardinals would prefer to have a final labor contract before we start spring training, regardless of our personal feeling, we intend to comply with both the spirit and letter of the commissioner's order."

Speaking for the players, Miller considered Kuhn's action "a constructive step."

Miller said the commissioner's intercession would assure opening the season as scheduled.

"There's been no threat of a strike by the players," Miller emphasized. "The whole thing has been an owners' lockout."

22

Kuhn Rules Against Charles Finley's
Sale of Players (1976)

SOURCE: Letter from Commissioner Bowie Kuhn to Charles O. Finley, George Steinbrenner, and Richard O'Connell, June 18, 1976, Harold and Dorothy Seymour Papers, #4809, Box 1, Folder 13, Division of Rare and Manuscript Collections, Cornell University Library

On June 15, 1976, the trading deadline, Oakland A's owner Charlie Finley began the process of rebuilding his dynasty by selling stars Rollie Fingers and Joe Rudi to the Boston Red Sox for $1 million each, and Vida Blue to the New York Yankees for $1.5 million. Although player sales were legal, Commissioner Kuhn was concerned that sales of this magnitude damaged the credibility of baseball by allowing wealthy clubs to dominate the labor market at the expense of the A's, which he felt would have no chance to compete after losing three star players at once. In the letter presented here Kuhn outlines his reasons for voiding the sale.

Finley responded by suing Kuhn in federal court. On March 17, 1977, the court found in favor of Kuhn. Finley appealed the decision and lost again, on April 7, 1978.

To: Charles O. Finley

George Steinbrenner

Richard O'Connell

Following is the text of my decision today in the matter of the assignments of the contracts of players Blue, Fingers & Rudi:

Pursuant to the major league agreement and rules, I conducted a hearing yesterday into the question whether the recent assignments of the contracts of Oakland players Joe Rudi, Rollie Fingers and Vida Blue to the New York and Boston clubs should be approved by this office or whether such transactions should be disapproved as inconsistent with the best interests of baseball, the integrity of the game and the maintenance of public confidence in it.

While the clubs and players' association argued that the assignments were in accordance with the terms of applicable rules, none of the participants made a persuasive argument as to the overriding considerations of whether these transactions are consistent with baseball's best interests, the integrity of the game and the maintenance of public confidence in it. I cannot accept the narrow view that these considerations should be ignored.

Shorn of much of its finest talent in exchange for cash, the Oakland club, which has been a divisional champion for the last five years, has little chance to compete effectively in its division. Whether other players will be available to restore the club by using the cash involved is altogether speculative although Mr. Finley vigorously argues his ability to do so. Public confidence in the integrity of club operations and in baseball would be gravely undermined should such assignments not be restrained.

While I am of course aware that there have been cash sales of player contracts in the past, there has been no instance in my judgment which had the potential for harm to our game as do these assignments, particularly in the present unsettled circumstances of baseball's reserve system and in the highly competitive circumstances we find in today's sports and entertainment world.

Nor can I persuade myself that the spectacle of the Yankees and Red Sox buying contracts of star players in the prime of their careers for cash sums totaling $3.5 million is anything but devastating to baseball's reputation for integrity and to public confidence in the game, even though I can well understand that their motive is a good faith effort to strengthen their clubs. If such transactions now and in the future were permitted, the door would be opened wide to the buying of success by the more affluent clubs, public suspicion would be aroused, traditional and sound methods of player development and acquisition would be undermined and our efforts to preserve competitive balance would be greatly impaired.

I cannot help but conclude that I would be remiss in exercising my powers as commissioner pursuant to the major league agreement and major league rule 12 if I did not act now to disapprove these assignments. If, as contended by the participants, the commissioner lacks the power to prevent a development so harmful to baseball as this, then our system of self-regulation for the good of the game and the public is a virtual mirage. I think the commissioner's power is clear and binding and its exercise vital to the best interests of the game and accordingly the assignments here involved are disapproved.

The players will remain on the active list of the Oakland club and may today be in uniform and participate in Oakland games.

Commissioner Bowie K. Kuhn

23

Kuhn Describes New Basic Agreement (1976)

SOURCE: House Select Committee on Professional Sports, *Inquiry into Professional Sports*, 94th Cong., 2nd sess, part 1, 17–20

After an extended period of negotiation, the owners and players finally signed a new Basic Agreement on July 12 during the All-Star Game proceedings in Philadelphia. The most significant element in the agreement was the new reserve system under which certain players could become free agents. Players signing contracts after the 1976 season could enter the free-agent pool after spending six years in the majors and could reenter the pool five years later. Players currently under contract could also become free agents under certain circumstances. In addition, some veteran players could officially request a trade and specify certain teams to which he could not be traded.

A brief section at the end of the agreement, unnoticed at the time, would later have a tremendous impact on baseball history. Owners who recalled the holdout of Dodgers stars Sandy Koufax and Don Drysdale in 1966 added a clause that outlawed collusion between players in salary negotiations, which would also apply to the owners. In the 1980s this clause cost the owners hundreds of millions of dollars in fines as they were found guilty of collusion on three occasions. Appendix I, Article XVII, of the 1976 Basic Agreement, which defines the workings of the reserve system and includes the anticollusion clause, is reprinted in James B. Dworkin, Owners Versus Players: Baseball and Collective Bargaining *(Boston: Auburn House, 1981), 105–12.*

This year Baseball is enjoying one of its most successful years in terms of fan attendance and interest. Overall attendance as of July 18, 1976 reached a level of 18,370,021. This is an increase of more than 1,638,000 over the same period in 1975. Many individual clubs as well have set new attendance records in the first half of the 1976 season.

Not only is this a year in Baseball of expanded attendance and excitement over new stars and pennant contenders, but it is also a year in which Baseball has negotiated a significant labor settlement. This settlement has established a new, innovative reserve system.

This new labor pact was the product of compromise and intense negotiation. But, the significant point is that this settlement was achieved at the bargaining table, not in an antitrust suit. This recent agreement is proof-positive that the present status of Baseball under our laws is appropriate; proponents of a radical change cannot carry the burden of proof that must be met to justify altering a system that works.

On Monday the owners adopted this new labor settlement. We hope that the players will likewise ratify this agreement in the near future.

Although the agreement is quite complex and has not yet been put in final form, a summary of the basic provisions can be presented. This summary will demonstrate the degree of success and reconciliation that these labor negotiations have achieved. The agreement attempts to perform the difficult feat of accommodating the legitimate need of the clubs for an effective player control arrangement, with the desire of the players for a more competitive market for their services. This agreement is bold and imaginative; further, all parties recognize that such a fundamental amendment of our traditional labor arrangement must be considered experimental. We are hopeful that the agreement will strike a proper balance without irreparably compromising either side's interests.

The highlights of the new labor agreement are as follows:

1. Creation of a new reserve system. —The most significant provision of the new agreement provides for major modifications of the reserve system as it has historically operated.

As you may know, an arbitrator in the recent *Messersmith* dispute interpreted the existing uniform player contract as permitting a player to become a free agent by playing out the option year of his contract, and the federal courts have supported his decision.

Even in the face of the *Messersmith* decision, it is quite significant that the Players' Association in the recent negotiations have acknowledged that a meaningful system of control over player contracts is essential to Baseball; this is consistent with their position in the *Flood* case:

"Basically * * * it was our position that the reserve rule system was illegal in that its restrictions were just about total, that it was inconceivable to us that you could have a game of baseball with no rules, but that it seemed quite reasonable to us that modifications which were less restrictive than the present system could be made, were practical, and presumably could make the system safe from attack in terms of its illegality."

With both sides in agreement that some effective form of reserve system is necessary, a compromise system has been established to replace the traditional reserve system. The new agreement provides that a player who signs a contract after ratification of the agreement will have the right to become a free agent after he has acquired six years of major league service. A player will again have the right to free agency every five years thereafter. In order to prevent those clubs with the greatest financial resources from becoming dominant by signing a disproportionate number of the talented free agents, there will be detailed provisions that regulate the process whereby a club selects negotiation rights to players in the free agent pool.

2. Player right to demand to be traded. — A player who signs a contract after ratification of the agreement will have the right to request his club to trade him after he has completed five years of major league service and will have the right to designate six clubs to which he would not accept a trade. If the club cannot effect a trade, then the player becomes a free agent.

3. "Reentry" provisions for players who sign contracts prior to the ratification of the new basic agreement. — The procedures described in paragraph 1 above, will govern the process whereby those players who play out their contracts and become free agents under their current contracts will be able to negotiate with clubs. Here again, the agreement attempts to limit the degree to which money can be the primary determinant of a team's strength and success.

4. Increased Players' Financial Benefits. — Finally, there have been increases in the players' minimum salary and in expense and travel allowances, and the clubs' contribution to the players' benefit plan has been raised from $6.5 million annually to $8.3 million.

It is not surprising that the owners and players had such constructive negotiations this year. A brief examination of our labor negotiations since 1966 shows that the owners and players have been able to reach agreements on a wide range of matters.

(a) The 1968–69 basic agreements. — The first basic agreement for the years 1968–69 raised the minimum salary from $7,000 to $10,000 and increased various expense allowances. The owners agreed to several scheduling and travel rules that had been sought by the players. A grievance procedure was instituted in which the Commissioner of Baseball served as arbitrator. It was agreed that if a player's contract was

renewed under the renewal option clause, his salary could not be reduced by more than 20%; before this, a 25% reduction was permitted. Finally, the owners agreed to give the Players' Association notice of prospective rule changes and to discuss such changes with it and they agreed to participate in a joint owner-player study of the reserve system and possible alternative to it.

(b) The 1970–72 and 1973–75 basic agreements. — The second and third basic agreements, covering the periods 1970–72 and 1973–75, respectively, continued the trends towards more liberal financial benefits for players. The minimum salary rose from $13,500 in 1972 to $16,500 in 1975. Termination pay provisions were liberalized significantly in 1970, and the 1970 agreement added the requirement that there could be no more than a 30% aggregate salary reduction over a two-year period. In each agreement, travel and living allowances were increased substantially, and a cost of living escalation guarantee was instituted in 1970.

Each of the two agreements also contained nonfinancial provisions of note. In 1970, it was agreed that the arbitrators who would preside over grievance proceedings would be selected jointly by players and owners, and in 1973 a provision allowing resort to arbitration to resolve salary disputes was added.

Finally, the 1973 agreement contained a significant modification of the reserve system. This provision specified that no player with ten years major league experience, the last five of which were spent with his present club, could be traded without his consent and that no player with five years major league experience could be sent to a minor league club without his approval.

These changes demonstrate that the new agreement is a continuation of a history of tough, but fair, bargaining over the fundamental issues of player rights and management prerogatives. This labor history demonstrates conclusively, we believe, that no change in Baseball's status under the antitrust laws is needed or warranted, since Baseball has been able through collective bargaining to reconcile owner and player interests while still protecting the fans' interests. Experience in other sports has shown that a constructive reconciliation of player and owner interests simply is not achieved in the antitrust courtroom or within the four corners of a judicial decree. Rather, it is hammered out at the bargaining table under the strictures of the federal labor laws. . . .

There are other aspects of Baseball's system of self-regulation that are not subject to the antitrust laws. As you know, since the days of Commissioner Landis the Major League clubs have empowered the Commissioner of Baseball to decide what is in the "best interests" of Baseball. I believe that the record of the Commissioners' actions pursuant to this mandate demonstrates that they have in fact sought to balance fairly the interests of the fans, the players and the owners.

One example is the Commissioner's decision earlier this year to order the spring training camps to open. I might note that I took that action in the face of rather intense opposition of some of the clubs. But I felt that it was in Baseball's best interests.

Another example, of more immediate interest, is the decision by the Commissioner to prevent the assignment of the player contracts of Vida Blue, Rollie Fingers and Joe Rudi. Since this matter is currently in litigation before the courts, with discovery proceedings and hearings on motions for summary judgment and preliminary injunction scheduled shortly, I am advised by my counsel that it would be inappropriate to discuss the details of this matter at any length at this time. However, I understand that, after this initial round of educational hearings, the Committee will return to the subject of Baseball in later hearings, and I may be able to brief the Committee more fully on this matter at that time.

24

Baseball Announces First Free-Agent Draft (1976)

SOURCE: Press release from the Office of the Commissioner, October 29, 1976, "Economics—Free Agency—1976" file, National Baseball Hall of Fame Library

After the 1976 Basic Agreement defined the parameters of free agency in mid-July, players, owners, and fans alike braced for the impact. A common view was that wealthy teams would sign all the best players and dominate pennant races for years to come. The idea that teams would damage themselves by overpaying for mediocrities and over-the-hill stars did not occur to many.

In the following press release, baseball officials tried to put a positive spin on the process they had fought bitterly against for years. In doing so, they correctly anticipated the excitement that the opening of the free-agent market would have on the "hot stove league."

FOR IMMEDIATE RELEASE
October 29, 1976

BASEBALL'S FIRST FREE AGENT NEGOTIATION SELECTIONS SCHEDULED FOR THURSDAY; A.L. EXPANSION DRAFT IS FRIDAY

To baseball fans, the most important parts of the off-season have always been the rumor, expectation and reality of trades plus the buildup of rookie phenoms and rehabilitated veterans. To executives, the period starting late in October and lasting into the latter part of February meant much the same plus time to catch a deep breath from one season and to plan for the new year ahead.

That's all changed now. The new collective bargaining agreement between the major league clubs and the Major League Players Association [*sic*] provides a new event on the annual fall baseball calendar.

The debut of the Free Agent Negotiation Selections will be at 10 a.m. Eastern Standard Time on Thursday (Nov. 4) at New York's Plaza Hotel.

Attention promises to be heavy since the selections represent the first step in determining the future home of each player who went through the 1976 season under a contract renewed by his club.

Twenty-four players were on the tentative list one week before the draft although any of them could decide to sign with his 1976 club prior to midnight Sunday. Each player not signed by then becomes potentially available to any of the 24 established teams, including his 1976 club. Expansion entries Seattle and Toronto do not participate until next fall.

The selections will limit the number of clubs eligible to negotiate with each player to a maximum of 13—the first 12 clubs to select negotiation rights plus the player's 1976 team if it desires.

The National League won a coin toss so Montreal will select first. The leagues will alternate choices with the order of selections within a league being the reverse of the won-lost percentage achieved by each team this season. It is possible—although perhaps unlikely—one player could be tabbed by the maximum of 12 clubs before the first round is completed with the initial selection of the American League champion New York Yankees.

Otherwise each team will have at least one chance to select negotiation rights to the player it regards as the most valuable potential addition to its roster.

Picks will continue until all players have been selected the maximum 12 times or until each team has passed.

Then the clubs will begin trying to sign the players. The size of the talent pool—unless it drops below 14 players before Monday—makes it possible for each team to sign two players even if the club doesn't stand to lose anyone. Four teams have more than two players on the list. They may sign up to whatever number they lose.

Oakland had seven players on the list as of Thursday (Oct. 28), while Baltimore and California had three each and Minnesota two. Philadelphia has two and the Chicago Cubs, Cincinnati, Pittsburgh, San Diego, San Francisco and the Yankees one apiece.

The order of selection for the initial year:

1. Montreal	9. San Francisco	17. Pittsburgh
2. Chicago White Sox	10. Texas	18. Oakland
3. Atlanta	11. Chicago Cubs	19. Los Angeles
4. Milwaukee	12. Cleveland	20. Baltimore
5. St. Louis	13. Houston	21. Philadelphia
6. Detroit	14. Boston	22. Kansas City
7. San Diego	15. New York Mets	23. Cincinnati
8. California	16. Minnesota	24. N.Y. Yankees

Here are the players scheduled to be included unless signed by the club they finished with in 1976 (shown in parenthesis) prior to Nov. 1:

CATCHERS (1): Gene Tenace (Oakland).

INFIELDERS (11): Sal Bando (Oakland), Bert Campaneris (Oakland), Dave Cash (Philadelphia), Paul Dade (California), Tito Fuentes (San Diego), Bobby Grich (Baltimore), Richie Hebner (Pittsburgh), Willie McCovey (Oakland), Tim Nordbrook (California), Billy Smith (California), Eric Soderholm (Minnesota).

OUTFIELDERS (5): Don Baylor, also plays first base (Oakland), Reggie Jackson (Baltimore), Gary Matthews (San Francisco), Joe Rudi (Oakland), Royle Stillman (Baltimore).

PITCHERS (7): Doyle Alexander (New York Yankees), Bill Campbell (Minnesota), Rollie Fingers (Oakland), Wayne Garland (Baltimore), Don Gullett (Cincinnati), Steve Stone (Chicago Cubs), Wayne Twitchell (Philadelphia).

Another meeting vital to American League clubs will be held at the Plaza Hotel next Friday (Nov. 5) at 10 a.m. EST. That is the expansion draft which will provide 30 players for each of the two new teams, the Seattle Mariners and Toronto Blue Jays.

3

The Dawn of Free Agency

The transition to the free-agency era did not go smoothly. While the play-ers—even those who remained with their clubs—benefitted as salaries rose astronomically, owners struggled to find the path to success. The New York Yankees, led by free agents Catfish Hunter and Reggie Jackson, dominated the AL at the end of the decade, but too many teams made poor decisions by signing modestly talented or aging players to extravagant, multiyear contracts. The biggest winner of all was Nolan Ryan, whose .512 career record and four no-hitters convinced the Houston Astros to give him baseball's first million-dollar salary for the 1980 season.

Several individual players enjoyed spectacular moments, led by Jackson, who earned the nickname "Mr. October" by slamming a record five home runs (including three in the final game) in the 1977 World Series. The following season Pete Rose excited baseball fans by amassing a 44-game hitting streak, while Bucky Dent appalled the Red Sox nation by depositing a Mike Torrez pitch just over the "Green Monster" to help his Yankees win a playoff to con-clude one of the greatest pennant races ever. Two years later the Philadelphia Phillies and Ryan's Astros staged a thrilling, bizarre NLCS destined to be re-membered for generations. All of these memories, however, were endangered when the players went on strike in the summer of 1981. The split-season for-mat imposed after the 50-day strike alienated many fans, especially those of the Cincinnati Reds, who were locked out of the playoffs despite earning the NL's best overall record.

25

Pam Postema Seeks to Become First Female
Major League Umpire (1977)

SOURCE: *Sporting News*, January 8, 1977

In the midst of the winter session at the Al Somers Umpire School—which had trained the majority of major league umpires—a Sporting News *reporter arrived to write a profile on one of the students. The student, Pam Postema, was attempting (along with one other woman) to graduate from the school and become a professional umpire. In her autobiography* You've Got to Have Balls to Make It in This League: My Life as an Umpire *(New York: Simon and Schuster, 1992), written with Gene Wojciechowski, Postema criticized herself for participating in the story and umpire Harry Wendelstedt for his hypocrisy. Postema bitterly recalled that Wendelstedt, like most of the instructors at the school, was condescending and overly critical during her training, although she received one of the top scores at its conclusion. In the article, however, Wendelstedt and Somers are cautiously supportive of her career ambitions.*

Following her graduation, Postema was hired by the Gulf Coast League. She progressed at a steady pace and made it to the American Association, one of the top minor leagues. She remained at the Triple-A level for six years and was released because she had failed to earn promotion to the major leagues.

Ohio Gal Breaks Somers Ump Barrier
By Brad Willson

DAYTONA BEACH—How far in the future is a feminine major league umpire? Most career baseball men would reply anything from "never" to "very far, if ever."

Christine Wren, 27, who completed her second season as an umpire in the Class-A Northwest League in 1976, is farther along that road than any other female.

Graduated from Bill Kinnamon's umpiring school in California three years ago (she was among the top 10 in a class of 400), Ms. Wren may have some company soon.

Pam Postema, an attractive farm lass from Ohio, has taken at least a step toward her ambition. She convinced Al Somers, ultra conservative dean of the Somers Umpire School here, that she has a chance.

Ten years ago, Somers wouldn't have discussed the possibility of a woman umpire in Organized Baseball. Only two years ago, he said, "There'll never be a woman student in my school. It's just not a job for a woman."

Twenty-two-year-old Pam, 5-8, and 150, will be the first woman in the school which has produced 60 percent of the major league umpires. A lone girl among 100 males.

Even two months ago, when she wrote to Somers, asking for an application, he "forgot" to answer her letter. She persisted. More letters. Phone calls. All in a friendly, but determined tone.

Finally, Somers and his chief instructor, National League veteran Harry Wendelstedt, invited her here for an interview.

The tall, onetime third baseman on a boys' softball team has an engaging smile and a direct gaze from hazel eyes.

Somers and Wendelstedt, who run a tight ship, frankly were skeptical. Pam was nervous. But she made a good impression.

After she'd been duly enrolled for the six-week course which started January 2, the first girl in the 37 years Somers has been training umpires said:

"I know it's not going to be a hop, skip and a jump from the school to even a job in the bush leagues. I feel to get consideration when it's placement time, I have to be among the top 15 students."

Somers and Wendelstedt invited her to come down from Gainesville, Fla., for a personal interview before accepting her tuition check.

Wendelstedt was very frank. "We're not making concessions; not changing our program for you. People think calling balls and strikes or safe and out is the big part of umpiring. Can you take the pressure when players and/or fans think you've missed a pitch? Can you do 400 deep knee bends in a game behind the plate?"

Later, he said, "I believe she's sincere. I don't feel she's in it for the publicity as some women might be."

A waitress in a big restaurant chain in Gainesville, Postema lives with her sister, Peggy, 23, a graduate student at the University of Florida.

Wendelstedt kept posing questions: "Can you stand the pressure? Do you understand the problems a young, single, attractive girl will face being in class and on the field with some 100 young men of different backgrounds and from 30 or 35 states?"

Somers pointed out there are no facilities for women at the five-diamond complex of the Montreal Expos' minor league complex where field work is scheduled from 10:00 a.m. to 3:30 p.m. daily.

Over the 22 years Somers has run the school himself and for the earlier years he worked for the late Bill McGowan, he and Wendelstedt have had to send many students home before the school was a week old.

"In the past two springs, we've had to send nine boys packing because we felt they were unfitted, emotionally, for one of the toughest jobs in the game," Wendelstedt pointed out.

Postema's rebuttal:

"Growing up on a farm in Willard, Ohio, is pretty much of a man's world. I know I have to be ready. Keep my cool. Granted, many girls wouldn't fit into the situation I'm bucking. Baseball isn't ready for women players . . . but maybe it's ready for a woman umpire. All I want is the chance. All I ask is to be treated like any other student.

"Women have made it as auto race drivers, jockeys, horse trainers and harness drivers. A couple of years ago, that would have shaken up guys like A. J. Foyt and Cale Yarborough."

Will Pam be in the lineup with men in the spring games which are an important part of the field work?

"Why not?" she replied. "When I played third in games with boys back home, they admitted, grudgingly, that I had a pretty good arm."

Somers, more so than Wendelstedt, conceded he's relaxed some of his opposition to the possibility of a woman umpire.

"We'll have some problems we never had before with all male classes," Wendelstedt said. "But I told her I'd do everything I could—just as I will any student—to help her. It's a challenge to me as an instructor and, if she should make it, it will be to my credit that I could meet the challenge."

Somers added, cautiously, "There wasn't a future for women at the time Bernice Gera tried to force the issue. Now, well, maybe there is. Times change. We'll have to wait and see. Yes, I'd have to say she has a chance. Otherwise, we wouldn't have accepted her as a student."

26

A Profile of the Society for American Baseball Research (SABR) (1977)

SOURCE: *Sporting News*, March 5, 1977

In retrospect, it may seem odd that it took until 1971 for a group such as SABR—the Society for American Baseball Research—to be organized. Since 1951 Congress had investigated professional baseball numerous times and produced thousands of pages of information on the sport's history. The congressmen relied in part on a number of law review articles and studies by graduate students on baseball, and research in this area continued. Two PhD students, Harold Seymour and David Quentin Voigt, wrote doctoral dissertations on baseball history and in the 1960s published them as the first volume in their respective multivolume histories of the sport. By 1971 at least seven other major books—the first three volumes of The Fireside Book of Baseball *(1956, 1958, and 1968), edited by Charles Einstein;* Eight Men Out *(1963) by Eliot Asinof;* The Glory of Their Times *(1966) by Lawrence Ritter;* The Baseball Encyclopedia *(1969); and* Only the Ball Was White *(1970) by Robert Peterson—focused on baseball history had been published, to mostly rave reviews.*

Still, it was not until 1971, when L. Robert Davids wrote a brief letter to The Sporting News *inviting fellow "statistorians" to meet in Cooperstown, that an organization was formed. Only fifteen people met with Davids at the initial meeting, but afterward the group grew rapidly. In the following article Bill Madden felt the need to make clear that SABR members were researchers first, and not collectors of memorabilia.*

The Sports Collector by Bill Madden

Live, Die with SABR

NEW YORK—Every so often upon leafing through other columns in THE SPORT-
ING NEWS—particularly those of Bob Broeg, Leonard Koppett and C. C. Johnson
Spink—my curiosity is provoked by passing references to The Society for American Baseball Research. And amid the various avenues of the hobby scene, I am
frequently surprised to find more and more collectors who are members of this
organization.

All of which caused me to wonder: Just who are these people? What sort of organization is this SABR (as it's most commonly called)? It isn't that its members are
deliberately secretive in this, their research hobby, but rather they are merely more
inclined to share their findings with other baseball aficionados instead of proclaiming themselves as experts.

Although researching baseball and all its debate-provoking statistics has long
been a hobby for most observers of the game, it wasn't until 1971 that L. Robert Davids of Washington DC decided to organize some of these "fans."

"It was March 19, 1971—the 100th anniversary of the birth of Joe McGinnity—when
I wrote letters to about 35–40 people," Davids recalled. "I felt if we get this many people organized, pay dues, help each other, etc., we could even have our own publication. Well, only 16 could meet that August at Cooperstown, but a couple of weeks later
the officers were sitting around my dining room table and drafting a constitution.

"I remember saying then that while it's true we're small now, we might some day
have as many as 50 members. Well, we had 80 by the end of 1971 and as of January
1, we were up to nearly 430."

Indeed, SABR, which charges $10 per year and issues a bi-monthly bulletin in ad-
dition to other special publications, has become a rapidly-growing outlet for baseball hobbyists and students. But as Davids points out, collectors form only a small
portion of SABR's membership.

"We emphasize research," Davids said. "Basically our organization was formed
for people who have a genuine interest in baseball. We draw our members from all
walks of life. There are college professors, airline pilots, bartenders, doctors, lawyers, policemen—even religious leaders such as a Jewish rabbi, a missionary in England and a Catholic priest in Japan. Collectors, I'd say, are only about 10 percent of
our membership."

Still, as Hall of Fame historian Cliff Kachline points out, "SABR serves as an outlet for people making baseball research their hobby. The SABR Journal and the other
publications like 'This Date in Baseball History' have become collector's items."

Much of the research conducted by SABR members is through the tedious means
of old newspaper clippings. Among the SABR projects currently underway or recently concluded are the compilation of all the inside-the-park home runs hit since
1920, a manuscript by Robert Huckabee of New Bedford, Mass., on the old Federal League of 1914–15 and Davids' point-by-point evaluation of Chuck Klein's

career aimed at justifying or renewing consideration of the old Phillies' slugger for the Hall of Fame.

There's also an attractively laid out collection of major league debut games, compiled by Bill Loughman of Elmhurst, Ill. Loughman's project, called "First Things First," is a series of one-page newspaper clippings, box scores, pictures and personal data on the first major league appearance of hundreds of former players. Eventually, he hopes to have it bound and made available to collectors.

The recent election of Amos Rusie to the Hall of Fame can also be traced to the efforts of SABR. One of the organization's prime concerns has been the 1871-through-1911 period of baseball history. In a recent survey of candidates from that era for the Hall of Fame, SABR members overwhelmingly ranked Rusie first among those deserving of enshrinement. Understand, of course, the survey was conducted after a thorough researching of all the candidates' statistics.

"Some of our members are a little overzealous when it comes to pushing a certain candidate for the Hall of Fame," Davids concedes. "But when it comes to the 1871–1911 period we feel that since these players are out of the memory range of most of the members of the Hall of Fame Veterans' Committee, it's important that someone research them. We have what I would call some real experts on 19th century baseball who have specialized their studies on how the players of that era performed."

"SABR pushed for both Sam Thompson (elected in 1974) and Rusie," added Kachline. "I don't believe in campaigning for a particular candidate for the Hall of Fame, but somebody should be responsible for bringing forth facts that otherwise might have been obscured through the years."

One such fact recently discovered by SABR involved another new Hall of Fame electee—Joe Sewell.

"Everyone has made mention of Sewell's fewest-strikeout records," said Kachline. "The record book credits him with only 114 in his entire career. But actually that figure should be 113. Bob Davids went back through the newspaper clippings and discovered that on June 29, 1923, Sewell was charged with a strikeout when actually it was his teammate, Rube Lutzke, who struck out in that game. You can be sure Sewell's plaque at Cooperstown will have the right total."

Two other areas of baseball history under close scrutiny by SABR are the old Negro Leagues and minor league playing feats. John Holway, who authored "Voices From The Great Black Baseball Leagues" (the Negro League counterpart to Larry Ritter's "Glory of Their Times"), and fellow SABR member Merle Kleinknecht are painstakingly compiling averages and statistics on the old Negro Leagues from newspaper clippings of those cities which had teams. And in an upcoming SABR Journal there will be many previously unpublished lifetime minor league statistics. Are you aware of the fact that Buzz Arlett holds the lifetime minor league record for home runs (432)?

A fascinating group, SABR. Anyone wishing to join up with this fast-growing researchers' hobby should write to SABR, P.O. Box 323, Cooperstown, N.Y. 13326. They welcome new members and contributors, even if you didn't know that on May 9, 1916 Bruno Haas of the A's walked 16 Tigers in his major league pitching debut.

27

Reggie Jackson, Billy Martin Nearly Come to Blows (1977)

SOURCE: *Boston Globe*, June 19, 1977

In the spring of 1977 Reggie Jackson was the focus of the baseball world. During the off-season Jackson had signed a five-year, $3.75 million contract with the New York Yankees. The flamboyant star immediately declared that he would lead his new club—which had been swept in the 1976 World Series—to a Series title. Jackson's arrogance offended many of his teammates and his combative manager, Billy Martin. During spring training Jackson gave an interview in which he declared that he was "the straw that stirs the drink" and attacked Yankees catcher Thurman Munson—a respected presence in the locker room and on the field—as an inadequate leader. After the article appeared in Sport *on May 23, the already-high tension between Jackson and his manager and teammates escalated even further.*

In a game against the Boston Red Sox, the antagonism was exposed before a nationwide TV audience. During a 10–4 loss to the Red Sox in Boston, Jackson hesitated while fielding a single by Jim Rice, who hustled to second on the play. An enraged Martin immediately replaced Jackson, who physically attacked Martin upon his arrival in the dugout. The incident became a symbol for the combustible Yankees club, famously referred to by New York reliever Sparky Lyle as "the Bronx Zoo."

Martin, Reggie Erupt . . . So Do Sox, 10–4

By Bob Ryan
Globe Staff

Not since Shirley Temple has there been such scene-stealing. Leave it to Billy Martin to upstage, in their own park, a Red Sox team that hit five homers and pounded 16 hits to send an enraptured gathering of 34,603 away cheering an authoritative 10–4 victory over his Yankees.

Numbered among the five home runs were two apiece by Carl Yastrzemski (with two and one on) and Bernie Carbo (both opposite-field solo shots). The fifth was a TV camera clout by George Scott, his fourth home run in as many games. The pitching was entrusted to a struggling, and admittedly, exhausted, Reggie Cleveland, and a swaggering Bill Campbell.

But the headline incident of the sweltering afternoon occurred in the Red Sox sixth inning. The Sox were leading, 7–4, and Fred Lynn was aboard via a bullet single when Jim Rice came up with a "scuse-me" blooper to right. By the time Reggie Jackson picked up the ball and made a throw, there were men on second and third.

Martin, not enthralled with Jackson's effort, sent Paul Blair out to replace him. When Reggie reached the dugout, he and Martin exchanged pleasantries, and quicker than you could say "Stanley Ketchel," the two men had to be restrained from going after each other. In the dugout. On national TV. With Yankee general manager Gabe Paul seated five feet away in an adjacent box seat.

Before the incident concluded, Yogi Berra had tackled Martin. Jackson headed for the clubhouse, where he was met by Paul. Martin sat down quietly in the dugout, turning his attention to the field, where the Red Sox were busy ensuring that, no matter what happens this afternoon, Boston will be in first place tomorrow morning.

The activity on the field was hardly sleep-inducing. A 2–0 first-inning Yankee lead (three hits, a fielder's choice and a wild pitch), for example, almost instantaneously turned into a 3–2 deficit when Captain Carl took the first pitch from Mike Torrez and directed it into the center field bleachers with Rick (3-for-5) Burleson and Fred Lynn aboard. "That," said Don Zimmer, "was the big hit of the game. Two runs down, you can't be sure when you'll get back in, but Yaz got us back in the game with one swing." Yastrzemski, by the way, finished the day 4-for-5, raising his average to .318.

Never again would the Red Sox trail, but that hardly meant Zimmer would spend time on the bench doing crosswords, either. The Yankees are hard to hold in this cozy ballyard, and Cleveland, who has been battling flu-type effects for a week, was lucky he could struggle out to the mound each inning.

"I was tired after four warm-up pitches," Reggie admitted. Zimmer, meanwhile, had his game plan in motion. "I just wanted five innings out of Reggie," he said, "and then I was coming in with Campbell."

Reggie's limit was the sixth, and so with one out, a run in, the lead down to 7–4 (Carbo's first inside-outer and a hit-and-run triple to left by Denny Doyle having sparked a three-run Sox fourth), and Yankees on second and third, in came the Man of a Thousand Pitches to face Carlos May. Campbell fanned May on a 3-and-2 screwball, and, after walking pinch-hitter Lou Piniella, he retired Mickey Rivers on a grounder to Scott to end the inning.

He was hardly in possession of his best stuff on this occasion, however, and he was right back in trouble when Willie Randolph and Thurman Munson opened the seventh with singles. But Chris Chambliss, who thrice flied to deep center (call them long, longer and ICBM) hit into a snappy 4-6-3 double play, and Blair, batting with a man on third instead of the departed Jackson, grounded to third. The eighth (Graig Nettles double and two-out walk to pinch-hitter Cliff Johnson) was only slightly less sedate, but the ninth was tension-free.

Still, this was just another flimsy three-run Fenway lead until Scott homered in the seventh, and Burleson singled and Yastrzemski hit a 3-2 Sparky Lyle offering for his 12th homer in the eighth.

Again, the Sox made impressive fielding plays, with an extraordinary third-inning Doyle stop and backhand flip to Cleveland to nip Rivers rating the First Star. Runner-up was a shoe-top grab by Carbo of a Nettles liner in the first. And once again the Yankee outfield hung itself, with Roy White overrunning Doyle's third-inning chopper into a triple and Jackson turning Rice's flare into The Case of The Loafing Right Fielder.

What's in store for today? Perhaps an exorcism. We've had everything else in this series.

28

Hall of Fame's Negro League Committee
Dissolved (1977)

SOURCE: News release, from the National Baseball Hall of Fame Museum, October 3, 1977, "Hall of Fame" file, National Baseball Hall of Fame Library

One of the rules of the Negro League Committee (NLC) stated that "Committee shall serve until it shall dissolve itself of its own motion or until further notice from the Board of Directors" (of the Hall of Fame). According to the news release below, on October 3 the NLC did just that, in order to accommodate a new Veterans Committee that would be empowered to elect Negro League players as well as eligible major league players and executives.

It is unclear why NLC members would voluntarily dissolve the committee—or if, in fact, they did so at all. The end result was disastrous for Negro League players and their fans. Between 1971 and 1977 nine players—conveniently, one at each position—were selected for enshrinement. Only two Negro League players were chosen by the new Veterans Committee between 1978 and 1994. The following year the Board of Directors succumbed to pressure and permitted special annual elections for Negro League players for a five-year period (later extended through 2001), permitting the election of an additional six Negro League representatives.

The future prospects for Negro League candidates to be promoted to the Hall of Fame did not seem promising at this time. In August 2001 the Veterans Committee was once again reorganized, to comprise all living Hall members, Spink Award winners (baseball writers), and Frick Award winners (baseball broadcasters). Every two years the committee—which includes almost no specialists in Negro League history—will have the freedom to select another Negro League player.

However, the Hall of Fame announced on July 26, 2005, that in 2006 a special election for Negro League players would be held. Players would be both nominated and elected by selected experts in the field who participated in an in-depth study of African Americans in baseball from 1860 to 1960 sponsored by the Hall of Fame. Seventeen players and executives—including the Hall's first female inductee, Effa Manley—earned their long-overdue induction.

The Board of Directors of the National Baseball Hall of Fame has added six new members to the Veterans Committee and approved a number of changes in voting procedures, it was announced Monday by President Ed Stack.

Hall of Famers Roy Campanella and Al Lopez were among the six added to the Veterans Committee, which was expanded from 12 to 18 members. The others are Gabe Paul, President of the New York Yankees; Buzzie Bavasi, former President of the San Diego Padres; Joe Reichler, Special Assistant to the Commissioner; and Bob Addie, former sports writer for the *Washington Post*.

The Board, upon considering the recommendations of a special committee appointed by Commissioner Bowie Kuhn to review the election rules of the various voting bodies of the Hall of Fame, took the following action.

1. Authorized the Veterans Committee to elect up to two candidates per year to the Hall of Fame although no more than one from any of the following three groups:

a. Players who have been retired 25 years or more after at least ten seasons in the Major Leagues.

b. Baseball executives, managers and umpires who have been retired from organized baseball for at least five years. The five-year waiting period is reduced to six months for anyone who has reached the age of 65.

c. Players with at least ten years in the Negro Leagues or a combination of ten years in the Negro and Major Leagues.

2. Empowered the Veterans Committee to consider any Major League player who retired prior to 1946, but limited voting on players who retired in 1946 or thereafter to those who received at least 100 votes in one or more elections of the Baseball Writers' Association of America.

The Veterans Committee will now consider candidates from among the former players of the old Negro Leagues, in addition to Major League players who have been retired for 25 or more years. For the past seven years former stars of the Negro Leagues were elected by a special committee. This committee had voted its self-dissolvement last February.

In still another step, the Hall of Fame Board decided that from time to time they will make eligible for action by the Veterans Committee certain outstanding Major League players who were not able to complete the 10 year eligibility requirement because of illness or death.

Subsequently, the Board of Directors waived the 10 year eligibility requirement for Addie Joss, mainstay of the Cleveland Indians pitching staff in the early 1900s. Joss' career ended in his sudden death at the start of the 1911 season in what would have been his tenth in the majors. Joss won 160 games, losing only 97, had a remarkable 1.88 earned run average and pitched 45 shutouts, including two no-hitters, one a perfect game.

The Board of Directors did not recommend any changes in the voting procedures on recently retired players, although it adopted the Committee's suggestion that the Baseball Writers Association review its election process with consideration given to problems created when members do not cast a full ballot. The BBWAA is charged with the responsibility of an annual vote on players retired between five and 20 years. It takes a 75 percent affirmative vote from either election body to enter the Hall of Fame.

29

Jackson's Three Homers Lead Yankees to World Series Title (1977)

SOURCE: *New York Daily News*, October 19, 1977

The New York Yankees were outscored in both the ALCS (by the Kansas City Royals) and the World Series (by the Los Angeles Dodgers). The Dodgers slugged more home runs in the Series than the Yankees as well. These team accomplishments were rendered meaningless by Reggie Jackson, who with three swings in the sixth and final game shattered several long-standing World Series records and earned for himself the nickname "Mr. October." Jackson joined fellow Yankee Babe Ruth as the only men to homer three times in a Series game, and he became the only player to total five home runs in one Series. Jackson also validated the judgment of the Yankees' flamboyant owner George Steinbrenner, who had been criticized for grossly overpaying for Jackson's "$3 million bat."

JAX'S 3 HOMERS RIP L.A.

Reggie a Record-Setter in 8–4 Win
By Phil Pepe

The strange and incredible saga of the '77 Yankees, which began in turmoil and continued in turbulence, ended in dramatic triumph last night as Reggie Jackson, the eye in the storm of many controversies throughout the season, rose spectacularly to the occasion, setting several World Series records with his $3-million bat.

Only hours after Billy Martin was given a vote of confidence, a substantial bonus for a job well done, and assurances he would be back in '78, Jackson, with his characteristic flair for the dramatic, crashed three home runs in successive times at bat, all on the first pitch, to drive in five runs and lead an 8–4 victory over the Dodgers as the Yankees won the World Series in six games.

The victory thus returned the world championship to New York, "Where it belongs," said owner George Steinbrenner, where it has been on 20 other occasions, but not since 1962.

Jackson's three clouts earned him the Series MVP Award and put his name in the record books along with another Yankee slugger of the past. Babe Ruth is the only other player to hit three home runs in one Series game, accomplishing it in 1926 and 1928 against the Cardinals.

But no player in history, not even the fabled Babe Ruth, ever connected on three successive times at bat as Jackson did last night. And no player in history, not even the fabled Babe Ruth, ever hit five home runs in one World Series as Jackson did in this one, connecting in his last nine official at bats, four of them in succession.

Jackson's hitting overshadowed the pitching of Mike Torrez, who hurled his second complete game victory, and Chris Chambliss' two-run homer in the second which wiped out a two-run lead the Dodgers took in their first at bat. It also vindicated the money Steinbrenner spent to make Jackson a Yankee in the re-entry draft.

Labeled the "best team money can buy," the Yankees proved it on the field with their dramatic five-game win over the Royals in the AL playoffs and their six-game Series victory over the best the National League had to offer.

This victory, said Billy Martin, "made everything worthwhile," all the problems, all the turmoil, all the doubts about his future.

"The players," Martin said, "deserve all the credit." And Reggie?

"I'm really happy for him," Martin said. "He was sensational."

Chambliss' homer tied the score and Reggie Smith's third home run of the Series put the Dodgers back on top in the third. Then Jackson took over.

Thurman Munson led off the fourth with a single and Jackson jumped on Burt Hooton's first pitch and drove it on a searing line into the first row of seats in right field.

As he circled the bases, the television camera focused on his face and Jackson looked into the camera and mouthed, "Hi, mom," twice. Then he ducked into the jubilant Yankee dugout and the first one to greet him was Billy Martin, with whom he had feuded several times during the turbulent season, and the manager patted the slugger on the cheek.

The Yankees scored another run in that inning without Jackson. Chambliss got a double on a misplayed pop that fell between Bill Russell and Dusty Baker in short left. Graig Nettles, doing his job, moved Chris to third by pulling the ball to the right side and Lou Piniella got the run home with a long sac fly to left.

But it was Reggie again, batting against Elias Sosa in the fifth, to put the game in cold storage. A single by Mickey Rivers, a force play on an attempted sacrifice and Munson's fly to left, brought Jackson up with one on, two out. Again he hit the first pitch and ripped a carbon copy line drive home run into the rightfield seats to make it a 7–3 game and put his indelible stamp on this climactic game, on this World Series.

A MONSTER SHOT

The redoubtable, irrepressible Jackson, who also set World Series records for total bases (25) and runs scored (10), would get one more chance at history. And he would not blow it.

Leading off the eighth against knuckleballer Charlie Hough, Jackson again jumped at the first pitch and drove it to center, a monster shot that landed halfway up the stands some 450 feet away.

Now the Yankees held a 8–3 lead and the issue was all but decided, the crowd beginning to celebrate early, moving down to jump on the field and celebrate this long-awaited championship.

The Dodgers prolonged things slightly, delaying the inevitable, pecking away for a run in the ninth, on Vic Davalillo's bunt single, but when pinch hitter Lee Lacy bunted in the air, back to the mound, and Torrez engulfed the ball in his huge mitt for the final out, the victory was won and the celebration began in earnest.

In the manager's office, Sparky Lyle had come in to escape the madding crowd in the Yankee clubhouse. The television was on, and the man on the tube was saying, "There were tears in my eyes as the Yankees won the world championship" and Lyle looked up at the television and said to the screen, "You ain't alone, sucker."

Now Martin came in and he, too, admitted he had shed tears, tears of joy, tears of relief.

"I had to," Martin said. "It was a long row, but I'm happy, even the guy who won $1 million in the lottery can't be as happy as I am right now."

He was asked to put his happiness into words, but words came hard.

"I can't," he said. "It's something you wish for all your life and now it's here."

In the jubilant and wet clubhouse, wet from champagne and wet from tears, Yankees were going around embracing one another and George Steinbrenner, his head and shirt soaked from champagne, was hugging his champions and talking about next year already.

"We'll be back next year," he said and when somebody asked him about changes, he said, "Changes? We don't need any changes. We're world champions. And we'll be back next year."

Cliff Johnson, a bottle of champagne in his hand, shouted, "What else do you want us to win? Is there anything else you want us to win?"

There was nothing else.

And in a corner, somebody told Jackson that the Series record he broke for total bases had been held by Billy Martin.

And Reggie Jackson, struck by the irony of it all, threw his head back and laughed.

"Reggie and Billy," he said, "Billy and Reggie."

And the soap opera had come to an end.

30 _____

Yankees Complete "Boston Massacre" (1978)

SOURCE: *Boston Globe*, September 11, 1978

After play had concluded on August 21, 1978, the Boston Red Sox held an eight-and-a-half-game lead over both their hated rival, the New York Yankees, and the Milwaukee Brewers. Over the next two weeks the Red Sox treaded water with an 8–7 mark, and the Yankees took advantage of Boston's lethargy by going 13–3. On September 7 Boston still held a four-game lead over New York as the Bronx Bombers headed to Fenway Park for a critical four-game series.

Not even the biggest Yankees fans could have anticipated the outcome of what has come to be known as the "Boston Massacre." Not only did New York sweep the four games to tie

Boston in the pennant race, but they humiliated their hosts by a combined 42–9 score. In the following article Peter Gammons assesses the mental state of the staggering Sox.

Yankees Reach the Top

New York Sweeps, 7–4, Ties Red Sox for First

By Peter Gammons
Globe Staff

Historians can mull over what happened. "We took a shellacking," Don Zimmer was to say. Germany vs. Poland. Yale 54, Harvard 0. Roosevelt-Landon.

Comedians can pass out AAA guides describing the best foliage routes the first week of October and compare it to being opposed for re-election by a Prohibition Party candidate or dedicate it all to the 60th anniversary of the last time Boston had a world baseball champion.

But it is gone. Over. Four straight. Yesterday's 7–4 Yankee victory was like watching the last 900 seconds of a football game tick off. The Earl Scruggs Review—18 singles and seven walks—finished the Yankees' weekend humiliation of the Red Sox. The line now is "it's a new, 20-game season." So, as the one man Boston could ever want to start a new, 20-game season, Luis Tiant, goes against Jim Palmer and the Orioles tonight, the question is: Can the Red Sox pull their minds and bodies together or was this weekend indeed the last days of Tsar Nickolas?

It doesn't take Branch Rickey to know that what was once a 14-game lead is now a flat-out, dead-heat tie in the American League East (also for the best record in baseball). It doesn't take Connie Mack to know that the Yankees, from the brilliant defense of Graig Nettles and Bucky Dent to the offensive heroics of Lou Piniella and Willie Randolph, are playing as well as the game can be played—22-5 with a 2.09 ERA in their last 27 games, while Boston is 2-9, 26 errors in their last 11. Tonight one of the teams will be in second place, the Yankees are idle.

El Tiante and Palmer have faced each other 10 times, Tiant winning four, Palmer three. "They (the Yankees) are a money club," Rick Burleson said after yesterday's Quaker meeting. The Red Sox . . . [in original]

By the time Bobby Sprowl had nervously walked four Yankees in his $^1/_3$ of an inning and Bob Stanley had gotten racked in a bizarre three-inning, 10-hit performance, people were asking for "They Don't Shoot Horses, Don't They?" on the megaboard. The linescore was Yankees 42-67-5, Red Sox 9-21-12. Hell, last year Boston hit 16 homers in three games here and outscored the Yankees, 30–9, which tells you something about Boston's Gorman Thomas Offense (67 hits and 42 runs) and the Yankees hit the Wall once and went over it once.

Piniella had 10 hits, Thurman Munson eight, and Munson hasn't changed. In one at-bat he gave a ball to the kid in the stands and smashed his bat over the dugout, then afterwards threw a plate of ravioli at a photographer. Randolph was on base 16 times.

Nettles, who roamed third base like Ray Nitschke, had six hits and took away 10 more, the only man who closes the shortstop and the up-the-middle holes simultaneously. New York hit .396 and Boston made 12 errors. Not one Boston starting pitcher finished the fourth. Only one got five outs. Fourteen pitching changes. George Scott is 0 for 25. Baserunners have 21 stolen bases in 24 attempts since Aug. 13. It's become so bad that it's hard to separate what is physical and what is psychological. But it has to be turned around with El Tiante.

Yesterday belongs in the Bob Quinn or Mike Higgins eras. Should Zimmer have started Sprowl, with 1 ½ years' professional and one game's experience instead of Tiant? Sprowl did something pitchers go careers without doing—walked Mickey Rivers on four pitches—and walked Randolph. He got Munson to ground into a double play, but Reggie Jackson hit a ball off the end of his bat through the middle, 1–0. Two walks later, and Zimmer brought on Bob Stanley. "I didn't throw right, that's all," Sprowl said. As barroom demagogues ripped Zimmer for taking him out so soon, Zimmer replied, "I didn't want him to get into any more trouble." Stanley's first pitch was roped into right by Nettles, it was 3–0, soon to be 6–0, and Ed Figueroa (16-9) and Rich Gossage (23 saves) plowed through.

The Red Sox got a homer from Fred Lynn, to left. They got two runs on Carlton Fisk's league-leading 38th double and Garry Hancock's fly ball. Jack Brohamer's double got in a run. But in the five hits, the one single came with two outs in the ninth—Butch Hobson's rope off the Wall.

Meanwhile, as the Yankees took extra bases and hit cutoff men, the Red Sox wandered around lost. Stanley didn't cover first when the beleaguered Scott made a superb diving stop. Fisk couldn't throw Rivers out with time in the first. Hancock misjudged a fly ball. Burleson, trying too hard, had one ball after another tick off his glove. Stanley slipped fielding a bunt. Another Fisk throw kicked off. He didn't throw one. "So we got whipped," said Zimmer. Someone asked him who had the advantage in the 20-game season. "I'll ask you," Zimmer replied.

The Yankees have left, and what they did was as embarrassing as it was boring. Their injured—Munson, Jackson—played and played well. Boston finally got Jerry Remy back, at 33¹/₃ RPM. Dwight Evans may be healthy again. And Luis Tiant faces Jim Palmer.

"We've got to kick ourselves in the butt," said Burleson. When they tried this past weekend, they missed. Now there are 20 games left and for the first time since May 23 someone else can claim first place (and the best record in baseball). Now the comedians and historians must sit down. Luis Tiant and Mike Torrez have the podium.

31

Yankees Defeat Red Sox in Classic Playoff Game (1978)

SOURCE: *Boston Globe*, October 3, 1978

After the "Boston Massacre" the Red Sox continued to stumble. On September 22 they were two games behind New York. Both clubs finished the season on a tear, but the Red Sox won their final eight games, while the Yankees lost their final game after a six-game winning streak. That loss brought New York back into a tie with Boston for the AL East pennant. A one-game playoff was scheduled in Fenway Park, with the team earning its 100th victory of the season to play the Kansas City Royals in the ALCS.

Boston took a 2–0 lead over the Yankees' invincible pitcher, Ron Guidry, going into the top of the seventh inning. With two outs and two men on, Red Sox starter Mike Torrez faced the weakest batter in the Yankee lineup, shortstop Bucky Dent. To the eternal disgust of Red Sox fans, Dent managed to pull a Torrez pitch barely over the "Green Monster," giving New York a 3–2 lead. The Yankees scored again in the seventh and got a Reggie Jackson home run in the eighth, which enabled them to withstand a two-run Boston rally in the bottom of the inning and claim a 5–4 win.

Even for Red Sox fans long-accustomed to postseason failures, this experience marked a new low. Leigh Montville, teetering on the boundary between black humor and self-pity, offers the latest addition to Red Sox history in his column below.

LEIGH MONTVILLE
So What? We're Used to Waiting

Hit me. Hit me again.

I am from Boston. I can take it.

Dance me around the room. Kiss me on the ear. Whisper sweet nothings, night and day, and tell me in the end that there is someone else. No problem. I understand.

I am from Boston. I can take it.

Rattle your punches off my rib cage. Dribble my ego behind your back. Drive me as far as we both can imagine, open the door, roll me out and tell me to walk. I don't mind. It's OK. It's fine.

I am from Boston. I can take it.

I am bred to disappointment the way a thoroughbred is bred to run. I know how to fall. I curl my body into a fine fetal position. I stick my thumb into my mouth. I absorb the impact, mutter something about "not meaning anything, anyway," bounce up smiling. I've been there before, Charlie.

I am from Boston. I can take it.

I don't need any sympathy about any Red Sox today. I don't need any welcome wagon, Salvation Army words about "good show" and "stiff upper lip" and "maybe next year" and all the rest. Maybe I would if I had been surprised, if this had been some lightning shot out of the blue, if something like this never had happened in this town before, but . . .

I am from Boston. I can take it.

The Yankees won in the end? The Yankees always win in the end, don't they? The Red Sox lost? The Red Sox always lose in the end. But it was close? Very, very close? It always is very, very close.

I know how these things go. I have seen the Red Sox, I have seen the Yankees. I have seen the Bruins, I have seen the Montreal Canadiens. I have seen the Patriots and I have seen rush-hour confusion on the Expressway and I have seen my local politicians and I have seen more than any one man can see.

I am from Boston. I can take it.

Was Bucky Dent's 306-foot home run over a fence 305 feet away supposed to be a surprise? Was the miracle story, the story of the bat handed to him a moment before the hit really supposed to be a shock? Was the fact that Bucky Dent wouldn't even have been hitting in that situation if someone else weren't injured supposed to be an added kick?

I thought it all simply was normal.

The early euphoric Red Sox lead? Normal. Dent's seventh-inning home run, the ninth batter in the lineup just changing the direction of the game? Normal. Reggie Jackson's eventual winning homer? The Red Sox' wild, but not-good-enough comeback? The final two outs—Jim Rice's fly ball that was 10 feet away from being a homer, Carl Yastrzemski's pop fly with the winning run on third? Normal. Normal. Normal.

I have seen the seventh games in '67 and '75. I have seen Enos Slaughter sliding home. I have seen Luis Aparicio, tripping, rounding third, a pennant lost by only half of a game. I know the filling inside life is only air, not whipped cream. I know the stories about the end of a lollipop only being a fuzzy stick are true. Normal. I know.

These Red Sox were not any different than the Yankees. They were just as good. They might have been better. They had better hitting. They had pitching that was just as good. They had a shakier bench and more inconsistent relief pitching, but overall they were just as good. Maybe better.

They had a season that gave this town some long stretches of baseball that were as good as any that we have seen. They had that overpowering start, that full-blown comeback, a string of excitement that was more than anyone could have expected. They won 99 games, a figure that would have been enough to put them into any playoff just about anywhere.

They simply happened to be playing in the one division with a team that could win 100 games. They simply were the Red Sox.

"No matter what the Yankees do, no matter how far they go, I am going to sit at home, convinced that we could have done the same," Red Sox shortstop Rick Burleson said in the gloom of the end. "I don't care what you say. I am convinced."

"They are as good as we are," Yankees third baseman Graig Nettles said. "Sure they are. But, the fact is that nobody is going to remember that. They are second. Nobody remembers who finishes second. They remember, maybe the teams that play in the World Series, but before that? Nobody remembers who finishes second."

Also normal.

I think I would be bothered, maybe, by all of this if I were from New York and things had gone the other way. I think if I came from any other place in this country I would have been bothered by fate and No. 9 hitters and changes in the wind and the fact that a right fielder somehow found a ball he couldn't even see. I might even have been found kicking a can in the early hours of this morning, strangling my cat or high-walking the tallest building I could find. I might have been found doing a lot of things.

I am, however, from Boston. I can take it.

So shake me up. Shake me down. Take me to the final five minutes of the movie and break the projector. Stick out a foot as I toddle toward the finish. Pound my head. Bend my mind. Hit me. Hit me, again.

I am from Boston. I can take it.

Just give me a minute to catch my breath this time.

Will you, huh?

32

Miller Comments on Umpires' Strike (1979)

SOURCES: Letter from Marvin Miller to MLBPA player representatives, May 3, 1979; and letter from Marvin Miller to Red Smith, May 31, 1979, Marvin Miller Papers, Series II, Box 8, Folder 6, Robert F. Wagner Labor Archives, Tamiment Library

Shortly after signing a contract with major league baseball, the Major League Umpires' Association hired Richie Phillips as their new executive director. The aggressive Phillips immediately declared the contract insufficient and persuaded the umpires to stage a one-day strike on August 25, 1978, to make clear their dissatisfaction. The strike accomplished little, and the MLUA officially went on strike on March 7, 1979. The contract was renegotiated and the strike ended on May 17, with the umpires returning to work two days later.

In spite of Phillips's militant stance, even some conservative critics like C. C. Johnson Spink of the Sporting News *acknowledged (in a September 16, 1978, editorial) that some of the umpires' complaints were valid. Over the next twenty years Phillips and his union would achieve significant salary increases and considerable leverage in future negotiations. The major leagues battled with Phillips until 1999, when they finally managed to break the union and rid themselves of their second-worst nemesis after Marvin Miller.*

The following letters by Miller, written just before and after the resolution to the strike, articulate his belief that the owners were using the MLUA conflict as a dry run for the upcoming battle with the MLBPA and the negotiations to renew the Basic Agreement, which expired at the end of 1979.

MEMORANDUM

to: All Player Representatives
from: Marvin J. Miller
subject: Umpires Dispute with Clubs and Leagues
date: May 3, 1979

There has been a great deal of newspaper, radio and TV comment concerning the umpires' dispute. Additionally, I have received numerous comments and complaints from Players throughout both leagues concerning the quality of the umpiring being performed by those who have undertaken to attempt to replace the experienced Major League Umpires.

I am certainly not an authority on the quality of umpiring, but I believe that the players are highly qualified to judge what they see. It is clear from the complaints I have received from players that many feel the umpiring this season is far more faulty than normal, and that more than a few games have been decided, not by the performance of the players, but by clearly improper decisions of umpires. If so, this is a serious matter since it carries the potential that divisional championships, league pennants and even the World Series would be decided in that fashion.

With respect to the merits of the dispute, I do not have all the facts. But one thing is clear: the assertions of the owners and their representatives, the league presidents, that the Major League umpires are in violation of their Basic Agreement are in error. The umpires' Basic Agreement contains only *minimum* salaries (as does the players' Basic Agreement). The umpires' Basic Agreement each year is supplemented by separate, individual salary contracts with each umpire (as is the case with players). 50 of the 52 Major League umpires *have no 1979 salary contracts.* The umpires without contracts are hold-outs and can not be considered as violating the umpires' Basic Agreement any more than a player, holding out because he is not satisfied with a proposed salary contract, could be declared in violation of the players' Basic Agreement. Furthermore, a United States District Court has refused the owners' request that it find the umpires in violation of the umpires' Basic Agreement.

Many players who have expressed concern about the umpiring have asked what types of things they can do, if they choose to do so. Players are, of course, free to express their opinions, verbally or in a written statement; they are free to do so individually or as a team; they can state their views, orally or in writing, to the officials of their club, to the League President, the Commissioner or to the press. If a player, or players wish to show support for the umpires who are not working, they are free to do so. I would urge only two precautions. Any activity should be on the player's own time—that is, outside of the hours he is expected to be in the ballpark. And there should be no concerted refusal to play since the players' Basic Agreement is in full force and effect until December 31, 1979.

Finally, the press has printed stories that the owners are only marginally concerned about the money differences with the umpires, but instead are taking a hard line to frighten the players and the Players Association in connection with our upcoming negotiations. This is supposed to make us all tremble??

Please make the contents of this memo known to the players on your club. If there are any questions, please call.

Best regards.

May 31, 1979
Dear Red:

Lee MacPhail sent me a copy of his May 25th letter to you.

Please permit me to disassociate myself from the views contained therein. The thrust of the letter is simply contrary to what is known about the dispute with the umpires and the settlement, contrary to what the umpires and their counsel have reported, and in conflict with literally hundreds of press reports throughout the dispute. How did your four very brief paragraphs draw all that fire?

As to the substance of Lee's complaint, I find no merit. The matter of whether the owners and their league presidents embarked on a so-called "hard-line" course with the umpires in a futile attempt to impress the players is only of passing interest. The consensus of the press in all parts of the country clearly ran along these lines. When Lee wrote that such an idea is "utter foolishness" he condemned virtually the entire sports media.

Lee's assertion that the forthcoming negotiations with the Players Association "was simply not an issue at any time during the negotiations with the umpires" is contradicted by the umpires. When all other issues were resolved, the dispute (and strike) continued over the amount of retroactive payments to be paid for the period of the strike. And, according to the umpires, the problem was the owners' fears of the impact that agreement on such payments would have on the negotiations with the Players in a similar situation.

The final five paragraphs in Lee's letter are not persuasive either.

1. The allegation that there was *no* improvement in the umpires' pension plan: There is a savings plan feature in the umpires' pension plan. Formerly the umpires could contribute zero to 5% of their salaries and their contribution was matched by the leagues. Now, the leagues will put in 5% even if an umpire chooses to put in less or nothing. As an example, an umpire who had put in 2 ½% had 5% credited. Such an umpire could now put his 2½% elsewhere and still receive a 5% credit. That hardly qualifies as no improvement.

2. The attempt to minimize the substantial gains in per diem allowance and paid vacations: The fact that the leagues may have felt these were areas that deserved attention and that they may have offered to "discuss" per diem before the strike began can not obscure the fact that this was coupled with a refusal to negotiate about salaries, the one area that the umpires had a right to bargain about. Similarly, it can not obscure the fact that the settlement produced significant salary increases *and*, in addition, paid vacations and substantially increased per

diem allowances. Interesting is the absence from Lee's letter of any reference to the leagues having obtained an injunction only last August against any strike dealing with matters already covered by the Basic Agreement explicitly or implicitly (such as per diem allowances and paid vacations), or any reference to the unsuccessful attempt to obtain a similar court order this year to bar concerted action on salaries as well. The fact that the umpires could not legally have taken concerted action with respect to paid vacations and per diem allowances is significant in confirming the validity of your statement that the umpires get more than they were asking for—not more than they may have wanted, but more than they had a legal right to negotiate about.

3. The allegation about "lost" pay does not really meet the issue. The umpires' counsel has stated that, despite the strike of over a month and a half, each of the umpires will at least be made whole with respect to his 1979 income by virtue of the higher salaries received, sums received which were actually labeled as retroactive pay, an additional bonus (not labeled as "retroactivity") and the higher per diem payments.

4. The allegation re "sophistry" is amusing since the allegation itself fits the definition of "sophistry": deceptive reasoning. It matters not what may have been said in the course of the negotiations. The fact is that the umpires were legally able to propose salary increases only. Their proposal requested a certain amount of dollars. The settlement provided for an even greater amount of dollars.

5. This "argument" really really puts the icing on the cake. Lee has now offered the opinion that without a strike the umpires could have obtained salary increases, increased per diem payments and paid vacations "in 1980 when the pension issue would have come up." The umpires' Basic Agreement provides that it shall continue in full force and effect until *December 31, 1981*. Having enjoined the umpires from concerted action concerning per diem allowances and paid vacations in August, 1978 and having further attempted to stretch the injunction as a bar to concerted action on salaries in April, 1979, and having ordered the umpires to sign their contracts or not report in February, 1979 and later advised them they were no longer employees, the umpires should have been reassured; they should have known that all these improvements would have come to them in January, 1980 when the leagues could continue to allege that the Basic Agreement prevented the umpires from taking action for two more years after January, 1980! Alice In Wonderland is composed of hard facts compared to that.

Sincerely,
Marvin J. Miller
cc: Lee MacPhail

33

The Player Relations Committee's Perspective
on Negotiations with the MLBPA (1980)

SOURCES: Various press releases from the Player Relations Committee, National Baseball Hall of Fame Library

The Player Relations Committee, tired of losing to Marvin Miller and the union both at the negotiating table and in the sports pages, fired PRC director John Gaherin in early 1977 and replaced him in February 1978 with General Electric negotiator Ray Grebey, who had a tough, union-busting reputation. The gauntlet was thrown down on October 31, 1979, when the PRC announced that it would exercise its right to terminate the 1976 Basic Agreement on December 31.

The players responded by agreeing not to play exhibition games, and set a strike date for May 23—the first time the union had threatened to strike during a season. In the meantime Miller and Grebey sparred in the press. The primary issues involved compensation to teams that lost players to free agency, and (as usual) salaries. The negotiations became so heated that both sides agreed to allow Ken Moffett of the Federal Mediation Service to bring the combatants to compromise. At the last minute an agreement was made to continue the season and to appoint a joint committee to study the issues in dispute. In December 1982 Moffett would quit in order to replace the retiring Miller as MLBPA executive director, a position he would hold for less than one year.

Printed below are portions of a number of press releases by the PRC between March and May, which presented management's side of the controversy. For an analysis of the union's perspective on these negotiations, see Charles P. Korr, The End of Baseball as We Knew It: The Players' Union, 1960–1981 *(Urbana: University of Illinois Press, 2002), 186–209.*

MONDAY, MARCH 24, 1980

Ray Grebey, Director of the Major League Baseball Player Relations Committee, Inc., and spokesman for the 26 Major League Clubs, emphasized today that negotiations on a new owner-player Basic Agreement have been productive and that "the process of collective bargaining is working."

His statement came as negotiators moved here [Scottsdale, Arizona] for a series of bargaining sessions this week.

Grebey said his assessment is supported by the fact that both sides have made or withdrawn a number of proposals.

"This is the time-consuming process of bargaining," Grebey said. "Study, analysis and give and take by both sides. It's not a one-way street. . . ."

THURSDAY, MARCH 27, 1980

Major League Baseball has invited the Federal Mediation Service to enter into the current Baseball negotiations for a new Basic Agreement and Benefit Plan.

Ray Grebey, Director of the Major League Baseball Player Relations Committee, said the Washington office of the Service has agreed to enter into the talks between his Committee and the Association.

Grebey . . . said the Mediation Service was asked to participate "in an effort to continue the collective bargaining now proceeding and to avoid a work stoppage threatened by the Players Association." Grebey stated that there is no reason for interruption in collective bargaining and that the Major League Season should open on schedule while talks continue.

"There is no reason for a strike in the absence of a signed agreement," he continued, "and especially in the light of high player salaries and the benefits offered Players in the current negotiations.

"It has been pointed out before that in 1976 Baseball played half a season without a signed agreement, Basketball currently is playing without one and Football once went three seasons without one. In all cases, a settlement was reached without interruption of their seasons."

Negotiations between the two Baseball factions were continuing here today.

TUESDAY, APRIL 22, 1980

Major League Baseball disclosed today, that the average salary for [a] Major League player in 1980 has reached the figure of $149,700 for the season.

The average is based on the 25-man opening day rosters of the 26 Major League teams.

It represents an increase of 23 percent over last season's average of $121,900 and an increase of 191 percent since 1976. The rise in the cost of living from December 1978 to December 1979 was 13.4 percent and from December 1976 to December 1979, 32 percent.

The average 1980 salary for 1979 Free Agent players signed for the current season is $228,300.

Ray Grebey . . . offered the following observations on the salary figures:

"When these salaries are considered—along with the ingredients that go to make up Baseball's Basic Agreement as well as the players' total employment guarantees and opportunities—it is difficult to understand why there should be a players strike.

"What would the players be striking to gain? The clubs' current proposals for a settlement include immediate vesting and improved benefits in the best pension plan in professional sports.

"When the Baseball negotiations are viewed against the backdrop of what is happening in the economy and to the workers and fans who enjoy Baseball, a conclusion must be reached that there is no reason for an interruption in the Baseball season," Grebey continued. "The 26 clubs have consistently sought to achieve and will continue to seek a negotiated settlement without a work stoppage, as threatened by the players.

"When one considers the number of fans being affected by layoffs and plant closings—as compared with the wages, benefits and working conditions provided the

Major League Baseball player, the conclusion is obvious. Take a look at the plant closings in the auto industry plus the productivity and contract language worked out in the New York transit settlement and in the steel industry.

"Baseball is being played now while negotiations take place—as has been the case in the past," Grebey said. "Therefore, strike talk and threats of interruption of the season can only create crises and a confrontation that is totally unnecessary."

THURSDAY, MAY 8, 1980

Talk about an "impasse" in Major League Baseball's negotiations with its players on a new Basic Agreement today was labeled "totally unwarranted" by Ray Grebey. . . .

Grebey issued the following formal statement on the matter:

"I have been reading for some time now article after article quoting the Director of the Players Association and a number of players threatening a strike on May 23. They also are quoted as saying that if players play the season without a contract, the clubs can 'declare an impasse' and institute whatever Free Agent Draft system they want. The Players Association should know better and know that the threats they are making are totally unwarranted. . . .

"The Association knows full well that even though no agreement was reached by the start of the 1980 season, the players and the 26 clubs have been operating under the terms of the expired 1976–1979 Basic Agreement, consistent with established Federal Labor principles.

"All this hard talk about strikes and impasse is unwise and can be harmful. The 26 clubs do not seek a strike nor an impasse. We seek a sound agreement that is in the best interest of the players, the clubs and the fans at the earliest possible date."

MAY 16, 1980

The Major League Baseball Player Relations Committee has characterized the latest offer of the Players Association in their bargaining for a new Basic Agreement as "an effort to avoid bargaining on the remaining issue."

The proposal in question, offered by the players yesterday, would delay any resolution on the remaining issue of Free Agency player compensation for at least two years while a study is made of the situation.

"The idea of a committee to study the question may have some cosmetic public relations appeal but it is another way of not dealing with the issue," commented Ray Grebey. . . .

"The clubs feel that now is the time to deal with this issue, not two years from now," he added.

MAY 23, 1980

The new Basic Agreement and Pension and Benefit Plan negotiated by Major League Baseball and the Players Association was described today by Ray Grebey, Director of the Major League Player Relations Committee, as "a negotiated settlement representing compromise by both sides and a product of real collective bargaining."

The agreement must be ratified by the 26 Major League Clubs and the Players Association membership.

"This is a settlement with something for everyone," Grebey said. "Everyone comes out a winner—especially the fans—since Baseball will continue to be played without interruption.

"It was the position of the 26 Major League clubs from the start, that a negotiated settlement could be reached without any interruption in play.

"In order to resolve the existing differences on compensation," Grebey said, "the Clubs and the Players Association agreed on a compromise which leaves the Free Agent Re-Entry Draft unchanged in 1980. But, in 1981, the Clubs' proposal for compensation becomes a part of the Basic Agreement and it cannot be removed without agreement of the two sides."

Grebey said a Study Committee of four will be appointed (two representing management and two the players). The study group will meet by August 1; gather, study and review information; and make a report to the Major League Clubs and the Players Association by January 1, 1981.

During a 30-day bargaining period to follow, the Clubs and the Players will try to reach an accord which would become part of the Basic Agreement.

If they do not reach an agreement by February 1, the Clubs may put into effect their current proposal for compensation for player selection rights. At that point, the Players have the right to reopen the portion of the Basic Agreement covering such compensation and to call a strike over the issue, if necessary.

Clubs must be notified of such intention by March 1, 1981, and the notice must include the date of the proposed strike, which must not be later than June 1, 1981.

If the players choose not to strike at that time, there can be no strike over compensation during the remaining life of the Basic Agreement. However, the Players may offer, prior to March 1, 1981, to waive their right to strike with a request for the Clubs to permit a substitute strike in 1982, not later than June 1.

There is no obligation on the part of the Clubs, however, to accept such a request.

"This makes the Clubs' proposal for compensation a part of the Basic Agreement in 1981 and it cannot be removed without agreement of the two sides," Grebey said.

"Also included in the new agreement," Grebey said, "are increases in player pension benefits of considerable importance. For instance, a player with 10 years of Major League Service will get $17,856 a year if he takes his pension at the age of 50.

"At the same time, the Clubs' contributions to the Pension Plan are based on the level of benefits and not tied to any fixed ratio of revenues."

Grebey listed these other improvements in contract language in the new agreement:

1.—Liberalization of schedule regulations, including an increase in the limit on consecutive scheduled playing dates to 20.

2.—Clarification of the definition of "salary" to eliminate contract adminis-tration problems.

3.—Agreement on improved health and safety regulations.

4.—Increases in players' expense allowances.

5.—An improved scale of minimum Major League salaries starting at $30,000 in 1980 and increasing to $35,000 in 1983.

34

Philadelphia Defeats Houston in NLCS Game Despite Controversial Call (1980)

SOURCE: *Philadelphia Inquirer*, October 12, 1980

The Houston Astros were involved in two of the most memorable League Championship Series of the 1980s. The first occurred in 1980, when the Astros, who were in the postsea-son for the first time, battled the Philadelphia Phillies. In the first game the Phillies won 3–1 behind the pitching of Steve Carlton. The final four games of the series, incredibly, all went to extra innings. The Astros won Games 2 and 3, which gave them the opportunity to earn a trip to the World Series with a third consecutive victory. Their chances increased as a result of a bizarre, controversial play in the fourth inning. Philadelphia was mount-ing a rally when center fielder Garry Maddox hit a broken-bat blooper toward Houston pitcher Vern Ruhle. Ruhle appeared to catch the ball on the fly, then completed what ec-static Astros fans believed was a triple play. After a lengthy delay umpires eventually ruled that only a double play occurred—even though replays seemed to indicate that only one out was properly recorded.

In spite of the adverse decision and the roar of a rival crowd, the Phillies rallied to win this elimination game and then win the final game of the series. They then proceeded to win the only World Series in their franchise's history.

Phils Come Up with a Surprise Ending in Wild and Crazy 5–3 Win over Astros

5th-Game Shootout Tonight
By Jayson Stark
Enquirer Staff Writer

HOUSTON—Anyone who had ever seen a Phillies playoff game knew how this was going to turn out.

It had everything any classic Phillies playoff loss should have—the critical blown umpire's call, the collapse of the star pitcher, the inning after inning of offensive fu-tility, the story line leading them to another tragic loss that seemed almost beyond their control.

Through all of the awful ways they have found to lose in October, none could have been worse than this. They couldn't just lose like the Yankees or the Angels or the Reds. They had to die with a strange, ugly scent in the air.

They would have to stir through the winter uncomfortably. Not only would they have to bear the pain of defeat. They would also squirm in the deeper agony of injustice.

But somehow, this time the ending was to be different. Somehow, the Phillies rallied once in the eighth, and then again in the 10th. And they beat the Astros, 5–3, in a third straight draining, extra-inning chiller yesterday. Somehow, they are still alive to play the Astros in a fifth game tonight. But it had to be seen to be believed.

"If we'd lost that game, it would have gone right into the long, bizarre saga of lost Phillies playoff games," said Mike Schmidt. "I just think it's better for everybody concerned that we won it. I think everybody can breathe a sigh of relief—except maybe the Astros."

They threw something off their backs yesterday, the curse that always stopped them one step from greatness. They were never supposed to have the heart to win the big ones, were they? Well, it would be hard to say that now.

"I think we disproved all that today," said Dallas Green, "as long as nobody turned the TV off too early."

It would have been easy to turn that set off after the fourth inning. It was in the fourth that Garry Maddox thunked the now-notorious broken-bat looper toward the mound. The films of that looper have since been viewed more times than *Star Wars*.

We know now, after 2 billion replays, that Houston pitcher Vern Ruhle fielded it on one very short hop. We know now that what was ruled a double play, and almost a triple play, should really have been only an out at first. We know now that the Phillies were indisputably robbed.

The Phillies knew that even then. There were 20 minutes of stomping around the field. Phillies threw bats. Phillies threw helmets. Schmidt even marched over to the stands to argue with league president Chub Feeney himself.

But none of that put any runs on the board. And what it did do was disturb the inner tranquility that Steve Carlton needs to be awesome. Carlton had to sit there for 30 minutes watching. And he never was the same.

"Steve has few idiosyncrasies," said Tim McCarver. "But one of them is delays. He hates delays."

Carlton immediately gave up a run in the fourth. Lonnie Smith, starting in left for Greg Luzinski, first misplayed Enos Cabell's catchable double. Then, after Art Howe's sacrifice fly, Smith lost the handle on the ball as he tried to throw it and dribbled it exactly three feet in front of him. He picked it up to throw out a runner at third, but it was still 1–0, Houston.

Then Carlton gave up another run in the fifth, a Luis Pujols triple starting it, a Rafael Landestoy single knocking it in. And finally, Carlton walked the bases full in the sixth. So Green reluctantly had to go to the bullpen early on a day when he was desperately trying to avoid using Tug McGraw. . . .

The Astros helped by blowing innumerable chances to bust it open. They had left seven men on in the fifth, sixth and seventh. They had had another run taken away on the sacrifice-fly blunder.

LEAD-OFF SINGLES

And so the Phillies weren't so out of it on the scoreboard, at a mere 2–0, as they began the eighth. Then Greg Gross and Smith led off the eighth with singles. Pete Rose bounced an RBI single just beyond Joe Morgan's dive. The throw went to third, Rose moved up a base and it was second and third for Schmidt.

Schmidt nearly struck out on an 0-2 pitch by reliever Dave Smith, foul-tipping it instead off catcher Luis Pujols' ankle. Pujols had to be led away and Schmidt trudged around edgily through what he called "the longest 0-and-2 count I ever had in my life."

He choked up and worked the count to 3-2. "I always choke up a little on two strikes, especially when I have to make contact," he said. "Believe me, I've struck out choking up a lot of times."

Finally, he bounced one up the middle. Morgan backhanded it, looked home, looked to third and then just held on. 2–2.

ROSE SCORES

Enter lefthander Joe Sambito. He struck out Bake McBride for the first out. But Manny Trillo lined a 1-2 pitch to right that Jeff Leonard may or may not have shoestringed.

Ump Bruce Froemming ruled he caught it; and Schmidt was doubled off first for the second sacrifice fly–double play of the day. But Rose had made sure. He waited until the ball came down, then tagged and scored.

"I yelled to him, 'Tag up,'" said third-base coach Lee Elia. "But he already was gonna do that. Only Pete Rose has the instincts to do that. A lot of people would overlook that. Pete was gonna make sure this was a 3–2 ball game."

The Phillies' bench was bedlam, but it wasn't over. Landestoy came up to lead off the bottom of the ninth, and 44,952 people were making so much noise the guys at NASA must have thought one of their rockets had just gone up.

Warren Brusstar, the fifth Phillies pitcher, said he never heard them. But he walked Landestoy, and the din grew louder.

"I really thought I got squeezed (by home-plate ump Doug Harvey)," Brusstar said. "But it's still my fault. That's the worst thing you can do as a pitcher—walk the leadoff hitter. And he's not the type of hitter who's going to hit the ball real hard, either."

Sambito bunted Landestoy to second. Terry Puhl belted Brusstar's second pitch down the right-field line, and it was tied.

Brusstar rallied himself to get out of the inning (with a line-drive double play by

Cabell). But he strode to the dugout with a very sinking feeling. Negating the most significant comeback in the Phillies' history could do that to you.

"I felt like I'd let the ballclub down," Brusstar said. "It was awfully frustrating."

But with one out in the 10th, Rose stroked his second hit to left. Schmidt went from 3-and-0 to 3-and-2, then crushed a line drive right at Jose Cruz in left. He turned toward the Astros dugout and raised both arms as if to say, "Can this really be happening?"

LUZINSKI DELIVERS

There were two outs, McBride the hitter. But Green ran up Luzinski to bat for him. Green had benched the Bull because Ruhle isn't a guy who gives up a lot of homers, so he felt Smith might be more productive. But he felt this was the spot.

"I was thinking gapper or home run," said Green. "And we got what we had to have out of it."

Luzinski ripped the second pitch down the line in left. It took one hop, hit the wall and caromed right to Cruz. But Rose was pumping toward third by then. Elia said he saw "a look" in Rose's eyes. That look told him, "He wanted it." Elia saw Cruz' throw to Landestoy, the cutoff man, sink a little low, and sent him.

The throw was there before Rose was. But it short-hopped Bruce Bochy, the catcher who had replaced Pujols. As Bochy strained to retrieve it, Rose slammed into him like Larry Csonka on fourth and one. The ball skipped away, and it was 4–3.

CHARLIE HUSTLE

"I had no choice but to do precisely what I did," Rose said. "I had to run into him because I couldn't reach home plate with my foot. . . . But I had an advantage on him because the ball came in on a short hop. The catcher couldn't brace for the throw."

Manny Trillo doubled in an insurance run. And suddenly, there was McGraw out there in the 10th, in his fourth straight game. He fanned Morgan, his nemesis the day before, with a surprise screwball. The side went down 1-2-3.

And, for once, a typical Phillies day had an atypical Phillies ending.

35

Analysis of Kuhn's Role in Settling Strike (1981)

SOURCE: *Boston Globe*, July 9, 1981

The issues that nearly caused a strike in 1980 had yet to be resolved by the following year. The owners insisted on a system in which teams losing free agents would receive compensation in the form of another player, while the MLBPA argued that such a system would effectively end free agency and reduce salaries. A committee of MLBPA representatives and owners met between January 29 and February 17, when the owners ended negotiations and unilaterally imposed their "Personnel Selection Rights" two days later. After further negotiation, again joined by federal mediator Ken Moffett, failed to achieve a resolution, the players went on strike on June 12. The strike lasted fifty days, delaying the All-Star Game until August 9 and the resumption of the regular season until the following day.

Commissioner Bowie Kuhn, always a controversial figure, was widely attacked in the media for his apparent unwillingness or inability to stop the strike. In his autobiography Kuhn lamented that he did not have the power to unilaterally force a union to negotiate or capitulate, and did not control the owners either. He noted that he deliberately avoided calling a press conference during the strike, but "did give in-depth interviews to writers periodically," including Peter Gammons, whom he later described as a "friend." Note the brief reference to Yale president and future commissioner A. Bartlett Giamatti.

So, What's Kuhn Doing about It?

His Powers Limited, He Still Spends Hours Advising Both Sides in Strike

By Peter Gammons
Globe Staff

The unkindest cut of all came from a man in California who wrote, "If Bowie Kuhn were alive today, this strike would never have occurred."

In his 13 years as baseball commissioner, Bowie Kuhn has heard better. He has also heard worse. "I am a Harry Truman admirer," Kuhn says, "and have learned to take Truman's 'if you can't take the heat, get out of the kitchen' philosophy. What I am in this position is a kind of super umpire. When things go wrong, fans scream at the umpire. When they don't like the flow of a game, they scream at the umpire. So it is with the commissioner."

Only, while sometime in the next year Billy Martin or Earl Weaver will never believe it as he launches into a theatrical tirade, these stakes are higher, and they are very different. Carl Yastrzemski, who understands business and baseball, asked "what is Bowie Kuhn doing in all this?" as the strike began. So did other players, fans, writers, cartoonists and even good and great presidents of institutions such as Yale. They see, hear and read about people named Marvin Miller, Rusty Staub and Ray Grebey arguing about the Grande Olde Game while Kuhn sits in the negotiating bleachers and two-steps through the indignities of NLRB courtrooms.

"I think it's difficult for the fans to understand how the commissioner has such an extensive amount of power in so many areas of baseball—stopping trades, suspending individuals—yet not have equal power in a strike," Kuhn said yesterday. "But no sports commissioner has the power to tell a union not to strike or, in effect, what to do. In this specific case I've always supported compensation in the game. But if I can't put pressure on the players, I don't think I can put pressure on the owners."

Kuhn has tried to work behind the scenes since the June 12 strike. He sleeps only 5–5½ hours a night, spends countless hours in meetings and admits he is busier now than he is during the regular season. "I try to lend what assistance in terms of ideas that I can," the commissioner maintains. "I try to make sure that the Player Relations Committee is maintaining its flexibility, or that it's not trying to break the union. That's really the best that the commissioner can do."

What Kuhn's lampooners have failed to understand is that Judge Kenesaw Mountain Landis came in the days of Calvin Coolidge, long before Andy Messersmith, Brad Corbett and unions. "If I had the power that he (Landis) had, I guess there wouldn't be a strike," says Kuhn. "But certain aspects of the game have changed."

What they also have failed to comprehend is that while Kuhn has virtually unlimited power "in the best interests of baseball," this is not a baseball matter. This is a labor matter and, unlike his predecessors who were so often management people, Kuhn has tried to maintain a public posture in the middle. "As I said, I do not have the power to tell the union not to strike. Occasionally I'm asked, 'Why is the commissioner being blamed? He didn't call the strike—the union called the strike.' I think they (the players) made a mistake, but I understand some of their fears. I understand why they want to protect themselves. I think they've exaggerated the situation at times, but I understand—and respect—their desire to protect their rights and the rights of players coming into the game.

"But there are two common areas of confusion. First, I'm confused with Ray Grebey. But I don't negotiate. Ray Grebey and the other members of the Player Relations Committee negotiate with the players. Second, people think the commissioner has some kind of godlike or Zeus-like power, which he does not. This is not like the everyday part of the game. This is not someone who did something unfairly, some trade, someone convicted of drug possession. This is governed by the labor laws of the United States government."

Kuhn is also often compared to NFL Comr. Pete Rozelle. "Again in this area there is not a great deal of power he can have over the football Players' Association," Kuhn claims. "I don't know the specifics of his role with the NFL Management Council, so I can't comment further."

Kuhn's stance on compensation and competitive balance—which can be translated to the apparency that a Minnesota can never win unless Calvin Griffith sells to big money and the obvious effect that is now having on the fans of that area—has been shrugged off as parroting the owners' line. But Kuhn has a legitimate concern about the quality of ownership, and the fear that the Grande Olde Game will be ravaged by five-year depreciation kings and egomaniacs, hardly crusaders of the fans' interests.

"When competitive balance is achieved, it should be more attractive to the present or future owner. It's a little early to know where we will go as far as revenue sharing is concerned, but the mere fact that more and more owners are saying that it needs deeper consideration means that it is a possibility down the road. I think you'll see a gradual—not dramatic—movement towards some form or forms of revenue sharing," [says Kuhn.] Which is at the heart of competitive balance.

Kuhn shrugs off claims that whatever he does is geared to remaining in office. "I've never had to politic," he says. "I'm not in this position because I needed a job.

This is not all I could do, after all. I like the people and I like the game. I was asked to take this job, and 13 years later, here I am."

He also feels that the media vastly overrated his meeting last month with alleged dissident owners George Steinbrenner, Edward Bennett Williams and Eddie Chiles. "I often wish I were 100 people. Part of what you deal with is 26 clubs, 150 minor league teams, umpires, the union, media, government . . . it's very hard to maintain constant lines of communication so everyone can know what you're thinking. One of the toughest things about this job is taking a position, sticking to it and letting everyone know exactly why you've done so. One of the things about the meeting with Eddie Chiles was that he really didn't know where the commissioner is coming from." But Kuhn asserts that that meeting was just one meeting with three men with one train of thought. He observes that he could have three or four other meetings with groups of different specific interests.

Some of his allies among owners have suggested that Kuhn is sick and tired of the demeaning remarks and wisecracks he has been subjected to and will step down next year. "Anything is a possibility theoretically," he responds, and goes back to Harry Truman and the heat.

At the present, he claims to be far more concerned about the effect of the strike on the game and the commissioner's office itself. On the latter: "Public perception of the commissioner is very important. I'm very much aware of that. I have thought a lot about this, but I think in time the fans will see that compensation is good for the game and the fan.

"I'm extremely concerned about the long-term effect of the strike on the game. While I would say that my mail tends to be reassuring, it has been strongly that way. There is some bitterness at times, but a lot of the letters say 'here's an idea,' often legitimate, and I also think that the American public realizes that unions are going to strike."

He has not yet decided about the All-Star Game, or more important, the minimum number of games that constitute a legitimate season.

He would like to see less media coverage ("Normally we're dying to have the media cover any of our events, but this isn't really one of our events, and I think coverage can be counterproductive in certain ways."), and "to get out of the courtroom and back to the negotiating table." He does not think, as the media have claimed, that there will be an owners' rebellion at today's meeting; he does, however, see optimism. "This session (today) is basically therapeutic. As the Players Executive Council reiterated its unified support for its negotiators, so I think you'll see the owners reiterate their support for the Player Relations Committee. The effect will be making both bargaining teams more effective, and maybe something can be accomplished from there."

Whatever, Bowie Kuhn will rise at 5 a.m. tomorrow. "Maybe someday down the line," he said, "the public perception of the commissioner's job will be that Bowie Kuhn did what he could."

36

Strike Ended After Fifty Days (1981)

SOURCE: *New York Daily News*, August 1, 1981

*The longest strike to date in major league history ended with a middle-of-the-night nego-
tiating session on July 31. Bitter rivals Marvin Miller and Ray Grebey managed to compromise on a compensation plan for the best free agents, and settled on a number of lesser
issues discussed in the article below. The reporters also note the likelihood that the owners would try to salvage the season by instituting a split-season format, whereby current
divisional leaders would be declared winners of the first half of the season and would face
winners of the second half of the season, which would begin on August 10, in a preliminary
round of playoffs. The suggestion, not yet official, was already generating controversy.*

Tempers Stay Hot Although Strike's Over
By Mark Liff and Bill Madden

For the first time in 50 days, major-league ball payers were running bases,
shagging fly balls and taking batting practice in major-league ball parks yesterday—only hours after clandestine and feverish bargaining brought a welcome end
to the baseball strike.

Weary negotiators announced the settlement at 6 a.m. in the Doral Inn, four hours
after they had hammered it out and gleefully began notifying striking players and
expectant club executives. The major-league season will resume Aug. 9 in Cleveland
with the All-Star Game. Regular play will commence the following day, Aug. 10.

In an interesting twist designed to recapture widespread fan support, the agreement provides for an optional split-season. If the owners choose, the season would
be divided into two parts, with the current divisional leaders in each league meeting winners of a makeshift "second season" that would begin on Aug. 10.

Owners will vote this week on the split season concept. Clubs like the Mets, which
were out of the pennant race when the season stopped June 12, have welcomed such
an idea, although other divisional contenders, such as the Orioles, Phillies and White
Sox, are known to oppose it.

"Baseball is back in the headlines and they're gonna play ball," said Ray Grebey,
the owners' chief negotiator. "We'll do everything we can to restore fan confidence.
It's a victory for nobody and it's a loss for nobody."

Marvin Miller, executive director of the players' association, said he never thought
the season would be cancelled. "Their (the owners') losses were ready to pile up.
There was network (television) pressure on them, pressure from sponsors and pressure from (city) mayors. That's a lot of pressure."

The bitter personal battle between Grebey and Miller nearly overshadowed the
upbeat settlement mood. Miller refused to pose for photos with Grebey at a press
conference—and Grebey had to be restrained from bolting the session, calling it
"nothing more than a paid commercial" for the players.

Striking players will not be penalized for days missed during the strike, although the owners, until the final minutes, refused to credit this time. Accredited service time is counted toward free agency, salary arbitrations and pension.

Compensation for teams losing free agents, which had been the main stumbling block to a settlement, was resolved with the players apparently winning many of their demands. The agreement provides that teams stock a pool of talent from which clubs select compensation. The players had held fast to this demand.

Those in the top 20% to 30% statistically require two amateur draft picks—one from the signing club and one in a special selection round—as compensation. There no longer is any limit to the number of clubs which may select rights to players and "ranking" players selected by fewer than four clubs are free to negotiate with any team.

Teams cannot lose more than one player from the pool in any given year. Teams can protect from 24 to 26 players in their organization, depending on the number of free agents they sign. Players with no-trade contracts and those whose contracts require their consent before trades must be protected.

Up to five clubs also may opt out of the free agent draft for a three-year period. They cannot lose a player nor can they attempt to sign free agents.

The owners claim they won their demand for direct compensation through a fund that would pay $150,000 to clubs losing players from the pool for the first time. The fund is to be created by equal contributions from the clubs.

The owners also claim as a major victory an additional year of labor peace by extending the contract through 1984. Minimum salaries have been raised in that new final year, as have been in-season meal allowances.

The owners further agreed to make additional payments to the players' benefit plan for the extra year. In addition, the owners said they will make a $2.34 million contribution to the pension fund, which was due on July 13, the original date of the All-Star Game.

In exchange for these and other concessions, the players agreed to withdraw their charge with the National Labor Relations Board that the owners failed to bargain with them in good faith. The players had contended that they needed the owners' books to formulate their bargaining policies.

The 17-page typewritten agreement, with a five-page exhibit, was first shaped by Miller and Grebey during a day-long secret session in the offices of the National League in Rockefeller Center. Miller and Grebey were noticeably absent when formal negotiations were to have begun at 2 p.m. in the Doral Inn under the auspices of federal mediator Kenneth Moffett.

In a scenario similar to that of a year ago, when a temporary settlement averted a strike, Miller and Grebey were without most of their supporting casts: Grebey was accompanied by American League President Lee MacPhail and Miller by Donald Fehr, the association's chief counsel.

As this clandestine session continued to progress toward a settlement, Moffett was left the task of explaining to the press. "As you know, some people have not been here today," he said sheepishly. "There have been some sidebar meetings going on."

37

Cincinnati Excluded from Playoffs Despite Achieving Best Record (1981)

SOURCE: *Cincinnati Enquirer*, October 4, 1981

The Cincinnati Reds finished the 1981 season with the best overall record in baseball, 66-42, which earned them a four-game lead over Los Angeles and a six-game advantage over Houston. Unfortunately for the Reds, this was a split season, which meant that in defiance of logic, baseball's best team would miss the playoffs. When the strike hit, the Reds were ½ game behind the Dodgers in the standings. Over the remainder of the season, Cincinnati again played outstanding baseball, but on the season's penultimate day, lost to ensure that they would finish behind the Astros. Houston, which had a losing record in the season's first half, beat Cincinnati by one game in the second half. Reds fans—and reporters—were angry at the situation. So were their counterparts in St. Louis, whose Cardinals finished with the NL's second-best record overall but failed to make the postseason.

Baseball's Best Record Gets Reds Armchair Seat

By Tim Sullivan
Sports Reporter

John McNamara wanted to throw something, but he didn't want to be destructive.

He felt like crying, but he was too angry for that.

In his most frustrated hour, the manager of the Cincinnati Reds was powerless even against his own emotions.

The Reds will finish the regular season this afternoon with the best overall record in baseball, yet the gerrymandered split season setup has made them spectators for the playoffs. Saturday's 4–3 loss to the Atlanta Braves—the Reds' third straight defeat—made Houston the National League West's second half champion.

Should the Reds win and the Astros lose today, the Reds will have lost both halves of Bowie Kuhn's split season by one-half game. In both halves they have played one fewer game than the champion.

Entering today's season finale, the composite standings look like this:

Cincinnati	65	42	.607	____
Los Angeles	63	46	.578	2½
Houston	60	48	.556	5½

The Dodgers and Astros will open the National League West playoff Tuesday.

"It's been a mess, the whole thing," McNamara said. "You never get over things like this.

"To be cheated out of the thing by someone's lame-brain idea is ridiculous. You strive for this thing all your life and lose it because of this. . . . It's going to take a hell of an adjustment. There's not any way you can lose it gracefully."

The Reds' last hope was dashed on a day that seemed full of promise. George Foster's first-inning home run gave Tom Seaver a 3–1 lead, but the Reds' ace and Cy Young candidate couldn't hold it.

Bob Horner, the Braves' circular slugger, had knocked in the game's first run with a first-inning sacrifice fly. He brought the Braves to within a run with a fourth-inning homer, tied the game with a sixth-inning homer and scored the winning run after singling in the eighth.

Reds reliever Tom Hume, who took over after the Reds pinch hit for Seaver in the seventh, gave up Horner's single and Chris Chambliss singled Horner to third. Dale Murphy then hit a shot that second baseman Ron Oester caught with Chambliss dangerously off base.

Oester threw in the direction of first baseman Johnny Bench, hoping for a double play, but the throw grazed Chambliss and bounced away while Horner scored.

"Chambliss cut back and it hit him in the shoulder," Oester said. "It's just one of those things."

The Reds threatened to tie the game in the bottom of the eighth, when Dave Concepcion and Foster hit one-out singles to finish Atlanta starter Rick Mahler. Reliever Rick Camp fell behind Bench, 3-and-1, but retired him on a fly ball to shallow center and then struck out Ray Knight to end the inning.

Camp earned his 17th save of the season with a perfect ninth inning and left the Reds to wonder what might have been.

"We had our chances to win," Seaver said. "You can moan all you want about the split season, but we had our chances to win."

His was the minority sentiment.

"It seems like the way the thing was drawn up and everything has gone against us all year long," catcher Mike O'Berry said. "It's tough to take when you think you're the best team and the playoffs start and you're sitting home watching it."

O'Berry, who had his first three-hit game of the season, added, "I would have taken my usual 0-for-3 for a win."

Since the Reds don't have the luxury of exchanging hits for victories, they will have all winter to wonder whether they really were baseball's best team.

"We may not have had the best team, but I think we deserve a chance to prove that," Knight said. "Our record speaks for itself. As of right now we're the best team in baseball, the last three days excluded."

"Are we the best? Playing in the National League, I would say yes," Foster said. "There are not too many teams that have been able to beat us overwhelmingly or beat us any time they wanted to."

"I can't speak for the American League," McNamara said, "but this club can play with any ballclub in the National League. The only club that dominated us was the Cardinals and we didn't see them in the second half. We must have done something right to have the best overall record. We got penalized because we played both halves of the season."

The Reds' plight may not mean much to the Astros or the Dodgers, but it was enough to move Atlanta manager Bobby Cox to sympathy.

"I'm sorry for Mac," he said. "I would be a whole lot mad in his place."

He could not have been much angrier than McNamara was.

"It'd be poetic justice if they have the final World Series game in Montreal with Kuhn in his pinstriped suit and snow up to his hips," McNamara said. "I hope the playoffs go on to Halloween so he can wear a mask or something for the final game of the World Series. That would be appropriate."

38

Miller Attacks Future Commissioner for Strike Commentary (1982)

source: Letter from Marvin Miller to A. Bartlett Giamatti, February 4, 1982, Series II, Box 3, Folder 31, Marvin Miller Papers, Robert F. Wagner Labor Archives, Tamiment Library

On June 16, 1981, the New York Times *published a column by Yale president A. Bartlett Giamatti entitled "Men of Baseball, Lend an Ear." Giamatti, an unabashed romantic, urged the players to abandon their strike because of the significance of baseball to American culture, without taking into consideration the issues that fueled the strike in the first place. To Giamatti, all that mattered was that the national pastime was endangered.*

Marvin Miller waited until December 28 to send Giamatti an angry two-paragraph response. After receiving a reply, Miller wrote a more detailed letter to Giamatti on February 4, 1982. The letter illustrates the conflict between the public perception of baseball as a timeless, precious American game, and the harsh reality of the sport as a business featuring, in the words of George F. Will, "men at work." It also explains Miller's frustration with commissioners like Bowie Kuhn and Giamatti who steadfastly claimed to represent baseball fans, not the owners who hired and paid them. Miller needed to destroy these myths in order to advance the mlbpa's *agenda, but he never fully succeeded.*

February 4, 1982

Dear Mr. Giamatti:

Your letter of January 12th was received. You wrote that I had indicated that your *Times* piece had all the issues wrong. I expressed no such thought. My criticism was that you did not address the issues; that instead you failed to deal with them and falsely portrayed what was involved ("the strike is utter foolishness"; it is "the triumph of greed" . . . ; etc.).

You wrote of your surprise that I found the tone of the piece "anti-libertarian and anti-union" and complained that examples had not been offered to support this view. Examples were omitted simply because they stick out of your piece like a sore thumb.

The owners, intent on turning back the clock by unilaterally changing the contract to weaken or destroy free agency rights, purposefully provoked a strike. The "unbiased educator" proclaims the strike as "utter foolishness." The owners, aware that the only way to bull through their regressive plan, counted on disunity among the players and a rapid "back-to-work" movement. The "unbiased educator," three days into the strike, calls for a back to work movement. Applying the appellation "anti-union" to you was a mild understatement. Your professed innocence is mind-boggling.

For 90 years until 1976 baseball players were property. For more than a decade prior to 1976 the typical player entered his profession by being "drafted"—usually from high school—by one major league organization. His choice was to sign a contract drawn up only by the owners' lawyers, at whatever salary the organization chose to pay him, or not to play in organized baseball anywhere in the U.S., Canada, Japan, or any of the Caribbean nations. Once he signed such a contract he was the property of the organization—never again free to change employers unless his employer traded him, sold him for cash or, when it was felt he could no longer play, released (discharged) him.

In 1976, through a variety of circumstances, the players succeeded in reforming the reserve system and gained certain limited freedom. In 1980–1981 the owners decreed that such limited freedom was to be made meaningless by imposing free agent compensation. The "unbiased educator," now objecting to the term "anti-libertarian" applied to him, promptly condemned the strike and lent his pen to a strike-breaking effort which, if successful, would have returned the players to, or close to their former status as pieces of property.

Given the above, you are clearly wrong in describing my letter as either gratuitous or nasty. Under the circumstances my letter was mild rather than nasty and, as a response to your union-busting article, was anything but gratuitous.

The last paragraph of your letter was neither anti-union nor anti-libertarian. It was plainly ignorant.

Major league baseball has never been in a better condition. By any measure—attendance and fan interest, gate receipts and television revenue, number of major league teams and number of major league players, profits, spiraling upward market value of franchises, number of would-be franchise purchasers, closeness of pennant races, number of teams (and number of different teams) which are real pennant contenders, the all-time record rate of 1982 season-ticket purchases, etc., etc.—all attest to this fact. Hence, my conviction that your statement that baseball is "such a mess" is evidence of your ignorance of the facts.

The concern I expressed in my prior letter with respect to the future of education in at least one section of the ivy league has not been allayed.

Very truly yours,

Marvin J. Miller

4

A Lull in the Storm

The mid-1980s was a period of relative peace and prosperity in baseball—on the surface. There were no major strikes or lockouts, but owners were angry enough to oust Bowie Kuhn from office and install Peter Ueberroth (the organizer of the phenomenally successful 1984 Los Angeles Olympics), who helped negotiate a new Basic Agreement in 1985. He also initiated a new strategy with the owners that would soon come back to haunt them. Ueberroth reversed a Kuhn decision to ban legends Willie Mays and Mickey Mantle from baseball events due to their association with casinos, and had to deal with an embarrassing trial in which several players were revealed to be cocaine addicts.

On the field the game was as compelling as ever. The action was led by Pete Rose, who finally broke Ty Cobb's career hits record, and young pitching phenoms Dwight Gooden and Roger Clemens, who captured the nation's attention by striking out 20 players in a game. The 1986 postseason featured two nail-biting League Championship Series that were topped in drama by a World Series featuring Gooden and Clemens, which the ill-fated Boston Red Sox failed once again to win. The public assigned most of the blame to Bill Buckner, whose error on a simple ground ball concluded Boston's collapse in the sixth game. Buckner's perceived crime was dwarfed the following year by Los Angeles Dodgers executive Al Campanis, whose racist comments in a nationally televised interview revealed once again that baseball had not yet dealt with its most pervasive problem.

39

Bill James on "Sabermetrics" (1982)

SOURCE: Bill James, *The Bill James Baseball Abstract 1982* (New York: Ballantine Books, 1982), 3.

In 1977 a Topeka, Kansas, man named Bill James self-published 1977 Baseball Abstract, a sixty-eight-page collection of nineteen articles in which James attempted to use statistics to answer a number of questions about the game. Did popular pitchers like Nolan Ryan really increase attendance? Was there any appreciable difference in the length of games depending on the umpiring crew? Was there a better way to rank defenders other than by fielding percentage? Traditional baseball men thought they had answers to these and many similar questions, but until James they had not attempted to measure or analyze them statistically, or devise new formulas to better understand how baseball was really played.

In 1977 few people cared about such issues, but James persisted, and after five years he finally signed a contract with a major publisher to make his Abstract available to a wider audience. Since then James's influence on baseball has risen considerably. A growing number of managers and general managers take into account results gathered through "sabermetrics" (James's term, taken from the acronym SABR—the Society for American Baseball Research, an organization whose members helped spread and improve on James's work) when making personnel moves or enacting game strategies. Baseball journalists who grew up on the Abstracts and other books by James started to incorporate his philosophies into their writings. In 2002 the Boston Red Sox completed the cycle, hiring James to help them surpass the New York Yankees.

Printed here is the introduction to the 1982 Abstract, in which James discusses the concept of sabermetrics. An index of James's writings is available at http://members.cox.net/sroneysabr/JamesIndex.

INTRODUCTION

If you sometimes get the feeling between here and the back cover that you are coming in on the middle of a discussion, it is because you are. This is the sixth annual edition of a book which throughout its first five years has been read by a number of people who could congregate peacefully in the restrooms in the left field bleachers in Yankee Stadium. In spite of our size, or perhaps because of it, we have advanced the discussion some from the point at which it began. I have tried very hard to hide that fact by writing careful introductions to the methods in use, but I can't, really; it's like when you walk into a room where people are talking about you, there's always a millisecond pause before they launch energetically into their discussion about Chinese earthworms or the declining quality of plastic food storage bags. There's a millisecond missing from this book. I can't hide it.

This is a book about baseball. It is a book about how you can get answers to baseball questions. It is not my purpose to convince you that Andre Dawson should have been the MVP or shouldn't have, to convince you that Reggie Jackson is through or that he isn't, to show you that Pete Rose will get 4,200 hits or that he won't. It is my purpose to equip you with tools you can use to work on those answers for yourself.

This is a book about *sabermetrics*. Sabermetrics is a coined word, the first part honoring the SABR (Society for American Baseball Research), the second part indicating measurement. Sabermetrics is the mathematical and statistical analysis of baseball records.

Sabermetrics does not begin with the numbers. It begins with issues. The numbers, the statistics, are not the subject of the discussion; they are not the subject of this book. The subject is baseball. The numbers bear a relationship to that subject and to us which is much like the relationship of tools to a machine and to the mechanic who uses them. The mechanic does not begin with a monkey wrench; basically, he is not *interested* in the damn monkey wrench. All that he wants from the monkey wrench is that it do its job and not give him any trouble. He begins with the machine, and with the things which he sees and hears there, and from those he forms an idea—a thesis, if you must—about what must be happening in that machine. The tools are a way of taking the thing apart so that he can see if he was right or if he needs to try something else.

People say things. People say that baseball is 75% pitching. People say that pennant-winning teams must be strong up the middle. People say that good pitching will stop good hitting. People say that a ballplayers' prime is from 28 to 32. People say that you should guard the lines in the late innings of a close game. They say that you never want to get thrown out at third base with no one out or with two out in an inning. They say that Sal Bando hits well in the clutch, and that you can tell this by his RBI counts. They say that power hitters may get the glory, but that it is small "constants" like hitting the cut-off man and hitting behind the runner which win pennants. Whitey Herzog was once quoted as saying that Frank White saved the Royals two runs a game. People say that when you draw in the infield it adds 100 points to a hitter's average. Sabermetrics is the field of knowledge which is drawn from attempts to figure out whether or not those things people say are true.

What has always seemed curious to me is that there are so few of us involved in it. Baseball is drowning in records, and people think about them and talk about them and write about them a great deal. Why doesn't anybody *use* them? I really don't know. But that, in essence, is what I am about here.

40

"Destiny Has Finally Overtaken Bowie Kuhn" (1982)

SOURCE: Letter from Peter Seitz to Bowie Kuhn, November 8, 1982, Peter Seitz Papers, #5733, Box 21, Folder 39, Kheel Center for Labor-Management Documentation and Archives, Cornell University

In the aftermath of the 1981 strike, a number of owners were furious with Kuhn—which was not unusual. For the first time, however, some of these owners acted to secure consent

among their peers to rid themselves of Kuhn. Nine owners, mostly from the National League, signed a letter asking for the commissioner's resignation, but the letter's existence was revealed and was shredded at an owner's meeting in December. Nevertheless, the opposition to Kuhn remained.

The NL franchises at the forefront of the anti-Kuhn group were Atlanta, Cincinnati, Houston, New York, and St. Louis. In spite of public and private efforts to sway these owners, and numerous expressions of support for Kuhn by various luminaries (all mentioned by Kuhn in his autobiography), in a November 1 meeting the NL voted 7–5 to re-elect Kuhn—a negative vote since a three-quarters vote was required. Kuhn reluctantly agreed to serve the balance of his term, through August 1983, but remained in office until October 1984, when Peter Ueberroth, fresh from his triumphant orchestration of the 1984 Los Angeles Olympic Games, took office.

In the letter presented here one of Kuhn's former foes, Peter Seitz, addressed Kuhn's dismissal while venting anger at his perceived treatment at the owners' hands nearly eight years after the fact.

November 8, 1982

Dear Mr. Kuhn:

In time, as it happened to Cardinal Wolsay, Sir Thomas More, Archbishop Cramner, Billy Martin (the itinerant and ubiquitous manager) and to Seitz (your one-time and quondam arbitrator), destiny has finally overtaken Bowie Kuhn. I take no pleasure in welcoming you into the company of the erstwhile makers and shakers. Indeed, I feel some remorse, despite the fact that there were some rather important occasions when your convictions were at odds with my own. The Messersmith Case, by now, is as ancient history as the Carthaginian Wars. I bear no discernable scars and I am wholly free of feelings of animosity. However, the fact that you are stepping down (as I did, under somewhat different circumstances) prompted this letter.

I believe that each of us, in the roles assigned for us to play, acted conscientiously in the achievement of what we conceived to be our designated missions. In my case, I was cast out by the Major Leagues with the same grace and empathy as John Milton's Jehovah when he cast out Satan from Heaven in *Paradise Lost*. The fact that I did make some small contribution to dispute settlement in Baseball (it is my impression that aside from the Catfish Hunter and Reserve System cases, the clubs benefitted more from my decisions than the Players' Association) was utterly ignored. I was dismissed unceremoniously with the conventional pink slip without a word of kindness except from John Gaherin who, being a gentleman, could not act otherwise. The dismissal was ignominious and shameless in character and took no account of my professional career and general acceptance as an arbitrator. Perhaps the manner of dismissal told the public more of the character of those who ran the Major Leagues of Baseball than it told them of my competence and integrity. Nevertheless, at the time, the brutality and rudeness of the action hurt deeply and it is only now, years later, when you yourself were asked to step down, that I considered it appropriate to voice these feelings and reactions.

According to the conventional rhetoric, Professional Baseball is regarded as the quintessential American sport. I believe that it could be! However, I doubt that there was anything essentially American in the mean and vindictive manner of my dismissal as arbitrator. Those who regard professional baseball as *The* American sport should, at least, recognize and live up to some of the ideals of amateur athletics. It pains me to say that too many of the club owners seem to have little acquaintanceship with the manners of amateurism in sports and are content with standards and ideals that amateurs would regard as squalid.

At the age of 77 my indignation at the crude, vulgar and offensive manner in which the owners saw fit to disparage my professionalism and integrity is considerably mellowed by time; but, nevertheless, I find it therapeutic, on this occasion, to express myself on the subject and, hereafter, to hold my peace.

I know you by reputation to be an honorable person; and I am sure that your contributions to the sport have been many and valuable—even if, like Fiorello LaGuardia, when you did make a mistake, it was a "beaut." The fact that we had strongly contradictory views on the Messersmith Case,* however, does not dissuade me from hoping that your departure from your post as Commissioner will not be characterized by the meanness and rudeness which accompanied my dismissal.

Baseball has some fine conventions which deserve preservation. Normally, a hapless pitcher, being removed from the mound in the course of an inning will get a few kind words from the Manager for his efforts, perhaps a reassuring pat on the back and even an opportunity to doff his cap in deference to the applause of the more sensitive and appreciative customers. This is part of what makes baseball a sport rather than a cock-fight. I am afraid that too many of the franchise owners, your former clients, are unaware of this.

I wish you good fortune in your future endeavors.

Very truly yours,

Peter Seitz

*At the hearings, you may recall (the one period when we met) you lectured me sternly and resonantly on the subject that arbitration was never intended to be and was the wrong way to resolve disputes concerning the Reserve System; and that such disputes should be settled by collective bargaining. I agreed with you and inquired whether you had any suggestions for me as to how to get the dispute from the arbitration table to the negotiating table (which the clubs you represented had *already* refused to do at my suggestion). You were unable to provide me with any guidance!

41

Kuhn Orders Mickey Mantle to Choose Between
Baseball and Casino (1983)

SOURCE: *New York Daily News*, February 9, 1983

In late 1979 Willie Mays signed a contract with Bally's Park Place Casino in Atlantic City to help in promotional activity. Commissioner Kuhn acted swiftly and asked Mays to "disassociate" himself from baseball as long as he was employed by the casino in order to avoid the appearance of a link between baseball and gambling. Mays refused and stopped working with the New York Mets. The media attacked Kuhn for insensitivity and hypocrisy, since several team owners held interests in racetracks, but Kuhn—who insisted that Mays had not been banned from baseball, but merely asked to make a choice—held firm.

Three years later another baseball legend found himself in a similar predicament. When Kuhn learned that Mickey Mantle had signed a $100,000 contract with the Claridge Hotel and Casino, he gave Mantle the same ultimatum. Mantle, who maintained that he had received no comparable offers from baseball, accepted Kuhn's ruling and honored his contract. The following column is typical of the response of the media to Kuhn's actions against Mays and Mantle. Kuhn's ruling was reversed in early 1985 by new commissioner Peter Ueberroth.

Phil Pepe
Mick's Dollar and Sense Decision

In his last few seasons as a Yankee, the numbers on Mickey Mantle's contract always read the same—$100,000—right up until he retired after the 1968 season. At the time, it was the maximum paid to any baseball player, a ceiling established by club owners as an unwritten rule long before Marvin Miller and free agency and arbitration.

If he were still playing today, there would be no telling how much money a Mickey Mantle would bring on the open market. "How could you pay me?" Mantle said yesterday. "It would be like Joe DiMaggio once said. I'd walk into the owner's office and say, 'Hi, partner.'"

In the 14 years since he hung up his uniform, nobody in baseball—or out of baseball—has come along and offered to pay Mantle anything like $100,000. Now along comes the Claridge Hotel and Casino, and they are willing to pay Mantle $100,000 a year—the same amount he received for bashing baseballs—just to be a good-will ambassador for the hotel. Essentially, what Mantle will do is host some high rollers at golf tournaments sponsored by the hotel.

"It's not," said Mantle, "as if I'm going to stand outside the hotel and say, 'Psst, hey, buddy, come in here and gamble.'"

For this, Mantle has been told by the commissioner of baseball that he must disassociate himself with the game he loves so much, the game he graced with his awesome power and blazing speed.

The reason for the commissioner's decision is that the Claridge Hotel and Casino is in the gambling business and baseball cannot have anyone associated with gambling. It, to use the catch-all cliche, "is not in the best interests of the game."

It does not matter that the Claridge Hotel and Casino is in Atlantic City, where gambling is perfectly legal. It does not matter, either, that there are baseball owners and players who own race horses and one owner who owns a race track in Florida and that, the last time I looked, the principal activity at a race track was gambling. It does not matter that the Riviera Hotel in Las Vegas, another gambling establishment in a city where gambling is legal, invited 45 members of the Baseball Hall of Fame to participate in its annual golf tournament last year, paid them to attend and awarded prize money to the winners.

The distinction between gambling at a race track and gambling at a casino is something I cannot comprehend. The distinction between getting paid to appear at a golf tournament sponsored by a gambling establishment and getting paid to host a golf tournament sponsored by a gambling establishment is something else I cannot comprehend.

What we seem to have here is a classic case of the double standard—one rule for baseball's lords, another for its serfs.

Under the circumstances, Bowie Kuhn had no choice but to rule against Mantle after he imposed a similar ban on Willie Mays, who took a job with Bally's Park Place Hotel and Casino. He had set a precedent with Mays. Could he do otherwise with Mantle? The real question is: Should he have set the precedent with Mays? Was that not a double standard?

Not so, said Kuhn, who has been very diligent in his years as commissioner in the area of gambling.

"When I came into baseball (in 1969), there were several owners who had holdings in casinos. I ordered them to divest themselves immediately. But there was an established precedent, a grandfather clause, if you will, of baseball people being involved in horse racing. I didn't like it, but I didn't feel I had the right to do anything about it," Kuhn said.

"When George Steinbrenner purchased Florida Downs, I let it stand because it was 'grandfathered,' but I said, 'That's it, it will go no farther.' I think what I've done is consistent.

"You've got to be practical. I have nothing against a player going to a casino or playing in a golf tournament sponsored by a casino. The difference is Mickey and Willie are involved in a regular pattern of employment.

"What bothers me is that people think I enjoy making these decisions. I hate having to do it. I have the greatest respect and admiration for both Willie Mays and Mickey Mantle, but I feel I had to do what I did. And I didn't ban Willie Mays from baseball. He and Mickey Mantle are welcome at all baseball functions. I have just prohibited them from being employed by a ball club."

Kuhn informed Mantle of his decision in a letter hand-delivered to the former Yankee star at the Waldorf-Astoria yesterday morning. In his letter, Kuhn said that he was disappointed one of baseball's greatest stars had taken this job, that he hoped Mantle might align himself with Panasonic, as Reggie Jackson has, or with Mr. Coffee, as Joe DiMaggio did.

"I've been out of baseball 14 years," said Mantle. "I didn't get an offer from Panasonic or Mr. Coffee."

The real pity is that there are no jobs in baseball for a Mickey Mantle or a Willie Mays that can pay them the amount of money they are getting from the casinos. Mantle says he has been offered coaching jobs.

"But they don't pay much," he said. "Can you imagine me working for Billy (Martin) for $15,000 and he's making $500,000?"

To his credit, Mantle says he holds no hard feelings toward the commissioner.

"I expected it," Mantle said. "He had to do what he did after Willie. It's all right. He's not taking anything away from me. I haven't done anything in 14 years except go to spring training."

And when you think about it, that's the saddest part of all.

42

Miller Questions Actions of His Successor (1983)

SOURCE: Memorandum from Marvin Miller to MLBPA Executive Board, March 7, 1983, Marvin Miller Papers, Series II, Box 4, Folder 1, Robert F. Wagner Labor Archives, Tamiment Library

Just three months after Ken Moffett replaced the retiring Marvin Miller as executive director of the MLBPA, Miller began to question Moffett's motives and competence. As soon as Moffett took office on January 1, he hired two lawyers to work with Donald Fehr, one of whom went on vacation almost immediately, soon followed by Moffett in February. In early March Miller, acting in his contractual capacity as advisor to the union, drafted a three-page memorandum on various issues confronting the MLBPA, including the new TV contract and the proposed lengthening of the postseason. He was appalled to learn from Moffett that the memorandum would not be distributed to the players, on Moffett's orders, as Miller had intended. Miller responded by drafting the following memorandum and sending it directly to the player representatives.

To Miller's further dismay, the players—and Fehr—ignored the second memorandum. However, as Moffett's poor performance became increasingly apparent, in November the players asked Miller to come back as interim executive director, with his first duty being the firing of Moffett and his lawyers. Miller would stay in office for a year, to be replaced in January 1985 by Fehr. Miller discusses this episode in pages 320–29 of his autobiography.

MEMORANDUM

To: Executive Board
From: Marvin J. Miller
Subject: THE PLAYERS' RIGHT TO KNOW

The strength of the Players Association for the past 17 years has been dependent upon a free flow of information between our office and the elected Player Representatives and players. I am concerned by an apparent sudden departure from this policy. *Deliberate withholding of information from the elected Player Reps, and thereby from the players, has occurred in the past several days.*

On March 3rd I wrote a memorandum to the Player Reps (copies to Ken Moffett and Don Fehr). It contained facts and views on some current matters of importance to players (TV network contract, owners' proposal of adding post-season games, and the relationship of these issues to the pending TV litigation). The memo also requested guidance from the executive board as to its intention when I was asked to serve as consultant, i.e. advisor to the executive board, to the director, to both?

You have not seen that memorandum because, on Ken Moffett's order, you are not to be permitted to read it. I have been so advised directly by Ken and by David Vaughan, one of the two additional lawyers hired by Ken. Vaughan, acting under Ken's order, took away the memo from the secretary to whom it had been dictated and refused to return it to me.

That same day I was informed of the following:

1. The office door locks have been changed. Not one of the four or five extra sets of keys can be found.

2. No staff member is permitted to provide any information requested by me, not even the names of recently elected Player Reps.

3. If the memo is seen by Player Reps, Ken assures me he will undertake to discredit it by impugning my motives.

This weird and childish behavior boggles the mind. It has been triggered solely by my desire to communicate some facts and views to the Player Reps and to receive their guidance about my role as consultant. The suppressed memorandum, as you will see when you eventually read it, contains nothing which even remotely justifies such irrational and exaggerated behavior. I trust that you will form your own judgment by reading the memo itself. As soon as it is typed, it will be sent to you, regardless of the "order" to destroy it.

Given the events of the last several days, the March 3rd memo itself becomes relatively unimportant. What is more significant to the future of the Players Association is the need to stamp out, at its inception, a policy of barring Player Reps and players from receiving information on matters affecting the players' interests.

If the censorship arose from fear that the memo would jeopardize the unity which has characterized the Players Association, and has been its strength, it is up to the players to instruct the new director that constructive criticism does not foster disunity. Censorship does. What divides and destroys an organization is an assumption that its elected representatives are not capable of using their own judgment to reach decisions. An executive director of the Players Association who does not respect and trust the players will receive no trust in return. *That* would be disastrous.

The events of the past few days obviously have involved personal indignity. I doubt that players had this type of treatment in mind as a fitting climax to 17 years of service. Nevertheless, that is trivial compared to the need for players to make clear that they will not tolerate *any suppression* of information, *any censorship*, or *any preselection* of what the players are to be permitted to read or hear.

Everyone makes mistakes, including leaders of organizations. In a democratic organization, the members and elected officers can be counted on to correct errors by participating in policy decisions. They can do that, however, only by having access to all the facts and views available on matters of interest.

The future welfare of the players and the Players Association could well be determined by your degree of success in re-establishing a free flow of information and the mutual trust and respect that accompanies it.

Best regards.

43

Kuhn Announces New Policy on Drugs; Union Responds (1984)

SOURCE: Memo, "Joint Drug Program & Discipline," June 28, 1984; letter from Donald Fehr to Bowie Kuhn, August 6, 1984, Marvin Miller Papers, Series II, Box 3, Folder 1, Robert F. Wagner Labor Archives, Tamiment Library

Throughout the 1980s one of the most vexing problems facing baseball was the use of illegal drugs, particularly cocaine, by major league players. Although addiction was not unknown previously, the number of players arrested, convicted, fined, and jailed increased at a phenomenal rate during the first half of the decade. The best-known case involved Steve Howe, a talented relief pitcher who unsuccessfully fought his convictions—but was successful in overturning the frequent suspensions by four different commissioners over a decade's span. In December 1983 four players for the Kansas City Royals were found guilty of cocaine possession and received brief jail sentences. Commissioner Kuhn's attempt to suspend them for the entire 1984 season was overturned by an arbitrator.

Angered by what he saw as the MLBPA's casual attitude toward the problem, Kuhn asked PRC director and former AL president Lee MacPhail and Don Fehr, the acting executive director of the union, to agree on a plan to treat and punish drug offenders. The plan, concluded on May 10, did not satisfy Kuhn, who wanted tougher sanctions. Over the next month minor changes were made to the plan, which was approved on June 27 but later rescinded by the owners on October 22, 1985. On the following day Kuhn released a separate document listing the penalties for various stages of drug usage. Five weeks later, Donald Fehr responded with a letter reminding Kuhn that such penalties had to be negotiated with the union.

June 28, 1984
TO: ALL MAJOR LEAGUE CLUBS & PLAYERS
FROM: COMMISSIONER BOWIE K. KUHN
RE: *JOINT DRUG PROGRAM & DISCIPLINE*

THE JOINT DRUG PROGRAM

As you are all aware, agreement has been reached on a Joint Player/Management program dealing with drug use. We all recognize that this program is new and experimental and that it addresses only certain categories of drug cases. At the same time, a great deal of thought and effort has gone into it and I urge all concerned—players and Clubs alike—to put aside any misgivings, to use the program to the fullest and to give it a chance to work. As Commissioner, I support it fully and sincerely, including its assurance of amnesty to players coming within its terms.

NEW DRUG RULES

While the new drug program significantly broadens the situations in which players will be entitled to amnesty, it is vital to the integrity of Baseball and the public's confidence in it that serious categories of drug cases, which the program is not designed to cover, be subject to serious disciplinary penalties. It is also important that all concerned be aware of the penalties which will be invoked with respect to these cases. The combination of the procedures established in the joint program and specific rules for drug involvement not covered by the joint program will, I believe, considerably strengthen our ability to effectively deal with drug use problems.

Accordingly, the following rules will henceforth apply:

1. The possession or use of illegal drugs is strictly prohibited. The procedures established in the joint player/management drug use program shall be followed in all applicable cases. Matters excluded from the joint program shall be handled in accordance with these rules.

2. Any player convicted of or pleading guilty to a crime related to the distribution of a controlled substance will be suspended without pay for a minimum of one year up to a maximum of permanent ineligibility.

3. Any player who facilitates the use by others of a controlled substance will be suspended without pay for a minimum of one year up to a maximum of permanent ineligibility.

4. Any player convicted of or pleading guilty to any crime related to the possession or use of a controlled substance will be suspended without pay for one year.

5. Any player found in possession of or using any controlled substance on

the playing field or the premises of a stadium will be suspended without pay for one year.

6. Any player who has previously been disciplined under these rules and thereafter again is found in violation of any of them shall be subject to such discipline as in the opinion of the Commissioner may be appropriate under the circumstances which may include permanent ineligibility.

7. Any player involved with a controlled substance covered by the joint program who for any reason is excluded from the procedures of the joint agreement (that is, players who have been on the Rehabilitation List for more than 60 days and those who fail to comply with the recommendations of the Joint Review Council) shall be subject to such discipline as in the opinion of the Commissioner is appropriate.

8. In addition to the sanctions set forth above, any player disciplined as the result of involvement with a controlled substance may thereafter be placed on probation for such period as may be determined to be appropriate under the circumstances. During this probationary period, the player will be subject to mandatory, unannounced testing for the purpose of assuring that the player is no longer involved with a controlled substance. The probationary terms may also include such provisions as may, in the opinion of the Commissioner, be appropriate as regards aftercare or community service.

9. Any player involved with a controlled substance not covered by the joint program shall be subject to such discipline as in the opinion of the Commissioner may be appropriate provided, however, that any player who voluntarily seeks help for such a problem *will be accorded amnesty and not be subject to discipline.* Such players will, however, be subject to appropriate probationary terms which may include testing, aftercare and community service. The amnesty referred to above does not extend to subsequent failure to comply with the probationary terms or for any renewed involvement with such controlled substances.

6 August 1984
Dear Bowie:

This has reference to your memorandum of 28 June to all clubs and players (copy attached) concerning action you intend to take for players who are not covered by the new joint drug agreement. Please be advised as follows:

First, as you are well aware, these "new drug rules" are the unilateral creation of the Commissioner's office, and do not reflect any agreement or understanding with the Players Association. As I explained when you advised that you were considering issuing new "rules," these rules amount to nothing more than a statement of present intention by you with respect to hypothetical future situations.

The Basic Agreement requires that any discipline imposed, whether by a club, league, or the Commissioner, be for "just cause." Just cause is a standard which cannot be readily applied in the abstract. On the contrary, management must prove, on the facts of each individual case, by clear and convincing evidence, that just cause is present for the penalty imposed. In any particular future case, should your office impose discipline which, in our view, does not meet the just cause standard, you can expect that a grievance will be instituted, whereupon you will be obligated to prove, on the facts of that case, that just cause is present for your action.

Suffice it to say that we are not persuaded that you would be able to meet that burden in many of your hypothetical examples. But we will only argue individual cases when and as they arise—not hypothetically. We hope, with the approach signaled by the new joint drug agreement, that we will have few, if any, future cases raising these issues.

Sincerely,

Donald M. Fehr

44

Official Report on Baseball in the 1984 Olympic Games (1984)

SOURCE: U.S. Olympic Committee, *Official Report of the Games of the XXIIIrd Olympiad Los Angeles, 1984*, vol. 1, 658–660, http://www.la84foundation.org/6oic/OfficialReports/1984/1984v1pt3.pdf

For more than a century baseball had been known as the "national pastime" of the United States. During that period baseball also became very popular in Japan and throughout much of Latin America. Nevertheless, the International Olympic Committee had never agreed to admit baseball as a medal sport because of its limited international appeal. As this excerpt from the baseball section of the Sports Administration and Competition Management chapter in the Official Report of the Games *notes, baseball had appeared as a demonstration sport during six Olympics previously. As the host Olympic nation for the 1984 Games, the United States had the right to designate two sports for demonstration status, and on April 10, 1981, the IOC approved the choice of baseball and tennis as the demonstration sports in 1984.*

The extraordinary financial and popular success of the Los Angeles Games helped convince the IOC to grant medal status to baseball for the 1988 Seoul Games. In 2005, however, both baseball and softball were scheduled to be eliminated following the 2008 Games, largely due to major league baseball's refusal to conform to Olympic drug testing standards and to suspend their season to permit its players to participate in the Olympics.

Baseball

More than 385,000 spectators attended eight days of Olympic baseball at Dodger Stadium in Los Angeles, giving the demonstration sport the third highest attendance of the Games behind football and athletics.*

*Soccer and track and field —Ed.

The long-standing and constant support of the Los Angeles Dodger professional baseball organization contributed immeasurably to the success of the event. Not only did the Dodgers offer use of their 56,000 capacity facility in the middle of their season, but they also assisted greatly in the planning stage and provided the majority of the staff necessary to operate the venue.

The initial push for the inclusion of baseball in the 1984 Games began in 1979 when the Extraordinary Congress of the International Amateur Baseball Association (AINBA) was held in Los Angeles. AINBA made a presentation to the LAOCC's Demonstration Sports Commission, which recommended baseball and tennis as its choices for demonstration status in the 1984 Games. When the IOC gave its approval for the two demonstration sports on 10 April 1981, a four-team, six-day tournament format was dictated. Included in this original plan was the stipulation that medals would not be presented to the winners, athletes could not march in Opening or Closing Ceremonies and teams would not be able to stay in the Olympic villages. The LAOCC continued to lobby for inclusion of baseball as a full medal sport. At the 1983 IOC Session in New Delhi, the number of teams was expanded to six and permission to conduct awards ceremonies and present special gold, silver and bronze medals similar to those awarded in official Olympic sports was granted. By May 1984, many of the LAOCC's original demands were met as the IOC approved an increase in the number of participating teams to eight and allowed baseball players to stay in the Olympic villages and to march in Opening and Closing Ceremonies.

Although baseball had been a demonstration sport in six other Olympic Games, previous formats consisted mainly of one-game exhibitions played in makeshift ballparks. The inclusion of an eight-team, eight-day tournament for baseball in the 1984 Games and the tremendous spectator interest was seen by the AINBA as a major step forward for international amateur baseball.

The LAOCC executed an agreement in principle with the Dodgers in September 1981, calling for the Dodgers to provide Dodger Stadium as the site for the baseball demonstration and act as a managing partner with the LAOCC in assuming responsibility for the housing, feeding, transportation, security, entertainment and training of the athletes during the Games. In return, the Dodgers would receive a percentage of the gross receipts derived from baseball ticket sales and reimbursement for day-of-game expenses. The Dodgers were entitled to offer their season ticket holders right of first refusal to purchase tickets to their regular seats during the Games. In late 1983, the LAOCC was able to revise downward its village housing estimates allowing baseball athletes village privileges under the following conditions: a maximum of 20 athletes and five officials per team were permitted; the needs of each team would be administered by its own NOC* without an increase in the size of the NOC staff; and the cost for each athlete would be $100 per night (compared to $35 per night for athletes in medal sports). The contract with the Dodgers was then amended and the LAOCC reassumed responsibility for athlete housing, feeding,

---

* "NOC" stands for National Olympic Committee —Ed.

entertainment, security, transportation and training in return for the Dodgers' paying two-thirds of the housing costs for the athletes by 1 March 1984. The Dodgers were responsible for operating the stadium during the Games, while the LAOCC managed key departments such as Technology, Language Services and Accreditation, necessary for the Olympic Games functions but not within the scope of the Dodgers' usual operation.

Selection criteria for the six teams originally called for the tournament called for automatic berths for the defending world champion (Korea) and the host country as well as one berth each for European and Asian entries and two for the Americas exclusive of the United States. Several alternatives which had been selected as reserves against non-participation provided additional choices when the tournament was increased to eight teams. When a final schedule was determined, the eight teams were divided into two groups for divisional round-robin play. Two games were played each day with the top two teams in each division after round-robin play advancing into semi-final games. Japan outscored the United States, 6–3, in the championship games, while Chinese Taipei shut out Korea, 3–0, for third place.

45

Ueberroth Pressures Cubs to Install Lights at Wrigley Field (1984)

SOURCE: Letter from Peter Ueberroth to Andrew McKenna, December 18, 1984, "Stadium: Chicago (Wrigley) 1980–1989" file, National Baseball Hall of Fame Library

The Chicago Cubs had the best record in the NL in 1984, earning them the home-field advantage over the San Diego Padres in the NLCS. The NL ruled, however, that because the Cubs could not play night games, Chicago would host the first two games and the remainder of the series would be played in San Diego. The Cubs lost to the Padres in five games.

This account is a myth; at the time the divisions alternated home-field advantage. However, Commissioner Ueberroth seized this opportunity to make clear to the Cubs ownership the importance of night postseason games to its television partners. The letter reproduced here was cited as evidence in the case of Chicago National League Ball Club, Inc., v. James R. Thompson, The City of Chicago and Lake View Citizens Council, *in which the Cubs hoped to overturn the local statute forbidding the installation of lights at Wrigley Field. Although Judge Richard L. Curry ruled against the Cubs on March 25, 1985, the momentum had started to turn against the traditionalists. On February 23, 1988, the Chicago City Council voted to approve a limited number of night games at Wrigley.*

December 18, 1984

Re: *NIGHT BASEBALL IN WRIGLEY FIELD*

Dear Andy:

We have had a number of discussions about the need for the Cubs to undertake all appropriate steps to assure that future National League Championship Series and World Series games in which the Cubs may be participants can be played at night. While I think you fully understand Major League Baseball's position on this matter, I write to be certain that our communication has been clear and complete. I can assure you that the views expressed in this letter are shared by all other Clubs with whom I've discussed this matter.

As you know, Baseball is contractually obligated to ABC and NBC to schedule certain LCS and World Series games at night. Obviously, this is not possible so long as Wrigley Field is not equipped with lights and the Cubs are prevented by state and local law from playing at night. I should make clear that Major League Baseball's sole interest in such nighttime scheduling relates to LCS and World Series games, and not to regular season games.

If Baseball were required by the absence of lights in Wrigley Field to play all post-season games scheduled there in the early afternoon instead of in prime time, the other Major League Clubs would stand to lose many millions of dollars in television revenue which Baseball would be forced to rebate to the networks. As you know, the Clubs are heavily dependent upon this revenue to meet the costs of operations. It would simply not be fair to impose this financial burden on the other Clubs.

The problem is not simply one of money. Baseball has an obligation to continue to schedule games at times when the greatest number of fans nationwide have the opportunity to view its showcase events. In these times of the fractionalizing of television audiences, any other course would be foolhardy. There is also the near certainty of confusion and schedule dislocation when darkness causes suspension or postponement of rain-delayed or extra-inning games begun in daylight.

As I have repeatedly told you, the solution to this problem lies squarely at the Cubs' doorstep. In the wake of last year's experience, I cannot in good conscience let the matter go unresolved, to be dealt with by a last-minute gerrymandering of the schedule with an assist from Lady Luck. The time for you to address the problem is now, when there is a chance to develop careful answers that will as nearly as possible accommodate the interests of all.

I must warn you that in the absence of appropriate solutions being worked out by the Cubs, Baseball will have no alternative but to resolve the situation on its own. In order to avoid the drastic consequences above referred to, this could include the requirement that the Cubs' post-season games be played elsewhere than at Wrigley Field, perhaps not even in Chicago.

This office stands ready to help your Club in any appropriate way as you address this situation.

Sincerely,
Peter Ueberroth

46

New Basic Agreement Signed, Ending Two-Game Strike (1985)

SOURCE: *Baltimore Sun*, August 8, 1985

The 1985 Basic Agreement negotiations were the first not to feature either Bowie Kuhn or Marvin Miller in fifteen years. Peter Ueberroth was anxious to demonstrate his independence from the owners while consolidating his power over them, while new MLBPA executive director Donald Fehr (previously the general counsel for the union) was trying to escape the immense shadow of Marvin Miller, who while retired participated in the proceedings. As usual, neither side seemed willing to compromise, and as promised the players went on strike on August 6. According to historian Robert Burk, Ueberroth convinced Fehr to exclude Miller from the talks, and Fehr and management negotiator Barry Rona quickly came to an agreement. Although many players and owners criticized the deal for being too conciliatory, the general consensus was that, for the first time, owners had struck the better deal in forcing players to have three years of service, up from two, to qualify for arbitration and in gaining the right to reduce pre–August 31 rosters. Burk observed that Ueberroth could afford to be more generous than the owners would have liked because of his idea to institute a plan whereby owners would agree not to bid for free agents. Later known as collusion, this strategy would soon envelop baseball in a series of lawsuits and would cost baseball hundreds of millions of dollars. It also cost Ueberroth the legacy he sought.

Strike Ends; Play Resumes Today
By Kent Baker
Sun Staff Correspondent

NEW YORK—Negotiators in the 2-day-old baseball strike reached a settlement yesterday, and the game is scheduled to resume today with a full schedule.

Commissioner Peter Ueberroth announced the agreement at approximately 12:30 p.m. yesterday, but the details of the contract were delayed by legal questions on both sides and still were being completed late last night. They eventually were announced about 11 p.m.

The scheduled news conference was postponed several times.

The details of the settlement include contributions of an average $32.6 million a year to the players' pension and benefit plan. This is considerably less than the $60 million players sought, but higher than the $25 million the owners had offered as the strike deadline approached.

The players compromised on the salary arbitration issue, because beginning in 1987 a player must have three years of service to be eligible for the process. Certain other criteria were changed, but the details were not spelled out.

Minimum salaries will increase to $60,000, a 50 percent boost, and cost-of-living raises are included in the course of the five years that the agreement runs. In addition, national association players (minor leaguers) will be guaranteed one-third of that minimum salary, or $20,000.

In addition, compensation for free agents again will include only amateur draft picks. No longer will a club be able to receive a major-league player in the compensation pool after losing a player to free agency.

The new formula is that a club losing a free agent will be able to receive two amateur players if the free agent they lose is ranked in the top third of his group, one amateur player if he ranks in the middle third and none if he ranks in the bottom third.

Negotiations appeared on the verge of ending two nights ago, when Ueberroth stepped in and requested that the two sides continue talking. His influence apparently played a primary part in the settlement.

Orioles owner Edward Bennett Williams said the two parties were "close when Ueberroth arrived" at the negotiations about an hour before the settlement was announced.

"He has a presence that hangs on the negotiations like the ghost of Banquo," said Williams. "When both sides are disappointed, you know it's a fair settlement."

But later in the evening, Ueberroth was passing the credit to the negotiating teams headed by Don Fehr for the players' union and Lee MacPhail for the owners. "They found the path. They did it," the commissioner said.

"They put baseball back on the field. I want you to know clearly I had no role. It was done by these two teams of people, and there was integrity on both sides. It was something that needed to be done right because of the players' careers and the owners' futures. And they did it."

Early in the negotiation process, when Ueberroth advanced suggestions to end the dispute, both sides had tended to downgrade him. Marvin Miller, former executive director of the Major League Players Association, had dismissed Ueberroth as an "amateur mediator," and MacPhail, head of the owners' Players Relations Committee, had called him "a man who is doing what he sees as proper."

Some teams will play doubleheaders tonight to make up for games lost last night. So in effect, the strike cost the schedule only one night of games.

The National League will play single games today, and the American League will play five doubleheaders, including the Orioles at Toronto.

American League president Bobby Brown said, "Ultimately, games from Tuesday will be made up."

But the schedule in the National League was convenient for single games, because teams had another series with the teams they were currently playing. In the American League, current series were the last of the year between those particular opponents.

In addition to the Orioles–Blue Jays doubleheader in the AL, Boston will be at Chicago, Cleveland at New York, Detroit at Kansas City and Milwaukee at Texas in doubleheaders today.

MacPhail said, "The owners were trying hard to get a salary cap on arbitration, but in effect, the result was a compromise. The owners dropped the cap in favor of the extra year of eligibility."

Fehr, acting executive director of the players' association, concurred.

He also said, "We've been advised by the clubs that they are contemplating some sort of revenue sharing in response to the association's final proposals, which involved dispensing a portion of the disputed pension money to clubs in smaller markets.

"To what extent we're not sure," Fehr said. "Obviously, we're interested in that."

MacPhail said the best-of-seven League Championship Series and the World Series will not be affected and that the players will lose two days' pay unless those games are made up on an open date.

Fehr said the delay in the official announcement constituted nothing more than the time required to get the agreement on paper.

"There were no major glitches or hurdles," he said. "It takes a number of hours to draft an agreement. We had reached it orally (around noon) and then adjourned to the players' association office to get it down on paper."

MacPhail said the owners gave some in the settlement.

"It doesn't go a great distance to accomplish what we wanted, but it's a start. It's a five-year agreement, and we'll go from here. A lot of people just decided that there was not going to be another 50-day strike."

Despite Ueberroth's disclaimers, MacPhail said, "The commissioner did an excellent job of keeping things going. He kept urging us to bargain and to keep the rhetoric down. He was interfering as little as possible in the negotiation process, because we had to live with an agreement we made ourselves."

47

Players Testify in Pittsburgh Drug Case (1985)

SOURCE: *Pittsburgh Press*, September 8, 1985

In December 1983 four Kansas City Royals players were found guilty of illegal drug possession and received brief jail sentences and (after a successful appeal to an arbitrator by the union to reduce season-long expulsions) brief suspensions from baseball. Commissioner Kuhn, in one of his final acts, agreed with the union on a Joint Drug Policy, which specifically prohibited mandatory drug testing and allowed for players who admitted a problem to escape punishment, while permitting the commissioner to punish players found guilty of a drug offense in court. As more players were arrested for drug possession, owners pressed Commissioner Ueberroth to abandon the JDP. The dramatic drug trials in Pittsburgh in September 1985, in which more than twenty players received immunity for their testimony, was for some owners the last straw. Their determination to defeat and ultimately crush the union was greater than ever before.

Players Blame Cocaine Addiction on Lonely Road Trips and Money
By Toni Locy
The Pittsburgh Press

Their uncommon ability to play a very common game—baseball—introduced major leaguers Lonnie Smith, Keith Hernandez and Enos Cabell to a life on the road, a life which included the frequent use of cocaine.

Although they all said they began using the drug during trips to other ballparks, they each gave their own version of why. "Money is the problem," Smith said. Boredom was cited by Cabell and, for Hernandez, it was a matter of simply joining in with other players.

All the reasons, they indicated during two days of testimony at the cocaine-trafficking trial of Curtis Strong, resulted from their season-long travels, playing 81 of 162 games coast-to-coast in six months, away from family, friends and home.

Testimony also indicated that each came to grips with his addiction—or "problem" as they preferred to call it—in time, and all three testified that they have kicked their cocaine habits:

Smith, a career .300 hitter, said he was forced into rehabilitation after he stayed up all night snorting cocaine and was "too jittery" and "uncontrollable" to play the next day.

Hernandez, a former co–Most Valuable Player and batting champion, testified that he awoke one morning with a serious nose bleed and the shakes.

Cabell, a 12-year veteran of the major leagues, said he decided to stop using cocaine in 1984, when use of the drug by ballplayers became a controversial issue. He said he realized that he was "getting older" and had "too much to lose" by continuing to use cocaine.

All three testified under a grant of immunity. Also identified during the trial as cocaine-users were nine other players and one ex-player, most of them, at one time, members of baseball's elite, the sport's best, brightest and highest-paid players.

Jeff Leonard, 29, an outfielder for the San Francisco Giants, and Dave Parker, 34, a former Pittsburgh Pirate now playing with the Cincinnati Reds, are expected to testify after Cabell.

Former Pirate John Milner, who is no longer playing baseball, also is expected to take the stand.

In addition, the following players have been identified in testimony as cocaine-users:

Joaquin Andujar, 32, a star pitcher for the St. Louis Cardinals; Bernie Carbo, 38, a retired outfielder who played for six teams; Lary Sorensen, 29, a pitcher for the Chicago Cubs.

Dick Davis, 32, a former Pirate now playing in Japan; Gary Matthews, 35, a former All-Star outfielder for the Chicago Cubs; Dickie Noles, 28, a pitcher for the Texas Rangers; J. R. Richard, 35, a retired pitcher who led the National League in strikeouts in 1978 and 1979; and Al Holland, 33, a pitcher for the California Angels who tied for best relief pitcher of the year in 1983.

And more names of ballplayers who have used cocaine are expected to surface this week, when testimony resumes before U.S. District Judge Gustave Diamond.

Cabell will re-take the witness stand to be cross-examined by Strong's attorney, Adam O. Renfroe Jr.

The ballplayers are the only witnesses in the case against Strong, a former Philadelphia caterer accused in a 16-count indictment of selling cocaine to National League ballplayers from June 13, 1980, to May 14, 1984.

Strong, who was known as "Chef Curt," was indicted by a federal grand jury May 30, along with six others.

Davis's name surfaced twice when Smith and Cabell testified that he introduced each of them to Strong in Philadelphia.

According to testimony, Smith met Strong early in the 1981 season in a room at the Stadium Hilton near Veterans Stadium in Philadelphia.

Davis, Smith and Strong were in Davis's room when Strong pulled out several packages of cocaine wrapped in "girlie magazine papers," Smith said.

Smith and Cabell were the only players so far to testify that they purchased cocaine directly from Strong.

Under questioning by U.S. Attorney J. Alan Johnson, Hernandez said he "placed orders" with Smith to make the buys for him. Smith said he also made cocaine purchases for Andujar.

Specifically, Smith testified that he bought cocaine from Strong in Pittsburgh Aug. 13, 1982, Sept. 29, 1982, and April 12, 1983, when he was playing for the St. Louis Cardinals.

Unlike Smith—who said he initiated the purchases from Strong—Cabell said he was always contacted by the caterer.

Under questioning by Assistant U.S. Attorney James J. Ross, Cabell testified that he purchased cocaine from Smith in Pittsburgh June 13, 1980, Sept. 1, 1980, June 5, 1981, and May 14, 1984, when he played for the Houston Astros and San Francisco Giants.

Hernandez reiterated statements made by Smith, testifying that he saw Strong in the lobby of the Hilton Hotel and Towers on one of the Cardinals' trips to Pittsburgh.

He also testified that "40 percent" of all major-leaguers used cocaine in 1980, which he described as "the love affair year, the romance year" between baseball and cocaine.

"Cocaine is everywhere," Hernandez said. "It's in every city in the country. It's just not in the big cities, it's everywhere."

During his cocaine use, Hernandez said he never purchased cocaine from another player. "If they had it, they would share. It would be more like if it was bought it was, 'Pick me up a gram,' if someone had a connection," Hernandez said.

Renfroe asked Hernandez if cocaine was prevalent in every team in baseball, and the player replied: "I can't say it's in every ball club."

Hernandez said he did not purchase cocaine directly from Strong, because he was afraid baseball officials were wise to drug abusers and were watching Strong.

In his questioning of Smith and Hernandez, Renfroe attempted to depict the players as drug dealers themselves and also over-paid.

Smith testified that his yearly salary with the Cardinals was $225,000 the first year, $500,000 the second, and $700,000 the third. He said he started out at $60,000 with the Phillies and presently is earning $750,000 a year.

Renfroe attempted to needle Smith by saying the ballplayer was "comfortable sitting in the witness stand making $750,000 a year."

"No, I don't feel comfortable," Smith responded, noting his lifestyle consumes his salary.

The defense attorney also delved into Hernandez's finances. Hernandez said he presently earns about $800,000 a year with the Mets.

He testified that in 1974, when he signed his first baseball contract, he made $17,000 a year. His salary increased gradually until 1980 when he jumped from $75,000 a year to $300,000 to $400,000 annually.

Hernandez also said that he did not believe he was traded by the Cardinals to the Mets because of his drug problem.

Renfroe also attacked Hernandez on his memory lapse as to the players he used cocaine with during 1980, the time he described as his "mass use" year. "It's very vague," Hernandez said several times. "I can't remember who I did cocaine with or where I got it."

Hernandez, who was the players' representative for the Cardinals and presently with the Mets, said he did not know that Smith had such a bad cocaine problem.

Renfroe asked numerous questions about the duties and responsibilities of the player representatives, to which Hernandez replied: "You are overstating the position."

The ballplayer said the job entailed giving advice when it was sought and usually advising players with problems to call the players' union.

48

Pete Rose Breaks Cobb's Career Hits Record (1985)

SOURCE: *Cincinnati Enquirer*, September 12, 1985

Pete Rose, one of the most nakedly ambitious, statistics-conscious baseball players of all time, surpassed a record once considered unassailable—Ty Cobb's lifetime total of 4,191 hits—on September 11 after twenty-three years of unrelenting effort. Some journalists fretted that Rose, who had returned to the Cincinnati Reds in late 1984 as a player-manager, was simply hanging on after his days as a productive player had passed to top Cobb, but Rose was such a popular player that Reds fans could not have cared less. Columnist Tim Sullivan, in his article below, wrote from the perspective of Rose's adoring Cincinnati fans.

Numbers Don't Tell Full Story
Tim Sullivan

Now that Pete Rose has the record we have anticipated so long, it should be remembered that he never needed it.

It is the milestone of his baseball career, not the measure. It is his landmark, not his legacy.

No, anyone who would appraise Pete Rose would be wrong to do so by the numbers. For he is not so much a ballplayer as he is an emotion, an attitude, a symbol. "Pete Rose," Commissioner Peter Ueberroth said, "*is* baseball."

He is, at least, what baseball ought to be. In our time, perhaps in all time, no one has played this boy's game so boyishly.

He perfected the head-first slide and has turned even the inning-ending putout at first base into a stylish celebration. The wonder of Pete Rose is that baseball has no drudgery for him. If he is a hot dog, it is because he plays the game with so much relish.

"He should bypass the Hall of Fame," Steve Garvey says, "and go straight to the Smithsonian."

He is, in short, an original. Four thousand, one hundred and ninety-two hits no better define Pete Rose than five acts define Hamlet. In both cases, the play's the thing.

Rose's pages in the record books, to borrow a line he once used for his paycheck, could be piled so high that a show dog couldn't jump over them. Yet future generations could not fully appreciate him without film; the All-Star collision with Ray Fosse, the playoff bout with Bud Harrelson, the autumn evening in 1975 when he turned to Carlton Fisk and said, "Ain't it great just to be playing a game like this."

Just as easily, though, the footage could come from lesser contests, for Pete Rose views *every* game with glee—the arctic nights in San Francisco, the Saharan afternoons in St. Louis, the two-night doubleheaders of long-lost pennant races.

"I live for baseball," he says.

The record he reached Wednesday is merely the measure of that devotion. It represents 23 seasons of fighting fatigue and ignoring aches, of wanting things a little more and a lot longer than the next guy.

It does not mean he is the greatest hitter of all-time. It does not even mean he is the greatest hitter of his own time. "It will mean," Rose says simply, "that I'm the guy with the most hits."

This does not diminish the accomplishment; rather it makes it all the more extraordinary. It is a triumph of desire over talent, of endurance over opportunity.

It is exactly what Pete Rose deserves.

49

Clemens Breaks Record with Twenty Strikeouts in a Game (1986)

SOURCE: *Boston Globe*, April 30, 1986

In 1986 Roger Clemens launched his phenomenal career by winning the first of his six Cy Young Awards with a dominating 24-4 record, helping the Boston Red Sox make the World Series for the first time in eleven years. His brilliance was demonstrated early, when he broke a single-game strikeout record first established in the nineteenth century by fanning 20 Seattle Mariners in a nine-inning game. Clemens' achievement was not tarnished by the ineptitude of his opponent, who as reporter Dan Shaughnessey predicted, set an American League record for team strikeouts in 1986. Clemens' record has been tied twice since the feat—by Clemens again in 1996 and by rookie Kerry Wood in 1998. Randy Johnson of the Arizona Diamondbacks also fanned 20 players in nine innings in a game against the Cincinnati Reds on May 8, 2001, but since the game went into extra innings and Johnson failed to complete the game, he is not credited with tying the record.

Clemens Fans a Record 20

Sox Pitcher Baffles Mariners, 3–1

By Dan Shaughnessy
Globe Staff

Smoke Got In Your Eyes. In one of the most sensational pitching performances in baseball history, Red Sox right-hander Roger Clemens last night struck out a major league record 20 batters en route to a three-hit, 3–1 victory over the Seattle Mariners at Fenway Park.

Has any pitcher ever been more overpowering? In 111 years of major league baseball, Clemens is the first hurler to strike out 20 batters in a nine-inning game. He walked none.

"The people who were here tonight (13,414) saw history that won't be broken," said ancient Mariner Gorman Thomas (one strikeout and a homer for Seattle's run).

"When the last out was made, I wanted to tip my hat. He was that good. It's the finest effort you'll ever see."

Watching the Mariners try to hit Clemens was like watching a student driver navigate Storrow Drive at 4:30 on Friday afternoon. Slumping Seattle is on a record-setting strikeout pace, and Clemens was at the top of his high-octane game. You didn't need Dick Albert, Jimmy the Greek Snyder or Carnac the Magnificent to tell you what was going to happen. But no one could have envisioned the magnitude of Clemens' mound mastery.

Sir Roger struck out the side three times. The Mariners put only 10 balls in play, and only two of those were pulled.

"I was playing catch with Geddy (Sox catcher Rich Gedman) all night long," said Boston third baseman Wade Boggs. "It was an easy night."

Clemens threw 138 pitches, 97 for strikes. A Toronto radar gun clocked several serves at 97 miles per hour, and his fast ball averaged 95 m.p.h.

Red Sox manager John McNamara said, "I saw Catfish Hunter pitch a perfect game and I saw Mike Witt pitch a perfect game and Tom Seaver pitch some great games—but that was the most awesome display of pitching I've ever seen."

In addition to setting the coveted nine-inning strikeout record, Clemens tied the American League record with eight straight punchouts (matching Nolan Ryan and Ron Davis), broke the single-game Red Sox strikeout record (17 by Bill Monbouquette in 1961), and shattered the Fenway mark (16 by Jack Harshman of the White Sox in 1954). If you're looking for a little more perspective, remember that they've been playing baseball at Fenway for 75 years.

The ninth inning was electric. Clemens struck out Spike Owen swinging, then fanned Phil Bradley on three pitches for the magic No. 20. Ken Phelps grounded to short to end it.

"The ninth was all on adrenaline," said Clemens.

After Phelps grounded out, Clemens was mobbed by his teammates. He worked his way over to the backstop and hugged his wife, Debbie. "I wanted to give her the ball, but she was afraid somebody would take it from her," said Clemens. "So I kept it."

The record-smashing outing came very close to being a heartbreaking loss for Clemens. He trailed, 1–0, after Thomas' centerfield homer in the top of the seventh, and the frustrated Sox had run into three outs while trying to score on Seattle righty Mike Moore.

Dwight Evans broke the spell with a two-out, three-run homer, his first homer since the opening pitch of the season.

But Evans' blast will serve as little more than a footnote when baseball bards sing of this night. It was not an evening for hitters or fielders.

"This will be something I'll cherish for a long time," said Clemens. "And I hope it stands for a while."

The fireballing righty was the last person the Mariners wanted to see. They came into the game with 166 strikeouts, 55 more than the league runners-up (Texas, 111). Seattle is on a pace which would shatter the major league strikeout record (1,203) by more than 200.

Clemens (4-0, 1.62 ERA) was perfect in the first three innings. Owen, Bradley and Phelps all went down swinging in the first. Thomas led off the second with a hard liner to Jim Rice in left, then Jim Presley and Ivan Calderon (called) struck out. In the third, rookie Danny Tartabull grounded to second, Dave Henderson was called out on strikes and Steve Yeager flied to left. Clemens was in danger of walking five of the first nine hitters, but never threw ball four.

Clemens' no-hitter/perfect game was punctured in the fourth when shortstop Owen led off with a single to right on an 0-2 curve ball. Clemens punished the Mariners by whiffing the next eight hitters.

Don Baylor had a big assist in the eight-strikeout record. After Clemens got Bradley and Phelps swinging, Baylor (playing first while Bill Buckner DH'd) dropped a Thomas popup in foul territory.

Baylor's blunder served history well. Thomas was called out by Vic Voltaggio on a 3-2 pitch as Clemens closed the door on the fourth.

Clemens was at his best in the fifth when he fanned Presley with a 2-2 heater, then blew Calderon away on three pitches and got Tartabull on a 2-2 looker. All three Mariners were called out on strikes. Seen that lately? Clemens had 12 strikeouts at the end of five.

With an assist from Baylor, Clemens had become the third pitcher in Sox history to fan six straight batters. The immortal Buck O'Brien turned the trick against the Senators on April 25, 1913, and Ray Culp punched out six straight Angels on May 11, 1970.

O'Brien and Culp fell out of the Sox record book when Henderson fanned on a 2-2 pitch leading off the sixth. Seven straight.

Yeager was next and fell behind 0-2, then looked at a 2-2 curve ball. Eight straight, four swinging, four called. Clemens had tied the league record shared by Ryan (1972 and 1973) and Davis (1981).

Owen broke the string by flying to center to end the sixth. Through six innings, Clemens had fanned 14 and thrown 92 pitches, 60 for strikes. The Mariners had put only four balls into play.

The fires were still burning in the seventh. Bradley and Phelps struck out swinging.

Enter Thomas. With the count 1-and-2 and the crowd on its feet and roaring, Thomas interrupted the euphoria. He drove a fly which landed in the first row of the center-field bleachers. Clemens trailed.

Evans got it back, with interest, in the bottom of the seventh.

With two outs and no one on, Steve Lyons slapped a single to left. Glenn Hoffman walked (Ed Romero ran for Hoffman), then Evans drove a 1-0 pitch off the back wall in center for a 3–1 lead.

"That picked me up," said Clemens.

He picked up strikeouts No. 17 and 18 (setting the ballpark and club records) in the eighth, and went into the major league record book in the ninth. It was Clemens' 20th big league victory.

50

Mets Win Dramatic, Sixteen-Inning Game Over Astros, Win NLCS (1986)

SOURCE: *Houston Post*, October 16, 1986

In 1986 the National League's version of Roger Clemens was Houston Astros pitcher Mike Scott, whose unhittable (and, according to NL batters, illegal) forkball produced a record of 18–10 with a 2.22 ERA and 306 strikeouts. During the NLCS Scott was even more dominant, permitting only one run and eight hits in two complete-game victories, and striking out nineteen. If the New York Mets were to advance to the World Series, they had to win the sixth game of the NLCS in order to avoid facing the invincible Scott the following night.

The Mets made their task more difficult by falling behind 3–0 in the first inning, and failing to score until the ninth, when they rallied to tie the game against Bob Knepper. Both teams scored once in the fourteenth inning. New York seemed to clinch a trip to the World Series by crossing the plate three times in the top of the sixteenth inning, but Houston rallied for two runs and had a man in scoring position when Mets pitcher Jesse Orosco ended the epic match by striking out Kevin Bass.

METS GET OFF SCOTT FREE

N.Y. Wins in 16 to Sidestep Date with Astros' Ace

By Ivy McLemore
Post Sports Reporter

Sometime in the future, the hurt will disappear and certain names will be forgotten. But the memory of one of baseball's finest masterpieces will linger.

It was the best of times and the worst of times for the Houston Astros, whose 1986 season finally ended Wednesday. For them, there are no tomorrows, only the haunting remembrances of a storybook season that offered one of the most horrifying endings imaginable.

Before the disbelieving eyes of a record Astrodome playoff crowd of 45,718 and millions of witnesses on national television, the New York Mets scored three runs in the 16th inning to take a 7–6 victory over the Astros and capture the National League pennant in the longest postseason game in baseball history.

This was a game for the ages, one in which the Astros blew a 3–0 lead in the ninth inning, one in which they needed a mammoth homer off the left-field foul pole by Billy Hatcher to tie the score in the 14th, and one which finally expired when Kevin Bass struck out with the potential tying run on second base in Game 6 of the NL Championship Series.

Although the Mets took a 7–4 lead in the 16th on run-scoring singles by Ray Knight and Lenny Dykstra and a wild pitch, the Astros battled back with two runs in the bottom of the inning on run-producing singles by Hatcher and Glenn Davis.

With runners on first and second and two out, Bass worked the count to 3-and-2 against Jesse Orosco. He swung and missed at the game's final pitch, ending a 4-hour, 42-minute ordeal filled with emotional highs and lows.

Afterward, the mood in the Astros' clubhouse was one of shock, not despair.

"The fans won more than anybody today," Davis said. "It would be hard for any fan not to have been excited in this game."

Of more than a dozen Astros questioned after the game, none could say without question that the better team won. In retrospect, there was a feeling among the Astros that they beat themselves.

"We didn't get the key hits and the key outs and we made some fundamental mistakes," Manager Hal Lanier said. "Other than that, it was a great ballgame, the most emotional one I've ever been involved in because it drained you."

In his mind and his heart, Lanier firmly believed the Astros were three outs away from the World Series when Bob Knepper took a 3–0 lead into the ninth. With Mike Scott scheduled to pitch Game 7, Lanier thought the Astros were on the brink of jubilation.

But it wasn't to be.

"I know we would've won no matter what (Mets second baseman) Wally Backman said," Lanier said. "With Mike Scott on the mound and the way he had been pitching, I knew we would have won."

The game tilted in the Astros' favor in the first inning and remained there until the ninth. Knepper did a splendid job of protecting a three-run lead he received by allowing only two hits through eight innings.

Bill Doran sparked the Astros' early outburst when he led off the first with a single to center. Hatcher hit into a fielder's choice at second, but scored when Phil Garner lined a 1-and-2 pitch from left-hander Bob Ojeda to the left-center field wall.

Davis followed with a run-scoring single to left. After Bass walked, Jose Cruz delivered a bloop single down the right-field line that swelled the Astros' lead to 3–0.

Then came the first of several plays that will make the Astros' winter less comfortable. With Bass at third and Cruz at first, Alan Ashby missed a suicide squeeze attempt on a 1-and-1 pitch that left Bass an easy out off third. Ashby followed with a liner to short.

"One of the things I'm going to stress more next spring is bunting," Lanier said. "As a team, we didn't bunt as well this year as I thought we could have."

The Astros muffed a scoring chance when Doran rounded third too far in the fifth on Hatcher's infield single and was tagged out to end the inning. Davis was stranded in the next inning when he doubled with one out, but could not advance on two grounders.

Knepper, outwardly showing more emotion and determination than he had in any of his previous 39 starts this season, worked the count to 1-and-2 on Dykstra to lead off the ninth before yielding a pinch-hit triple which landed beyond Hatcher's outstretched glove in center.

Mookie Wilson followed with a line single which deflected off the top of Doran's glove at second and went into right field. One out later, Wilson scored on Keith Hernandez's double to center that narrowed the Astros' lead to 3–2.

That was all for Knepper, who remained standing in the same spot in the Astros' dugout for the next two hours as he watched another seven innings unfold. As the Astros went down swinging, Knepper stood leaning over the railing, his hands clasped.

"We didn't get the big play when we needed it," said Knepper, explaining the Astros' heartbreaking playoff failure. "We didn't get many key base hits.

"You never know what would have happened, but I thought we would have gone to the World Series if we had won either of these last two games. To the Mets, facing Mike Scott tomorrow night would have been a big mental challenge."

Dave Smith had trouble with the location of his pitches when he came on in relief of Knepper in the ninth. He walked Gary Carter and Darryl Strawberry to load the bases before working the count to 2-and-2 on Knight.

Plate umpire Fred Brocklander, the target of the Astros' wrath after blowing a critical call at first base in Game 5, called Smith's next pitch a ball. Lanier promptly popped out of the Astros' dugout for a conference with his pitcher, giving Brocklander an earful along the way.

"As a manager, and for my pitchers, I want to get the calls consistent," Lanier said. "Knight complained after two strike calls on the outside corner, then Dave (Smith) made the same pitch and he did not call it. That's when I went out to talk to Dave and have my say with Fred. Considering what I told him, I'm surprised he didn't kick me out."

Knight ultimately hit a 3-and-2 pitch for a sacrifice fly that tied the game. After Backman was intentionally walked to re-load the bases, Smith worked the count to 3-and-2 to pinch hitter Danny Heep, who couldn't check his swing on a pitch that might have forced in the Mets' fourth run of the inning.

The home crowd spent much of the overtime session on its feet, waiting for the pendulum to swing the Astros' way one more time.

It never did.

Backman's run-scoring single against Aurelio Lopez in the 14th followed a single by Carter, a walk to Strawberry and a fielder's choice by Knight and gave the Mets a 4–3 lead.

Hatcher responded by slamming a 3-and-2 pitch off the foul pole near the upper deck in left for one of the longest, most emotional homers in Astrodome history. Hatcher ran backward toward first as he watched his homer stay fair by inches to send the crowd into bedlam.

"I thought we were going to win," Hatcher said. "We played as hard as we could. I just wish there had been a man on base (on the homer) so we could be playing tomorrow."

Two innings later, the Mets wrapped up their first NL pennant since 1973 against Lopez and reliever Jeff Calhoun. Strawberry's leadoff double, which fell between

Hatcher and Doran in shallow center, set the tone for a frustrating inning that typified the series.

Orosco survived a scare in the bottom of the inning to earn his third victory of the series—all in relief. Rick Aguilera and Roger McDowell combined for eight scoreless innings out of the New York bullpen Wednesday.

More than an hour after the game, Lanier sat in his clubhouse office and patiently answered questions as he had all season. In the final analysis, he said he was proud his team went out in style.

"If it had to end this way, I'm glad we came back the way we did," he said. "I think the players should be proud of the year we had and I think the fans in Houston should be proud, too. Most people picked us fifth or last in spring training. I think we surprised them."

To say the least.

51

Buckner Error Helps Mets Avoid Elimination from World Series (1986)

SOURCE: *Boston Globe*, October 26, 1986

Bill Buckner was stigmatized as a "goat" after his error in the bottom of the tenth inning of the sixth game of the World Series contributed to the New York Mets' come-from-behind 6–5 victory. The 37-year-old Buckner was one of several Boston Red Sox players who helped convert a 5–3 lead to a defeat. With two out in the tenth, the Red Sox—only one out from their first Series title in sixty-eight years—permitted the next three batters to hit singles, making the score 5–4. A wild pitch by Bob Stanley allowed the tying run to score and advanced the potential winning run, Ray Knight, to second base. Only after this had occurred did Buckner fail to field an easy ground ball by Mookie Wilson, permitting the ebullient Knight to cross the plate with the winning run.

The Red Sox still had a chance to win the Series. In the seventh game they earned a 3–0 lead, but the Mets tied the game in the sixth inning and went ahead for good in the following inning. Their 8–5 victory, and the World Series championship, was earned through clutch hitting and pitching, not handed them on a silver platter by Bill Buckner as many bitter, superstitious Red Sox fans still believe.

Mets Steal Win from Sox, 6–5, in 10th

Error by Buckner Allows Knight to Score Winning Run; Boyd to Pitch 7th

An error by first baseman Bill Buckner gave the Mets a tenth-inning, 6–5 victory over the Red Sox last night, sending the World Series into a seventh game tonight at Shea Stadium. Buckner's error sealed the Sox' fate after what appeared to be an all-but-certain Sox victory. The Sox had opened the tenth with a towering home run by Dave Henderson that seemed to guarantee that they would win their first World Series in 68 years.

They Were Just One Pitch Away

By Leigh Montville
Globe Staff

NEW YORK — One pitch away from a world championship. One pitch from an end to 68 years of frustration. One pitch.

Not close enough.

In a heartbreak that ranks with all of the heartbreaks ever recorded in the long book of Boston Red Sox heartbreak history, the Olde Towne Team let that world championship bounce away in the red dirt of Shea Stadium last night. One wild pitch. One error by first baseman Bill Buckner. One pitch away. The New York Mets scored three runs in the bottom of the 10th and final inning after allowing the Red Sox two in the top of the inning to post a wild, 6–5 win in the sixth game of this World Series and force a seventh game tonight at 8:35 (NBC-TV).

Never have the Red Sox come this close and failed. Never in the Bucky Dent game or the Enos Slaughter game or the Jim Burton game or all the recorded games of frustration had the finish been this close to a championship. Never. Not since 1918. Never.

"We didn't get that final out," manager John McNamara said. "That's all I can say. We needed that one more out, and we didn't get it.

"Yes, it's disappointing, but at least we have another chance tomorrow. That's something they (the Mets) didn't have."

How much of a heartbreak was this? A simple recitation of the roller-coaster events of the 10th is enough to show how bad this one was. In the top of the 10th, Dave Henderson, apparently God's favorite baseball player of this October, homered to left. The Red Sox added another run, and they had a 5–3 lead and an apparent win.

What more could they want? Relief ace Calvin Schiraldi was on the mound. There was dancing in the dugout. There was a party in half the houses in New England — tell the truth — crepe paper being strung everywhere, the civic reception and parade virtually ready to go.

Schiraldi took care of leadoff hitter Wally Backman with a fly ball to left. One out. Schiraldi took care of slugger Keith Hernandez with a fly to center. Two outs. Two outs!!!!!

The moon suddenly fell out of the sky and landed on the Red Sox' heads. Kerplunk! Kaboom! Ouch and double ouch!

How to describe the unraveling? Gary Carter singled to left. So what? Pinch hitter Kevin Mitchell singled to center, Carter moving to second. Big deal. Third baseman Ray Knight, husband of pro golfer Nancy Lopez, swinging with two strikes, singled to center to score Carter and move Mitchell to third. Uh-oh. The lead now was 5–4 and the tying run was on third.

Schiraldi was taken from the game and replaced by Bob Stanley. Wouldn't this be the story of stories? Wouldn't that be the perfect final picture, Stanley hugging catcher Rich Gedman as the 68 years of frustration ended? Here was the man who has endured the longest run of wrath from the Fenway Park fans. Couldn't he celebrate the loudest?

The batter was Mookie Wilson, the Mets' left fielder, a man who will swing at most pitches thrown anywhere near the plate, a swinger's swinger.

Stanley pitched. Mookie swung. Foul ball. Stanley pitched. Ball one. Stanley pitched. Ball two. Stanley pitched three straight times. Mookie fouled all three pitches backwards. The count was stuck at 2-2.

On the next pitch, Stanley ran the ball inside. Mookie jumped backward. Gedman reached for the ball, but not far enough. Wild pitch. Kevin Mitchell ran home as if he were yelling ollie-ollie-in-free and setting the Mets and the entire city of New York free in a giant game of hide and seek. Tie game, 5–5.

Knight now was on second with the winning run. Stanley still was on the mound. Mookie still was at the plate. The count now was 3-2. Stanley pitched again. Mookie fouled the ball backward again. Stanley pitched again. Mookie fouled again.

On the next pitch, Mookie hit a weak ground ball toward first. Half the crowd of 55,078 began to record the easy, unassisted out in the scorebook. The other half breathed nervously, relaxing for the inevitable 11th inning.

Red Sox first baseman Bill Buckner bent low to pick up the ball. Bill Buckner, the man of a million aches and hurts, didn't bend low enough. The ball skipped directly through Buckner's legs and down the first base line. Knight, running all the way with two outs, virtually cartwheeled to the plate, landing so hard to officially score the run that he thought he hurt himself.

Pandemonium landed as if it were a giddy disease. The Mets gave curtain call after curtain call, handshake after handshake, while the Red Sox walked off the field with the dumbstruck look of accident victims. The worst. The absolute worst.

"Thinking about the team's history . . . ," manager McNamara was asked in the interview room.

"I don't know anything about history," he said with a toneless voice, "and don't tell me anything about that choke crap."

Due to the lateness of the game, added to early deadlines at most metropolitan newspapers, story after story was ripped up in a hurry. How many leads had been written about this game that had the Red Sox winning, 5–3, and ending all that frustration? How many actually made the newspapers? How many happy stories, traded for sad? How fast? How unbelievably fast?

"Not yet," he was told. "It all will depend on what happens in the final game. If the Red Sox win that game, the story will be a sidelight. But if they don't . . ."

Never easy with this team. Never easy.

52

Dodgers Executive Questions Whether Blacks Have "Necessities" to Manage (1987)

SOURCE: Transcript of *Nightline*, episode #1530, April 6, 1987, "Jackie Robinson/Hagler-Leonard Fight," Journal Graphics

The fortieth anniversary of Jackie Robinson's historic major league debut was celebrated throughout baseball. The ABC news program Nightline *honored the occasion by interviewing several people knowledgeable about Robinson and his significance to both baseball and American history, including Dodgers executive Al Campanis, who played with Robinson in the minor leagues.* Nightline *host Ted Koppel—who by his own admission knew little about baseball—was discussing Robinson with journalist Roger Kahn and Campanis when Koppel introduced the topic of the paucity of African American managers in the major leagues. To Koppel's astonishment, Campanis proceeded to defend baseball's dismal record of minority hiring by stating, among other things, that blacks "may not have some of the necessities" to manage or serve as executives in baseball. Koppel gave Campanis several opportunities to redeem himself, but Campanis failed to take advantage of the opportunity. After the national uproar over Campanis's comments, the Los Angeles Dodgers fired Campanis. The issue of minorities in management was addressed by baseball, but little if any progress was made. Campanis died in 1998 at the age of eighty-seven.*

Following is a partial transcript of the Nightline *episode. Interestingly, the program was interrupted, as originally intended, with news of the conclusion of the Sugar Ray Leonard–Marvin Hagler championship fight. Two days later, after Campanis had been asked to resign, Koppel hosted another* Nightline *show on prejudice in baseball, featuring Commissioner Ueberroth and Reggie Jackson.*

TED KOPPEL: Mr. Campanis, how long did it take before anyone on the team that first year, in 1947, actually helped Jackie Robinson, I mean, from a human point of view? Obviously, you played together. It was a great team. But how long before anybody helped him as a human being?

AL CAMPANIS, Vice President & Director, Dodgers Player Personnel: Well, Mr. Koppel, it's a privilege and an honor for me to reminisce about Jackie Robinson. I played with him in 1946, and I can truthfully say that he's probably one the best athletes that I've ever seen play the game of baseball. He had not played very much baseball. He was basically a football and baseball star. But when he joined the Montreal club, he had such great aptitude that in a short while he became the best ballplayer in the International League. In 1947, as you had indicated, Jackie was moved to first base, because they had a second baseman named Eddie Stanky, and he played first base in the National League. He became the Rookie of the Year and played in a strange position, [hitting] I think, .297, and had an outstanding season. He again played second base—back to his position that he played in the International League the following year, after they had traded Eddie Stanky. Jackie Robinson became a most valuable player. He had outstanding aptitude, learned how to make a double play. He was a venturesome, daring base runner, and he was a wonderful sight to behold.

KOPPEL: Now, Mr. Campanis, I know it's noisy there in the Astrodome, but let me try my question again. How long was it before other people on the team began to treat him like a human being, began to help him as a human being?

MR. CAMPANIS: I believe when he indicated by his baseball prowess that he could contribute and play a type of game that would help the team win, that the whites, so to speak, began to accept him as a person. And, after awhile, when someone helps you win a ballgame, you get to accept him very readily.

KOPPEL: Mr. Kahn, what about the point that Mrs. Robinson made in that recorded piece a moment ago, that even to this day—now, I understand Frank Robinson, for example, was a manager at one point—but to this day, we have—I don't even know—are there any black managers today?

MR. [ROGER] KAHN: Currently?

KOPPEL: Currently.

MR. KAHN: I don't believe so. But more significantly, are there any black general managers? Managers are employees. Are there any black club owners? Jack—I asked Jack once, "Would you like to manage?"—after he was through playing. And he said, as a matter of fact, although he had some tough associations with baseball, yes, he thought he would, thought he'd be a good one. And said, "Once I got a call from Vancouver," (which was in the deep minor leagues) "and they asked if I'd be interested, and I told them I would be. They never called me back." So, although we can all rejoice in the progress that baseball has made in integration, I think if Jack were alive today, Jack would say, "How come there are no blacks running ball clubs?"

KOPPEL: Mr. Campanis, it's a legitimate question. You're an old friend of Jackie Robinson's, but it's a tough question for you. You're still in baseball. Why is it that there are no black managers, no black general managers, no black owners?

MR. CAMPANIS: Well, Mr. Koppel, there have been some black managers, but I really can't answer that question directly. The only thing I can say is that you have to pay your dues when you become a manager. Generally, you have to go to the minor leagues. There's not very much pay involved, and some of the better-known black players have been able to get into other fields and make a pretty good living in that way.

KOPPEL: Yeah, but you know in your heart of hearts—and we're going to take a break for a commercial—you know that that's a lot of baloney. I mean there are a lot of black players, there are a lot of great black baseball men who would dearly love to be in managerial positions, and I guess what I'm really asking you is to, you know, peel it away a little bit. Just tell me why you think it is. Is there still that much prejudice in baseball today?

MR. CAMPANIS: No, I don't believe it's prejudice. I truly believe that they may not have some of the necessities to be, let's say, a field manager, or perhaps a general manager.

KOPPEL: Do you really believe that?

MR. CAMPANIS: Well, I don't say that all of them, but they certainly are short. How many quarterbacks do you have? How many pitchers do you have that are black?

KOPPEL: Yeah, but I mean, I gotta tell you, that sounds like the same kind of garbage we were hearing 40 years ago about players, when they were saying, "Aah, not really—not really cut out—Remember the days, hit a black football player in the knees, and you know, no—" That really sounds like garbage, if, if you'll forgive me.

MR. CAMPANIS: No, it's not—it's not garbage, Mr. Koppel, because I played on a college team, and the center fielder was black, and the backfield at NYU, with a fullback who was black, never knew the difference, whether he was black or white; we were teammates. So, it might just be—why are black men, or black people, not good swimmers? Because they don't have the buoyancy.

KOPPEL: Oh, I don't—I don't—it may just be that they don't have access to all the country clubs and the pools.... From everything I understand you're a very decent man and a highly respected man in baseball. I confess[ed] to you, before we began this program, baseball is not one of my areas of expertise. I'd like to give you another chance to dig yourself out, because I think you need it.

MR. CAMPANIS: Well, let me just say this, Mr. Koppel. How many executives do you have on a higher level or higher echelon in your business, in TV, I mean . . .

KOPPEL: You're absolutely right, but I . . .

MR. CAMPANIS: . . . or anchormen? How many black anchormen do you have?

KOPPEL: Fortunately . . .

MR. CAMPANIS: Let's just . . .

KOPPEL: Yeah, fortunately, there are a few black anchormen, but if you want me to tell you why there aren't any black executives, I'm not going to tell you it's 'cause blacks aren't intelligent enough. I'm going to tell you it's because it is that whites have been running the—have been running the establishment of broadcasting just as they've been running the establishment of baseball for too long and seem to be reluctant to give up power. I mean, that's what it finally boils down to, isn't it?

MR. CAMPANIS: Well, we have scouts in our organization who are black, and they're very capable people. I have never said that blacks are not intelligent. I think many of them are highly intelligent, but they may not have the desire to be in the front office. I know that they have wanted to manage and some of them have managed, but they're outstanding athletes, very God-gifted, and they're very wonderful people, and that's all I can tell you about them.. . .

MR. CAMPANIS: Well, Mr. Koppel, I think that Jackie Robinson probably did more for the acceptance of a black athlete than anyone that I have ever . . . have seen or known, but what you've got to realize that when you had the problems from the Civil War, it becomes a thing that doesn't happen overnight. I think Robinson . . . Jackie did a tremendous job in making the black athlete acceptable in the areas in which it had never occurred before, namely, playing professional major league baseball. And if you look back and think about the fact that it took so long for an athlete, just . . . you've got to realize that it's going to take a little time also for executives and managers. They have to sort of get into this just about the rate that Jackie did, which took a long time.

KOPPEL: I guess I don't need to remind you, Mr. Campanis, when Jackie Robinson joined, you were a kid.

MR. CAMPANIS: No, no, no, we played together.

KOPPEL: Yeah, I mean, but you were a kid, you were a youngster, right? You were what, in your 20s?

MR. CAMPANIS: In was in my mid-20s, right.

KOPPEL: Mid-20s, all right, well, you're a man in your mid-60s right now. How many generations is this going to take, do you think?

MR. CAMPANIS: Well, I don't have the crystal ball, Mr. Koppel, but I can only tell you that I think we're progressing very well in the game of baseball. We have not stopped the black man from being an executive. They also have to have the desire, just as Jackie Robinson had the desire to become an outstanding ballplayer.

KOPPEL: Just as a matter of curiosity, Mr. Campanis, what is the percentage of black ballplayers, for example, in your franchise?

MR. CAMPANIS: I would say, I think Roger mentioned the fact that about a third of the players are black. That might be a pretty good number, and deservedly so, because they are outstanding athletes. They are gifted with great musculature and various other things, they're fleet of foot, and this is why there are a lot of black major league ballplayers. Now, as far as having the background to become club presidents or presidents of a bank, I don't know. But I do know when I look at a black ballplayer, I am looking at him physically and whether he has the mental approach to play in the big leagues.

5

Rose, Giamatti, and Collusion

The late 1980s marked one of the most tumultuous periods in baseball history. In three separate cases independent arbitrators concluded that the owners, following the lead of Commissioner Ueberroth, had colluded to artificially deflate player salaries. The owners were fined $280 million and many players were granted free agency, including Kirk Gibson, who parlayed his freedom into a legendary performance during the 1988 World Series with his new club, the Los Angeles Dodgers. Gibson and teammate Orel Hershiser (who set a record by throwing 59 consecutive scoreless innings that season) were among the few bright spots in an otherwise dark era.

If collusion wasn't bad enough, the revelation that baseball legend Pete Rose had bet millions of dollars on baseball while managing the Cincinnati Reds, in violation of baseball's cardinal rule, shook baseball to its core. The subsequent investigation, led by lawyer John Dowd, provided ample proof of Rose's guilt, but failed to convince many of Rose's most devoted fans. The difficult investigation took its toll on new commissioner A. Bartlett Giamatti, who died of a heart attack just one week after announcing Rose's permanent expulsion from baseball in 1989. Giamatti's friend and successor, Fay Vincent, presided over the World Series that year, which was interrupted by a devastating earthquake. Even the 1991 Series, considered by some to be the most exciting ever, could not totally erase the memories of the previous three years.

53

Arbitrator Decides Against Owners in
"Collusion I" (1987)

SOURCE: Thomas T. Roberts, "The Matters Put at Issue by Grievance No. 86-2," September 21, 1987, Marvin Miller Papers, Series II, Box 1, Folder 25, Robert F. Wagner Labor Archives, Tamiment Library

After the signing of a new Basic Agreement in August 1985, Commissioner Peter Ueberroth and the owners decided to institute a policy of refusing to sign top free agents following the season. The strategy was too successful—the MLBPA and the press could not help but notice the lack of signings, especially of star players like Detroit's Kirk Gibson. The union filed a grievance, and on September 21, 1987, arbitrator Thomas Roberts ruled that the owners were guilty of collusion. Ironically, the anticollusion clause had been added to the Basic Agreement in 1976 at the owners' insistence, in memory of the joint holdout by star pitchers Sandy Koufax and Don Drysdale. The clause prevented players and owners from acting in concert to artificially inflate or suppress salaries.

This case (better known as Collusion I) was the first of three collusion cases successfully brought against the owners by the union in the 1980s. In his decision Roberts—who had been fired by the owners in August 1986 and reinstated the next month when the firing was declared illegal—ruled that seven of the free agents, including Gibson, would regain free-agent status. Of these "free-look" (later called "new-look") free agents, only Gibson received an offer.

MAJOR LEAGUE BASEBALL ARBITRATION PANEL

THOMAS T. ROBERTS, CHAIRMAN
Panel Decision No. 76, Grievance No. 86-2

In the Matter of the Arbitration Between MAJOR LEAGUE BASEBALL PLAYERS ASSOCIATION And THE TWENTY-SIX MAJOR LEAGUE BASEBALL CLUBS

THE MATTERS PUT AT ISSUE BY GRIEVANCE NO. 86-2
Grievance No. 86-2 was filed by the Players Association on January 31, 1986. It asserts the twenty-six Major League Clubs "have been acting in concert with each other with respect to individuals who became free agents under Article XVIII after the 1985 season." Article XVIII of the Basic Agreement (negotiated by the parties in 1976) establishes a system of free agency available to eligible members of the bargaining unit. This contractual provision recites that free agency is limited to players who have achieved a total of six years of major league service and who have additionally provided the proper notice of free agency intent or who have been released or not tendered renewal contracts. Paragraph H of Article XVIII is entitled "Individual Nature of Rights." It reads:

"The utilization or non-utilization of rights under this Article XVIII is an individual matter to be determined solely by each Player and each Club for his or its own benefit. Players shall not act in concert with other Players and Clubs shall not act in concert with other Clubs."

Paragraph H of Article XVIII was originally proposed by the Clubs during the 1976 negotiations in response to a fear that individual players might join to "package" or sell their newly created free agency rights in a manner reminiscent of the earlier joint holdout attempt of Dodger players Sandy Koufax and Don Drysdale. The Players Association responded to their proposal by insisting the clubs be subject to the same constraint and thus in the clause as finally adopted appears a similar prohibition running against concerted club action. As presently constructed, the provision recognizes the tradition of individual salary negotiations in major league baseball but it is designed to guarantee that individual players negotiate with individual clubs.

THE HEARING BEFORE THE ARBITRATION PANEL

Grievance No. 86-2 was heard in arbitration over thirty-two days of presentation commencing on June 25, 1986 and continuing through May 20, 1987. A total of 5,674 pages of verbatim transcript was produced and 288 exhibits received. Finally, post-hearing briefs were submitted and on August 31, 1987 the arbitration panel met in executive session.

DECISION OF THE ARBITRATION PANEL

Following the completion of the 1984 championship season sixteen of the twenty-six major league clubs signed free agents who had been playing for other clubs. In addition thereto, several other players eligible for free agency generated considerable interest from clubs other than their employer during the 1984 season. The experience during the winter of 1985–1986 was entirely different, however. Twenty-nine of the 1985–1986 re-entry free agents (plus three players who had not been tendered renewal contracts) signed with their former clubs. Only one of those twenty-nine players (Carlton Fisk) received a bona fide offer from a club other than his employer during the 1985 season (i.e., his "former" club) until such time as his former club announced it did not desire to re-sign the player. The clubs showed no interest in the available free agents at any price until such time as their former club declared the player no longer fit into their plans.

The Players Association characterizes what occurred in the free agency market during the 1985–1986 off season as a "boycott" in which all twenty-six major league clubs participated with an intent to destroy free agency. It is argued no club would turn its back on free agency unless confident all of the other clubs would do likewise. The Players Association states the clubs thus carried out an understanding designed to once and for all do away with free agency, a goal entertained since the December 23, 1975 decision of Chairman Seitz in the Messersmith-McNally case.

In their turn, the Clubs contend that what occurred during the 1985–1986 winter was nothing more than the culmination of a predictable evolution to a more sober and rational free agent market from that present during the 1970s. It is argued no agreement existed among the clubs concerning free agency and in fact each of the clubs individually made rational independent decisions regarding the employment of free agents, decisions based upon legitimate baseball, business management and financial factors. The clubs declare that what occurred was the result of the general economic condition of the industry, certain changes in the Basic Agreement, and the least attractive pool of free agents in recent years. The clubs add that the depressed level of activity in the 1985 free agency market was simply the culmination of a ten-year trend rather than the sudden result of a conspiracy.

The positions taken by the parties in this case put directly at issue the meaning, intent and application of Article XVIII (H). As noted, that clause was negotiated in 1976 with the stated purpose of precluding either players or clubs from entering into an agreement, plan or understanding regarding their rights under Article XVIII. The provision declares that the utilization or non-utilization of free agency shall be an individual matter determined solely by each player and club for his or its own bene-fit. With regard to free agency, players may not act in concert with other players and clubs may not act in concert with other clubs. Thus, in the context of the present in-quiry any agreement or plan involving two or more of the clubs and governing the manner in which they will or will not deal with free agents is contractually forbid-den. It is not required that such an agreement or understanding be in writing and accompanied by all the formalities of a contract. A common scheme or plan direct-ed to a common benefit is in violation of the bargain of the parties.

Article XVIII (H) is not designed to prohibit the established practice of the clubs whereby their representatives regularly meet to exchange information, express views and seek the counsel of the Player Relations Committee. The clubs, the Player Rela-tions Committee, the Players Association and player agents remain free to exchange information. What is prohibited is a common scheme involving two or more clubs and/or two or more players undertaken for the purpose of a common interest as opposed to their individual benefit.

It is appropriate to pause here and recall something of the history of the free agent market subsequent to its creation in 1976. In that regard the evidence discloses that the arrival of free agency on the major league scene generated considerable enthu-siasm and a resultant lively bidding for the services of the relatively few players el-igible for such status. In 1976, for example, eleven of the twenty-six clubs signed a total of sixteen significant free agents. Player contract prices began to rise and multi-year contracts were negotiated. This is not to say, however, that all clubs viewed the free agent market as a panacea. Indeed, some of the clubs have never become active in the competition for free agents while others have shied away after experiencing initial disappointing results. Yet this pattern of history does not explain the sudden and abrupt termination of all efforts to secure the services of free agents from oth-er clubs as present during the winter of 1985–1986.

The clubs argue that the experience of the free agents following the completion of the 1985 championship season was the direct result not of a conspiracy launched by management but rather the deteriorating economics of the game, the increased cost of free agents and the number of "disastrous" club experiences with free agents coupled with a trend in recent years toward the development of young players through the farm system procedure. These contentions will be considered separately.

In the course of the 1985 negotiations the clubs for the first time distributed to the Players Association and to one another a statement of their financial situation including profit and loss balances. This was followed by the urging of the Commissioner that the clubs develop policies and practices designed to solve their economic problems. It is to be noted, however, that Article XVIII (H) provides no exemption from its precepts based upon fiscal needs or constraints. Acting in concert with regard to free agency rights is prohibited whatever may be the economic situation of the individual clubs. Nothing in that provision would prevent any of the twenty-six clubs from offering a free agent a salary and contract term consistent with its budget. In 1985, however, no free agent received an offer at any price until and unless his former club declared a lack of interest.

The contention is advanced by the clubs that the quiescence of the 1985 free agent market was set in part by the conviction of the owners that most players who signed long-term contracts thereafter exhibited a pronounced decline in performance, frequently accompanied by long periods on the disabled list. It is argued this perception caused all of the clubs to reduce the guarantee of such contracts to a term of two years for pitchers and three years for position players. While the contracts of all free agents are not long-term, most premier free agents make such an agreement a condition of signing. Indeed, it may be said that multi-year contracts are a direct result of the availability of free agency. It follows from this that if free agency can be weakened or destroyed the long-term contract will disappear. This may be a happy result from the perspective of the clubs but it may only be accomplished within the constraints of the provisions of the basic agreement, including the precepts of Article XVIII (H).

A certain number of clubs have always emphasized minor league development and a strong scouting system. In more recent years a view has emerged that young players have not become as productive as many veteran players but at substantially more modest salaries and this phenomenon has been reflected in the quality of the amateur draft. A number of clubs have thus turned from free agency to the perceived advantages attendant to the utilization of young players developed in the farm system coupled with the incidental benefit of avoiding forfeiture of a first or second round draft pick. It is further argued that a rampant resort to free agency has also been dampened by the demise of the free agency re-entry draft process and its attendant publicity. Additionally, the 1985 Basic Agreement introduced a new system of deadlines imposed upon free agent negotiations so that if a club now fails to offer a free agent employee salary arbitration by December 7 (or if an offer of salary arbitration has been made and not accepted) that club must sign the player by

January 8 or lose the right to negotiate with him until May 1. Once again, however, these contractual realities of contemporary baseball life do not provide assurance that a free agent will remain with his former club. Only a common understanding that no club will bid on the services of a free agent until and unless his former club no longer desires to sign the free agent will accomplish such a universal effect. In the case at hand, just such a result was obtained. This, in itself, constitutes a strong indication of concerted action.

As noted above, and confirmed by history, not all clubs have been active in the free agent market. The Kansas City Royals, for example, have never signed a significant free agent from another club. The same is true of the Minnesota Twins, Oakland Athletics and Seattle Mariners. A number of other clubs have, however, tasted of free agency with the signing of at least one significant player. The Toronto Blue Jays signed free agent Dennis Lamp in 1983, the San Francisco Giants signed Joel Youngblood in 1982, the St. Louis Cardinals signed Darrell Porter in 1980, the Los Angeles Dodgers signed Dave Goltz and Don Stanhouse in 1979, the Milwaukee Brewers signed Roy Howell in 1980, the Philadelphia Phillies signed Pete Rose in 1978, and in the same year the Pittsburgh Pirates signed Lee Lacy while the Montreal Expos signed Elias Sosa. The Boston Red Sox have not signed a significant free agent since 1979 and the New York Mets have not done so since 1980. The Chicago Cubs signed Dave Kingman in 1977 and Bill Campbell in 1981. The Cleveland Indians have signed but one significant free agent, i.e., Wayne Garland in 1976.

More recent free agency activity has seen the Houston Astros sign Omar Moreno in 1982, the same year the Chicago White Sox signed Floyd Bannister. In 1983 the Cincinnati Reds signed Dave Parker and the Detroit Tigers signed Darrell Evans. 1984 saw three significant free agents move to the Baltimore Orioles, i.e., Don Aase, Lee Lacy and Fred Lynn.

The five clubs who have been the most active participants in free agency are the Atlanta Braves, the California Angels, the New York Yankees, the San Diego Padres and the Texas Rangers. In 1981 the Angels signed Reggie Jackson and Frank LaCorte was signed in 1983. The Braves signed Bruce Sutter in 1984 while the Yankees signed Bob Shirley and Steve Kemp in 1982, plus Ed Whitson in 1984. Also in 1984 the Padres signed Tim Stoddard and the Rangers signed Cliff Johnson, Dave Rozema and Burt Hooton.

In the winter of 1984–1985, twenty-six of the forty-six re-entry free agents changed clubs. The situation was dramatically different during the winter of 1985–1986. Prior to the commencement of spring training in 1986 twenty-nine re-entry free agents plus at least three "non-tender" free agents (Dave Kingman, Al Cowens and Joel Youngblood) signed major league contracts. All but four of that total of thirty-two free agents (i.e., Juan Beniquez, Al Holland, Dane Iorg and David Palmer) signed with their former clubs. True enough, after the commencement of spring training nine other free agents signed with new clubs. It is to be noted, however, that in each such case the free agent had not been signed by his former club. Indeed, with the exception of Carlton Fisk no free agent received an offer from a new club until and unless his former club was no longer interested.

The situation of Kirk Gibson will serve as an example of the foregoing. Gibson became eligible for free agency while employed by the Detroit Tigers. The Kansas City Royals sought to initiate discussions with his agent and went so far as to entertain Gibson on a hunting trip at the conclusion of the 1985 season. The interest of the Royals in Gibson suddenly cooled, however, concurrently with a meeting of the owners at St. Louis, Missouri, in October of 1985 and a gathering of the general managers in Tarpon Springs, Florida during November of 1985. These meetings were convened contemporaneously with a public announcement of the Royals that they were not going to make an effort to sign any free agents, including Kirk Gibson. The Atlanta Braves also initiated discussions with Gibson's agent but abruptly terminated the exchange. Other established performers on the field received no offers at all except from their former club. These players included Donnie Moore, Tony Bernazard, Tom Brookens, Jamie Easterly, Phil Niekro, Joe Niekro and Aurelio Lopez. Carlton Fisk received a single private overture from the owner of the New York Yankees but that contact was not even revealed to the other members of the management of the New York Yankees. The climate of the market had abruptly changed.

To return for a moment to the commencement of spring training in 1986, it is to be noted that only four free agents had by that time changed clubs. Of that number, Al Holland and Dane Iorg were never offered employment by their former clubs while David Palmer and Juan Beniquez declined such offers. None of the four were offered salary arbitration by their former club prior to the December 7 contract deadline. This removed the former club from a negotiating position until at least May 1, 1986 and Palmer as well as Beniquez ultimately signed for a salary less than the offer of their former club. The result of all this was a preemption of free agency negotiating rights by the former club, a result that could only be obtained through common consent in violation of Article XVIII (H).

The clubs argue that those free agents signed following the completion of the 1985 championship season enjoyed the benefits of a free competitive market as witness[ed by] the contracts of Donnie Moore (one million dollars per year for three years), Carlton Fisk ($875,000 for 1986) and Kirk Gibson (four million dollars payable over a span of three years). It is further claimed the clubs offered generous salaries to their own free agents because of a fear the players might be lured away by other clubs. The approach of the clubs to free agency negotiations during this period was, however, not consistent with the existence of a free market. Their conduct demonstrated a conviction and belief that none of the other clubs would interfere in the negotiations with their own players until and unless they announced they no longer desired to retain the services of the player. No enthusiasm remained to sign their own players before they could declare for free agency. Nor are we speaking here of only "significant" free agents. Each and every free agent had the same experience, i.e., no offers until their former clubs stated they were no longer interested. This is precisely the result forbidden by Article XVIII (H).

The individual clubs have attempted to explain their conduct during the 1985–1986 winter as a uniform disenchantment with free agency and not a form of prohibited concerted action. Thus, it is said the Atlanta Braves adopted the philosophy of their new General Manager (Bobby Cox) that a team is most effectively developed through its farm system while Vice President Mike Port of the Angels introduced a change of emphasis to scouting and internal development so as to avoid the need to surrender a high draft choice in return for signing a free agent. Port also testified that in 1985 the Angels had no need for a starting pitcher or a catcher. The clubs state that in 1985 the Rangers adopted a written commitment to scouting and minor league development while the San Diego Padres signed only re-entry free agent Dane Iorg because President Ballard Smith was seriously concerned about the financial health of the franchise. The Milwaukee Brewers lost 5.4 million dollars in 1985 and could not afford to sign a free agent while the Kansas City Royals decided to stand pat after winning the 1985 World Series. Director of Player Personnel Al Campanis of the Los Angeles Dodgers testified he was pleased with the composition of his team and saw no reason to become involved in a bidding war for available free agents. Similar testimony was presented on behalf of the New York Yankees, the Baltimore Orioles, the Chicago Cubs and the Cincinnati Reds. Indeed, each and every club representative who testified at the hearing denied a common agreement or understanding. Yet it must be noted that the 1985 class of free agents was unattractive only to clubs other than the club for whom they were employed during that season. It is further to be recalled that those players who declare for free agency are not all superstars. It is reasonable to anticipate that interest in the services of at least some of them will be expressed by a team other than the club by whom they were employed at the time they elect free agency. They surely had a value at some price and yet no offers were advanced.

At the conclusion of the 1985 championship season and early on during the off-season that followed, a series of meetings of the management of major league baseball were convened. Thus, a regularly scheduled quarterly meeting of the owners or their representatives took place at Itasca, Illinois on September 27, 1985, a meeting chaired by the Commissioner. Also in attendance were the two League Presidents, representatives of the Player Relations Committee and counsel. A report was made by a subcommittee of the Long Range Planning Committee concerning the player development systems in place and the cost of those enterprises. The next meeting of the owners took place on October 22, 1985 during the World Series at St. Louis, Missouri. On that occasion a vote was taken to terminate the Joint Drug Agreement previously entered into with the Players Association and a further report of the subcommittee of the Long Range Planning Committee was received. Additionally, the retiring Director of the Player Relations Committee, Leland S. MacPhail, distributed a memorandum (dated October 16, 1985) that had as its message the undesirability of long-term contracts because players signed to such agreements frequently do not thereafter perform to the level of their ability or suffer injuries that force them to leave baseball while still enjoying the salary benefits of the contracts.

MacPhail urged the clubs to "exercise more self-discipline in making their operating decisions" and resist the temptation to "give in to the unreasonable demands of experienced marginal Players." MacPhail declared, "We must stop day dreaming that one free agent signing will bring a pennant. Somehow we must get our operations back to the point where a normal year for the average team at least results in a break-even situation, so that Clubs are not led to make rash moves in the vain hope that they might bring a pennant and a resulting change in their financial position. This requires resistance to fan and media pressure and is not easy." The Commissioner then asked that the comments of MacPhail be given serious consideration and following an informal poll certain club representatives stated their intent to avoid long-term contracts.

The Major League Baseball General Managers met at Tarpon Springs, Florida on November 6, 1985. At that session the Commissioner repeated his concern regarding the financial commitment made by the clubs under long-term player contracts and stated, "It is not smart to sign long-term contracts." He further described such signings as "dumb." There followed the annual Major League Baseball Meeting in San Diego, California on December 11, 1985. At that meeting Mr. MacPhail, on behalf of the Player Relations Committee, distributed a list of the players who had declared for free agency. As noted herein, the distillation of the message of these meetings resulted in every major league club abstaining from the free agency market during that winter until an available free agent was "released" by his former club upon the announcement that the former club was no longer interested in his services. That result was obtained through the conduct of the clubs uniformly established and maintained. The right of the clubs to participate in the free agency provisions of the Basic Agreement no longer remained an individual matter to be determined solely for the benefit of each club. The contemplated benefit of a common goal was substituted. This action constituted a violation of the prohibition against concerted conduct found in Article XVIII (H) and Grievance No. 86-2 is therefore sustained. Pursuant to the stipulation of the parties, argument and evidence regarding an appropriate remedy will be entertained at hearings to be scheduled at the earliest convenience of counsel and the Chairman of the Arbitration Panel.

AWARD

1. The Clubs violated Article XVIII (H) of the Basic Agreement following the completion of the 1985 championship season by acting in concert with regard to the free agency provisions of the said Article XVIII.

2. The question of the construction of an appropriate remedy shall forthwith be set for hearing before the Arbitration Panel.

DATED: September 21, 1987
THOMAS T. ROBERTS, Chairman
BARRY RONA (I Dissent)
DONALD M. FEHR (I Concur)

54

Owners Lose Collusion II in 1986 Free Agency Case (1988)

SOURCE: *Sporting News*, September 12, 1988

Less than a year after the initial collusion ruling, arbitrator George Nicolau found the owners guilty of collusion against the 1986 class of free agents in what is now known as Collusion II. In his August 31 decision Nicolau found that the owners had jointly decided not to bid on free agents, even such star players as Andre Dawson and Lance Parrish. Dawson changed clubs only when he offered to sign a blank contract for the Chicago Cubs, for whom he would win the NL MVP Award in 1987. Parrish signed with the Philadelphia Phillies for a below-market value, and Phillies management was subsequently punished for this transgression by the other owners. Nicolau would determine the monetary penalty at a later date.

Collusion: Owners Are Batting .000

By Murray Chass

NEW YORK—In baseball terms, the players are batting 1.000 and the owners .000 in the World Series of collusion. The players, however, continue to wait for their winning shares—the damages to be awarded for the owners' illegal practices.

For the second time in less than a year, an arbitrator has ruled that baseball's club owners were guilty of conspiring against free agents in violation of the collective bargaining agreement.

George Nicolau, the arbitrator, provided no immediate remedy for the owners' collusive action toward free agents following the 1986 season. However, in an 81-page opinion released August 31, Nicolau was more severe, and more pointed in identifying club executives and specific examples of violations than Thomas Roberts was in finding the owners guilty of collusion against 1985 free agents.

Any monetary damages and second-chance free agency will be determined in subsequent hearings before Nicolau. Roberts currently is hearing the remedy phase of Collusion I. Lawyers estimate that if the two arbitrators accept the players' arguments, they could award damages in the area of $75 million.

In his decision, Nicolau said the clubs' lack of interest in the group of 79 free agents after the 1986 season could not be attributed to individual actions. The case centers on eight players—Andre Dawson, Lance Parrish, Doyle Alexander, Bob Boone, Rich Gedman, Ron Guidry, Bob Horner and Tim Raines. Another key figure is Jack Morris, who offered his services to several clubs, but found no takers and returned to the Detroit Tigers before the deadline by agreeing to salary arbitration.

Dawson and Parrish signed with new clubs after January 8, 1987. Horner wound up playing in Japan and the five others were in limbo until May 1987, when they were able to rejoin their old clubs. Since then, Dawson has waived his right to renewed free agency by agreeing to a Chicago Cubs contract through the 1989 season.

"What transpired in 1986," Nicolau wrote, "occurred because everyone 'understood' what was to be done. By common consent, exclusive negotiating rights were, in effect, ceded to former clubs. There was no vestige of a free market, as that term is commonly understood. The object was to force players back to their former clubs and the expectation was that all would go back in a replication of 1985, requiring nothing more to be done."

The arbitrator, who also is hearing Collusion III involving 1987 free agents, flatly rejected the owners' contention that their 1986 behavior differed from the previous year because there was significant bidding for some free agents. That contention, he said, is "contrary to the evidence and insupportable."

The evidence presented during 39 days of hearings over seven months, Nicolau went on, "convincingly establishes that everyone knew there was to be no bidding" for free agents as long as their former clubs "coveted" them. Then, in a litany of specific examples involving various clubs and players, Nicolau wrote:

"Surely John McHale of the Expos knew . . . (Roy) Eisenhardt of the A's surely knew . . . Surely Giles (Bill Giles, president of the Phillies) knew . . . Surely Green (Dallas Green, former president of the Cubs) knew . . . (Stan) Kasten, the Braves' president, surely knew. . . ."

The arbitrator also found that Bobby Brown, the American League president, and two A.L. club owners, Bud Selig of Milwaukee and Jerry Reinsdorf of the Chicago White Sox, telephoned Giles, president of the Philadelphia Phillies, trying to dissuade him from signing Parrish, who had played out his contract with Detroit.

Club executives refrained from comment on the decision, leaving that task to Barry Rona, executive director of the Player Relations Committee. However, speaking of his telephone call to Giles, Brown said, "I felt it wasn't inappropriate to tell him that Detroit was trying to sign their catcher and I would hate to see him leave our league. He was our All-Star catcher. I felt I was stating a couple of obvious facts. I can't think what he thinks. That's his prerogative. But I saw nothing wrong with telling him those two things."

Concluding his opinion, Nicolau said, " . . . there was a patent pattern of uniform behavior, a uniformity simply unexplainable by the rubric of financial responsibility or by any other factors on which the clubs have relied in this proceeding. In my opinion, their conduct with respect to the 1986 free agents was in deliberate contravention of club obligations as embodied in Article XVIII (H), for which an appropriate remedy is fully justified."

The article cited is the part of the collective bargaining agreement that says, "Players shall not act in concert with other players and clubs shall not act in concert with other clubs."

Donald Fehr, executive director of the Major League [Baseball] Players Association, hailed the decision, saying it shows a "story of deceit, dissembling and conspiracy."

Rona took exception to the decision, just as he did with Roberts' ruling last

September 21. At that time, Rona said Collusion II would be different because there was a "different set of facts." However, Nicolau found "there was no markedly different factual pattern in 1986."

Rona noted that the events covered in the Nicolau decision occurred before the clubs received Roberts' ruling in the 1985 case. Immediately after the Collusion I decision, Rona said, the clubs, though they disagreed with it, said they would comply with the decision. The union, however, filed a grievance charging continued collusion in 1987, and that's the case Nicolau is hearing now.

Commissioner Peter Ueberroth, Rona added, had restated baseball's policy on clubs' participation in the free agent market. Such participation, Rona quoted Ueberroth as saying, is "an individual matter to be determined solely by each club."

Ueberroth had no comment beyond Rona's statement.

Fehr said that he and other union lawyers, including Steve Fehr, who argued the players' case before Nicolau, would decide whether to ask for a second-chance free agency for the 1986 players. Roberts offered such a chance to seven of the 62 free agents from the 1985 case, and Kirk Gibson moved from the Detroit Tigers to the Los Angeles Dodgers. The 55 other players didn't get a second chance, Roberts said, because they had been free agents again subsequent to the 1985–86 off-season.

The union, Donald Fehr said, also will ask Nicolau to restore players to the financial position they would have been had there been no conspiracy. Third, he said, "We want to reestablish both the salary structure and the length of contracts so that as we go into collective bargaining in 1990, the association as a group is not disadvantaged by the collusion."

Calling the owners' action "one of the most shameful episodes in baseball history," Fehr said, "Not once since this started have you had a management official acknowledge this breach of faith with the players and the fans."

Richard Moss, former general counsel for the union, said he was eager to see what the commissioner and the league presidents would do. Singling out A. Bartlett Giamatti, the National League president and the man generally expected to succeed Ueberroth as commissioner, Moss added, "Mr. Giamatti has given a lot of speeches and has written articles lately about the need for morality in the baseball industry, saying that those who cheat and violate rules should be severely disciplined. I would think that he would suspend or otherwise punish owners, general managers and their labor relations advisers who put them up to cheating and violating the collective bargaining agreement as soon as it was signed. If he doesn't, I will be suspicious about his definition of morality."

Giamatti declined to respond. "I don't have a comment," he said. "I'm sorry that the perception is there, but I don't have a comment. I don't want to get into any arguments or contentious comments. I don't want to be at loggerheads with anybody."

55

Kirk Gibson, Orel Hershiser Rally Dodgers to Surprising Lead in World Series (1988)

SOURCE: *Sporting News*, October 24, 1988

The Los Angeles Dodgers were not expected to win the National League pennant, but their only two star players, Kirk Gibson and Orel Hershiser, insisted. Hershiser ended the season with a record-setting fifty-nine consecutive scoreless innings (even though the Dodgers lost the final game in extra innings after he threw ten shutout innings), verifying for the nation the legitimacy of his nickname, "Bulldog." He pitched in four of the seven NLCS games, earning a save and winning the final game with yet another shutout. Gibson's statistics were less spectacular—25 home runs and 31 stolen bases with only 76 RBI for the regular season—but the adrenaline-fueled, intense style he adapted from his days as a star college football player helped inspire his teammates to exceed their talents.

Unfortunately for the Dodgers, Gibson was thought to be out for the Series because of a pulled hamstring and bad knee. Gibson rose to the challenge in the first game of the Series against the seemingly invincible Oakland A's by hitting a game-winning pinch-hit home run in the bottom of the ninth inning off star Oakland reliever Dennis Eckersley. In the article below Paul Attner analyzes the impact of Gibson and Hershiser on the Dodgers' unlikely path to postseason success.

Just Trying to Do "Best We Can"

Gibson, Hershiser Carry Dodgers to Stunning 2–0 Start in World Series

By PAUL ATTNER
National Correspondent

LOS ANGELES—The words dripped with sarcasm as they came spitting from Tommy Lasorda's mouth.

"We are just honored to be in the World Series with Oakland," said Lasorda, bleeding Dodger blue. "We know they've won 108 games and we weren't supposed to be on the same field with them. But we are just trying to do the best we can."

Of course, when you already have won the first two games of the World Series after it seemed that almost everyone had picked Oakland to take no more than five contests to wrap things up, you can afford to be a bit spunky. And Lasorda, a master of situations and emotions, was having a marvelous time shoving the Dodgers' stunning start down the throats of misguided prognosticators.

How dare they choose against his self-proclaimed Destiny's Darlings? How dare they not be believers, even after the way Los Angeles upset the New York Mets in the National League Championship Series? If nothing else, the two victories had earned the kind of respect for the Dodgers that Lasorda believed they warranted, and that couldn't be taken away, no matter what happened the remainder of the Series.

But how was Oakland or, for that matter, mere observers, supposed to know that this strange and intriguing season for the Dodgers would continue, that Orel Hershiser would maintain his pitching magic and that a gimpy slugger named Kirk Gibson would create one of the finest moments in World Series history?

"Surprised?" said Lasorda, that sarcasm still evident. "Believe it or not, those two have been doing this for us all year."

Well, Hershiser, who stopped the Athletics, 6–0, with a three-hitter in Game 2, certainly has been this overpowering since the start of August. In his last 10 starts, he has pitched an astonishing eight shutouts and took another shutout into the ninth inning. Over his last 92 $2/3$ innings, he had given up just three earned runs. Coupled with his shutout of the Mets in Game 7 of the NLCS, his whitewashing of the A's made him the first pitcher in history to record complete-game shutouts the same year in both the league championship series and the World Series.

Dave Parker had all three hits off Hershiser and only three Oakland runners got as far as second base off Hershiser, whose nickname, Bulldog, reflects his determination on the mound, not his demeanor off it. This calm, humble man with the snapping sinkerball was on such a high that against the A's, he even got three hits himself—something a pitcher hadn't done in a World Series game since 1924.

"We know when he is out there we don't need to score many runs to win," said outfielder Mickey Hatcher, one of a bunch of pesky Dodgers who lend support to L.A.'s stars. "But his hitting, well, it's lucky."

Hershiser readily agreed. "I was just trying to get my bat on the ball," he said of his two doubles and one single. "I got more tired from running the bases than from actually pitching." And this from a man who already had tossed 33 $2/3$ innings in the postseason.

Oakland could accept losing to Hershiser. After all, he is baseball's premier pitcher this season, a given for the N.L. Cy Young Award. But the A's still aren't sure what happened to them in Game 1, when Gibson transformed this World Series from an Oakland showcase to a two-team race.

It's easy to snarl at Gibson's regular-season statistics and wonder, "Can this really be a legitimate MVP candidate?" After all, 25 homers, 76 RBIs and a .290 batting average are nice numbers, but they hardly are a full season's production for, say, someone like Jose Canseco.

But to measure Gibson's true value to his team—and isn't that what an MVP really is all about?—one needs a yardstick like the playoffs. Here, under a microscope almost daily, the guts and drive of this fascinating man can be dissected, relished, and, yes, understood for their immeasurable worth.

Mock Gibson's regular-season numbers if you will, but you'd better bow to what he had accomplished in postseason play. Gibson, bothered by a pulled left hamstring, probably shouldn't have been playing, or at least not starting, in the NLCS and World Series. But, until he could barely walk, he demanded to play, convinced that a half-healthy Gibson was still important to the Dodgers.

And who's to argue: He looked woeful until the 12th inning of Game 4 against the Mets, then he hit a game-winning home run. The following afternoon, he hit a three-run homer to wrap up Game 5. And in Game 7, his sacrifice fly produced the game-winning RBI as the Dodgers won an unexpected pennant.

But Gibson twice dived recklessly into second base, once on a steal attempt, once to break up a double play. In the process, he aggravated the hamstring pull and sprained his right knee so badly that, when the World Series opened October 15, he could hardly hobble to the park, much less think about playing.

So, of course, he merely performed another miracle. In one of the most dramatic moments you'll ever see in sports, he limped up to home plate in the bottom of the ninth with one man on, the Dodgers down, 4–3, and the best reliever in baseball, Dennis Eckersley, on the mound.

Down the road in Hollywood, where fantasies are transferred onto celluloid, Gibson obviously would force the count to 3 and 2, and then, with everyone standing and cheering and praying, drill a home run into the right field stands to win the game and send the Dodger fans into ecstasy. After the homer, he limped around the bases in such obvious pain that the fans winced each step of the way.

In the real world, of course, Eckersley would overpower the weakened Gibson and Oakland would take a one-game lead in the Series.

But since we are dealing here with Kirk Gibson, a man who lives for these kinds of situations, reality and fantasy suddenly got all mixed up with one swing of the bat. The ball did indeed clear the right field fence on a 3-and-2 pitch, he did indeed hobble around the bases, the Dodgers did indeed win and he did indeed eventually limp to his locker, where a coach already had posted a sign proclaiming it the home of Roy Hobbes, the fictional hero of "The Natural."

Gibson most likely should be known as Roy Hobbles, but all the imagination of the Hollywood writers couldn't have topped this real-life baseball moment. . . .

56

Baseball's First Retractable Domed Stadium Debuts in Toronto (1989)

SOURCE: Toronto *Globe and Mail*, June 6, 1989

The debut of the Toronto SkyDome marked the culmination of a design first dreamed of back in 1955, when Brooklyn Dodgers president Walter O'Malley suggested that a new Dodgers stadium be built with a retractable dome. Olympic Stadium in Montreal was intended to have such a dome, but financial mismanagement and a strike by construction workers prevented its installation until 1987. The mechanism used to open the dome failed two years later, and the dome remained closed. Since then four major league stadiums have been built with either retractable or convertible domes.

The technology in Toronto worked perfectly, and media came from as far as Japan to gawk at the new-age stadium, which also featured a luxury hotel with windows facing the field and other innovative features calculated to maximize income. In spite of the revolutionary nature of the SkyDome, its debut did not inspire awe in the author of the article below.

NO PLACE LIKE DOME

Fans Greet SkyDome Opener Warmly
By Gary Loewen
The Globe and Mail

The pleasant scent of freshly mowed grass didn't waft up from the green plastic imposter covering the playing field and the snack stands surely broke some sort of unofficial ballpark bylaw by failing to purvey Crackerjack to baseball fans.

But all shortcomings aside, the much-ballyhooed SkyDome drew favorable reviews last night in its big-league debut.

Its retractable roof opened wide to the night sky, the stadium may have cost its prime tenants, the Toronto Blue Jays, a victory last night against the Milwaukee Brewers. The park's bigger dimensions swallowed up pinch-hitter Bob Brenly's fly ball in the eighth, turning a two-run homer into a long out.

The Brewers hung on to win, 5–3, in front of the biggest crowd—48,378—to witness a baseball game in Toronto.

Brenly said there was no doubt his fly would have been a home run at Exhibition Stadium.

"I've never had any luck hitting in this park," he deadpanned.

Earlier in the day, with its state-of-the-art retractable roof sealed shut, the SkyDome resembled a giant armadillo just emerged from Lake Ontario—potentially the star of a B-grade horror classic, say, "The Grey Godzilla that Gobbled Hogtown."

In the SkyDome's case, the homeliness proved to be only shell deep.

First-time visitors, most of whom heeded urgings to take public transit, gawked in awe as they entered the facility, remarking on the clean sightlines and the aesthetics.

The fans were well-behaved, too, as if visiting a fastidious great aunt's immaculately tidy home.

At worst, the SkyDome, with its lid on tight, offers the sensation of an over-sized shopping mall. It has neither the claustrophobia of the Seattle Kingdome nor the economy-sized garbage bags that line the outfield walls of Minnesota's Metrodome. A temple of gloom it's not.

The roof remained closed yesterday until about 4 p.m. when promising weather forecasts lured the panels open. After the one-hour procedure (a computerized system eventually will cut it to 20 minutes) the sun streaked in and the wind swirled.

It will take a few nights of experimentation with the convertible top to determine the effect of the atmospherics on the flight of balls, Jay manager Cito Gaston said. Most domed stadiums are a hitter's paradise, although the Houston Astrodome is an exception.

Gaston, who lives year-round in Toronto, offered the most glowing tribute to his team's new home. Like a kid waiting for Christmas, he had eagerly anticipated this day and put off visiting the stadium until all the trimmings were up.

"I haven't been here until today. I wanted to come down and see it all at once.

"It's amazing. I guess I don't have the words to describe it," Gaston said of the dome, adding that no other ballpark in North America was comparable.

"This is the best right here. This has got to be the ultimate. This is really something."

Gaston can be forgiven for getting caught up in last night's electric atmosphere, akin to a season-opener or a playoff game.

There was a scare yesterday afternoon that the show would not go on. American League umpiring supervisor Marty Springstead insisted a black cloth be installed over a section of centre-field seats to create a backdrop for pitches.

Springstead also was concerned about a gap between the turf and the warning track, which made footing dangerous. A molding, yet to be installed, will correct the problem.

"It's like building a house—there are always flaws. It's going to take time to iron things out," he said.

The game started as scheduled at 7:46 as a lightning-like streak of flashbulbs greeted Jim Key's historic first pitch.

It was clear from the outset that, not only was this park a decided improvement on Exhibition Stadium, it also was louder. With its circular design, cheers and applause—not to mention, construction workers' hammers—were contained, creating a livelier atmosphere.

Indeed, up until game time, laborers pounded and primped and preened—and posed for pictures—causing the teams to miss batting practice. While the bowels and passageways of the SkyDome remained construction zones, the field itself was set for action.

The players themselves were quietly excited about the prospect of playing in an ultra-modern home. A couple of Jays wondered aloud what kind of a poke it would take to reach the impressive, three-storey centre-field scoreboard.

Certainly, it would take a Ruthian blast. Fred McGriff, George Bell and Glenn Braggs hit homers, but none came close.

"This would be a pretty good place for a ballpark," Jay pitching coach Al Widmar said with a half-smile, surveying the new grounds.

57

Pete Rose Banished from Baseball (1989)

SOURCES: www.baseball1.com/bb-data/rose/agreement.html, www.baseball1.com/bb-data/rose/statement.html, and www.dowdreport.com

The most serious investigation into gambling in baseball since the Black Sox scandal concluded on August 24, when Cincinnati Reds manager Pete Rose agreed to accept permanent expulsion from major league baseball in order to avoid an official finding that Rose had bet on baseball, including on his own team. The investigation began in February, when a Sports Illustrated *reporter informed Commissioner Ueberroth that the magazine had information of Rose's gambling activities. Ueberroth and incoming commissioner A. Bartlett Giamatti, who replaced Ueberroth on April 1, hired Washington DC attorney John Dowd to conduct a thorough investigation of the allegations, which Rose vehemently denied.*

From the beginning Rose and his lawyers fought the investigation, even winning an injunction in a Cincinnati court barring Giamatti from exercising his powers as commissioner under the "best interests of baseball" clause to investigate Rose, which was soon overturned. By August it became obvious that Dowd had abundant evidence that Rose had bet on baseball, but in order to quickly conclude the sordid affair, Giamatti and Reuven Katz, Rose's attorney, agreed that Rose would accept expulsion if major league baseball did not explicitly state that Rose had violated Major League Rule 21, which banned gambling on baseball. It came as a shock when, in a press conference immediately following the announcement of Rose's punishment, Giamatti stated that he believed Rose was guilty. In his autobiography, Giamatti's deputy commissioner Fay Vincent, a lawyer, noted that Giamatti was not in violation of the agreement but was simply stating a personal opinion. Nevertheless, the incident fueled suspicions among many fans that Giamatti was biased against Rose. In January of 2004, after fourteen years of denial, Rose finally admitted his guilt in a widely promoted autobiography, but denied placing bets from the Reds clubhouse as alleged in the Dowd Report.

Interestingly, a March 8, 2002, article in the New York Daily News *found that the same investigation also revealed that two umpires, Frank Pulli and Rich Garcia, had placed bets with bookies. The umpires were placed on probation for two years, but received no other punishment, and the incident was kept secret.*

AGREEMENT AND RESOLUTION

On March 6, 1989, the Commissioner of Baseball instituted an investigation of Peter Edward Rose, the field manager of the Cincinnati Reds Baseball Club, concerning allegations that Peter Edward Rose engaged in conduct not in the best interests of baseball in violation of Major League Rule 21, including but not limited to betting on Major League Baseball games in connection with which he had a duty to perform.

The Commissioner engaged a special counsel to conduct a full, fair and confidential inquiry of the allegations against Peter Edward Rose. Peter Edward Rose was given notice of the allegations and he and his counsel were generally apprised of the nature and progress of the investigation. During the inquiry, Peter Edward Rose produced documents, gave handwriting exemplars and responded to questions under oath upon oral deposition. During the deposition, the special counsel revealed key evidence gathered in the inquiry to Peter Edward Rose and his counsel.

On May 9, 1989, the special counsel provided a 225-page report, accompanied by seven volumes of exhibits, to the Commissioner. On May 11, 1989 the Commissioner provided a copy of the Report to Peter Edward Rose and his counsel, and scheduled a hearing on May 25, 1989 to give Peter Edward Rose an opportunity to respond formally to the information in the report. Peter Edward Rose received, read and is aware of the contents of the Report. On May 19, 1989, Peter Edward Rose requested and subsequently received, an extension of the hearing date until June 26, 1989. Peter Edward Rose acknowledges that the Commissioner has treated him fairly in this Agreement and has acted in good faith throughout the course of the investigation and proceedings.

Peter Edward Rose will conclude these proceedings before the Commissioner without a hearing and the Commissioner will not make any formal findings or determinations on any matter including without limitation the allegation that Peter Edward Rose bet on any Major League Baseball game. The Commissioner has determined that the best interests of Baseball are served by a resolution of this matter on the following agreed upon terms and conditions:

1. Peter Edward Rose recognizes, agrees and submits to the sole and exclusive jurisdiction of the Commissioner:

A. To investigate, either upon complaint or upon his own initiative, any act, transaction or practice charged, alleged or suspected to be not in the best interests of the national game of Baseball; and

B. To determine, after investigation, what preventative, remedial, or punitive action is appropriate in the premises, and to take such action as the case may be.

2. Counsel for Peter Edward Rose, upon his authority, have executed a stipulation dismissing with prejudice the civil action that was originally filed in the Court of Common Pleas, Hamilton County, Ohio, captioned *Peter Edward Rose v. A. Bartlett Giamatti*, No. A8905178, and subsequently removed to the United States District Court from the Southern District of Ohio, Eastern Division, Docket No. C-2-89-577.

3. Peter Edward Rose will not avail himself of the opportunity to participate in a hearing concerning the allegations against him, or otherwise offer any defense to those allegations.

4. Peter Edward Rose acknowledges that the Commissioner has a factual basis to impose the penalty provided herein, and hereby accepts the penalty imposed

on him by the Commissioner and agrees not to challenge that penalty in court or otherwise. He also agrees he will not institute any legal proceedings of any nature against the Commissioner or any of his representatives, either Major League or any Major League Club.

5. The commissioner recognizes and agrees that it is in the best interests of the national game of Baseball that this matter be resolved pursuant to his sole and exclusive authority under the Major League Agreement.

THEREFORE, the Commissioner, recognizing the benefits to Baseball from a resolution of this matter, orders and directs that Peter Edward Rose be subject to the following disciplinary sanctions, and Peter Edward Rose, recognizing the sole and exclusive authority of the Commissioner and that it is in his interest to resolve this matter without further proceedings, agrees to accept the following disciplinary sanctions imposed by the Commissioner.

a. Peter Edward Rose is hereby declared permanently ineligible in accordance with Major League Rule 21 and placed on the Ineligible List.

b. Nothing in this agreement shall deprive Peter Edward Rose of the rights under Major League Rule 15 (c) to apply for reinstatement. Peter Edward Rose agrees not to challenge, appeal or otherwise contest the decision of, or the procedure employed by, the Commissioner or any future Commissioner in the evaluation of any application for reinstatement.

c. Nothing in this agreement shall be deemed either an admission or a denial by Peter Edward Rose of the allegation that he bet on any Major League Baseball game.

Neither the Commissioner nor Peter Edward Rose shall be prevented by this agreement from making any public statement relating to this matter so long as no such public statement contradicts the terms of this agreement and resolution.

This document contains the entire agreement of the parties and represents the entire resolution of the matter of Peter Edward Rose before the Commissioner.

August 24, 1989

STATEMENT OF COMMISSIONER A. BARTLETT GIAMATTI

The banishment for life of Pete Rose from baseball is the sad end of a sorry episode. One of the game's greatest players has engaged in a variety of acts which have stained the game, and he must now live with the consequences of those acts. By choosing not to come to a hearing before me, and by choosing not to proffer any testimony or evidence contrary to the evidence and information contained in the report of the Special Counsel to the Commissioner, Mr. Rose has accepted baseball's ultimate sanction, lifetime ineligibility.

This sorry episode began last February when baseball received firm allegations that Mr. Rose bet on baseball games and on the Reds' games. Such grave charges could not and must never be ignored. Accordingly, I engaged and Mr. Ueberroth

Roberto Clemente, exhibiting his ability to hit bad pitches, lines a double off the Mets' Jon Matlack for his 3,000th—and final—major league hit. National Baseball Hall of Fame Library, Cooperstown, New York.

Before a national television audience, Hank Aaron slugs his record 715th home run off the Dodgers' Al Downing on April 8, 1974. National Baseball Hall of Fame Library, Cooperstown, New York.

Frank Robinson became
major league baseball's first
African American manager
in 1975 for the Cleveland
Indians. National Baseball
Hall of Fame Library,
Cooperstown, New York.

These two photographs, taken immediately before and after the bottom of the tenth inning in the sixth game of the 1986 World Series, represent twenty-three of the most painful minutes in Boston Red Sox history. National Baseball Hall of Fame Library, Cooperstown, New York.

Peter Ueberroth was a great success as the primary organizer of the 1984 Olympic Games, but his brief term as baseball commissioner was stained with his initiation of collusion against players. National Baseball Hall of Fame Library, Cooperstown, New York.

Al Campanis was a respected executive with the Los Angeles Dodgers until he destroyed his career by making racist remarks on *Nightline* in the spring of 1987. National Baseball Hall of Fame Library, Cooperstown, New York.

A. Bartlett Giamatti was beloved by many baseball fans for his romantic views on baseball, and was mistrusted by Marvin Miller and other union officials for the same reason. National Baseball Hall of Fame Library, Cooperstown, New York.

After Giamatti's tragic death, his friend Fay Vincent began his term as commissioner with the support of the owners, but Vincent lost much of that support, and his job, within three years. National Baseball Hall of Fame Library, Cooperstown, New York

Jack Morris was already regarded as a tough, clutch pitcher prior to the 1987 World Series, but his ten-inning shutout in the seventh game of the Series forever clinched his reputation. National Baseball Hall of Fame Library, Cooperstown, New York.

appointed John Dowd as Special Counsel to investigate these and other allegations that might arise and to pursue the truth wherever it took him. I believed then and believe now that such a process, whereby an experienced professional inquires on behalf of the Commissioner as the Commissioner's agent, is fair and appropriate. To pretend that serious charges of any kind can be responsibly examined by a Commissioner alone fails to recognize the necessity to bring professionalism and fairness to any examination and the complexity a private entity encounters when, without judicial or legal powers, it pursues allegations in the complex, real world.

Baseball had never before undertaken such a process because there had not been such grave allegations since the time of Landis. If one is responsible for protecting the integrity of the game of baseball—that is, the game's authenticity, honesty and coherence—then the process one uses to protect the integrity of baseball must itself embody that integrity. I sought by means of a Special Counsel of proven professionalism and integrity, who was obliged to keep the subject of the investigation and his representatives informed about key information, to create a mechanism whereby the integrity we sought to protect was itself never violated. Similarly, in writing to Mr. Rose on May 11, I designed, as is my responsibility, a set of procedures for a hearing that would have afforded him every opportunity to present statements or testimony of witnesses or any other evidence he saw fit to answer the information and evidence presented in the Report of the Special Counsel and its accompanying materials.

That Mr. Rose and his counsel chose to pursue a course in the courts rather than appear at hearings scheduled for May 25 and then June 26, and then chose to come forward with a stated desire to settle this matter is now well known to all. My purpose in recounting the process and the procedures animating that process is to make two points that the American public deserves to know:

First, that the integrity of the game cannot be defended except by a process that itself embodies integrity and fairness;

Second, should any other occasion arise where charges are made or acts are said to be committed that are contrary to the interests of the game or that undermine the integrity of baseball, I fully intend to use such a process and procedure to get to the truth and, if need be to root out offending behavior. I intend to use, in short, every lawful and ethical means to defend and protect the game.

I say this so that there may be no doubt about where I stand or why I stand there. I believe baseball is a beautiful and exciting game, loved by millions—I among them—and I believe baseball is an important, enduring American institution. It must assert and aspire to the highest principles—of integrity, of professionalism of performance, of fair play within its rules. It will come as no surprise that like any institution composed of human beings, this institution will not always fulfill its highest aspirations. I know of no earthly institution that does. But this one, because it is so much a part of our history as a people and because it has such a purpose on our national soul, has an obligation to the people for whom it is played—to its fans and well-wishers—to strive for excellence in all things and to promote the highest ideals.

I will be told that I am an idealist. I hope so. I will continue to locate ideals I hold for myself and for my country in the national game as well as in other of our national institutions. And while there will be debate and dissent about this or that or another occurrence on or off the field, and while the game's nobler parts will always be enmeshed in the human frailties of those who, whatever their role, have stewardship of this game, let there be no doubt or dissent about our goals for baseball or our dedication to it. Nor about our vigilance and vigor—and patience—in protecting the game from blemish or stain or disgrace.

The matter of Mr. Rose is now closed. It will be debated and discussed. Let no one think that it did not hurt baseball. That hurt will pass, however, as the great glory of the game asserts itself and a resilient institution goes forward. Let it also be clear that no individual is superior to the game.

58

Commissioner Giamatti Dies of Heart Attack (1989)

SOURCE: *Washington Post*, September 3, 1989

The pressure of the Pete Rose investigation weighed heavily on Commissioner Giamatti. Supporters and opponents alike observed that Giamatti appeared to age throughout the ordeal. It is impossible to know exactly what affect the investigation actually had on the commissioner's health, but many believe that Giamatti's sudden death on September 3, less than two weeks after Rose accepted his banishment from baseball, was due in part to the stress he had endured over the six months of the investigation. Still, Giamatti's death came as a shock. Not only did baseball lose one of its most passionate fans, but it also thrust the sport into an era with uncertain leadership at a time when, after years of strife with the MLBPA and hundreds of millions of dollars in collusion-related penalties remaining to be paid, strong leadership was needed more than ever.

For Giamatti, It Ended at Head of the Class
By Shirley Povich

The name itself, A. Bartlett Giamatti, was uncommon enough. Parted in the middle and hybrid British-Italian, it was scarcely one to be associated quickly with the loftiest office in baseball. Yet in a game that cherishes its history and is always bringing its past into the present, no name ever commanded such force in baseball in so short a time, only 154 days in office.

It hardly suffices to speak of shock at the sudden death on Friday of Bart Giamatti. Shock of shocks perhaps, so startling was it in the near wake of the act that ensures Giamatti's own place in history as the commissioner who would determine that American Hero Pete Rose had become bad for baseball and had the daring to ban Rose for life.

The Pete Rose thing was barely less startling than Giamatti's own presence as the commissioner of baseball. Who could have forecast that A. Bartlett Giamatti would someday attain that office? Baseball long has prided itself on being America's most earthy sport, the game for the masses. Then what was this cum laude academician, this superscholar with his PhD in comparative literature, with an eight-year record as president of Yale, and nine honorary degrees, doing in the highest office of the game?

Ah, but there was something else in his resume. He was a certified baseball nut with not only affection but a passion for the game. At South Hadley, Mass., he was manager of the high school team, picking up and counting the bats, balls and gloves that were in precious supply. While teaching at Yale he flaunted his passion for the Red Sox by wearing a Boston cap in class.

Before he dropped in on Red Sox games as the commissioner of baseball, with retinue, he was there rooting for them as a private citizen, in a grandstand seat, lapping it up, and pulling for his heroes, Bobby Doerr, Ted Williams, Johnny Pesky, Joe Cronin and Vern Stephens.

On the night Giamatti died, Red Sox announcer Ken Coleman read to the Fenway Park crowd one of Giamatti's essays on baseball: "Baseball breaks your heart. It is designed to break your heart. The game begins in the spring when all else begins. And blossoms in summer, filling the afternoons and evenings . . . and then as the chill and rains come, it stops . . . and leaves you to face the fall alone."

He left a trail of his love for baseball long before he was voted into office as president of the National League and then commissioner. There is record that he earlier had said, "I have always found baseball to be the most satisfying and nourishing game outside of literature." And he could write about it. P. G. Putnam publishers selected his article on Tom Seaver's farewell as among the "Best Sports Stories" of that year. Even on the day of his induction as president of Yale he is remembered as saying: "The only thing I wanted to be president of was the American League."

He had long been doing baseball another service by example, by giving the message to all in the land that it was a game for scholars as well as the man on the street. This was sharp rebuke to those impatient folks unaware of the charms of baseball who were given to calling it a "dull game." Like the late Red Smith, who once retorted that "baseball is a dull game only for those with dull minds," Giamatti was an apostle of the fascinations of baseball, of the strategies and the nuances that made it a game for imaginative fans.

Giamatti was an original expressing his affection for baseball long before it became fashionable for others, notably op-ed columnists who pronounced and repronounced their love of the game. With them it became a form of baseball chic.

So rooted was Giamatti in the traditions of the game, so opposed was he to tampering with it. He was an outspoken opponent of the designated hitter, deplored AstroTurf diamonds and the lights at Wrigley Field. He was no opponent of the hot dogs that came with the seat he bought in Fenway Park before he got in on a season pass as NL president and commissioner.

He was tormented by the Pete Rose case, he said after banning Rose. "Of course I agonized over it. And I know Pete Rose and his family did." But he was also annoyed that for five months it was clouding the whole baseball season, a vile distraction for the pennant races. He wanted to get it over, never wanted baseball in the courts, and when the time came he got rid of Rose with all the finality of a click in the lock.

He allowed Rose the favor of omitting any accusation of betting on baseball in the agreement that Rose would accept the punishment. But he took pains to clear up all doubt of his own convictions when he said at his news conference: "Yes, I believe Pete Rose bet on baseball and I'm banning him for life. There was no deal . . . he's fired." There would be no overhanging confusion about what he really meant.

On that day he also revealed once more the charming pixie in him when he asked a writer to repeat the second half of his question, saying, "I was so enthralled by my answer to the first part, I wasn't paying attention to the last part."

What will be Bart Giamatti's remembered place in baseball? It is a pride that on the day he banned Pete Rose it was written here, "In the history of baseball commissioners, A. Bartlett Giamatti goes to the head of the class." His predecessor, Peter Ueberroth, has called him the "greatest of all baseball commissioners." This, after only 154 days.

In writing of Giamatti's death, Boston Globe journalist Michael Madden perhaps attained the most inspired of lines: "Say it ain't so." That could serve as the finest of eulogies to the illustrious, uncommon man of whom it was accurately written that his heart was in the ballpark.

59

World Series Interrupted by Devastating Earthquake (1989)

SOURCE: *Sporting News*, October 30, 1989

After the sordid Pete Rose affair and the shocking death of Bart Giamatti, the arrival of the 1989 World Series between the San Francisco Giants and the Oakland A's was most welcome. Commissioner Fay Vincent, in office for barely a month, happily presided over the Series, which began as expected with two easy wins by Oakland at home. The clubs moved across the bay to San Francisco to play the third game on October 17. At 5:04 p.m., just before play started, the unimaginable happened.

A powerful earthquake, triggered by the slippage of the Loma Prieta fault in the Santa Cruz Mountains, rocked San Francisco and the surrounding area. The quake, later measured at 7.1 on the Richter scale, killed sixty-five people and caused $7 billion in damage. Faced with the decision of what to do about the World Series—a trivial concern under the circumstances—Vincent earned the respect of baseball fans everywhere (but not San

Francisco mayor Art Agnos, who later complained that Vincent had pressured him to re-start the Series prematurely) for his decision to postpone the Series for a week. Vincent's subsequent description of the Series as "a modest little sporting event" was most appro-priate, and the column below reflects Vincent's perspective.

Art Spander
Vincent's Priorities Are in the Right Place

SAN FRANCISCO—His predecessor, Bart Giamatti, was a man of letters, and the reference is not merely to those such as ERA or RBI. We didn't know much about Francis Vincent, except perhaps that he was nicknamed Fay and that he had become commissioner of baseball in the most difficult of times.

Now we know enough. Now we know Vincent comprehends more than a feeling of what is merely right or wrong. Vincent is sensitive when sensitivity is demand-ed. Vincent has perspective.

It was a tough call for baseball, deciding what direction to go after the earthquake jarred us into reality at Candlestick Park. There were egos, dollar bills, wrecked homes and coroners' reports to consider. There was tradition. There was provincialism.

But Vincent, Giants Owner Bob Lurie, Athletics Owner Walter Haas and, yes, ABC-TV, deserve respect. So often we complain about the power television has over sport, but those parties made the right call.

They postponed the Series for a week, a week that would give us time to bury our dead, collect our thoughts and try in this region known as the Bay Area to re-turn to a semblance of normalcy.

A sports columnist, even one with a news background, feels helplessly out of place in responding to human catastrophe.

Our words are full of irony and sarcasm about trivialities. We worry about passed balls or fastballs, making light of men playing boys' games.

And then the real world intrudes. And we're caught with our adjectives down, looking stupid if we try to compare the collapse of a team with the collapse of a freeway and feeling stupid if we wonder whether a delay of the World Series will af-fect either team.

We needed time to think while San Francisco and Oakland and those coastal towns 75 to 90 miles away, Santa Cruz and Watsonville, needed time to recover.

Some argued that the World Series should be cancelled and the Oakland A's de-clared the winner, since they held a 2–0 lead in the best-of-seven affair. Some argued the Series should be moved. But Vincent and baseball did what was proper. Sooner or later, "life as usual" must resume. But not too soon.

Sure, we thought about 1963 and the assassination of President John F. Kennedy, when college football postponed its games, but the National Football League, under the direction of Pete Rozelle, did not. Rozelle was guilty of insensitivity.

We thought about the 1972 Munich Olympics and the kidnapping and murder of the Israeli athletes, when the International Olympic Committee refused to halt or delay the Games. Insensitivity.

But baseball—actually, the men who run it—could look around and see that structures had fallen and tears had fallen and that the wisest thing to do was to step back for a while.

"Our modest little sporting event," Vincent called the baseball championship of America. How wonderful to have someone in charge who is not overwhelmed by his organization's importance.

San Francisco had waited 27 years for a World Series game. Not since 1962, when Willie McCovey hit a low liner to the Yankees' Bobby Richardson, ending a rally and spoiling a dream, had there been Series competition at Candlestick Park.

The first two games of what had been labeled the Bay Bridge Series—a mocking title with the collapse of a section of the bridge in the earthquake—had been held at Oakland.

They had been boring and, perhaps because the Athletics were so efficient, taking both the Giants and fans out of the game early, they had been quiet.

There was a great deal of noise before the scheduled start of Game 3 at Candlestick. It was obvious that the spectators were in an emotional mood. And then there was too much noise, a low rumbling that at first sounded as if thousands of people were stamping their feet in unison.

I was in the upper deck at Candlestick, the auxiliary press section, sitting next to Rob Matwick, public relations director of the Houston Astros.

"What's going on?" Matwick asked nervously.

I laughed.

"An earthquake," I told him.

I'm 51 and have spent all my life in California. I know an earthquake when one happens.

But I've never known one like this. Candlestick swayed like a ship on a stormy sea. The quake lasted maybe 15 to 20 seconds, but it seemed like an hour.

And then it was over. Some 60,000 people cheered. They were Californians. They were Giants fans. They were survivors. Surely this was a sign from nature. No harm, no foul. "Play ball," they began to chant.

They'd been through big quakes before. So had I. In 1952, in Los Angeles, the one that destroyed the town of Tehachapi; a roller in 1964 in Mexico City; another major one in Los Angeles, when I was passing through in 1971; and certainly dozens of minor ones in San Francisco.

But nothing like this one, which had out-of-town writers terrified and had me a trifle nervous. Until it stopped. And then it was over. Or so we thought.

News traveled quickly. We learned a section of the Bay Bridge had fallen. The upper deck of a freeway had pancaked onto the lower deck.

Yet Candlestick Park, the most maligned stadium in America, held up. And you uttered a silent prayer, because with 60,000 people in the stadium, a failure of the structure is too frightening to consider.

Candlestick stood the test. Baseball stood the test. Praise all to whom praise is due.

60

Vincent Defends Controversial Television Contract (1989)

SOURCE: Senate Subcommittee on Antitrust, Monopolies and Business Rights, *Sports Programming and Cable Television*, 101st Cong., 1st sess., 1989, 31–39

After broadcasting major league baseball since the 1947 World Series, and after airing the popular Game of the Week *every Saturday afternoon during the season since 1953,* NBC's *contract with baseball expired following the 1989 season. To the dismay of many, in December 1988, Commissioner Ueberroth announced that major league baseball had signed a contract with* CBS *that would eliminate the weekly broadcasts and air only twelve regular-season games annually between 1990 and 1993, along with All-Star Games and all postseason contests. A popular cable network,* ESPN, *would air 175 games per season, six per week plus additional games on holidays. The angry response was led by Curt Smith, author of several books on baseball broadcasters, who argued that only half the country had access to cable and that this marked the first time that a sport had voluntarily reduced its exposure on network television. Smith's jeremiads helped convince new commissioner Fay Vincent to increase the regular-season broadcasts to sixteen, but Smith and his allies were not satisfied.*

Below is Vincent's statement before a Senate committee on November 14, 1989, on the CBS-ESPN *contract. Smith's most comprehensive attack on the contract is in his book* Voices of the Game *(New York: Fireside, 1992), 539–65.*

Beginning next year Baseball's exposure on local and national television will be expanded and deepened by our new telecasting arrangements. Local telecasts will continue to provide significant amounts of Baseball to the viewing public. The changes in the way Baseball will be telecast nationally will result in a large rise in viewing audiences. The combination of local and national telecasts will provide broader coverage of the game than ever before. . . .

LOCAL TELECASTS

It is important to emphasize at the outset that Major League Baseball, unlike many other sports, is followed by its fans principally through local game telecasts. Television ratings over the last decade have revealed the preference of our fans for local telecasts versus national telecasts.

To correct a widespread misunderstanding, the total number of local, free over-the-air telecasts of Major League Baseball games (including both home and visiting team telecasts) *has increased, not decreased*, each of the past five years. The total number of local, free over-the-air telecasts was 1,485 in 1984 and has increased each year to a total of 1,653 in 1989. Moreover, the number of free local telecasts exceeded the number of cable telecasts in 1989 by more than 55%. . . .

It is true that the number of local cable telecasts has increased each of the past four years. This does *not*, however, reflect a shifting of games from free television to cable television. In the aggregate, it reflects the telecasting of Baseball games on cable that were previously not being telecast at all. In recent years, our clubs have authorized an average of 60 telecasts on free television per year. Many would like to sell more free telecasts but have been constrained by commitments that local broadcast stations have been made to carry network (ABC, CBS, Fox and NBC) programming and syndicated programming. Our clubs have *not*, however, been limited to any significant degree by restrictions contained in national network contracts—either past or future. In fact, as will be shown in detail, the restrictions contained in our CBS and ESPN contracts are so slight that each of our clubs will have the ability to authorize at least 130 free telecasts per year. With only three of the 26 clubs placing more than 75 free telecasts per year, there obviously remains substantially more scheduling flexibility than required for local telecasts, even assuming . . . We therefore are perplexed by accusations that free telecasts are being "siphoned" to cable and limited by national contract restrictions. While the number of games on cable television may be increasing, they are simply not being lost by free, local television. . . .

CBS

Under Baseball's CBS agreement beginning in 1990, there will be a decrease in weekend afternoon national baseball telecasts compared to 1989 and previous years. The new agreement calls for 16 Saturday or Sunday (or Independence Day) afternoon telecasts, a number that was recently increased from 12. The elimination of a national, exclusive telecast every Saturday afternoon was, in part, a response to steadily declining national ratings. It was also the result of a competitive bidding process in which only one network expressed any desire to telecast a baseball game every weekend. It is important to note that no single club may be selected more than four times in a season for exclusive CBS telecasts; on all other days a club may change the start times of its free telecasts to avoid the exclusive CBS afternoon time period, just as clubs have done in the past with NBC Saturday telecasts. It should also be noted that the decrease in weekend national exclusive telecasts provides a corresponding increase in afternoon time periods available for free local telecasts, the demonstrated preference of Baseball fans. This will further increase the great flexibility the clubs have to schedule free local telecasts. . . .

Moreover, it should be emphasized that Major League Baseball has contractual obligations for the All-Star Game and all post-season games to appear on free television through 1993.

SUMMARY

For many years, the way that Baseball was marketed on television did not fit the viewing preferences of Baseball fans. Through our new agreements with CBS and ESPN, and especially through the great flexibility that has been preserved for fans to see their home teams on local stations, televised Baseball beginning in 1990 will be far more appealing to a far greater number of fans. We are hopeful that this in turn will generate greater attendance and contribute to an overall increase in the popularity of Baseball. Our new television arrangements are pro-consumer and pro-competitive and will provide the greatest amount of Baseball to the greatest number of fans.

61

Thirty-Two-Day Lockout Ends with New Basic Agreement (1990)

SOURCE: *Sporting News*, March 26, 1990

According to writer John Helyar, as early as December 1988 the owners, supported by Commissioner Giamatti, planned to lock out the players prior to the 1990 season in an attempt to force the union to bargain for a new Basic Agreement from a weakened position. Giamatti's friend and replacement, Fay Vincent, undercut the owners' unanimity within two days of the February 1990 installation of the lockout by meeting with three owners who had changed their minds and wanted to open the spring-training camps. Vincent also met with MLBPA executive director Don Fehr on several occasions, avoiding PRC negotiator Chuck O'Connor in the process.

The primary issue on the table was player eligibility for salary arbitration. Even though owners won the majority of arbitration cases, the end result was still soaring salaries, a trend slowed only by collusion. The union wanted up to half of all players with two years' service to be eligible, while the owners refused to allow players with less than three years' service to qualify. As the lockout continued, several players on the MLBPA board started to weaken in their resolve, so Fehr resurrected Marvin Miller to inspire them to remain united. On March 18 an agreement was finally reached, allowing the season to start only a few days late.

Ah, Spring: 4-Year Pact Opens Camps

17 Pct. Solution on Arbitration Brings End to 32-Day Lockout
By Murray Chass

NEW YORK — Fay Vincent, whose first World Series as commissioner was nearly wiped out by an earthquake last October, raised a question in February as the labor dispute between the owners and players shut down what was supposed to have been Vincent's first spring training.

"Do you think I'll have baseball in my administration?" he mused.

The sport's eighth commissioner had to wait for a month to get the answer: Yes, Fay, there will be baseball in your time.

That was guaranteed March 18 when negotiators, working from noon to midnight, reached agreement on a four-year contract that ended the owners' 32-day lockout and cleared the way for the opening of spring training camps.

Fittingly, peace was announced in Versailles—at least in the Versailles ballroom of the Helmsley Palace Hotel.

"I have a very pleasant duty," Vincent said at a news conference at 1:15 a.m. March 19. "It is simply to announce that tonight an agreement in principle has been reached between the players' association and the Player Relations Committee. It's been a difficult process, but we have reached an agreement in a satisfying bilateral fashion, and it is a good thing for baseball."

At the time Vincent spoke, the regular season was scheduled to begin in exactly two weeks. But those April 2 openers already had become casualties of the lockout, the second longest shutdown in baseball history. Only the players' 50-day strike in 1981 was longer among the seven work stoppages that have occurred in the last 18 years.

The agreements included the following points:

Season openers will be April 9, and each club will play a minimum of 158 games. The possibility of a full complement of 162 games will be worked out later.

Spring training was to begin March 20, the date of the vernal equinox. The first exhibition games were scheduled March 26.

Rosters will stay at 24 players this season, then expand to 25 in the 1991 season.

Salary arbitration rights were approved for the top 17 percent of players with two to three years of major league service. To qualify, those players must have been on a major league roster at least 86 days in the previous season.

The minimum major league salary will be $100,000.

Owners will contribute $55 million annually to the players' pension fund.

Steve Greenberg, the deputy commissioner, said officials were hopeful that each team would have a 162-game schedule this season. Games lost in the week of April 2–8 would be made up on off-days and as parts of doubleheaders—or perhaps during a week added at the end of the season.

The Major League Players Association proposed the extra week, but it was not immediately adopted. The owners' negotiators said they would have to discuss the matter with the CBS television network, which has rights to the League Championship Series and the World Series. The postseason games would be affected by a change in the regular-season schedule.

A representative of the owners got in touch with a CBS official the night the agreement was reached, but was told that the network would not reach a decision until the following day.

If the extra week were approved, a World Series that went the full seven games—and was not interrupted by rain or earthquake—would run until October 28 instead of October 21, as originally scheduled. Last year's Series ended October 29 after a 12-day delay because of the Bay Area earthquake.

"We expect there will be considerable effort made to avoid having an asterisk next to the season," Vincent said.

Although spring training camps were to open officially March 20, players who were already in Florida and Arizona began working out the previous day.

Hours before the camp gates were flung open, Bud Selig, owner of the Milwaukee Brewers and chairman of the PRC board, talked about the lockout, which had been in effect since February 15.

The lockout, Selig said, was "designed to produce an agreement before the season started. It was designed to prevent the interruption of the season, all the sadness of 1981, the heartache that we went through. It put pressure on both parties to get something done."

The players' union never did share Selig's view of the lockout, but both sides finally were able to agree on a new Basic Agreement to replace the one that expired last December 31.

Vincent was delighted over the settlement, but he said, speaking of the lockout's effect, "I think damage has been done and a lot of us regret that damage."

The key to the settlement was the compromise on salary arbitration eligibility for players with two to three years of service in the majors.

Until March 17, the owners had adamantly opposed eligibility for any players with less than three years' service. The players, who initially wanted the eligibility level to be returned to two years, most recently had proposed making 50 percent of the two-to-three group eligible, based on those players' service time.

The groundwork for the owners' foray into untouched territory was laid March 14, following a hearing before arbitrator George Nicolau on the union's request to have the clubs place $51.6 million into escrow as damages arising out of the Collusion II ruling by Nicolau. That case affected free agents following the 1986 season.

Chuck O'Connor, the owners' chief negotiator, and Donald Fehr, executive director of the players' union, talked briefly after attending Nicolau's hearing.

"Beginning with my conversation with Chuck," Fehr related, "a chain of events was set into motion."

Three days later, in a Saturday morning bargaining session, O'Connor began seriously exploring the possibility of making some of the two-to-three players eligible.

They continued the effort the following day at Vincent's office, but it was a far more treacherous exploration for O'Connor than it was for Fehr.

According to a source close to the talks, the negotiators would meet for five minutes or 20 minutes March 18, then break for three or four hours. During those breaks, the source said, the six owners on the PRC board could be heard debating loudly the wisdom of giving ground on the arbitration issue. (Selig termed the behind-closed-door noise "divergent opinions.")

Give they did, though, as did the union. As the owners crept up with their percentage, the players descended with theirs. A source said the owners reached 12 percent, the players 20. Finally, they agreed that 17 percent of the two-to-three players who had at least 86 days of major league service (172 days is considered a full year) in the preceding season would be eligible for salary arbitration.

That would make perhaps 15 players eligible in any given year, depending on the total number of players who would have the necessary qualifications.

On other major matters, the players accepted a $100,000 minimum salary and the $55 million a year in pension contributions. The union's most recent requests had been for $105,000 and $57 million. The 1989 figures were $68,000 and $39 million.

The two sides agreed to have 24-man rosters for 1990 and 25-man rosters beginning in 1991 and lasting until the National League expands by two teams. An announcement on those two new cities was to be made in 90 days. There were erroneous reports that the agreement also included provision for six expansion teams by the end of the century. There was no such provision.

There was no provision for expanded rosters for the month of April this season, a move the players requested because of the abbreviated spring training. However, when the players balked at starting the season April 4, as the owners proposed, the owners said the rosters would number 24 at the start of the season.

Eugene Orza, the union's associate general counsel, said that the roster issue would be discussed further, along with the scheduling of the makeup games.

Among other elements of the settlement, the two sides agreed that either could terminate the agreement after three years, the players received a guarantee of protection against collusion and both sides agreed to a study committee on industry economics and a labor-management committee to discuss labor differences.

Fehr acknowledged that "there is a measurably lower degree of hostility" at the end of these negotiations than there had been after the previous three negotiations in which he was involved.

But, he added, speaking of improved labor relations that is Vincent's stated goal, "The answer is yet to be told. After a passage of time under this agreement, under the administration we have in baseball now, if the players perceive an attitude of genuine respect and an effort to be fair, if there is respect for the agreements that are made, then the respect will come back and be genuine. That remains to be seen. The effort will be made. We certainly hope it turns out that way."

The new relationship between the owners and the players began at 5:54 a.m. March 19. That was when their negotiators signed the memorandum of understanding of the new collective bargaining agreement.

Not long afterward, Scott Sanderson, an Oakland pitcher who was a member of the players' negotiating committee, closed the second news conference by saying, "The players express their appreciation for Mr. Vincent and his part in all these negotiations and his respect for all the players and their respect for him."

62

Owners Lose Collusion III (1990)

SOURCE: *The National Sports Daily* (New York edition), July 19, 1990

Following the 1987 season the owners adopted a new strategy for keeping salaries down. An "Information Bank" was established, with the currency being information on salary offers to prominent free agents. Teams interested in a particular player could take a "withdrawal" in the form of knowledge of offers made to that player by his team and by other teams. In theory this would prevent owners from promising players considerably more than they had been offered by any other club, which would lower salaries not only to individual free agents but also to players in arbitration, since salary claims by both the player and the club were based on salaries received by players with similar statistics.

Unfortunately, as in the past, owners lacked the self-discipline to make the Information Bank work. A number of owners made dishonest "deposits" by claiming to have offered a player less money or fewer years than they actually did, and free-agent salaries rose slightly. The situation worsened when, on July 18, arbitrator George Nicolau ruled that the Information Bank was simply another form of collusion against 1987 free agents. In each of the three full years of Commissioner Ueberroth's term (1985–87), the owners followed his advice to reduce player salaries and were found guilty of collusion in each case.

The three collusion cases were ultimately settled in December for $280 million, to be distributed at the discretion of the union. A legal notice to be filed by players seeking to join in the settlement was reprinted in The National Sports Daily *on April 5, 1991. As of 2003 some players were still seeking a portion of the settlement through litigation with the MLBPA.*

Owners Guilty of Collusion Once Again
By Ken Gurnick of the *National*

Baseball's legal losing streak continued Wednesday when an arbitrator ruled that owners conspired to manipulate the free-agent market for a third consecutive season.

Arbitrators previously had ruled that owners deliberately agreed not to sign free agents following the 1985 and 1986 seasons in an unlawful attempt to depress player salaries. Wednesday's decision by George Nicolau covered players granted free agency following the 1987 season, when owners contributed to an information bank enabling them to share details of other teams' contract offers.

"I hope we've seen the last of this sorry tale," said Donald Fehr, the executive director of the Players Association, who echoed a management representative's conciliatory tone in the aftermath of the union's sweep.

In this case, commonly referred to as "Collusion III," Nicolau ruled that the information bank violated the collective bargaining agreement, which prohibits teams or players from acting in concert during negotiations. Teams discontinued the information bank before the 1988 free-agent market began, and the new collective bargaining agreement specifically prohibits information banks in the future.

Wrote Nicolau in his verdict:

"With (the previous cases) as a backdrop, the bank's message is plain: If we must go out into the free agent market and bid, let's quietly cooperate by telling each other what the bids are. If we all do that, prices won't get out of line and no club will be hurt too much."

Among the 76 free agents filing claims in the Collusion III case are Jack Clark, Gary Gaetti, Dave Righetti, Dave Smith, Jack Morris, Mike Witt, Paul Molitor, Frank Tanana, Dennis Martinez and Brett Butler. Based on previous collusion cases, some or all of these players could be granted free agency again as part of the remedy phase.

In addition, monetary damages will be assessed by the arbitrators. Tom Roberts, who arbitrated Collusion I, already has awarded players $10.5 million in just the first stage of that proceeding. The Players Association expects penalties to surpass $100 million for the three cases, although a settlement could be negotiated first.

"Over the next two to three weeks, the union will meet with the (management's) Player Relations Committee and the arbitrator to discuss procedures which could bring this episode to a conclusion as soon as possible," Fehr said.

Based on testimony taken in the actions, the conspiracy strategy was hatched by then-commissioner Peter Ueberroth, who was hired by owners with a directive to bolster profitability.

Barry Rona, who handled negotiations on behalf of management's Player Relations Committee during the Ueberroth years, would not comment on the third verdict.

63

Vincent Rules Against Steinbrenner in Spira Case (1990)

source: Fay Vincent, "Decision of the Commissioner," July 30, 1990, Marvin Miller Papers, Series II, Box 6, Folder 10, Robert F. Wagner Labor Archives, Tamiment Library

The ruling by Commissioner Vincent reprinted here summarizes a sordid affair in which Yankees owner George Steinbrenner was found to have conspired against one of his own players, Dave Winfield, with a former associate of Winfield's, Howard Spira. Spira convinced Steinbrenner—who had derisively nicknamed Winfield "Mr. May" for his perceived postseason failings—to pay him $40,000 for information against Winfield. In his autobiography Vincent detailed the investigation of the allegations and noted his astonishment that Steinbrenner chose to accept permanent expulsion from baseball over a three-year suspension. Vincent eventually reinstated Steinbrenner on March 1, 1993.

DECISION OF THE COMMISSIONER

On March 20, 1990, my office instituted an investigation of the circumstances surrounding the relationship between George M. Steinbrenner, III, the principal owner of the New York Yankees Baseball Club, and Howard Spira. This investigation was precipitated by press reports that Mr. Steinbrenner had paid Spira $40,000, culminating a three year working relationship.

SUMMARY OF DECISION

I conclude that Mr. Steinbrenner's payment to Mr. Spira in January 1990, and his undisclosed working relationship with Spira and the private investigation of Spira's allegations conducted by and at Mr. Steinbrenner's direction between December 1986 and September 3, 1987, constitutes conduct that is not in the best interests of Baseball. Such conduct constitutes a violation of Major League Rule 21(f), which is incorporated in the Major League Agreement to which Mr. Steinbrenner is a signatory.

My decision in this case derives from two fundamental and, in my view, indisputable premises:

(1) An owner of a Major League Baseball Club may not initiate and maintain for months, without the knowledge of the Commissioner, a working relationship with a known gambler in furtherance of a private investigation aimed at a ballplayer or an affiliate of a ballplayer; and

(2) An owner of a Major League Baseball Club may not pay a gambler for information intended to be used in a dispute involving the owner and a ballplayer.

In his testimony before me, Mr. Steinbrenner conceded errors of judgment both at the beginning of his dealings with Mr. Spira and at the end with the payment to this individual. In essence, then, this decision is largely the result of admitted misconduct by Mr. Steinbrenner, although there is ample evidence from other sources supporting the conclusion I have reached.

Some may argue that nothing very serious is involved in this case; that Mr. Steinbrenner erred but not egregiously; that there are worse problems in Baseball and that these errors do not warrant a strong punitive response. I strongly disagree. I sat through the two days of Mr. Steinbrenner's testimony and I am able to judge the degree of candor and contrition present in this case. I am able to discern an attempt to force explanations in hindsight onto discomforting facts. And I am able to evaluate a pattern of behavior that borders on the bizarre.

Since 1921, the Commissioner of Baseball has been charged with the responsibility of insuring that all those affiliated with the game of Baseball conduct themselves in a manner that instills public confidence in the game and its participants. Mr. Steinbrenner's dealings with Spira are unacceptable under this code of conduct, which I am committed to enforce.

When Mr. Steinbrenner began his association with Spira and private investigation of Mr. Winfield, he in effect disregarded the Office of the Commissioner. He ignored the proper course of conduct, which was to advise Commissioner Ueberroth promptly and fully of the overture by Spira. Rather, even accepting Mr. Steinbrenner's version of the facts, he waited several months—perhaps as many as nine—before partially advising the Commissioner's Office. I find that conduct unacceptable. No Commissioner can permit or encourage an owner to run his own investigation into serious matters that are within the jurisdiction of this office, and Baseball has long forbidden the kind of association with a known gambler that permeates this case.

Furthermore, there is no issue of notice or warning here. Mr. Steinbrenner admitted to me that in these circumstances he would not again do what he did in 1986–1987. He would come to me or my successor. Moreover, he cannot have had any doubt that my office was responsible for handling this kind of issue, for he came to this office at a later date. Mr. Steinbrenner knew what to do; he just failed to do it in a timely and complete manner.

I find the transaction that culminated in the payment to Spira to have been a serious error of judgment, and I must impose correspondingly serious sanctions as a consequence. Mr. Steinbrenner knew that the payment to Spira was ill-advised because all his advisers spoke against it. He knew Spira was or had been a gambler—it matters not which—and yet he made the payment. He knew Spira claimed he had been promised money for a job or both, and yet Mr. Steinbrenner made the payment, thereby validating the claim that Spira was being paid for providing information. He knew the payment, if exposed, would look bad and he knew, or at least should have known, that, if the payment were exposed, it would bring disrepute to him and therefore to Baseball. As a result, efforts were made to cover it up.

Mr. Steinbrenner admits an error of judgment but contends he never intended to hurt Baseball or to act "not in the best interests" of our game when he paid Spira. My response to this is twofold. First, his intentions cannot easily be discerned from the conflicting evidence before me. While Mr. Steinbrenner now claims he was extorted and feared possible violence directed against him and his family, neither of his two principal advisers, McNiff and William Dowling, testified there was extortion involved in the payment. McNiff is a former FBI agent with 30 years of experience and Dowling is a former prosecutor. Presumably they know extortion when they see it—even if Mr. Steinbrenner does not. I also note that Spira, who Mr. Steinbrenner contends provided solid information, claims he was promised future consideration in their first meeting in December 1986.

These claims of fear and of extortion are not credible. I note no tone of fear on the tape of the March 1990 conversation following the payment when Spira asked unsuccessfully for an additional $110,000. At that time, Mr. Steinbrenner never mentioned that he made the payment out of fear, nor did he claim he was extorted. Rather he said he paid Spira to help him out. And when Mr. Steinbrenner said a final "No" to the $110,000 demand, he exhibited neither fear nor confusion. He even argued he overpaid with the $40,000 in that Spira's information was described by Mr. Steinbrenner as not that helpful.

In sum, Mr. Steinbrenner has offered multiple and conflicting explanations of his decision to give $40,000 to Spira, ranging from charity to extortion. Based on my review of Mr. Steinbrenner's testimony and the transcripts of his and McNiff's discussions with Spira, I am persuaded that neither extreme was at work here. Rather, the payment was in consideration for Spira's help and was an exercise in expediency, for I have little doubt that Spira had become a nuisance to Mr. Steinbrenner and the Yankee organization and was a potential embarrassment to Mr. Steinbrenner. The interests of Baseball are not served by permitting an owner to deal with an admitted gambler (who boasts of ties with organized crime) for years, pay him $40,000 in a furtive fashion and ultimately claim to have been extorted.

Indeed, it is apparent to me that Mr. Steinbrenner does not appreciate the gravity of his conduct. By paying Spira, Mr. Steinbrenner placed himself at a minimum in the untenable position of having possibly financed the repayment of gambling debts or of bankrolling future wagering. No participant in Baseball, let alone the owner of a Club, should put himself in such a position.

None of the "defenses" raised by Mr. Steinbrenner and his lawyers is viable. For example, Mr. Steinbrenner's contention that his conduct cannot be held to be an infraction of Rule 21(f) because he did not intend to violate the rule misses the point. Undoubtedly few, if any, individuals found by my predecessors to have engaged in conduct not in the best interests of baseball intended to harm the game. I believe that he had no intention of harming the game, but it is Mr. Steinbrenner's conduct that I must consider here.

Equally unavailing is Mr. Steinbrenner's contention that he believed in good faith that what Spira was telling him about Winfield was true. The truth or falsity of Spira's allegations have no bearing on my decision that the initial dealing with Spira and the 1990 payment violate Rule 21(f). Although I am skeptical of Spira's capacity to tell the truth, I make no finding as to those allegations, as none is required for purposes of this decision.

If I were to accept the pleas of Mr. Steinbrenner and his vigorous counsel and agree not to punish this admitted mistake of judgment, I would be establishing bad precedent and making bad Baseball law.

Mr. Steinbrenner's team of lawyers have also raised assorted objections to the procedures employed and to the purported biases of Mr. [John] Dowd and myself. I have directly and indirectly through my counsel responded to and rejected this posturing. I will not belabor the point other than to state that Mr. Steinbrenner has been afforded a full and fair opportunity to present to me orally and in writing his views and testimony, all of which I have considered with an open mind. In my view, Mr. Steinbrenner's dilemma is not with the procedures I have utilized, but with his inability to rewrite history.

I now turn to the issue of disposition and sanctions. In my view, the situation before me is quite simple. I find the twin mistakes, one at the outset of the private investigation and one in the payment, to be serious instances of misconduct. I do not find the misconduct enough to warrant permanent expulsion from Baseball, although under all the circumstances here I have given that sanction serious consideration. Rather, I find that remedial action is in order. Mr. Steinbrenner must somehow be persuaded to pay closer attention to the legitimate interests of Baseball. No participant in Baseball, whether a journeyman player or the owner of a team with perhaps the richest tradition in our game, can be permitted to ignore the rightful responsibilities and functions of this noble and historic Office.

My greatest disappointment was Mr. Steinbrenner's testimony that it did not occur to him during this very sorry period that what he was doing could run afoul of the rules of Baseball. In essence, he heard no internal warnings because none went off. Even as he was authorizing that funds be drawn from the New York Yankees to pay off an admitted gambler, Mr. Steinbrenner did not think he was doing anything risky from the viewpoint of Baseball. Such thinking is insensitive to the considerations of what is in Baseball's best interests.

This case is an important one because it involves an owner of an historically important franchise. As is publicly known, he has been disciplined many times during his seventeen-year tenure in Baseball and is perceived as an owner who frequently ignores the established rules of the game. While I am willing to disregard his past disciplinary problems as indicating any wrongdoing here, I must be mindful of the importance of focusing Mr. Steinbrenner on his obligations to be more sensitive to the best interests of Baseball as a senior owner in the game.

In short, I must get the attention of this owner. He must learn to be more careful, to listen to his advisers, and to consider more carefully all the ramifications of his conduct. It is my sincere hope that the sanctions, which are provided for in the attached Agreement and Resolution, will have the result I intend. If they do not, I or my successor will be confronting Mr. Steinbrenner once again. And that cannot be in the best interests of Baseball.

Accordingly, I find that, on the basis of the record before me, but especially on the basis of his own sworn testimony, Mr. Steinbrenner has acted in the two cited instances not in the best interests of Baseball. In discussing an appropriate sanction with Mr. Steinbrenner, I have learned from him that he now accepts this key finding. As a result, I am prepared to accept his representations and his agreement to the sanctions which I am imposing on him pursuant to the terms and conditions of this attached Agreement and Resolution.

Pursuant to my authority under the Major League Agreement and Major League Rules, I am imposing separately certain terms and conditions on the Yankees pursuant to a Supplemental Order to be issued by my Office.

Dated: July 30, 1990

Francis T. Vincent, Jr.
Commissioner of Baseball

64

Jack Morris, Twins Win Classic Seventh Game of World Series (1991)

SOURCE: *Minneapolis Star-Tribune*, October 28, 1991

The 1991 World Series was the first in which two teams that had finished in last place in their division or league the previous season had met in the fall classic the following year. The Atlanta Braves had been a terrible team throughout the previous decade, and although the Minnesota Twins had won the 1987 World Series, they were not among the teams expected to contend for the 1991 AL pennant. True to form, these unexpected champions produced another surprise by playing one of the most dramatic World Series in baseball history.

The biggest star of the Series was Minnesota pitcher Jack Morris, who won more games in the decade of the 1980s than any other pitcher. Morris won two games in the Series, but he earned his greatest fame for pitching ten shutout innings in the seventh game, finally winning when Twins pinch hitter Gene Larkin hit a single with the bases loaded in the bottom of the tenth.

On Top of the World

Morris and Larkin Key Another Magic Carpet Ride
By Jeff Lenihan
Staff Writer

It was a scene only Andy McPhail and Tom Kelly could have visualized back in February. Those two men and, of course, a fellow named John Scott Morris, who yearned to go home.

Just after 11 Sunday night, Morris was somewhere in the bowels of the Metrodome, clutching the trophy awarded to the most valuable player in the World Series. On the playing field, his teammates reveled in their 10-inning, 1–0 victory, turning somersaults, tackling one another and pumping their fists toward a roaring crowd of 55,118 that had no intention of going home.

Perhaps the most dramatic and closely contested World Series in major league history was complete, and the ending could not have been more appropriate.

Morris, pitching for the third time in nine days, talked Kelly into letting him pitch the 10th inning, something no World Series starter had done in 22 years.

The Twins made Morris' perseverance worthwhile, giving him a run in the bottom of the 10th inning to secure their second straight extra-inning victory. The game's lone run scored in a fashion befitting this Series. Gene Larkin, limited to pinch-hit duties because of a knee problem, hit a bases-loaded fly ball over the drawn-in outfield for the game-winning single. As Dan Gladden trotted home, his teammates poured out of the dugout.

Morris, who grew up playing baseball on the playgrounds of Highland Park, joined Gladden halfway down the third base line and gave him an escort homeward, ensuring the outfielder stepped on the plate to make Minnesota's second world championship in five seasons official. Morris picked up Gladden as the Twins swarmed the field.

Morris, who allowed just nine baserunners, dueled John Smoltz, who pitched $7^1\backslash3$ scoreless innings before turning the game over to his bullpen.

In World Series history, only one other seventh game had been decided by a 1–0 score. That was in 1962, when Ralph Terry of the Yankees shut out the Giants. The game was the third in the Series to reach extra innings, setting a World Series record. Last night's game was also only the second seventh game to go into extra innings and the first since the 1924 Washington Senators, the forerunners of the Twins, beat the New York Giants 4–3 in 12 innings, with 36-year-old Walter Johnson pitching a complete game [*sic; it was not a complete game*].

The one-run game was the fifth of the Series. Only the 1972 Series, with six, had more. Last night marked the fifth time in the Series a team won the game in its final at-bat, the fourth time the winning run scored on the game's final pitch.

Facing a tired Alejandro Pena, Gladden led off the 10th with his third hit, a broken-bat looper that floated into the left-center field gap. Without hesitating, Gladden rounded first and dashed for second.

"I knew it was between the outfielders and it was going to bounce rather high," Gladden said. "I was just being aggressive."

Chuck Knoblauch pushed a sacrifice bunt to the right side that moved the winning run to within 90 feet of home plate. The game's biggest non-surprise was next; Kirby Puckett's second intentional walk in three innings. Kent Hrbek, 3-for-26 in the Series, was also given a free pass, loading the bases with one out and setting up the double play.

Larkin, whose only previous appearances in the Series were three pinch-hit attempts, hit a first-pitch fastball well over the head of Brian Hunter, who retreated but had no chance.

"I knew as soon as I made contact it was hit far enough to go over Hunter's head," Larkin said. "I said, 'We're champions. We're champions.' It was an unbelievable feeling."

No Game 7 in World Series history had gone as many innings without a run scoring. But it was not for lack of opportunity. The Twins mounted threats in the eighth and ninth, only to be thwarted by double plays. Morris, with the help of a decoy by Knoblauch, the rookie second baseman, somehow extricated himself from an eighth-inning jam when no exit seemed available.

Lonnie Smith led off the eighth by lining a 1-0 pitch into right field. Terry Pendleton then split Gladden in left and Puckett in center with a line drive into the gap. When Smith rounded second, it was clear the ball would not be caught and the game's first run would score.

Knoblauch gave Smith the impression that he had fielded a grounder and was throwing to Greg Gagne at second to start a double play. Smith slowed and only reached third.

Knoblauch and Gagne said the second baseman had tricked Smith, but Atlanta manager Bobby Cox insisted there was no decoy. "Why he held up," Cox said, "I don't know."

Said David Justice: "When Terry hit it and I saw where the ball was, I thought, 'Oh, yeah.' We definitely scored. Then I saw Lonnie pull up."

Smith was left at third when Morris responded with one of the gutsiest escape jobs in recent postseason history. With the infield in, Ron Gant dribbled a grounder toward first base and Hrbek, who stepped on the bag as the runners held. Kelly, Morris and catcher Brian Harper conferred on the mound and decided to walk Justice, a dangerous lefthanded hitter, to set up a double play. The Braves obliged as Sid Bream, having a Series as atrocious as Hrbek, hit a ground ball to Hrbek, who began a first-to-home-to-first inning-ending double play. Hrbek pumped his fist. Morris, crouching and screaming, pumped his several times as he danced off the mound.

"They had opportunities and we somehow got out of it," Morris said. "We had opportunities and they somehow got out of it."

Before Larkin's hit, the Twins had two hits in 38 at-bats with runners in scoring position since the end of Game 2. They had runners on the corners with one out in the eighth but Mike Stanton bailed out Smoltz when Hrbek lined into a double play. In the ninth, a single by Chili Davis, and a bunt hit by Harper created a scoring chance. But Shane Mack grounded into a double play, and after Mike Pagliarulo was walked intentionally, pinch hitter Paul Sorrento struck out.

"Tom told me I was out of the game after the ninth," Morris said. "I told him: 'I've got a lot left and tomorrow we don't play.'"

Said Kelly, "I told (pitching coach) Dick Such, 'What the heck. It's only a game.' And we sent him back out there."

Morris finished having thrown 125 pitches. He allowed seven hits and two walks, one of which was intentional.

Before the game was even an hour old, it already had a sudden-death quality about it. Both Smoltz and Morris worked 1-2-3 first innings, but neither retired the side in order again until Morris worked an easy sixth. At that point it was clear Morris was getting stronger, as he tends to do when, as Kelly says, "he smells the finish line."

Yet the question still seemed to be whether the 24-year-old Smoltz could keep up with the 36-year-old pitcher he had emulated as a teenager in Detroit.

Smoltz, who had not lost since Aug. 15, was 14-2 in the second half, and one of those losses came by a 1–0 score. Last night, Smoltz and the Braves were losers who didn't deserve to lose.

"I wish we could split the trophy in half," Kelly said. "I can't say who played better."

But it was the Twins, who took their last-to-first journey the final step, rejoicing. Nearly 30 minutes after the game, Morris led his teammates in a victory lap around the field. As the Metrodome speakers blasted "Twist and Shout," the players leaped into the air simultaneously.

In 1987, Kelly stayed in the dugout as Minnesota celebrated its first World Series victory. Last night, he joined the celebration, albeit briefly, then pumped his fist and waved his cap at the crowd as he left the field.

The on-the-field celebration scene seemed incongruous if one thinks back to January. The Twins were coming off a seventh-place finish and did not seem willing to do anything more than tinker with their existing roster. Kelly was not discussing his job security, but some of his closer friends, people like equipment manager Jim Weisner, had the feeling Kelly was very concerned about his future.

Morris was a free agent, but his chances of returning to his hometown did not seem good. And even when he put his name on a three-year contract, he probably could not have imagined this.

"This was a classic," Morris said. "Just a beautiful ballgame."

The same could have been said of the Series. And the season.

6

Selig, Fehr, and the Strike

The fuse lit with the hiring of Marvin Miller as MLBPA executive director in 1966 finally exhausted itself in September 1994, when acting commissioner Bud Selig announced to a stunned nation that he was canceling the remainder of the season and the World Series. Not even the broadcast of Ken Burns' epic documentary on baseball, or memories of the exciting postseasons of 1991 and 1993, could salve the wound caused by the interminable battle between players and owners.

The new ingredient that fueled the explosion was the successful coup against Commissioner Fay Vincent by Selig and other owners in 1992 after Vincent, in the activist tradition of Bowie Kuhn, unilaterally ordered the realignment of the NL. Enraged by two decades of losses against the players in courtrooms and arbitrators' hearings, in January 1992 the owners approved a form of revenue sharing and, more significantly, changed the definition of the commissioner's power, preventing Selig and future commissioners from exercising the "best interests" clause in many cases. Selig, in the face of outrage and ridicule from players, columnists, and congressmen, insisted that the office had been strengthened, not diminished.

The faceoff extended into 1995 and was temporarily resolved only after a federal judge ruled that the owners had illegally withheld payments to the players' pension fund and reinstituted the previous agreement. The start of the 1995 season was delayed, and the dispute was not officially resolved until a new Basic Agreement was signed in December of 1996.

65

Vincent Orders NL Realignment, Again Angers Owners (1992)

SOURCE: *Sporting News*, July 20, 1992

Commissioner Fay Vincent was widely acclaimed in the aftermath of the 1989 World Series. After that, however, he soon began to lose the support of the ownership. The first substantial backlash against Vincent came in June 1991, while the National League was deciding where to place two expansion teams. Vincent decided to compel the American League to supply players for the expansion draft, and in return awarded the AL 22 percent of the $190 million in expansion fees. Owners from both leagues were outraged, and one AL owner was quoted in a June 17, 1991, Sporting News *article as saying, "That's it. Fay Vincent is history."*

The next year was even worse for Vincent. On July 1 he threatened to suspend Yankees owner George Steinbrenner, manager Buck Showalter, and two other Yankees officials for testifying on behalf of reliever Steve Howe, who had appealed his latest suspension from baseball for cocaine abuse to Vincent. Just five days later Vincent announced his decision to realign the NL by transferring the Chicago Cubs and St. Louis Cardinals to the NL West, and moving the Atlanta Braves and Cincinnati Reds to the NL East. As logical as the transfer seemed geographically, the Cubs responded by suing Vincent—even though they were prohibited from doing so by the Major League Agreement—because their owners, the Tribune Company, feared losing revenue from the more-frequent West Coast telecasts of Cubs games on Tribune-owned superstation WGN. An injunction was granted, and Vincent dropped his plan. This did not satisfy Vincent's growing list of enemies.

In September 1993 both leagues announced their plans to realign the leagues into three divisions each. The Cubs got their wish and were placed in the NL Central along with the Cardinals, their traditional rivals. Another fear of the owners, interleague play, would be approved in January 1996.

A Shift in Power

Realignment Has Brought on Big Changes for Fay Vincent and the NL East
By Peter Pascarelli

Geography is the most-often mentioned argument for realigning the National League. But the unprecedented decision by baseball Commissioner Fay Vincent to send St. Louis and Chicago into the National League West and Atlanta and Cincinnati to the NL East has significance far beyond mere concerns for distances between division rivals.

By transferring the four teams, Vincent has drastically shifted the National League's balance of power to the East. Most managers and players in the league consider Cincinnati and Atlanta to be the best two teams in the league.

Meanwhile, by making the realignment decision himself, Vincent transformed what was not a burning issue into quite possibly a test case for the powers of the commissioner at one of the most critical junctures in major league baseball history.

The Chicago Cubs, who have stubbornly opposed moving to the West, have sought an injunction in federal district court to block Vincent's realignment order. And though it does not directly sue Vincent, the legal action represents another test of the commissioner's "best interest of baseball" powers at a time when some owners are openly pushing for Vincent's ouster.

The Cubs' suit contends:

- The fans will face "irreparable injury if the commissioner's unlawful action is not enjoined, because traditional team rivalries will be disrupted."
- A hardship will be placed on their fans because of the prospect of later starting times on TV (superstation WGN) and radio because of more games on the West Coast.
- Vincent's action "upsets the divisional alignment that has been in place for 23 years, since the National League divisions were first created in 1969."
- The National League's constitution forbids transferring a team to another division without the club's permission.

The complaint asks that a decision on the injunction be made by Monday so the league can draft a 1993 schedule by its July 31 deadline.

Although the Major League Agreement prohibits teams from suing the commissioner, that has not stopped owners from trying. And it should be noted that all previous lawsuits against commissioners have failed, with the most recent attempt made by George Steinbrenner in the 1980s.

Vincent's decision also underscores the continued erosion of each league's influence. And this realignment is believed by some to be the forerunner of what could be an eventual merging of the two leagues into four geographical divisions.

But regardless of what happens off the field, the NL East clearly will become the National League's power division should realignment go through. Cincinnati and Atlanta are largely young teams, and the Braves have one of the deepest farm systems in baseball. They join teams such as the New York Mets, with their financial capacity to spend for players, the young and talented Montreal Expos and the Pittsburgh Pirates, who are seeking their third consecutive NL East title.

The Cubs, meanwhile, are a middle-of-the-road club hovering near .500 with little young talent on the way. And the Cardinals, while possessing a solid young nucleus, are hardly in Atlanta's or Cincinnati's class. They join a division in which the Dodgers could face years of rebuilding, the Padres seem stalled at semi-contending status and the Astros and Giants are in limbo over their ownership. (And wouldn't it be ironic if the Giants moved to St. Petersburg, which presumably means the commissioner would institute yet another realignment for geographical reasons.)

"Things can change quickly in baseball, I realize that," Phillies General Manager

Lee Thomas said. "But today, it looks like Atlanta and Cincinnati are kind of head and shoulders above the rest of the teams.

"It means some of the rest of us are going to have to work harder. That's the first thing you think of. I mean, before this, you could see in a year or two where we could be as good as most teams in our division. But the Braves and Reds seem clearly above any of the clubs."

Phillies Manager Jim Fregosi was even more blunt. "It puts us further away. I don't think there's any question about that when you take the two best pitching staffs in one division and put them in the other.

"I don't know if this means we have to do something major. But the total package is that you want to win. And this makes that a much more difficult task."

Members of the Mets had similar thoughts. "Not to knock the Cardinals or Cubs, but our division is going to be tougher for sure now," Mets Manager Jeff Torborg said.

"In the short term, you'd have to say without diminishing the Cubs and Cardinals, that two of the stronger clubs are coming in," said Frank Cashen, the Mets' chief executive officer.

However, Dodgers Manager Tommy Lasorda had a different view. "Everyone's saying how the NL West is happy that they won't have to compete with the Reds and Braves anymore. But maybe the Reds and Braves are happy because they won't have to compete with the Dodgers."

The Dodgers-Reds rivalry has been among baseball's best for decades. Similarly, the Cubs have had a great rivalry over the past 10 years with the Mets. And Chicago and St. Louis have long traditions of rivalries with Philadelphia and Pittsburgh.

At the same time, the new lineup will create a natural rivalry between Atlanta and Florida. And Colorado has long had a number of Cardinals and Cubs fans.

Meanwhile, the political and legal ramifications of Vincent's decision could be felt for years. Already beset with opposition from a growing number of owners, Vincent did not help the situation with the realignment decision. He was sharply criticized by NL President Bill White who said, "The commissioner has jeopardized a longstanding working document, which has governed the National League for decades."

Five NL clubs—San Diego, Atlanta, Montreal, Pittsburgh and San Francisco—had requested the commissioner's involvement after the Cubs had used the veto power afforded them under the league constitution to block realignment, the debate being triggered by the addition of expansion teams in Florida and Colorado.

However, several clubs who favored realignment, did not want Vincent to overturn the league's decision-making process.

"I think we'll suffer somewhat from losing our traditional rivalries and also from the change in time scheduling, but we will go along with it because geographically and logically, it makes sense," said Fred Kuhlmann, chairman of the St. Louis Cardinals. "However, I would have preferred that our league process not be overruled."

Dodgers President Peter O'Malley hinted at taking the same legal action ultimately taken by the Cubs.

And though the outcome in the courts is uncertain, it seems clear that his handling of the realignment issue has further eroded support for Vincent.

There is also growing talk that should the courts uphold the commissioner's right to override league decisions, the historical separation of the league could be ultimately eliminated through some form of interleague play.

"The commissioner's decision poses interesting questions," Cashen said. "He has sweeping powers at a time when people are talking about realigning all of baseball."

Said one NL owner, who requested anonymity, "The leagues could be soon extinct."

There are already proposals to realign all 28 teams into geographical divisions, similar to the National Football League and National Basketball Association.

And ironically, there are more serious proposals being discussed by some owners to realign the leagues into three divisions of 5, 5, and 4 teams in order to add another rung of playoffs and hopefully attract added television revenue. Such future realignment would mean the Cubs, Cardinals, Reds and Braves would be moved again.

Left unsettled for now is what kind of schedule the NL will play next season when the league has 14 teams for the first time.

If it is the "balanced" schedule used by the American League—each team plays opponents within its division 13 times and opponents in the other division 12 times—the geography issue is meaningless. However, many owners strongly oppose the balanced schedule. And sources indicate the National League is leaning toward a "16-10" arrangement in which 16 games are played against division opponents and 10 against each of the other division's clubs.

66

Bud Selig Named Acting Commissioner After Vincent's Resignation (1992)

SOURCE: *Milwaukee Journal*, September 10, 1992

After more than a year of fending off increasingly agitated owners, Commissioner Fay Vincent confronted them at an owners' meeting in St. Louis. On September 3 they voted 18–9 to ask Vincent for his resignation. They were forced to take this action because there was no historical precedent, or an agreed-upon method, for firing a commissioner. Vincent initially refused to resign and vowed to fight for his job, hiring prominent attorney Brendan Sullivan to defend him. Just four days later, however, Vincent resigned. In his letter of resignation (quoted in his autobiography on pages 284–85), Vincent observed that "resignation—not litigation—should be my final act as commissioner 'in the best interests of baseball.'"

Vincent, and many baseball observers, did not believe that the rebellious owners had baseball's "best interests" at heart. Vincent had interfered with player-owner negotiations in the past, and with the current Basic Agreement due to expire following the 1993 season, owners wanted to be sure they were fully in control as they prepared to battle Don Fehr and the union. Bud Selig, the owner of the Milwaukee Brewers and a staunch anti-Vincent man, was chosen by the owners to become acting commissioner on September 9. He returned to Milwaukee the same day in order to watch Brewers star Robin Yount get his 3,000th career hit in front of his fans.

Selig an Easy Choice, Other Owners Declare

Werner, Bush Praise His Love for the Game, Ability to Mediate Problems

By Bob Berghaus
of The Journal Staff

San Diego Padres managing partner Tom Werner, waiting to see a historic moment on the field several hours after being a part of one off it, said he and his colleagues had an easy time deciding who was best suited to chair the baseball owners' executive council and run major league baseball until a new commissioner was named.

"As far as I was concerned the choice was Buddy, Buddy, and Buddy," Werner said, referring to Milwaukee Brewers President Bud Selig, who earlier Wednesday in St. Louis was entrusted to lead the 10-member council two days after commissioner Fay Vincent resigned under pressure.

Werner was in Milwaukee as Selig's guest to witness Robin Yount's 3000th hit, which he achieved in the seventh inning against the Cleveland Indians at County Stadium.

Werner had arrived at the park during the first inning with Selig, Texas Rangers owner George W. Bush and American League President Bobby Brown, after the historic meeting in St. Louis at which Selig became the first owner to assume the duties of the commissioner, just another of several hats he'll wear in "the best interests of baseball."

"There's not a man I think who cares more for the sport than Buddy does," Werner said. "I think his agenda is what's best for the game. I don't think he has a private agenda."

Selig tried to downplay his rise to the top of the baseball world at a news conference during the game, stressing that all members of the executive council would be involved in major decisions. Selig, though, does have authority to act on behalf of the council.

HIS WORKLOAD INCREASES

Selig also said he was not interested in the job permanently.

"I love what I'm doing here," he said, referring to the Brewers. "My heart lies here. It always has and always will."

By taking the position the 58-year-old Selig increased his workload significantly. As president of the Brewers he is in the middle of a drive to try to build a new stadium, for which the team plans to provide the majority of the cost. As for his other endeavors, Selig is heavily involved in several projects for the owners. He is chairman of the Player Relations Committee, the owners' negotiating arm and also is a member of the ownership committee. Selig also is co-chairman of the economic study group.

"There will be some demands on my time but it's something that I'm not overly concerned about," he said. "There is no timetable. Hopefully, it will be relatively short-lived."

Selig, stressing that the executive council will make all decisions that need to be made while he serves as chairman, could be involved in several key issues during the next few months. Among those are Vincent's proposed realignment of the National League; the possible move of the San Francisco Giants to St. Petersburg, Fla.; negotiating for a new television contract; and the chance of reopening the current collective bargaining agreement with the Major League Baseball Players Association before the Dec. 11 deadline.

There has been speculation that the owners may want to reopen the agreement and lock out the players as they did in 1990, to force concessions on free agency and salary levels. Vincent interceded that year and the lockout ended long before the owners would have liked. Because of his involvement last time, Vincent's opponents, of which Selig was one, feared a similar move by him and thus began applying pressure that eventually led to his resignation.

Selig insisted Wednesday night that the owners were not planning a lockout.

SAILING INTO UNCHARTED WATERS

"I've read (about) people who have said that all of these events sequence up to where we want to take a hard-line position," Selig said. "I don't understand the logic of that, frankly, but I don't have any further comment."

He couldn't give a timetable for naming a replacement for Vincent, nor would he discuss candidates.

"There is no prototype," he said. "It depends on what you're looking for. It depends on the candidates. I don't know. We're dealing in uncharted waters. I can't predict a time. The restructuring committee meets (Thursday)."

That committee will most likely come up with new duties for the commissioner that would take away much of his previous power and make him an executive officer who would report only to the owners.

The list of candidates includes Ron Brown, chairman of the Democratic National Committee; Richard Ravitch, president of the Player Relations Committee; Harvey Schiller, executive director of the U.S. Olympic Committee; Neal Pilson, president of CBS Sports; Paul Beeston, chief executive officer of the Toronto Blue Jays; Richard White, executive director of Major League Properties; and several general managers.

Selig also said deputy commissioner Steve Greenberg would stay on in charge of day-to-day operations in baseball's New York office. Selig said he would spend the majority of his time working in Milwaukee.

"We have to face all the issues and deal with them and what's good for all 28 of us. 28 franchises, 28 votes," Selig said. "There are a myriad of issues."

67

Owners Vote to Reopen Labor Negotiations

Early (1992)

SOURCE: *Louisville Courier-Journal*, December 8, 1992

According to the terms of the 1990–93 Basic Agreement, either the owners or the players had the right to start negotiating a new pact by informing the other side by December 11. The owners voted on December 7 to take that action during a meeting in Louisville. By re-opening the agreement ahead of schedule the owners obtained the right to force the play-ers' hand by locking the players out of spring training, but also gave the players the option of striking during the season. With no full-time commissioner in place, many felt that an-other interruption of the baseball season was unavoidable.

BASEBALL WINTER MEETINGS

Owners Reopen Labor Agreement; Lockout Possible

By George Rorrer
Staff Writer

Baseball owners voted 15–13 yesterday at the Galt House to reopen their labor agreement with the players' union a year earlier than scheduled, raising the likeli-hood of a work stoppage next season—the game's eighth in 22 years.

During a four-hour meeting, owners also voted unanimously to require a 75 per-cent vote in order to lock out players in the future. In 1990, owners locked out the players for 32 days before a collective bargaining agreement was signed.

"We are not seeking a confrontation," said Richard Ravitch, management's chief negotiator. "We would like to make some changes in the player compensa-tion system."

Ravitch said the owners want to begin negotiations immediately, but union pres-ident Donald Fehr said he wasn't sure when his group would be ready to start talks and wouldn't predict whether games would be halted yet again.

"History is not with us," he said. "Let us hope history is not a guide this time."

"But the fact the step had been taken makes a confrontation possible when oth-erwise there might not have been."

Ravitch said the current contract will be in force until Jan. 11, 1993, and it will recognize the basic format that determines compensation levels: players with six years' experience are eligible for free agency; those with three to six years are eligible for salary arbitration.

"There was a concern on the part of the owners that if they did not begin talking now, they would have no chance of affecting the economics of the 1994 season," Ravitch said.

Ravitch said he wants to negotiate "rationally, quietly and constructively," but he admitted a lockout is a legal option.

"I can only say that I hope and expect these negotiations will begin and proceed in absolutely good faith and produce constructive results in a manner that will not interfere with the 1993 season in any way," he said.

Fehr isn't sure that can happen. "I was approached with the suggestion that there wouldn't be a reopening," he said, "but that there would be a discussion of the problems over the summer as a gesture of good faith. I never heard back.

"What has to happen now is that the players will have to consider what position they're going to take, and what they will want from the negotiations."

By reopening the basic agreement, management not only gave itself the chance to lock out players but gave the union a chance to strike late in the season, when it can threaten large television payments from CBS.

"Sooner or later in the process, people have the tendency to set deadlines," Fehr said.

" . . . There are scenarios where the owners can put the players in a box."

Baseball was interrupted by strikes in 1972, '80, '81 and '85. Owners locked out the players in 1973, '76 and '90.

Ravitch listed reasons a lockout or strike will not take place.

"In the 1980s there was a period of ascending revenues and ascending optimism," he said. "Now there are real cares out there—TV contracts, decreasing attendance, concerns about the game, the public's attitude about it, the elasticity of the prices of concessions and tickets.

"There are problems with the distribution of the gross revenues among the various groups of players."

Fehr agreed that there are problems. "This has been an 18-month period which has seen an unusual amount of turmoil," he said, citing the sale of the Seattle Mariners to Japanese ownership, the rejection of a proposal to move the San Francisco Giants to Florida, a court fight over National League realignment, the forced resignation of commissioner Fay Vincent and the Marge Schott racial issue.

"Baseball needs another controversy like it needs another bullet in the head. . . . I thought this would be a year when people would try to make certain there was no confrontation."

Ravitch said he didn't think the closeness of the vote would give players reason to think management's bargaining position will collapse.

"There was no unanimity, obviously, so I can't speak for everyone collectively," he said, later adding: "I think owners are behind me 100 percent in my effort to achieve the bargaining objectives we have discussed."

Large-city clubs, led by the New York Mets, generally opposed reopening the agreement because they are profitable in almost all years. Mets co-owner Fred Wilpon even sent clubs a letter with reasons not to reopen.

The smaller clubs were in favor of the reopener and were joined by the Los Angeles Dodgers and Philadelphia Phillies, among others.

"It would be an easier task if all 28 clubs were of the same point of view," Ravitch said. "I can't deny that."

Fehr said the players must decide if they are willing to believe management's claims of financial hardship before they can accept such proposals as salary caps.

"We have long noticed and pointed out the disconnection between how the owners behave and what they say," he said, referring to the continued free spending on free agents.

68

Congressional Testimony Regarding the Resignation of Fay Vincent (1992)

SOURCE: Senate Subcommittee on Antitrust, Monopolies, and Business Rights, *The Validity of Major League Baseball's Exemption from the Antitrust Laws*, 102nd Cong., 2nd sess., December 10, 1992, 36–39, 105, 116–18

During a congressional hearing focusing on franchise relocation—an issue of significance to senators who wanted to attract teams or prevent teams from moving to a new city— former commissioner Vincent and current acting commissioner Selig testified on a variety of subjects related to relocation. Printed here are excerpts from each man's official opening statement dealing with the role of the commissioner as a businessman, baseball's antitrust exemption, and the still-controversial resignation of Vincent as commissioner.

STATEMENT BY FORMER COMMISSIONER FAY VINCENT

One of the major issues in baseball is whether baseball is or should view itself as anything other than a business like any other business.

When I was being attacked by certain owners, I was told that they wanted the Commissioner to be their Commissioner. They did not agree that the Commissioner should have any obligation to the public or to represent any other interests than the interests of the owners. One owner said the players had their union leader as did the umpires but no one represented the owners' interests.

Another view widely held by owners is that baseball should be run like any major corporation. The CEO or Commissioner should report to the owners who would be able to fire the Commissioner as the CEO in the corporate world can be fired.

The corporate analogy has great appeal to owners who have difficulty accepting or understanding why baseball is such a difficult enterprise. Thus, there is within baseball a major debate taking place over how baseball is to see itself, and what obligations, if any, baseball has to the public. My confidence in the wisdom of the resolution of this debate is well under control.

CONCLUSION:

It is my view that:

1. The existing antitrust exemption for Major League Baseball should be retained only so long as baseball can persuade you that it is a unique institution with special public interest obligations and not merely another business.

2. To the extent Major League Baseball acknowledges that the exemption is only justified by continuing recognition that baseball is a national trust—with obligations to this Congress and to the public that are not carried by ordinary businesses—the exemption should be continued and the performance of baseball closely monitored.

3. If the owners of baseball continue on their stated course of making baseball into their business and at the same time insist that the Commissioner is their CEO to be fired at will, I would no longer support the preservation of the exemption. If the exemption is to be surrendered let it be by the action of the owners. Only a strong Commissioner acting in the interests of baseball, and therefore the public, can protect the institution from the selfish and myopic attitudes of owners. . . .

STATEMENT OF ALLAN H. SELIG, PRESIDENT OF THE MILWAUKEE BREWERS BASEBALL CLUB

Mr. Chairman, I am pleased to appear before the Subcommittee today on behalf of Major League Baseball. For the last 23 years I have been the President and Chief Executive Officer of the Milwaukee Brewers Baseball Club. I currently serve in the position of Chairman of Baseball's Executive Council. The Executive Council consists of myself, eight other Club owners (four from each League) and the two League presidents. Baseball's governing documents provided that during a vacancy in the Office of the Commissioner all of the powers and duties of the Commissioner shall be exercised by the Executive Council. Those powers and duties include, of course, the Commissioner's authority to act "in the best interests" of Baseball. . . .

THE RESIGNATION OF FAY VINCENT AND
THE FUTURE GOVERNANCE OF BASEBALL

Some members of the Subcommittee have expressed concern over Fay Vincent's departure and what that departure means for the future of Baseball's Office of the Commissioner. Let me first say that the owners did not summarily dismiss Mr. Vincent for protecting the best interests of the Game and the public. When Mr. Vincent took office, he acknowledged that if he ever lost the confidence of a majority of the owners, he would resign. While Mr. Vincent had the full support of the owners when he took office under very difficult circumstances after the death of Bart Giamatti, he gradually lost that support. By September, 1992, 18 teams requested his resignation. Since he needed a majority of the Clubs to be re-elected to a second term, and since the decision on a second term could have been made as early as January 1993, Mr. Vincent recognized that he had become a lame duck Commissioner and that he had lost the confidence of two-thirds of the teams. As a result, he honored his initial pledge and resigned.

I cannot speak for all of the teams which lost confidence in Fay Vincent. Many Clubs had many reasons. However, perhaps the most commonly articulated concern was his inability to develop a consensus among the owners on the vital issues that face the Game today. Rather than pulling together under his leadership, the teams were drawing further and further apart, and were advancing their parochial interests. In the opinion of an overwhelming majority of the Clubs, Mr. Vincent was simply not the person to lead Baseball during what they all realized would be a very difficult and challenging period. Since his departure, we have appointed a restructuring committee which is hard at work and we are attempting to face the difficult issues and build consensus. It does not help the Game to have numerous teams for sale and to have teams on the verge of bankruptcy. Nor will it help if eventually only a few teams can afford all of the top players; fans will soon lose interest.

The Executive Council is now exercising the powers of the Commissioner's Office, including its "best interests" powers. Moreover, although the restructuring committee has not yet completed its work, I can say that there will still be a Commissioner who will continue to have strong powers to protect the integrity of the Game. There is in my view no reason to change the current laws to do something more.

69

Reds' Owner Marge Schott Punished for Racial Remarks (1993)

SOURCE: *Cincinnati Enquirer*, February 4, 1993

Marge Schott, a prominent auto dealership owner in Cincinnati, bought a controlling interest in the Cincinnati Reds in 1984 and was named president and CEO of the club the following year. Almost from the start she earned a reputation as a cantankerous, frugal woman with little feel for baseball or public relations. Her antics included allowing her beloved dogs, Schottzie I and II, onto the field, where they occasionally left deposits behind. By the early 1990s it became known that Schott frequently used racial and ethnic epithets in private, which she reinforced by occasionally using them in print and television interviews. Given baseball's poor record in hiring minorities as managers and executives, and with the Al Campanis incident still fresh in people's minds, Schott's comments required a rapid and firm response from the major leagues.

Excerpted below is the official opinion of baseball's Executive Council on its investigation of Schott. She was fined $25,000 and asked to relinquish control of the Reds for a year (she was reinstated in November). Schott did not learn her lesson—despite mandatory sensitivity courses—and in 1996 continued her verbal assault on minorities. In June 1996 she was ordered to give up her role with the Reds until the end of the 1998 season. Schott sold her stock in the Reds in September 1999, and she died in 2005.

Baseball: "Appropriate Remedy and Punishment"

Opinion of the Executive Council on suspending Reds President and CEO Marge Schott:

On December 1, 1992, the Executive Council of Major League Baseball instituted an investigation of Mrs. Marge Schott, the principal owner and general partner of the Cincinnati Reds baseball club, concerning allegations that Mrs. Schott engaged in conduct not in the best interest of baseball in violation of the Major League Agreement and Major League Rule 21. This investigation has focused on whether Mrs. Schott commonly and publicly conducted herself in a manner that is racially and ethnically offensive, while serving as a principal owner and employee of the Cincinnati Club. . . .

There is, for example, substantial and convincing evidence that Mrs. Schott frequently used the term "nigger" in the presence of Club employees when referring to African Americans in general and certain Cincinnati players in particular. There is also substantial and convincing evidence that Mrs. Schott has used the term in the public presence of persons with whom she had no prior contact. Two witnesses (one a policeman), neither of whom had met Mrs. Schott before, stated that Mrs. Schott had used the word in their presence while Mrs. Schott sat in her box at Riverfront Stadium during baseball games.

The Executive Council is aware of Mrs. Schott's assertions that she used the term "nigger" infrequently, or as a joking term, or as a result of generational difference, as well as the testimony of certain Reds' employees that they never heard her use this term. The totality of the evidence, however, overwhelmingly and convincingly supports the conclusion that Mrs. Schott frequently and repeatedly used terms such as "nigger," "lazy nigger," "damn nigger" and "dumb, lazy nigger," often while addressing employees of the Club. In this respect the Council notes when questioned by the Executive Council at the hearing, Mrs. Schott testified that she could not "recall things that went on 10 years ago, five years ago, two years ago or one year ago."

Substantial evidence was also obtained that Mrs. Schott has frequently referred to people of the Jewish faith in a derogatory manner, calling people of that faith "Jew bastards" and "dirty Jews" and stating that "Hitler had the right idea for them, but went too far." Finally, evidence was also obtained demonstrating that Mrs. Schott commonly referred to people of Japanese origin as "Japs."

Mrs. Schott has urged that her insensitive language was private free speech and therefore that the Council should not act against it. The witnesses, by and large, were employees of the Club and subjected to this language during their Baseball employment. And in at least two instances offensive language was used in a public location to strangers, in her box at Riverfront Stadium.

Mrs. Schott has also urged that "racial and other slurs are frequently used in a variety of baseball settings." We do not believe this is the case. In addition, Mrs. Schott's remarks reflect the most base and demeaning type of racial and ethnic stereotyping and many were made about players the Club had under contract, thereby indicating an insensitivity that cannot be accepted or tolerated by anyone in our industry or in society in general. . . .

70

"A Wild, Wacky Ride": Toronto 15, Philadelphia 14 (1993)

SOURCE: *Philadelphia Inquirer*, October 21, 1993

The 1993 World Series matched the defending champion Toronto Blue Jays and the upstart Philadelphia Phillies, a scruffy, blue-collar team that, like the Atlanta Braves and Minnesota Twins two years earlier, leapt from last place the previous season to the pennant the following year. Toronto arrived in Philadelphia with a two-games-to-one lead. The fourth game of the Series turned out to be one of the ugliest, craziest games in baseball history, as no pitchers on either side could consistently throw strikes or register outs. The game peaked in the eighth inning, when the Phillies' star reliever, Mitch "Wild Thing" Williams, surrendered five runs and his club's 14–10 lead.

Incredibly, this would not be Williams's lowest moment of the Series. Following a courageous 2–0 shutout in Game 5 by Philadelphia's Curt Schilling, the Series moved to Toronto. The Phillies entered the ninth inning with a 6–5 lead, only to see Williams lose the game on a spectacular Series-winning two-run home run by Joe Carter. Williams retired after the game. A complete box score and play-by-play account can be found at www.retrosheet.org.

Jayson Stark, the author of the article below, is one of the most colorful baseball reporters of the modern era. His passion for the oddities of baseball and for obscure statistics made him the ideal candidate to chronicle such a bizarre game.

A Wild, Wacky Ride as Phils Make It Their Kind of Game

Bad Pitching, Lots of Hitting, Unbelievable Statistics
By Jayson Stark
Inquirer Staff Writer

You want pitcher's duels and defensive epics? Sorry. You've got the wrong team.

You want clean, pristine baseball games that go zipping by in an hour and 54 minutes? Sorry. You've got the wrong team.

You want baseball the way it was designed in some manual by Branch Rickey? Forget it. You've got the wrong team.

This is the year the Phillies invited themselves to the World Series party. So hide the valuables. Cover up the chandeliers. This ain't gonna be pretty. As last night's rumblin', bumblin', stumblin' 15–14 loss to the Blue Jays proved conclusively.

Yes, the World Series found itself mixed up in an ultimate Phillies game last night. And if there were pockets of North America that weren't too sure what that entailed before, they know now.

It was a game that threatened to last until *Sunrise Semester* came on the air around dawn.

It was a game in which you couldn't even remember who the starting pitchers were by the fourth inning.

It was a game in which no lead, no ERA and no line in the record book was safe.

It started with two starting pitchers—Tommy Greene and Mel Stottlemyre's kid, Todd—who couldn't throw a strike.

It ended with Mitch Williams blowing a four-run lead to finish off the longest, highest-scoring World Series game of all time.

In the beginning, there were 62,000 people covering their heads to keep out of the rain. In the end, there were 62,000 people covering their heads to keep from watching the Wild Thing.

And in between, it was one of the most amazing postseason carnival rides ever witnessed.

Let us just begin to count the highlights and lowlights:

It was a night when the close relatives of the two starting pitchers had to hope they didn't get caught in traffic. Or else they were going to find themselves watching Al Leiter and Roger Mason. Fittingly, Greene and Stottlemyre managed to make their grand exits simultaneously. There was only one out in the top of the third inning at the time.

The last time both team's starters failed to make it through three innings in a World Series game was Game 1, 1966—the Orioles' Dave McNally versus the Dodgers' Don Drysdale. McNally gave up two runs that day. Nobody else on his team gave up any for the entire World Series. It didn't quite work out that way last night.

Two starts ago, in Game 2 of the playoffs against the Braves, Greene had such a rough night, people were debating whether he might have had the worst postseason start by any Phillie ever—2 1/3 innings, 7 hits, 7 runs. Last night, he managed to match that nifty line, column for column—2 1/3 innings, 7 hits, 7 runs. Try that on your Nintendo control panel sometime.

Stottlemyre made history of his own. No pitcher had ever gone out there and walked four hitters in the first inning of any World Series game ever until he showed up. One has now. Obviously, when the good mayor, Ed Rendell, talked about trying to get some swings against this guy, he was just another conscientious politician, making a promise he knew he could keep.

In their brief tenures, the two starters pooled together to give up 10 hits, 8 walks and 13 runs. They ran almost as many three-ball counts (12) as they got outs (13). And they just about did the impossible: they threw more balls (62) than strikes (57). So read your box score carefully this morning. It might explode.

Thanks to the efforts of Greene and Stottlemyre, among other people, this game moved along like a trash truck with four flat tires.

The first three innings of Game 4 of this World Series lasted 1 hour, 36 minutes. Just to put that in perspective, all *nine* innings of Game 4 of the first World Series—in 1903—lasted 1 hour, 30 minutes. Of course, there were fewer commercials back then. And possibly several more strikes.

When's the last time you saw each team blow a three-run lead in a World Series game? It happened in this game before the top of the third inning was even over. The Blue Jays led, 3–0, in the first inning. That lead lasted seven hitters. The Phillies led, 6–3, in the second inning. That lead lasted eight hitters. It was that kind of night.

Then there was the triumphant homecoming of Toronto's Leiter, a guy who spent many a happy hour cheering on those Phillies in his youth in Toms River, N.J. The folks from Toms River spent a few minutes last night cheering him as he got five straight outs. Of the next 11 hitters he faced, eight of them got on, two of them dispensed souvenirs for the paying customers in the right-field seats, and six of them scored.

Only in a game like this could David West get a standing ovation—just for getting an out. But he deserved it. He had to stalk into four World Series games over three years and face 11 hitters to get one. But he finally got Joe Carter to fly to right for the first out in the sixth inning last night—and lowered his World Series ERA from infinity to 162.00.

He was all the way down to 63.00 by the time his stint was through. And when's the last time a guy lowered his ERA by almost 100 points in one inning?

But that was just the half of it.

There was Lenny Dykstra, passing Joe DiMaggio—Joe DiMaggio?—on the all-time postseason home run list, by swatting Nos. 8 and 9 in a mere 109 at-bats.

There was Cito Gaston, dialing the wrong number on his bullpen phone and calling in the wrong relief pitcher in the fifth inning. He was the most shocked guy in the park when Mark Eichhorn arrived at the mound—since he was expecting Tony Castillo, who hadn't even warmed up yet.

Later there was Gaston allowing Castillo to hit for himself in the seventh inning. With his team down four runs. And nobody out. But in a game in which Greene and Leiter got hits and Stottlemyre got a bloody nose in his spectacular base-running debut, why the heck not?

And finally, of course, there was the Wild Thing—a guy Darren Daulton once called "the perfect ending to the perfect nightmare." Williams got a standing O when he headed for the bullpen in the sixth inning. He got a slightly different reception after he let a 14–10 lead expire in the eighth.

But no Phillies game—win or lose—would be complete without him, whether it's March or May or October. And the big question now is: After a game like this can the World Series ever be known as the, ahem, Fall Classic again?

71

Revenue-Sharing Plan Passed by Owners (1994)

SOURCE: *Baltimore Sun*, January 19, 1994

After months of conflict between owners of high-income clubs and owners of low-income clubs over the issue of revenue sharing, an agreement was reached in a Fort Lauderdale owners' meeting. The owners voted unanimously to create three groups of teams—high-, middle-, and low-revenue teams. Teams in the high-revenue group would contribute specified amounts of money to be redistributed to teams in the low-revenue group. Franchises in the middle group would neither contribute nor receive money from the pool. A similar plan with two groups of clubs was devised by Player Relations Committee president Richard Ravitch, but was rejected in August of 1993 and again earlier in January.

Teams in the lower economic bracket, who would receive less money than they wanted from the plan, approved the plan only on the condition that the players agree to a salary cap of some kind—a highly unlikely scenario, as all the owners knew.

Revenue Deal OK'd by Owners

Selig Calls 28–0 Vote "Remarkable, Historic"
By Pete Schmuck
Staff Writer

FORT LAUDERDALE, Fla.—The 28 major-league owners finally took the first step toward the economic restructuring of baseball last night when they ended a lengthy stalemate and agreed unanimously on a plan to redistribute revenue.

The long-awaited revenue-sharing plan is designed to help struggling small-market teams remain competitive in the face of spiraling costs and dwindling receipts, but the issue had taken on even greater significance as it divided the owners into big-revenue and small-revenue factions and delayed the start of collective bargaining with the Major League Baseball Players Association.

"In my judgment, this has been a remarkable and historic day," said acting commissioner Bud Selig. "The major-league clubs passed a unique and historic revenue-sharing plan, 28–0. Tonight was the result of thousands of hours of negotiations with Dick Ravitch and the Player Relations Committee—and many owners participated in a historic and meaningful revenue-sharing plan."

The owners would not release details of the plan, but it appeared to be a compromise between the modified PRC plan that came up one vote short of approval two weeks ago in Chicago and a large-revenue-team plan that garnered only 11 votes at that meeting. Somehow, Ravitch came away with a unanimous vote on an issue that had held the game hostage for several months.

"I think it is critically important that it was passed by a 28–0 vote," said Ravitch, "because it means all the teams have the same commitment and objective—to redistribute revenue between the clubs, maintain competitive balance and put the owners in a position to proffer to the owners an economic partnership that includes a salary cap. If there was not an agreement, we could not make that proposal."

The way Ravitch sees it, the plan will allow the most economically disadvantaged teams to draw on a pool of money contributed by the richest clubs, the formula based upon economic factors that will be re-evaluated annually. That means that a team that paid into the fund one year conceivably could draw on it the next.

"This plan is revenue and expense specific, not team specific," Ravitch said, "and it will be applied annually. It is not an agreement in which club X will pay. Clubs whose profiles meet certain characteristics are eligible to receive funds and other clubs that meet certain economic characteristics pay in."

No dollar figures were discussed, but the total pool is expected to be between $50 million and $60 million per year when—and if—the plan is fully in effect.

The Orioles almost certainly would be one of the teams required to contribute heavily to the fund.

Of course, revenue sharing is only half the battle. The owners only agreed to pursue a sharing accord because they viewed it as the first step toward a revenue-based salary cap. The decision to redistribute their income was made unilaterally, but the imposition of a salary cap will not be possible without the cooperation of the players association.

"This agreement will take effect when we get a Basic Agreement with a salary cap ingredient," Ravitch said. "It will last at least as long as the Basic Agreement and will transfer enough money to the small-market clubs so that every club will be financially able to meet the obligation to the players . . . because any cap also will have a salary floor."

There have been no assurances from the union that the players will be amenable to any ownership proposal that limits salaries, but Ravitch finally is in a position to create a specific agenda for full-scale negotiations on a new labor contract.

It also moves the owners and players a large step closer to another labor showdown, though both sides have agreed to keep the terms of the recently expired Basic Agreement in place through Opening Day.

Players association director Donald Fehr did not exactly join the owners in the round of applause they gave themselves after the agreement. He said from his New York home he has yet to see evidence of any economic partnership.

"I don't really have a reaction," he said. "It took Dick (Ravitch) a long time and he's entitled to a big raise. He has deliberately kept us in the dark and excluded us from this process. At some point, if he cares, I suppose they'll let us in on the details."

Fehr has long maintained that the union doesn't care how the owners distribute revenue, and he said nothing last night to indicate a willingness to cooperate on a salary cap.

"We didn't care as long as it didn't adversely affect the free market," Fehr said. "Now, they want the union's cooperation in adversely affecting the market. That's what a salary cap is."

If the agreement doesn't guarantee cooperation from the players union, it does leave the owners free to grapple with the issue that originally was expected to headline this meeting. The committee charged with presenting a candidate is expected to meet with baseball's Executive Council today to continue discussing possible candidates for the long-vacant commissioner role.

If they can agree on a candidate, then the Executive Council would likely present it to the full ownership later in the day for discussion and a possible vote. However, it seems unlikely that the process will move along that quickly.

In fact, speculation remains strong that the commissionership will remain under the custodial care of Selig, even though that might not meet with the approval of a congressional committee examining baseball's antitrust exemption.

Selig continues to insist that he does not want the job, but the lack of progress during Monday night's seven-hour Executive Council session only made it seem more likely he'll be asked to stay on.

One member of the Executive Council said yesterday that the discussion on Monday night never focused on a single "strong" candidate, though search committee chairman Bill Bartholomay had promised that a recommendation would be made. If that is true, it seems highly unlikely that the search for a commissioner can be concluded during the final scheduled day of meetings today.

Ravitch, however, indicated a lot could be accomplished today. He said last night that the owners would approve a resolution that would end all of the infighting over local television revenues and probably would address a restructuring plan that redefines the role of commissioner.

72

Selig, Fehr Testify on Redefined Powers of Commissioner's Office (1994)

SOURCE: Senate Subcommittee on Antitrust, Monopolies and Business Rights, *Professional Baseball Teams and the Antitrust Laws*, 103rd Cong., 2nd sess., March 21, 1994, St. Petersburg, Florida, 28–31, 56–59

The owners continued to meet and make major changes in the Major League Agreement following their agreement on revenue sharing. On January 19 they voted to give future commissioners full power to oversee negotiations with the MLBPA, and to require a 75 percent vote to approve labor contracts. Even more dramatically, the owners removed the commissioner's power to act in the "best interests of baseball" with regard to labor ne-gotiations. To the astonishment of many, the owners and acting commissioner Bud Selig maintained that they had strengthened the commissioner's powers by more clearly de-lineating them. MLBPA executive director Donald Fehr was not alone when he attacked this allegation, claiming that the owners' real intention was to weaken the office of the commissioner and make him a pawn of the owners. Fehr was joined by Senator Howard Metzenbaum, who in a subcommittee hearing said in response to Selig's argument about the commissioner's enhanced authority, "I say 'BS' to that."

Below are excerpts from the statements of Bud Selig and Don Fehr (respectively) on this issue.

I. BASEBALL'S RESTRUCTURING REPORT
AND THE COMMISSIONER'S POWERS

In January, 1994, the Major League baseball clubs voted to approve a small number of changes to the Major League Agreement, which sets out the fundamental understanding among the twenty-eight clubs with respect to how decisions will be made in baseball and how the game will be governed. Among many items, this basic charter established the Office of the Commissioner and provides certain powers to the Commissioner. After more than seventy years, baseball's governing document needed to be updated and clarified and the changes were overdue. The changes that were made strengthen the power and independence of the Commissioner. The chang-es contained in the adopted Restructuring Report guarantee every decision made by the Major League clubs and their owners will be in accordance with the highest standards of public confidence and integrity the millions and millions of baseball fans have come to expect from those who oversee our national pastime. . . .

Historically, the Commissioner of baseball has frequently—and correctly— referred to as having very broad powers to act under the Major League Agreement in the "best interests of baseball." In practice, however, these powers were infrequent-ly exercised and, especially in recent years, were uncertain in scope. For example, in 1992, Commissioner Vincent attempted to exercise the best interests powers to move the Chicago Cubs from the National League Eastern Division to the West-ern Division, notwithstanding a vote by the National League clubs, properly taken under the National League Constitution, that preserved the status quo. Although Commissioner Vincent may have believed he was doing what was best for baseball, a federal judge quickly told him he had no such power to act.

When baseball's Restructuring Committee was formed shortly after Fay Vincent's resignation to examine the entire area of the Commissioner's powers, it became clear that there were widely differing opinions as to how far the best interest powers ex-tended. While some thought they were extraordinarily broad, others thought that in any area specifically reserved for club voting, the Commissioner could not exercise best interest powers even in situations implicating the integrity of or public confi-dence in the game. Those holding that opinion felt that when a matter was specified for a club vote under the Major League Agreement or a League Constitution, the

Commissioner's best interest powers were inapplicable. The recent Chicago Cubs federal court opinion was used as authority for this view.

The overriding principle in the Restructuring Committee deliberations, however, was to make it clear that in all matters (with the exception of collective bargaining) that implicate the integrity of baseball or the public confidence in the game, business or otherwise, the Commissioner can exercise best interests powers to act, even if an action is taken by club vote under the Major League Agreement or League Constitution. As a result, depending on one's interpretation of the Commissioner's powers prior to restructuring, the Commissioner's best interests powers in January were either clarified, restored or augmented—but they clearly were not weakened. Those who have expressed concerns about the Commissioner no longer having the power to protect the public or to protect baseball's integrity should note that the Major League Agreement section setting out the Commissioner's powers never even mentioned the words "integrity" or "public confidence" until these modifications were made in January.

The uncertainties embedded in the Major League Agreement have hindered baseball's ability to move forward constructively in certain critical areas such as collective bargaining with the players. Of course, there was no Players Association, or even a federal collective bargaining law, in 1920 when the Commissioner's authority was first delineated. Our nearly 30-year history of collective bargaining with the Players Association reveals that the Commissioner's undefined and uncertain role in that process has repeatedly stalled and impeded productive discourse between the clubs and the players. The Players Association it seemed would negotiate with the clubs on the assumption there was another step available in the process—convincing the Commissioner to step in to make even more generous proposals or to force the clubs to abandon a negotiating stance not favored by the players. Baseball's fans have borne the brunt of the "crisis" bargaining that resulted because they have had to endure several unnecessary work stoppages.

Rather than exclude the Commissioner from labor relations with the players as most predicted the owners would, the clubs gave the Commissioner the responsibility to carry out the labor relations policies of the clubs. Since the clubs are the statutory employers of the players under the federal labor laws, baseball was mandated to place ultimate collective bargaining responsibility with the clubs. However, the Commissioner will be responsible for directing all future collective bargaining talks. Given the paramount role that our collective bargaining agreement with the Players Association plays in the overall economics of the game, this new responsibility will greatly enhance the Commissioner's power and influence over the direction of the industry. Moreover, with the Commissioner directing the clubs' collective bargaining efforts from the start, the delays and unnecessary work stoppages that have marked previous negotiations will hopefully be eliminated. This will be an enormous benefit to our fans.

Finally, for the first time, the League presidents cannot be elected without the direct approval of the Commissioner. Previously, the election of League presidents was the exclusive prerogative of each League's member clubs. Moreover, the Commissioner will have more direct authority over the League presidents and some functions formerly carried out by the League offices. Overall, restructuring has clearly and unambiguously centralized the administration of the business of baseball within the Office of the Commissioner.

Far from diluting the powers of the Commissioner, the long overdue restructuring plan recently approved by the clubs will preserve and strengthen the power and independence of the Commissioner. In the Commissioner's primary role of protecting the integrity of and public confidence in the national game of baseball, the Commissioner's power is now complete and unambiguous. Further, restructuring has given the Commissioner increased authority and responsibility to orchestrate baseball's centralized business operations, including the all-important collective bargaining with the players. These changes, I am confident, will enable the next Commissioner both to maintain baseball's status as a sport of unquestioned integrity and honesty and to take the game boldly into the 21st century as a thriving entertainment product that remains affordable and accessible to the great majority of fans. As such, the owners of Major League baseball clubs have again recognized that we have an obligation to the game of baseball and to its many, many wonderful fans that goes far beyond our own economic interests.

II. THE SELECTION OF A NEW COMMISSIONER

One of the first acts which I took as Chairman of the Executive Council when Fay Vincent resigned in September 1992, was to appoint a search committee for a new Commissioner. That Committee is chaired by William Bartholomay, the Chairman of the Atlanta Braves. The Committee's membership includes members of the Executive Council and the Co-Chairmen of Baseball's Restructuring Committee. In addition, I served as an ex-officio member since I had chaired the last two search committees for baseball. The Committee almost immediately hired an independent executive search firm and began its work in earnest. . . .

Over the sixteen months of its operation leading to the Major League meetings in Fort Lauderdale in January 1994, the Search Committee considered more than 380 candidates of extremely diverse backgrounds. There were scores of meetings and every member of the Committee interviewed numerous potential candidates in attempting to get down to a final group. The Chairman of the Committee alone interviewed 46 candidates.

The Search Committee came to the ownership meetings in Fort Lauderdale in January 1994 prepared to review finalists with the Executive Council and make a recommendation to the Executive Council and to the ownership. At that meeting, however, several owners raised concerns that the election of a Commissioner at this critical juncture was destined to doom that candidate to ultimate failure. This large group of owners raised those concerns at the meeting of all the clubs which followed our historic revenue sharing agreement. After a full and frank discussion in which all sides of the matter were discussed and at which virtually every owner spoke to express his or her opinion, the clubs requested that I continue as the Chairman of the Executive Council and that no candidate for Commissioner be presented for election at this time. I have stated from the time of my election as Chairman of the Executive Council and have repeated for the entire eighteen months I am not a candidate to be Commissioner and am not interested in serving as Commissioner. I can unequivocally state that remains my unwavering position.

The concerns expressed by the clubs were two-fold. First, the Restructuring Report which was approved provided that the Commissioner would be the head of all future collective bargaining negotiations with the Players Association. Major League Baseball hired Richard Ravitch to be its chief negotiator almost two years ago. He has worked diligently and industriously since that time to develop a collective bargaining strategy and to commence discussions with the Players Association in anticipation of reaching a new collective bargaining agreement with the players as soon as possible. To bring a new Commissioner into that environment and charge him or her with the responsibility for conducting labor negotiations would create confusion and ambiguity with regard to the role of Mr. Ravitch and would inevitably involve the insertion of a new person's style into a process which is now two years down the road.

On the other hand, if a new Commissioner were to be appointed and would announce upon appointment he or she had no intention of being involved in the collective bargaining process, it would undermine the intent of the Restructuring Report and would artificially constrain involvement of the senior executive officer in the game from the game's most important process. In addition, as negotiations progressed, there would be increasing pressure on a new Commissioner to become involved despite that person's relative newness to the negotiations and procedures. Putting a person into that situation as a first order of business was destined to create an untenable position, for the new Commissioner, the clubs and the players.

It is the intention of the clubs to elect a strong, independent and visionary Commissioner at the earliest possible juncture. It is our fervent hope that we can present such a Commissioner with a new collective bargaining agreement and ask that person to lead the owners, the players, the fans, and the umpires into the 21st century. To elect someone to that role now, before our labor negotiations have concluded, would hamper that goal.

PREPARED STATEMENT OF DONALD M. FEHR

This review of baseball's anomalous antitrust exemption began in the wake of the ouster of Commissioner Fay Vincent by the owners in September, 1992. Notwithstanding countless suggestions that the naming of a new Commissioner was imminent, the owners have now made it clear that they will not even consider naming a new Commissioner for many months yet, at the earliest. Even then, it is obvious that the recently adopted amendments to the Major League Agreement will place any new Commissioner in a vastly more restricted and much less independent role. Press coverage of the changes has suggested that the owners have turned the

Commissioner into a "ceremonial eunuch, and that the Commissioner's job hence-forth will be little more than to be the owners' 'lackey.'"

On behalf of his fellow owners, Mr. Selig protests that, to the contrary, the pow-er and independence of the Commissioner have been long misunderstood, that the Commissioner has in fact never had the power and independence that it was thought the Commissioner had to take action with respect to the owners' business decisions, and that the owners have actually enhanced the independence and authority of the Commissioner (assuming one is ever hired). Mr. Selig protests too much. Howev-er, he can be thanked for one thing: he has made it clear beyond peradventure of doubt that the owners have stripped from the Commissioner any power to restrain or prohibit their anticompetitive behavior. Thus, there can no longer be any sugges-tion, implied or otherwise, that a "strong, independent" Commissioner can some-how serve as a basis to continue the exemption.

What did the owners do? First, it was always thought that the independence of the Commissioner was in no small part because, as owners often said, he could not be fired. Of course, Fay Vincent was removed from office, and neither the report of the owners' restructuring committee nor the amendments to the Major League Agree-ment provide that a Commissioner may not be removed during his term of office. Thus, any future Commissioner now knows that his tenure in office is dependent entirely on the continued pleasure of the owners. He will know that he would not have the job if the owners had not decided to give it to him, and that if they change their minds, he can be removed. So much for independence.

Second, the Commissioner's authority to act to protect the "best interests" of the game was generally believed to have no practical limits, especially because any disputes as to the meaning of that term in the Major League Agreement were sub-ject to the exclusive jurisdiction of the Commissioner. However, now the best in-terests powers of the Commissioner have been "clarified" by adding new language to the Major League Agreement which provides, in essence, that such powers sim-ply do not extend to anything the clubs can vote on jointly as the Major Leagues, or individually as the American or National League. Thus, virtually all significant joint business decisions the owners make (e.g., national, local, cable and pay ca-ble television, number and location of franchises, relocation and expansion, stadi-um requirements, and sale of a club, to name a few) are now clearly outside of the Commissioner's authority. In virtually every area in which a Commissioner might identify and take action to protect a public interest at odds with the joint business decisions of the owners, it is now clear that the Commissioner will lack the author-ity to do anything.

Simply put, the owners' actions have made the Commissioner irrelevant to the analysis before this subcommittee. By no stretch of logic or imagination can the ex-istence of the Office of the Commissioner of Baseball serve as a justification to con-tinue the exemption. The owners have taken the Commissioner out of the game.

I cannot turn to the labor relations issues, however, without first commenting on a portion of Mr. Selig's prepared testimony. I hope that the Senators will each have the opportunity to read both Bud Selig's recent *New York Times* article*, and his written testimony submitted for this hearing. Not only did Mr. Selig acknowledge that the "emperor has no clothes," he says that the Commissioner has always (!) been without garments. Unfortunately, however, many people, including prior Commissioners, have simply misunderstood the scope of the Commissioner's real authority. Thus, he argues, since the Commissioner never had any real authority anyway, they have not taken any power and independence away from the Commissioner's Office, they have simply "clarified" the powers of the office.

With all due respect, this is a little much. One would think that at some time prior to the *New York Times'* article last week Mr. Selig, some other owner, any of the Commissioners, or any other representative of the owners would have made it clear that the Commissioner was not nearly as independent as was thought, nor were his powers as strong or broad as generally believed. For many, many years the owners were content to propagate the myth of the all-powerful commissioner, of the Commissioner as a sentry standing guard to protect the public. For Mr. Selig, on behalf of his fellow owners, to now come before the Congress and assert that the owners have now concluded that the general assumptions about the commissioner's powers were erroneous, and therefore the owners have not diminished the power, independence and authority of that Office, but have strengthened it is, at best, disingenuous.

THE EFFECT OF THE ANTITRUST EXEMPTION
ON LABOR NEGOTIATIONS

In the 24 years since the players and owners reached the 1970 Basic Agreement, there have been seven negotiations, resulting in a strike or lockout each time. In his statement, Mr. Selig asserts that it has been the "undefined and uncertain role" of previous Commissioners in labor relations that has made negotiations difficult, has "stalled and impeded productive discourse," and, evidently, has been the chief cause of the strikes and lockouts. Thus, the owners have eliminated any authority the Commissioner arguably had with respect to negotiations with the players, and have decided not to hire a Commissioner until the current negotiations conclude. However, the owners assure us that thereafter the Commissioner will be the owners' chief negotiator with the players, and thus will be even more influential than were past commissioners. Thus, Mr. Selig argues that with the next commissioner, and his clarified powers, "the delays and unnecessary work stoppages that have marked previous negotiations will hopefully be eliminated."

Quite bluntly, this is utter and complete nonsense. It is so completely wide of the mark that were it not for the fact that the players and owners are again involved in what, so far, appears yet again to be a very long and difficult negotiation, it would be laughable. What seems clear is that the owners evidently need a scapegoat for the

"Baseball's 'Best Interests' Phrasing Best Viewed Narrowly," March 6, 1994; reprinted on page 26 of this document. —Ed.

strife their bargaining positions have occasioned throughout the years, and the recently fired Commissioner, along with his predecessors, fits the bill.

The MLBPA does not negotiate with Commissioners; it negotiates with the owners, through whomever they designate. While a Commissioner has participated from time to time in our collective bargaining, he always did so—in so far as we were concerned, at least—as a participant on the management side, with the knowledge and consent of the owners. To suggest that a Commissioner did not represent the owners in such talks, or that the MLBPA did not regard the Commissioner at all times as part of management, is simply wrong. Every agreement we have made has been signed by management officials other than the Commissioner, and has been ratified by the owners.

Surely the owners knew at the time of those earlier negotiations what Mr. Selig has told the subcommittee today; that the Commissioner simply never had the power to dictate positions on business issues to the owners, including labor relations. Therefore, if a previous Commissioner was acting outside his authority, why did the owners not simply fire him, or ignore him?

73

Owners Withhold Pension Payment to Players (1994)

SOURCE:*Washington Post*, August 12, 1994

The relationship between the union and the owners all but grounded to a halt on August 1 when the owners, in a last-ditch attempt to force the MLBPA to reconsider a salary cap, reneged on their required pension contribution to the players. The players, who had previously announced a strike date of August 12, were not deterred. They refused to accept the owners' argument that skyrocketing salaries were the fault of greedy players and the arbitration system, and that increased costs were the primary obstacle to reestablishing competitive balance in the major leagues. Owners of small-market clubs countered that only the wealthiest clubs could afford to obtain and keep the best players needed to build a championship-quality team. The stalemate proved impossible to break, and on August 12 the players went on strike.

With Baseball's Last Out, a Strike

Players Walk Off Job After Failing to Agree with Owners
By Richard Justice

Major league baseball players packed their gear and said their goodbyes today as they prepared to go on strike after six months of sporadic and often bitter negotiations failed to produce a new labor agreement with team owners.

The strike officially began tonight after the Seattle Mariners defeated the Athletics,

8–1, in Oakland, but during the afternoon and evening, lights were turned off at Oriole Park at Camden Yards in Baltimore and other ballparks around the country for perhaps the final time this year. Hopes for an eleventh-hour settlement were futile. No meetings were held today between the negotiators for the players and the owners, and none are scheduled. The owners talked via conference call, and their chief negotiator, Richard Ravitch, said he planned to talk to Major League Baseball Players Association chief Donald Fehr Friday morning about scheduling the next meeting.

Fehr attended this afternoon's New York Yankees–Toronto Blue Jays game at Yankee Stadium and spent much of the remainder of the day briefing players by telephone.

"The players believe this is an unnecessary situation entirely created by the owners," Fehr said. "They think the owners wanted to force this shutdown and they got what they wanted."

Said Ravitch: "It's very sad that the players have decided to shut down this game. It's a tragedy for millions of fans and tens of thousands of people whose livelihood will be interrupted."

Fans headed to the ballparks yesterday for what might be the final chance to see their favorite teams this season. Many players made plans to return to their offseason homes. Key figures from both sides weighed in with their opinions. Even President Clinton and Vice President Gore chimed in, urging both sides to work toward a quick resolution.

"There are a lot of little kids there who want to see this season (completed) and there are a lot of not-so-little kids out there who know this is the most exciting baseball season in 40 years," Clinton said during a Rose Garden appearance.

In fact, the game is booming on many fronts. Fans have been going to the ballparks in record numbers to see a season marked by amazing individual and team performances. San Francisco's Matt Williams hit his 43rd home run Wednesday and was on a pace to break Roger Maris's single-season record of 61 home runs.

The Cleveland Indians—with a dazzling new downtown ballpark and a nucleus of outstanding young talent—are in line for a postseason appearance for the first time in 40 years.

It's the eighth time in 23 years that a labor dispute has interrupted a baseball season. This is potentially the most serious disruption since players struck for 50 days in 1981. Fifty-two days remain in the regular season, and sources on both sides say the disagreement is serious enough to threaten the World Series for the first time.

The players say they're striking as a preemptive move against the owners, who have threatened to declare a legal impasse during the winter and unilaterally impose a radically new system that puts a ceiling on player salaries. The players are striking now because, while they've collected most of their salaries, the owners still have millions on the line in ticket sales and national television revenues, particularly from postseason play.

The strike will affect not only the players, owners and fans, but also the hundreds of people who sell hot dogs, take tickets and work at stadiums. The Texas Rangers have ordered their front office employees to take a 10 percent pay cut next week and other teams, including the California Angels, apparently are considering layoffs if the strike lasts more than a couple of weeks.

Both sides seem prepared for a long strike. Neither side has strike insurance, but the owners, who will lose about $5 million per game, will use a line of credit with a consortium of banks. The players association can dole out $175 million to $200 million that has been withheld in trading card and other licensing revenues the past two years. Players will lose $6.7 million per game in salaries and benefits, and the first licensing payment will be made in mid-September. The next won't be made until next spring.

This strike, like most, is about money. The owners claim that nearly half of the 28 franchises are in financial trouble, and say they can no longer afford the free market system that has allowed the average player salary to more than triple in the past decade to the current $1.2 million.

The owners claim more than a dozen teams could lose money this season and that small-market teams such as the Pittsburgh Pirates, Seattle Mariners and Milwaukee Brewers can no longer afford to put competitive teams on the field.

The owners say the game's economic system is out of whack when the Toronto Blue Jays have more to spend on player salaries (around $55 million) than the San Diego Padres, Mariners and Pirates have in total revenue.

Those differences primarily are a product of television and radio revenues. A new television contract has cut each team's share from $15 million to $7.5 million per season, thanks to years of declining ratings for nationally televised regular season games.

That loss has accentuated a growing difference between what big-market and small-market clubs make from their individual television deals.

Owners say it's unrealistic to expect the Mariners, who earn $5 million to $6 million per season off local television and radio, to compete with the Yankees, who make $47 million a season. They say the Yankees simply can bid more for players and that fans in Seattle will lose interest because their team will never be in contention.

To remedy the problem, the owners proposed an economic system similar to the one adopted by National Football League teams a year ago. That system would give the players 50 percent of the industry's $1.88 billion in revenue for salaries and benefits. It would also impose a floor and a ceiling on what teams may spend on salaries. They hope that if there is not a wide disparity in payrolls, teams will be more competitive.

If the players accept the system—popularly called a salary cap—the owners have agreed to share more of their own revenue with one another. That plan would transfer an estimated $5 million to $9 million per season from the wealthy teams to small-market teams.

The catch: This plan to share revenue is triggered only by the union's agreement to accept a salary cap.

The players have suggested that more revenue sharing among the owners—currently only national television revenues are widely shared—would relieve the squeeze on small-market teams.

However, big-market clubs such as the Yankees and Los Angeles Dodgers refused to agree to revenue sharing unless they got something in return, namely a salary cap.

The players have refused to consider a salary cap because they believe it would mean restrictions on free agency and salaries. They point to the NFL's system and say the widespread release of well-paid veterans such as New York Giants quarterback Phil Simms and Washington Redskins wide receiver Art Monk is a direct result of teams forced to conform to the cap.

The NBA also has a salary cap, but it is vastly different in that teams are allowed to exceed the cap to keep their own players.

Baseball players currently receive 58 percent of industry revenue through salaries, and they say they're not about to accept less. The owners have countered that the 50 percent figure is negotiable, but one union source said his side simply believes a salary cap is "un-American."

"From the union perspective, this is an economic system that has worked very, very well," Ravitch said. "They like it. The players like it. They don't want to change it."

"The owners are not content with the American system," said Gene Orza, associate general counsel for the players union. "What the clubs want is a nice common mix of Adam Smith and Joseph Stalin."

Players say the owners historically have exaggerated their financial problems and that they're doing so again. This fight is similar to the ones the owners and players have fought seven other times, and all of those disputes ended with the owners making large concessions.

But the dynamics are different this time. There's no commissioner to intervene, as Peter Ueberroth did in 1985 and Fay Vincent did in 1990. Indeed, Vincent was forced out of office two years ago in part because many owners believed he was too conciliatory to the players.

The owners then agreed not to replace him until a new labor agreement was in place. Vincent's departure left hard-liners such as Milwaukee Brewers owner Bud Selig—the de facto commissioner—and Chicago White Sox chairman Jerry Reinsdorf in charge.

The owners have changed other rules as well. For the first time ever, they have a single negotiator—Ravitch, a former New York transit chief. No team owner has attended a single bargaining session.

That fact was decried Wednesday by New York Yankees owner George Steinbrenner, who told the *Philadelphia Inquirer* that owners should be allowed at the bargaining table and contradicted Ravitch's assertion that more competitive payrolls will translate to more competitive on-field play.

"Look at Montreal," Steinbrenner said. "The best record in baseball is the team with the second-lowest payroll. So you can shoot that theory in the butt. Look at Minnesota, they've won twice since we won. He's got to get off that argument. It doesn't wash."

Another change comes in how a new agreement is reached. Once a strike begins, any new agreement must be approved by three-fourths of the 28 owners instead of a simple majority. The change means that eight clubs can block any agreement and that the large-market and medium-market clubs, who might settle for an agreement similar to the one now in place, can no longer forge through an agreement unacceptable to the small-market teams. Eight of the so-called small-market teams stand to make significant additional revenue from the revenue sharing and salary cap.

74

Review of Ken Burns's Documentary *Baseball* (1994)

SOURCE: Austin *American Statesman*, September 18, 1994

The nation's loss was Ken Burns's gain. Only two days after acting commissioner Bud Selig announced the cancellation of the remainder of the season and the World Series, the first episode (or "inning") of Burns's epic documentary, Baseball, *aired on Public Broadcasting Stations across the country. Most reviewers raved about the eighteen-and-a-half-hour program, but some—most notably sportscaster and baseball historian Keith Olbermann—criticized Burns for ignoring baseball outside the New York City area and Boston, paying almost no attention to non–major league baseball (with the notable exception of the Negro Leagues) and for making scores of errors, especially his repeated failure to match the narration with historically appropriate pictures and film footage. Some of Olbermann's private e-mails regarding* Baseball *are in the "Baseball" file at the National Baseball Hall of Fame Library, including a list of errors.*

However, most baseball fans did not care if, for instance, Babe Ruth's sixtieth home run in 1927 was described as they watched Ruth hit the ball in a home uniform and cross the plate in a road uniform, without noting that no film of the historic home run is known to exist. They wanted to be reminded that baseball was still the national pastime, and in this regard Burns did not disappoint.

Baseball as a Metaphor for America

Ken Burns' New Series Goes for a Grand Slam
By Diane Holloway

Ken Burns, the baby-faced, 41-year-old documentary filmmaker best-known for the 1990 landmark *Civil War*, has a lot of nerve, doesn't he?

At a time when most people have given up on the strike-crippled baseball season, happily turned their attention to football and are eager to welcome the new television season, Burns is asking us to devote almost two weeks of viewing time to *Baseball*, a mammoth 18 ½-hour film on the history of America's favorite pastime.

Either the filmmaker suffers from delusions of grandeur or he has created a truly stunning television program. Fortunately for viewers and for Burns, *Baseball*, which airs in nine "innings" of two hours or longer (starting tonight at 7 on KLRU, Channel 18 Cable 9), is truly stunning.

(The maxi-series—only a fool would call it a miniseries—continues through Thursday this week, breaks for two days and returns Sunday through Wednesday of next week.)

Fanatical baseball fans will be transported by the sweep and detail of the production. Intelligent viewers who like history but don't give a hoot about baseball will like it, too. Think of it as a sequel to *The Civil War*, not a sports program, and you've got the gist.

"Several years ago, as filmmakers engaged in trying to evoke the most defining moment in American history, the Civil War, we became aware that a study of baseball offered the clearest way to explore the extraordinary and complicated country the Civil War made," Burns wrote in a companion piece to *Baseball*. "We have spent the last four years creating a film history that traces the entire sweeping, panoramic history of our country from the 1840s to today."

Burns has often expressed his profound belief in the value of the metaphor, and nowhere is that more evident than *Baseball*. Burns believes—and does a remarkable job of proving—that baseball represents America at its best and at its worst, at its most joyous and at its most painful. "The story of baseball is the story of immigration and assimilation, of the struggle between labor and management, of popular culture and the media, of myth and the nature of heroes, of the roles of women and class and wealth in our society," Burns said. "And most important, it is the story of race in America."

Indeed, race and racism play an important role in *Baseball*. Thursday night's 2 ½-hour "inning" is devoted entirely to "shadow ball," a reference to the parallel universe of the Negro Leagues. Although forced into existence by racism, the Negro Leagues flourished and produced such legendary heroes as Satchel Paige, Josh Gibson, Cool Papa Bell and Buck O'Neil, the first baseman for the Kansas City Monarchs. O'Neil provides wonderful commentary throughout the series but especially in Thursday's episode. He shines as brightly in *Baseball* as historian Shelby Foote did in *The Civil War*.

Next Sunday's episode deals with the tragic heroism of Jackie Robinson, the first black player to cross the color line in the majors. Hired by the Brooklyn Dodgers in 1947, Robinson endured constant abuse, including threats on his life. Although we think of him as a smiling sports star, his widow says in the program that her husband never felt appreciated and died an unfulfilled, unhappy man.

And lest we lull ourselves into thinking racism is merely a part of baseball's past, another episode includes former Los Angeles Dodgers executive Al Campanis's shocking interview on *Nightline* a few years ago in which he stated his racist rationale for why there are so few blacks in baseball management.

Baseball is also, as sportswriter Thomas Boswell says in the program, "America's family heirloom." Anyone who has children knows this is true. Fathers and mothers play ball with their children, and those children grow up to play ball with their own offspring. In Little League games across the country, millions of grandfathers, grandmothers, fathers and mothers cheer on the next generation of players and fans.

Burns presents dozens of important and poignant turning points, but he also presents terrific stories, interesting and obscure details (did you know the curve ball was invented in 1867 by a man named Candy Cummings?) and exciting moments. Yes, the sixth game of the 1975 World Series between Cincinnati and Boston, which many purists believe is the best game ever played, is covered—and covered beautifully.

In fact, great storytelling is the backbone of *Baseball*, and it is accomplished with Burns' brilliant use of old photos, old newsreels, thoughtful interviews, crisp narrative (delivered by John Chancellor) and personal musings by devoted fans. Among those who wax eloquent (although at times perhaps too poetic) are Bob Costas, George Will, Mario Cuomo, Shelby Foote (he's Burns' lucky charm) and Billy Crystal, to name a few.

Like the game itself, *Baseball* has a leisurely pace, sometimes seeming as if it could go on with endless extra innings. Tonight's first episode sets the pace, if not the tone. The task of introducing a two-week series is monumental and, at times, awkward, but once the storytelling is under way, the two hours flow smoothly.

Galloping through more than 50 years, the first inning deals with the beginning of unorganized baseball before the Civil War (dispelling the myth that Abner Doubleday invented it), the expansion of its popularity during the Civil War, the beginning of organized baseball (with teams such as the Brooklyn Trolley Dodgers, the New York Knickerbockers and the Cincinnati Red Stockings) and the establishment of the National League.

Viewers may wince when they hear that members of the clubs formed in the 1860s were not paid. The goal was to keep the game amateur and therefore pure. The seeds of a labor-management battle that continues in full force today thus were planted.

Tonight's episode also chronicles the ascendancy of such legends of Cy Young, Cap Anson and "King" Kelly.

Highlights of other episodes include entertaining and unusual portraits of some of the game's best players, including almost an entire inning devoted to Babe Ruth (Wednesday); and an extensive examination of 1941, perhaps baseball's best season ever, when Ted Williams hit .406 and Joe DiMaggio hit safely in 56 straight games.

The series concludes in the early '90s, perhaps optimistically looking forward to a long and healthy life for baseball. Actually, that may be a safe prediction, since the current major leagues could self-destruct and be replaced in the future by players from today's bumper crop of Little Leaguers.

Some people may feel Burns has placed the sport on too high a pedestal. While baseball can indeed be used as a metaphor for much that has happened in our social history, it is not, after all, a supreme being. And the sport is not (technically) a religion.

Nevertheless, watching *Baseball* is a splendid experience. If you don't want to watch the whole thing for two weeks, tape it and watch it on your own schedule. But if as many people come to their sets tonight as did for *The Civil War*, we could be in for another national TV-as-campfire experience, and we'll all be humming "Take Me Out to the Ball Game" for months to come.

75

Acting Commissioner Selig Cancels Remainder of Season, World Series (1994)

SOURCE: *Sporting News*, September 26, 1994

In the aftermath of Bud Selig's stunning decision to cancel the remainder of the season, including the World Series, few columnists stepped up to defend his actions. While the players garnered little sympathy, most baseball reporters reserved their wrath for the owners, whose mendacity in claiming massive losses even with surging attendance figures, the extra revenue generated by adding two expansion teams, and the luxury of operating in a robust economy, was difficult to comprehend. Veteran reporter Dave Kindred summarized his feelings in the column below.

This One's for You, Bud
Dave Kindred

There are good reasons for what we do and there are the real reasons.

The imp Muhammad Ali liked to tell a story about Abraham Lincoln. One night, Ali said, the old president enjoyed himself more than enough in the company of good Kentucky bourbon.

"Next morning," Ali said, "ol' Abe rubbed his eyes and looked around and said to his wife, 'I freed the *who?*'"

The lords of baseball closed down the game for what they declared are good reasons essential to financial survival. The real reasons, in one man's opinion: They did it for the macho glee of it. They did it to show they could strut as cockily as any kid wearing his cap backward. They did it to prove again who lives in the big house.

Little else explains why the owners' acting commissioner, Bud Selig, would bend fact so far as to say all 28 teams face financial catastrophe. That is ludicrous. Hardly more ludicrous, though, than Selig's repeated reference to his side's negotiators as "the Dream Team."

Here was a baseball man using a basketball analogy as if 125 years of his own game had given him no language sufficient to express his pride in negotiators who did nothing and did it for a long time.

All a reasonable person can hope is that Selig woke up the next morning and said, "I called off *what?*"

The lasting sorrow here, beyond any loss of the World Series, is that Bud & His Nightmare Boys have made the game smaller, if not in reality, certainly in spirit.

Practically anyone who has walked into a major league stadium has been in awe of the people, the place and the game that moved Red Smith, the late sports columnist, to write, "Ninety feet between bases is the nearest to perfection that man has yet achieved."

For some of us romantics, that feeling of awe is gone—perhaps forever.

Despite the lessons of baseball's robber-baron history, we looked upon ballparks as cathedrals of a sort, vessels of the human spirit. Not now, not for a while anyway. The owners have reminded us again that ballparks are cash registers for their personal use.

And now, in the mad tradition of burning the village to save it, the owners have torched the World Series on the premise that baseball is about to go broke, an argument threadbare for a century and patently absurd today.

Baseball sold more tickets for more games for more money in 1993 than ever before. It is a $3-billion growth industry with a dozen cities lusting to pay $125 million each to get in the big leagues. Never has baseball been more competitive, seldom has it been so vibrant. Were there interleague play, were there creative marketing, were there a partnership of owners and players, baseball would truly be in a golden age.

Still, Bud & His Nightmare Boys insist the game is hurtling toward the darkness of a financial abyss.

As it happens, and not so coincidentally, Selig's Milwaukee team may be one of the few truly in distress. As it also happens, there is a solution to his distress: Don't shut down baseball, just sell the team for, guessing here, $75 million more than he paid for it.

Or Selig could do what owners did in Atlanta, Cleveland and Baltimore. They cut payrolls, found good players and built ballparks. Now they're making money in markets not much different from Milwaukee.

All it takes is talent and imagination. Of course, some folks living in the big house don't have those necessities. They prefer a monopolist's system guaranteeing success. Thus, the 1994 salary cap/revenue sharing proposal, which, by the way, shows that owners trust no one, not even each other.

Teams agreed to share revenues only if everyone agreed to use the divvied-up money to pay players. That's why the cap scheme demanded that all payrolls be at least 84 percent of the average.

The incredible part of this is that most fans blame the players for the mess, when it's the owners' doing. And they did it while operating as this country's only billionaires' industry given immunity against antitrust laws protecting taxpayers from the dictatorial excesses of monopoly businesses.

U.S. Sen. Howard Metzenbaum of Ohio believes baseball owners have more power than executives in any other industry. Metzenbaum says, "If the CEO's of the auto industry, for example, had the same immunity from the nation's pro-competition laws, they could eliminate competition from imports, raise prices in lock step and even divide up the country—dictating that only Fords could be sold in New York, Chryslers in Chicago and General Motors cars in Los Angeles.

" ... Consider what the owners have done for us lately. They have inflated ticket prices, blackmailed cities for tax breaks, controlled TV coverage, blocked expansion and provoked the players to strike."

Basketball, football and hockey players seldom strike because they can play while lawyers argue. But baseball owners use the antitrust exemption to stand immune to such litigation. The players' only recourse is a strike.

Baseball's immunity originated in a decision by the otherwise brilliant Supreme Court Justice Oliver Wendell Holmes, who in 1922 ruled that baseball was a sport, not an interstate business. Congress 60 times has considered ending the exemption. But romance, tradition and other soft-headedness have always prevailed.

Now more than ever it is obvious that Congress should act; now more than ever it is obvious that the owners cannot be trusted to deal fairly with anyone.

We should remember words once spoken by Jerry Reinsdorf, who owns the Chicago White Sox. He said baseball is a business that should be run "for the owners, not the players or the umpires or the fans."

76

Congressional Research Service Offers Solutions to Labor Impasse (1994)

SOURCE: William A. Cox and Dennis Zimmerman, "The Baseball Strike and Federal Policy: An Economic Analysis," in Senate Subcommittee on Antitrust, Business Rights, and Competition, *The Court-Imposed Major League Baseball Antitrust Exemption*, 104th Cong., 1st sess., February 15, 1995, 111–15

With the expiration of the Basic Agreement on December 22, 1994, under federal collective bargaining laws the owners implemented their plan—in this case, instituting a salary cap and eliminating salary arbitration—unilaterally. The players filed a complaint with the National Labor Relations Board, claiming that the owners did not bargain in good faith and therefore were in violation of federal labor law. Their arguments gained strength on January 13, when the owners agreed to use replacement players if they could not sign a new pact with the union in time to start the 1995 season.

The threat of such a drastic action once again prompted Congress to hold hearings. The nonpartisan Congressional Research Service was asked to analyze the economic impact of the strike with regard to federal policy. The report excerpted below, which drew the ire of owners, concluded that relocating some small-market clubs to larger cities would help the owners more than any salary cap or revenue distribution would.

VI. POTENTIAL SOLUTIONS TO THE ALLEGED MARKET FAILURE

A. RELAX RESTRICTIONS ON RELOCATION OF FRANCHISES

One obvious solution is to allow financially strapped franchises to relocate to areas not currently served by MLB where expected profits would be greater. The owners' rules that prohibit relocation of franchises without league consent are the primary impediment to this option. Obviously the fans and public officials in cities losing teams would be unhappy, but their counterparts in the newly enfranchised cities will be delighted. One cannot say that total fan satisfaction will be increased or reduced, since one cannot add up such imponderables. Two factors suggest, however, that fan satisfaction may be higher after the move. The fact that an owner feels his prospects are better in a new location implies that he foresees more fans willing to support the team (whether at the stadium or on television). Another important attraction is the greater public subsidy the new location often is willing to extend, which may flow from a higher level of political and popular support.

In fact, the leagues' control over relocation was recently challenged in court by a partnership that had been refused approval to buy the San Francisco Giants and move them to Tampa Bay/St. Petersburg, Florida. The major leagues agreed to pay more than $6 million and apologize to these plaintiffs after a Federal district court decided that baseball's antitrust exemption did not extend beyond the reserve clause and permitted the suit to go to trial. Because of the out-of-court settlement, the antitrust issue raised in that case will not be addressed by higher courts. Possible violations of antitrust laws of the State of Florida remain under investigation by the Attorney General of that State after a ruling by Florida's Supreme Court adopted the Federal district court's narrow view of baseball's exemption and permitted the investigation to continue.

A major advantage to the option of easier franchise relocation to an unserved market is that it would not reduce the incomes of either players or the owners as a group. In fact, it is likely to increase those of both groups. This approach to counteracting growing competitive imbalance would have the additional effect of eliminating a longstanding anticompetitive practice.

B. EXPAND THE SUPPLY OF FRANCHISES IN LARGE-REVENUE MARKETS

Perhaps the optimal degree of equality in financial resources cannot be obtained by relocating weak franchises and raising the incomes of the poor. Greater inequality can also be achieved by lowering the incomes of the rich large-revenue teams. In industries operating under competitive conditions, the existence of businesses with exceptional profits like the New York Yankees would attract new firms into the location, which would capture some of those profits. A similar effect can be accomplished in baseball by loosening the constraints on the number of franchises and locating new ones in the markets that have the largest attendance and most valuable local radio and television rights. If additional teams were located in New York, Chicago, and Los Angeles, for example, the returns from attendance and broadcast rights of the Yankees, Cubs, and Dodgers would come down. Increasing the supply of franchises in large-revenue markets could make the large-revenue clubs economically similar to small-revenue clubs. If competitive balance is sensitive to equality of financial resources, this would be an effective policy.

This option would reduce the franchise values (and capital gains) of long-time owners of large-revenue clubs who have enjoyed unanticipated growth in local media revenues (and paid a franchise price that did not reflect those unexpected revenues). It also would reduce the franchise values (and impose capital losses) on recent purchasers who have not enjoyed unanticipated revenue growth. It would force these two groups of owners to relinquish part of their property's value to finance a solution to the problem. But one might ask why this loss would be more unfair than asking players to forego part of the value of their own talent and skill (their human capital) to solve the problem.

Of course, it is not necessary to impose capital losses on the owners of existing large-revenue franchises. Fees from the sale of these additional franchises could be used to compensate current owners for their losses. In fact, current owners could be given the right to sell franchises in their markets and keep all or part of the franchise fees.

C. INCREASED REVENUE SHARING

An alternative means of reducing inequality is to share more revenues among the teams. The existing sharing provisions allocate visiting American League teams less than 20% of gate receipts and visiting National League teams about 5%, shares which are considerably smaller than in football and basketball. Sharing of broadcast revenue is limited to national network television and some pay-per-view and cable broadcasts. The national network broadcast royalties in 1993 constituted about one-quarter of total team revenues (more for small-revenue teams), but a new contract has cut these amounts sharply in light of poor past ratings. The remaining source of shared revenue is from licensing trade-marked concessions. Local broadcast revenue could be but is not shared.

The optimal degree of revenue sharing for competitive balance is unknown, but is likely to lie between the current position of baseball's shared revenue and a system that allocates 1/28th of all revenue to each of the 28 existing teams. The independent members of the Economic Study Committee recommended that " . . . the current level of twenty-five percent shared revenues should be considered as a floor, and that significant increments in this percentage should be achieved promptly." [Economist Roger] Noll provides a very insightful discussion of the incentives created by different revenue sharing arrangements.

As discussed earlier, the salary cap/revenue sharing system that has been imposed by the owners essentially would finance increased revenue sharing from reduced player salaries. It is clear that many other options and combinations thereof are available that would take revenues to be transferred to financially weak franchises from the income of financially strong franchises instead of from the salaries of the players, or that would achieve any desired balance of sacrifice between players and owners to address the problems that they jointly face.

The effect of such options on player and owner factor shares and industry revenue growth depends upon several factors: the motivation of the owners—whether they are profit motivated or win motivated; upon whether the tax is levied on marginal payroll expenditures and revenues (only the portion above some predetermined level or team average) or on all payroll expenditures and revenues; and upon whether the distribution formula is based on marginal shortfalls in payroll and revenues (only the amount below some predetermined level or team average). In general, the impact on player salaries is greater the more the tax and distribution formulas operate on the margin.

D. SUMMARY

If the alleged market failure exists, it is related to excessive inequality of financial resources among franchises. Relaxed restrictions on player movement and pay may contribute to such a failure. Owner-imposed restrictions on the number and mobility of franchises also contribute to it. This suggests that options other than anti-competitive labor practices are available to correct the problem, and raises questions about whether MLB's antitrust exemption serves a useful public purpose.

The choice of remedy greatly affects the distribution of its cost between owners and players. The salary cap/revenue sharing option imposed by the owners, akin to increasing restrictions on player mobility, would have imposed the greatest share of the cost on players. If fully phased in for an uninterrupted 1994 season, it would have taken $198 million away from the players and used $38 million for increased payroll spending by small-revenue teams.

Expanding the number of franchises in large-revenue markets imposes most of the cost on a subset of owners. This option cannot be considered more or less fair than the salary cap/revenue sharing option; one would cut the value of the intangible capital of certain owners (their franchises), while the other would reduce the value of the human capital of players (their baseball skills). If the franchise fees paid by new owners were used to compensate the current owners for their loss, competitive balance could be enhanced with neither owners nor players being worse off. Relocating financially fragile franchises to more profitable locations currently unserved by MLB would also leave owners as a group and players better off. Relocation might, however, reduce the effectiveness of the relocation threat feared by communities and reduce the local public sector subsidies franchises receive through favorable lease and tax treatment. Finally, revenues to be shared with financially weak franchises might be raised from the income of financially strong franchises rather than from the salaries of the players.

77

Owners Compare "Myth" and "Truth" in Baseball Dispute (1995)

SOURCE: Senate Subcommittee on Antitrust, Business Rights, and Competition, *The Court-Imposed Major League Baseball Antitrust Exemption*, 104th Cong., 1st sess., February 15, 1995, 39–41

Furious at their treatment in the press, in the Congress, and by the Congressional Research Service, the owners responded by drafting their own version of the players' contentions and the owners' rebuttals. Their anger is evident in the phrasing of the players' "myths." Their objective was to convince their accusers, and the NLRB, that they did indeed make every effort to compromise with the union prior to unilaterally instituting their system.

SETTING THE BASEBALL RECORD STRAIGHT

Myth: The owners failed to provide financial information to the Players Association.

Truth: During the term of the 1990–93 Basic Agreement, the clubs and the players participated in a Baseball Economic Study Committee, which included people such as Paul Volcker. During that process, the clubs provided the MLBPA with audited financial statements and standardized financial questionnaires from each individual club for a period of 15 years. In addition, the clubs provided detailed information concerning "related entities" such as Turner Broadcasting and Anheuser-Busch. At the outset of the negotiations, the clubs provided audited financial statements and financial questionnaires for the 1993 season and detailed projections for 1994.

Myth: Major League Baseball is wildly profitable.

Truth: Since the advent of free agency, Baseball, as an industry, has essentially been a break-even operation, without taking into consideration interest expense and cost of capital. When the industry is at break-even, however, many markets (at least the eight to ten small ones) face serious losses.

Myth: Baseball's profitability is hidden in related party transactions.

Truth: The Baseball Economic Study Committee analyzed related party transactions carefully and concluded that those transactions did not alter the picture of Baseball's financial situation presented by the clubs' audited financial statements. In other words, related party transactions are not a source of hidden profitability.

Myth: Baseball has two sets of books.

Truth: Each club is audited by a Big 6 accounting firm. If there are two sets of books, all of those firms would have to be involved in a massive conspiracy.

Myth: All the Union wants is to maintain the "free market" system.

Truth: The economic system in Baseball is anything but a free market. The system requires that clubs pay a minimum salary; it prohibits clubs from reducing the salaries of some players by more than specified percentages; and it requires that the salaries of some players be determined by an arbitrator. The fact of the matter is that the MLBPA uses its collective strength to negotiate standard terms when those terms are to the advantage of its members. It resorts to "free market" rhetoric when it serves to increase player salaries.

Myth: The Major League players are prepared to live with whatever a free market system produces in terms of player compensation.

Truth: Baseball does not have a free-market system. If it did, every player would be in the market every year, negotiating *all* of his terms and conditions of employment without minimum salaries and salary arbitration. Marvin Miller has always said that the Union does not want every player to be a free agent (*i.e.,* they want to artificially limit the supply of players).

Myth: Major League players should have the right to look for employment with any club, and each club should be free to pay the player whatever it wants.

Truth: As noted above, the Union has always been in favor of limiting the number of players eligible for free agency at any time. Moreover, the NLRB has recognized that, for labor law purposes, the clubs are a single employer. As long as the MLBPA remains a union, the only right that players have under the federal labor laws is to collectively bargain their salaries with the clubs as a *single employer*. No employee has the right to force an employer to "compete" against part of the same employer.

Myth: The NFL and the NBA players hate the salary cap.

Truth: In fact, the NBA players agreed to extend the cap for another year without losing a day due to a strike. Before the NBA first negotiated the salary cap with its players in 1983, Baseball players made more than basketball players. Today, the average salary of a Baseball player is $1.2 million, while the average basketball player makes $1.8 million. The leader of the NFL players, Gene Upshaw, has often defended the salary cap system.

Myth: The Baseball specific exemption has caused labor problems in Baseball.

Truth: Even without the exemption created by *Federal Baseball*, Baseball's labor relations would be protected by the "nonstatutory labor antitrust exemption" available to all employers that engage in collective bargaining. Without a special exemption, the NFL had a strike in which it used replacement players, and without a special exemption, the NHL just lost half of its season due to a labor dispute. Without a special exemption, the NBA and the NFL have negotiated the type of salary cap system that the Baseball owners were forced to implement.

Myth: The owners could not have implemented their salary cap without their special antitrust exemption.

Truth: Unilateral implementation is part of the process of collective bargaining created by the National Labor Relations Act. At different points in their history, both the NFL and the NHL have unilaterally implemented terms and conditions of employment, despite the fact that they do not enjoy the exemption created by *Federal Baseball*.

Myth: The owners' adherence to their Ft. Lauderdale revenue-sharing agreement has been an impediment to collective bargaining.

Truth: For 10 years, Don Fehr told the owners that they could solve their problems with increased revenue sharing. The owners reached an agreement on additional revenue sharing last January. Ever since then, Don Fehr has been trying to undermine the agreement. Moreover, the owners have made at least two proposals to the MLBPA that would have required a substantial reworking (and a new vote) on the Ft. Lauderdale agreement.

Myth: The Union had to go on strike in August 1994 in an effort to prevent the owners' unilateral implementation.

Truth: The MLBPA went on strike in August 1994 because they thought that their leverage was maximized at that point and that the owners would quickly fold.

Myth: The owners entered the negotiations with a predetermined desire to implement the salary cap.

Truth: Over the course of the fall, the owners made two comprehensive economic proposals that did not contain a salary cap. Moreover, the MLBPA's adamant refusal to negotiate any meaningful change in the current player compensation system produced an early and persistent impasse in these negotiations. If the owners had really been intent on implementing, they could have done so much earlier. The owners were prepared to play the entire 1994 season under the terms of the old Basic Agreement that expired on December 31, 1993. The owners' desire to avoid implementation is further demonstrated by the fact that they consistently agreed to extend deadlines (*i.e.*, from December 5, 1994, to December 15, 1994, and finally to December 22, 1994). By December 22, 1994, the owners had no choice but to put some system in place in order to begin preparations for the 1995 season.

Myth: The repeal of Baseball's antitrust exemption would resolve the current labor dispute.

Truth: The repeal of Baseball's antitrust exemption would simply open an additional avenue of litigation for the MLBPA. Based on the behavior of the Players Association to date, this additional litigation avenue would just be another distraction that would keep the Union leadership from confronting the real economic issues in collective bargaining.

Myth: The MLBPA made several proposals that would have controlled salaries.

Truth: All of the MLBPA's proposals were nothing more than revenue-sharing plans. They did nothing to address the issue of player compensation. Even worse, they called for less revenue sharing than did the Ft. Lauderdale agreement.

Myth: The MLBPA's last proposal contained a significant tax on payrolls designed to limit the growth in player compensation.

Truth: The tax offered by the MLBPA was only applicable to clubs with payrolls above $65 million. The highest payroll in Baseball is $56 million. In short, the Union's tax was a tax on no one.

Myth: Major League Baseball is a cartel that needs to be regulated.

Truth: In terms of structure, Baseball is no different than any other professional sport. In fact, if it is a cartel, it has not been a very successful one, given that Baseball has essentially operated on a break-even basis.

Under true economic theory, Baseball is not a cartel. The need to present a balanced, competitive product on the field makes a professional sports league more like an industry which uses a "common pool resource" (like a group of fishermen that fish in the same area). The success of any sports league depends on fan interest and games between teams with a fairly equal chance of winning. The relative success of an individual team depends on its talent, relative to that of other teams. The common interest, however, depends on league balance. To try and analyze these conflicting economic motivations under a cartel model simply leads to incorrect conclusions.

78

Federal Judge Issues Injunction Against Owners; Strike Ended (1995)

SOURCE: U.S. District Court, Southern District of New York, March 31, 1995

The players' union filed an unfair practices charge against the owners with the National Labor Relations Board shortly after the termination of the Basic Agreement by the owners in late December. In early February the Player Relations Committee informed the NLRB that they would revoke the changes they implemented unilaterally with the exception of the abolition of salary arbitration. Three days later, on February 6, the PRC ruled that clubs no longer had the authority to sign players until a new agreement with the union was signed. The MLBPA refiled charges with the NLRB, claiming that this amounted to a violation of the anti-collusion clause and other issues. The NLRB ruled on March 27 to seek a temporary injunction against the owners, who promptly appealed the decision in federal court.

Four days later U.S. District Court Judge Sonia Sotomayor found in favor of the NLRB and upheld the injunction. The owners' appeal was denied by the U.S. Court of Appeals, and on April 2 the owners and the players agreed to start the 1995 season on April 25 under the conditions of the 1990 Basic Agreement.

Sonia Sotomayor, U.S.D.J.
ORDER

For the reasons discussed on the transcript of hearing before the Court this day, the Court issues an injunction directing and ordering Respondents, the Major League Baseball Player Relations Committee, Inc. and its twenty-eight constituent member clubs of Major League Baseball, 1) to restore the terms and conditions of employment provided under the expired Basic Agreement which was effective January 1, 1990, including its free agency/reserve systems with salary arbitration for eligible reserve players, Article XX (f) and all other of their constituent parts; 2) immediately to rescind by written notice to all club members any actions taken, including the February 6 letter from Charles P. O'Conner to Donald M. Fehr Re: Exclusive Representative Status of PRC and the February 6, 1995 Memorandum with its attached Questions and Answers sent by Charles P. O'Conner to All Major League Clubs Subject: Individual Club/Player Contract Negotiations, that are inconsistent with or conflict with the terms and conditions of employment, including all provisions of the free agency/reserve systems provided under the expired Basic Agreement; and 3) to bargain in good faith without unilateral changes to the Basic Agreement with the Major League Baseball Players Association (the "Union") in compliance with §8 (a)(1) and (5) of the National Labor Relations Act.

This injunction is to remain in effect until either (1) the Players and Owners enter into a new collective bargaining agreement that replaces the expired Basic Agreement, or (2) the final disposition of the matters pending before the National Labor Relations Board on the Complaint and Notice of Hearing of the General Counsel of the Board in Case No. 2-CA-28177, or (3) a finding of this court, upon petition of the Players or Respondents for a desolution of the injunction demonstrating that an impasse in good faith bargaining has occurred despite a reasonable passage of time negotiating in good faith the full mandatory bargaining terms of the expired Basic Agreement.

SO ORDERED.

Dated: New York, New York
March 31, 1995

7

Baseball Starts to Heal

The resumption of baseball in 1995 was welcomed by grateful but hesitant fans who made clear their disgust by failing to pass through major league turnstiles at the record rate of two years earlier. Even Cal Ripken's triumphant march toward breaking Lou Gehrig's record for consecutive games played did not reverse the attendance decline, despite claims to the contrary. Ripken's heroics in 1995 were surpassed in 1998 by an accumulation of incredible feats: a twenty-strikeout, one-hit pitching performance by a rookie; a perfect game; the heralded debut of an enigmatic Cuban refugee; and an incredible 114-win season by the New York Yankees, among others.

These accomplishments were dwarfed in the public eye by the efforts of two sluggers, Sammy Sosa and Mark McGwire, who staged a dramatic race for the honor of surpassing Roger Maris's record of sixty-one home runs in a season. Both men achieved that goal, but McGwire's new record of seventy home runs was tainted in some fans' eyes by the revelation that he used androstenedione, a supplement banned by the International Olympic Committee and the NFL, among many other sports organizations, but not by major league baseball. Confronted by the MLBPA, baseball failed to enact rules prohibiting the use of steroids or questionable supplements. The incredible offensive surge that started in the mid-1990s, credited by many with helping to bring fans back to baseball, nevertheless threatened the integrity of the sport more than any other incident since the Black Sox scandal eighty years earlier.

79

Baseball Approves Revision of Landmark Career Statistics (1995)

SOURCE: *Wall Street Journal*, May 19, 1995

The fourth edition of Total Baseball *was the first to be designated by major league base-ball as its official encyclopedia.* Total Baseball *differed from the previous book of record,* The Baseball Encyclopedia, *in its inclusion of hundreds of pages of articles and in its acceptance of some newer statistics such as "production" (the sum of on-base percentage and slugging percentage, now better known as* OPS*) and "total player rating," a summation of each player's relative worth in one number. It also embraced the efforts of dozens of dedicated "sabermetricians," who scoured the original records and in some cases found errors. The editor of* Total Baseball, *John Thorn, convinced major league baseball to accept these revisions as official, even when they resulted in the alteration of some well-known, even beloved, numbers.*

In 2001 major league baseball made another revision to the record. Jerome Holtzman, the official historian of major league baseball, reinstated the batting averages as they were originally recorded in 1876 and 1887, when the rules did not conform to statistical practice throughout the rest of baseball history. See Holtzman's essay "An Important Change to the Official Record of Major League Baseball" in Total Baseball, *7th ed. (Kingston, NY: Total Sports Publishing, 2001), 551–52.*

Baseball Rewrites Its Official Record Book
By Stefan Fatsis
Special to THE WALL STREET JOURNAL

Ty Cobb, the early 20th-century baseball star, died in 1961 with 4,191 hits and a lifetime batting average of .367. But recently, the famed Georgia Peach lost two hits and one point.

It's old news to baseball stat fanatics that record-keepers of the time erroneously double-counted a 2-for-3 performance by Cobb in a 1910 game. Now everyone else should get used to the lesser figures: They're now official.

Major League Baseball this year has endorsed the new, fourth edition of Total Baseball (Viking, $59.95), a 2,552 page agglomeration of statistics on everyone who ever played in a big-league game. (It's also the basis of Microsoft Corp.'s CD-ROM baseball guide.) Not a few of the numbers, including Cobb's, differ from those in the ninth edition of The Baseball Encyclopedia (Macmillan Books, 1992, $55), which had MLB's imprimatur, but lost it and stands to lose sales as well.

The dueling data may not seem like a big deal, but in baseball certain numbers—"56," "714," "755," "2,130," not to mention 4,191—are nothing less than talismanic. The slightest change in the record of some long-forgotten 19th-century player prompts impassioned debate among sabermetricians, as baseball statistics mavens are called, and Total Baseball's approach to revising data has stirred the pot.

Take Cobb. In 1910, the cantankerous Detroit Tiger won the American League batting championship, nipping Napoleon Lajoie by .385 to .384. When Cobb's extra two hits were discovered and deleted nearly 70 years later, his average that season effectively dropped to .383. The Baseball Encyclopedia never has taken note of the extra hits, but previous editions of Total Baseball went so far as to give Lajoie the title. Now it's been returned to Cobb, though the book lists his lower average and explains the discrepancy. Total Baseball's official revised policy: Player records change with proof of statistical error; awards and titles are forever.

(With two exceptions. Per a longstanding MLB edict, Total Baseball does recalibrate batting averages for 1876, when walks were counted as outs, and 1887, when walks were counted as hits, stripping that year's batting crown from Cap Anson.)

Not everyone is thrilled with the new approach. David Q. Voigt, a baseball historian who teaches at Albright College in Reading, Pa., argues that statistics should remain as recorded at the time, regardless of contradictory new evidence. Hence, Cobb should keep not only his 1910 title but his two extra hits. If walks were counted as hits in 1887, so be it.

"The past notions of reality have their own integrity. These have to be honored. If they made mistakes, OK," Mr. Voigt says. "What bothers me is these guys want certainty. You're not going to get certainty, not in the statistics of the game."

John Thorn, co-editor of Total Baseball, naturally disagrees: "To me, that's the equivalent of saying that if we disinterred Napoleon and found that contrary to all written reports he was not 5 foot 2 but 6 foot 2 we should keep this a secret."

Whatever your philosophical leanings, MLB's endorsement of the new data means that not a few numbers hammered into the plaques at the Baseball Hall of Fame in Cooperstown, N.Y., are now officially wrong. But the plaques, themselves considered historical artifacts, won't be recast.

"Some of these numbers acquire a kind of a poetry to them," chief research-librarian Tim Wiles notes. "When somebody takes them away or changes them and says we've improved baseball record-keeping, it's someone else's loss."

Not Lyle Spatz's. The records committee chairman at the Society for American Baseball Research (SABR, where sabermetrics gets its name) reports it was recently discovered that Roger Maris was credited with an extra run batted in in 1961, the year he broke Babe Ruth's single-season home-run record. Maris *really* had only 141 RBI that season, which would drop him into a tie for the American League title with Jim Gentile if it checks out.

Mr. Spatz is sure purists won't be happy. "I expect to hear from someone saying that you people are ruining baseball," he says.

80

2,131: Ripken Breaks Gehrig's Consecutive-Game Record (1995)

SOURCE: *Baltimore Sun*, September 7, 1995

Cal Ripken saved baseball. After the acrimony caused by the 1994 strike, attendance and television ratings plummeted, and many longtime fans swore off baseball forever. The prospect of Ripken surpassing Lou Gehrig's incredible record of 2,130 consecutive games played not only guaranteed soldout stadiums wherever Ripken's Baltimore Orioles played, but also helped to remind fans of the game's noble qualities. Without Ripken, many believe, major league baseball might have continued its disappearance from the consciousness of American sports fans.

The reality is a bit more complicated. True, Ripken was a very popular player, and certainly his achievement is worthy of celebration. Baseball has a new "unbreakable" record and another number has been added to baseball's statistical pantheon—2,632, the level reached by Ripken when he voluntarily sat out a game on September 20, 1998. However, Ripken also had many critics who pointed out the drop in his offensive performance and the decline of his defensive abilities, and who observed that any other player in Ripken's shoes would have been rested—and perhaps even benched—at numerous points during the streak. Moreover, the claim that Ripken saved baseball is mythical. In 1996 total major league attendance was more than 10 million less than in 1993, the last prestrike season. The average team drew more than 2.5 million fans in 1993, a figure not matched until 2006. Television ratings have also dropped in the face of competition from the NFL and the NBA, and also as a result of the explosion of alternative television options through the growth of cable and satellite television. As great as Ripken's feat was, it did not trigger the revitalization of baseball—no such revitalization occurred.

None of this mattered to those who witnessed the event in person or on radio or television. The column below reflects the adoration of Ripken expressed by his fans and by the baseball media.

Immortal Cal

He Touches Home with Victory Lap
By Ken Rosenthal
Sun Columnist

It was a victory lap for the ages. Rafael Palmeiro and Bobby Bonilla pushed Cal Ripken out of the Orioles' dugout, and off the game's all-time Iron Man went.

Down the right-field line, shaking hands with fans in the front row. Into the outfield, greeting the grounds crew and police officers. Above the center-field wall, where fans tumbled out of the bleachers as he leaped to slap them five.

Ripken's mother, Vi, leaned against his father, Cal Sr. Earlier, Senior had clapped and waved from his luxury box. Now he stood in his suit, hands behind his back, this incredibly tough man, biting his lower lip to fight back tears.

Junior had done it. One more time, the banner had dropped from the warehouse, revealing the number so many thought unattainable. The number 2,131. Never have four digits produced so many tears.

Grown men cried at Lou Gehrig's retirement ceremony 56 years ago, but those tears were born [sic] out of tragedy, the knowledge that Gehrig was seriously ill. These tears were born out of joy. And hometown pride. And love.

The game was delayed 22 minutes, 15 seconds. For a while, it seemed like play would never resume. For a while, it seemed Camden Yards would crumble from emotion.

He's just always there, you know? That's what was so celebrated, that's what this was all about. He's there when his team needs him. And there for a city that lost its football team and baseball glory long ago.

It's a simple virtue, perhaps, but in this harried age, simple can be remarkable. Such is the magic surrounding 2,131. A dozen years ago, Ripken was a local boy making good. Now, thanks to the streak, he's a national hero.

President Clinton shook both fists in exultation shortly after the celebration began. Vice President Albert Gore stood next to him, cheering. Sparklers and then fireworks went off on the stadium roof, evoking "The Natural."

In another box, Joe DiMaggio stood next to fellow Hall of Famer Frank Robinson. DiMaggio, two months short of his 81st birthday, was Gehrig's teammate. He, too, looked overcome by the moment.

Orioles second baseman Manny Alexander caught the popup that made the game official in the fifth inning. Instantly, the crowd roared. Police lined the outfield. And the Orioles' bullpen emptied, players and coaches running into the first base dugout, eager to join the celebration.

Ripken shook hands with his teammates, then left the dugout and jogged to where his wife, Kelly, was sitting. He removed his white Orioles jersey and handed it to her, revealing a black T-shirt underneath. On the back, it said, "2,130+, Hugs and Kisses for Daddy."

The TV cameras kept coming back to his mother, Vi. One moment, she was hugging her middle son, Fred. The next moment, she was holding her hands over her face. Always, she was crying.

Back on the field, Ripken picked up his son Ryan, 2, and kissed his daughter, Rachel, 5. Rachel wasn't having any of it. All night, she kept wiping her hand against her face, wiping off daddy's kisses. She wouldn't join him on the field, either.

It was so warm, so touching, so wonderfully, gloriously human. Ripken plays the game with such precision, he is sometimes described as a robot. Rarely does he show emotion. But on this night, he appeared relieved, and humbled, and so, so happy.

He touched hands with his brother, Bill, through the home-plate screen. Bill's wife, Candace, blew him kisses. The TV cameras showed Orioles general manager Roland Hemond crying. Hemond, a career baseball man who has seen it all.

Ripken earned this. Oh, how he earned this. In spring training, he said he wasn't sure how he would react to the attention surrounding the streak. Now the verdict is in: He reacted gracefully, exquisitely, remarkably.

Whatever the impact on his offensive statistics, however selfish his motives might have once appeared, no one will dare scoff at his accomplishment, the ordinary turned extraordinary, the methodical beauty.

There were eight curtain calls on this night, one after Ripken's home run—his third in three days—and seven during the fifth-inning celebration. The crowd chanted, "We want Cal! We want Cal!" Palmeiro and Bonilla gave their little push.

And, the victory lap began.

The closest thing you see to it in sports is during Olympic track and field, but how many Olympians win gold medals in their hometown? At one point, Ripken grabbed a man in the front row. Maybe an acquaintance. Maybe an old friend.

In left-center, he slapped palms with the Orioles' relievers, now back in the bullpen. He took a special moment with longtime bullpen coach Elrod Hendricks. As always, he kept going, and going, and going.

In front of the left-field bleachers, reaching up to fans in the first row. Down the left-field line, past the $5,000 seats to benefit research of Lou Gehrig's disease. And in front of the California Angels' dugout, where the evening's opponents awaited.

One by one, the Angels congratulated Ripken. The Whitney Houston song, "One Moment in Time," blared over the sound system. So much cheering. So much crying.

When Frank Robinson hit a ball out of Memorial Stadium, it was marked with a banner that said, "Here." The appropriate banner for Ripken would say, "There."

There for his team. There for his sport. There for his city.

There in heart. There in spirit. There in body, and in soul.

81

MLBPA Ratifies Basic Agreement, Officially Ending 1994 Strike (1996)

SOURCE: *Boston Globe*, December 6, 1996

The long national nightmare was over. After missing parts of two seasons and playing the 1996 season under a cloud, the owners and players finally settled their differences by signing a five-year agreement, retroactive to 1996, which would guarantee labor peace through the 2000 season. The new agreement had several important features, most notably the approval of interleague play for the 1997 and 1998 seasons, a luxury tax on several high-payroll teams, and increased revenue sharing in an attempt to increase competitive balance. In addition, fourteen players were granted free agency as a result of added service time accrued during the strike. Two of these players, Moises Alou and Alex Fernandez, would sign multimillion-dollar contracts with the Florida Marlins within the week, helping to propel the expansion franchise to a remarkable 1997 season.

Players' Ratification Brings Baseball Peace

By Larry Whiteside

GLOBE STAFF

The longest labor dispute in U.S. sports history is finally over.

Peace was officially restored to major league baseball yesterday in Puerto Rico when a five-year agreement, retroactive to this past season, was ratified by the Major League [Baseball] Players Association. Thus ends a four-year battle with an agreement that precludes work stoppages through the year 2000.

The agreement had been approved by major league owners in Chicago Nov. 27, contingent on the resolution of several minor issues. After a two-day delay, players gave their approval yesterday. The differences were worked out by the two negotiators, union leader Donald Fehr and Randy Levine, the owners' chief negotiator.

Fehr said from Puerto Rico that he was pleased that the ordeal was over but he was too exhausted to characterize the new contract, which included a couple of late changes.

"With this unfortunate period behind us," said Fehr, "my fellow players and I can once again focus on the game on the field. We are confident that baseball's best days lie ahead."

Levine, the second of two negotiators used by the owners during the dispute, was elated.

"I want to congratulate Don Fehr, the other lawyers and the players on this new contract," he said. "It was a lot of hard work by people. Now the owners and players have a chance to work in a real partnership. And that's good for baseball."

The long dispute had been a costly one for both sides. Players lost about $350 million in salary during the 232-day strike in 1994 and '95. Over a three-year period, the 28 major league teams suffered more than $800 million in operating losses.

After the '96 season, owners at first wanted to prolong the dispute unless certain demands were met in the contract. When the players refused, the owners quickly realized that the new contract was a lot better than playing another season under the rules of the old contract, which expired Dec. 31, 1993.

The executive council of the players' union met for three days in Puerto Rico before ratifying the agreement. They did so after several late changes.

The union agreed to permit interleague play on an experimental basis in 1997 and '98. Originally, the deal gave permission for interleague play in 1997 only.

Approval of the second year of interleague play was contingent on retaining the limit of up to 16 interleague games per team. If owners want to expand that schedule in 1998, they would have to allow the designated hitter in all interleague games, not just the ones in American League parks.

Also, 14 players will get credit for service time during the 75 regular-season days wiped out by the strike. Tim Naehring of the Red Sox is among those who will receive free agency tomorrow at 2 p.m., according to a source. He will be joined by Alex Fernandez of the White Sox, Jimmy Key of the Yankees and Moises Alou of Montreal, among others.

Apparently, clubs must act quickly, according to the source. The usual filing period for free agents has ended. Thus, teams must decide by tomorrow at midnight whether to offer salary arbitration to their former players in this category. Those players not offered arbitration cannot negotiate with their former teams until May 1.

Other items:

The minimum salary increases to $150,000 next season.

The players' share of ticket money from the first three games of each first-round playoff series drops from 80 to 60 percent, with the difference going into an escrow account.

There will be a 35 percent luxury tax on the portions of payrolls above $51 million for the five teams spending the most on players, a provision designed to decrease the payroll disparity between the large- and small-market teams.

There will be vastly more revenue sharing among the clubs, as high-revenue teams are forced to give up a higher percentage of their locally generated broadcast and ticket money.

Acting commissioner Bud Selig said from Milwaukee that there is no such thing as a perfect agreement, but this one has a lot of positives about it.

"One has to be satisfied that we've made progress," said Selig. "But there is much to be done. The concerns people have about the game are legitimate. When you think back to everything that has happened, this deal reflects a lot of the activity and hopes by both sides. Now it's up to us all to move forward."

82

Fehr Comments on Proposed "Curt Flood Act of 1997" (1997)

SOURCE: Senate Committee on the Judiciary, *Major League Baseball Antitrust Reform*, 105th Cong., 1st sess., 1997, 10–13

Since 1950 the U.S. Congress has considered amending or eliminating the antitrust exemption for baseball in place since the 1922 Supreme Court decision on the issue sixty times. Several bills were supported by major league baseball, but all died before coming to a vote. After the disastrous 1994 strike, which resulted in the cancellation of the World Series that year, however, Congress, as well as owners and the MLBPA, realized that the time had come for another attempt.

On January 21, 1997, Senators Orrin Hatch, Patrick Leahy, Strom Thurmond, and Patrick Moynihan introduced S. 53, titled the "Curt Flood Act of 1997" in memory of the player who sacrificed his career in an attempt to overturn the exemption. After several months of delays, the owners and players finally met and agreed on the language of the bill, although Stanley Brand, the lobbyist for the minor leagues, opposed the very idea of removing the exemption, even after the signing of a new Professional Baseball Agreement that ensured the stability of the minors. During a hearing on June 17—at which Brand failed to appear—Donald Fehr offered the following statement describing the need for the anti-trust exemption from the players' perspective. The bill, limited only to labor negotiations, was finally signed by President Clinton on October 27, 1998, but has had no practical effect. For an analysis of the legislation by the Congressional Research Service see Janice E. Rubin, "Curt Flood Act of 1998: Application of Federal Antitrust Laws to Major League Baseball Players" (Washington, DC: Penny Hill Press, 2004).

PREPARED STATEMENT OF DONALD A. FEHR

This Committee has spent considerable time in the last four years studying antitrust issues as they relate to baseball. On behalf of all major league players, I want to thank Chairman Hatch and Senator Leahy for their interest in and attention to these issues. My views on these matters are well known from my previous testimony before this and other committees, and need no repetition here.

As has often been noted, over the last 25 years, there have been eight consecutive work stoppages (strikes and lockouts) in major league baseball, more than in the other three major team sports (football, basketball and hockey) combined. We believe that this results, in significant part, from the belief of the major league owners that major league players, unlike their counterparts in basketball, football and hockey, have no rights under the antitrust laws. Major league players have sought, and continue to seek, the same rights under the antitrust laws as other professional athletes similarly situated, no more but no less.

The importance of the antitrust laws to the collective bargaining process in professional sports is often misunderstood. It is not necessarily the use of the remedy that is important; rather, it is the opportunity to resort to the remedy that matters. It has been the desire to have an alternative course of action available to them, an alternative course which would have a moderating influence on the bargaining process, that has been at the heart of the players' efforts in the antitrust area. As we learned too well in 1994, the players effectively had only one choice: accept the owners unilaterally imposed terms and conditions of employment, or strike. Unlike other similarly situated athletes, baseball players have no other alternative. And unlike other professional sports team owners, who know that their players are protected by antitrust laws, baseball owners have believed that major league players do not have such protection, and therefore believe that if they can break the union, the players have no recourse, and the owners can impose whatever conditions they choose. That does not foster labor peace. Accordingly, major league players have petitioned Congress to ensure that they have the same rights and protections under law as do other similarly situated athletes. We are prepared to continue that effort in order to avoid in the future what has been the seemingly inevitable disruption in the game every time we negotiate.

THE NEW COLLECTIVE BARGAINING AGREEMENT
Many people were surprised to learn that there was any mention of antitrust legislation in the new collective bargaining agreement. With both sides knowing that

this effort would continue until either a bill was passed or the next work stoppage was upon us, the parties chose to address this issue in the recently signed collective bargaining agreement . . . .

The players and owners were very careful to make certain that the bill they would jointly support would deal only with major league player issues; the scope and effect of the antitrust laws is not changed in any other respect. In other words, whatever the law is with respect to other issues or third parties, it will continue to be—this legislation will do nothing to change it.

The relevant portion of Article XXVIII reads as follows:

> "the Clubs and the Association will jointly request and cooperate in lobbying the Congress to pass a law that will clarify that Major League Baseball Players are covered under the antitrust laws (i.e., that Major League Players have the same rights under the antitrust laws as do other professional athletes, e.g. football and basketball players), along with a provision that makes it clear that passage of that bill does not change the application of the antitrust laws in any other context or with respect to any other person or entity."

LEGISLATION

Early in this Congress, Senators Hatch, Leahy, Thurmond and Moynihan introduced S. 53. That bill constitutes a much broader clarification of the application of the antitrust laws to major league baseball than the bill contemplated in the collective bargaining agreement. As was the case in prior bills, however, S. 53 made clear that it was not to affect the application of the antitrust laws with respect to franchise relocation issues or the Sports Broadcasting Act, nor was it to affect "the applicability or nonapplicability of the antitrust laws to the amateur draft of professional baseball, the minor league reserve clause, the agreement between professional major league baseball teams and the teams of the National Association of Baseball (sic), commonly known as the 'Professional Baseball Agreement,' or any other matter relating to the minor leagues."

We fully supported that bill, and continue to believe it to be wise public policy. But the hope was, and continues to be, that the collective bargaining agreement recently signed will lead to the enactment of legislation relating only to major league players quickly and cleanly, so that the owners and players can put this issue behind them and set their sights squarely on working together to repair and improve the game.

I have been advised that a substitute amendment recently circulated to S. 53, apparently in anticipation of an early agreement to legislative language effectuating the collective bargaining agreement, and to keep the process moving forward. That amendment was taken virtually verbatim from Article XXVIII of the new Basic Agreement. As such, we had no objection to it when it was originally offered, nor do we now. It was the Association's hope, however, that to the extent the owners and players could agree to legislative language that accurately reflected the intent of that amendment, and which the parties felt comfortable supporting, the legislative process would be further facilitated.

To that end, and at the strong urging of Senators Hatch and Leahy, the Association has attempted to develop with the owners an acceptable alternative to that amendment. On 16 May, 1997 representatives of the Players Association reached an agreement with representatives of Major League Baseball on language that the MLB representatives would take to the MLB owners for approval. My understanding is that they did so last week. Hopefully, by today, the Chairman has been advised of the owners' actions on this suggested language.

83

Impact of 1997 Professional Baseball Agreement on a Minor League Club (1997)

SOURCE: *Augusta Chronicle*, August 31, 1997, http://augustachronicle.com/stories/083197/spo_green.html

Once major league officials saw how the minor leagues boomed in popularity and profitability following the signing of the 1990 Professional Baseball Agreement (PBA), which obligated minor league affiliates to assume many of the expenditures previously paid by the parent clubs and required a substantial investment in stadium improvements, they reinforced the notion of financial self-sufficiency in the 1997 PBA. As in 1990, many minor league clubs complained about the increased economic burden required under the PBA. One example of a club's anticipated difficulties in meeting the requirements of the new PBA is noted in the article below.

Jackets Will Feel Effects of New Agreement in '98
By Rob Mueller
Staff Writer

When the National Association of Professional Baseball Leagues and Major League Baseball got together earlier this summer to hammer out long-range plans for the future, a radical plan for Triple-A realignment next season garnered much of the attention.

What slipped through the cracks in relative obscurity was the signing of a new 10-year Professional Baseball Agreement in June—a pact that truly will hit home for the Augusta GreenJackets and the rest of minor league baseball.

The new PBA between Major League Baseball and the National Association, the governing body of the minor leagues, takes the bulk of the financial burden off the parent clubs, placing it on their affiliates. The agreement takes effect in October, and runs through the 2007 season.

In return for a guarantee of stability regarding affiliation for the 156 existing minor league franchises plus two new Triple-A expansion clubs which begin play in 1998, farm clubs will foot the bill for the NA's Umpire Development Program, as well as equipment costs. Previously, major league clubs were solely responsible for umpire development and most baseball-related expenditures.

During negotiations, umpire development was the major league's greatest concern. With the victory, MLB estimates an annual savings of $5 million under the new contract.

"The industry as a whole faces an uncertain future, especially from a financial standpoint," NA president Mike Moore said. "We must work together to find solutions which will benefit the fans."

This after attendance at minor league ballparks nationwide reached the 17-million mark in July, the biggest fan boom in 45 years.

"When we got around the table and everyone's ideas were presented, the majors quickly realized that the stability and the present setup were to their advantage," Moore told *Baseball America*.

GreenJackets general manager Chris Scheuer estimates the new PBA will cost the club an additional $60,000 in 1998.

In the South Atlantic League, as well as the six other Class A leagues, clubs can expect to pay around $20,000 for umpire development. Scheuer said he expects to spend an additional $40,000 on equipment—baseballs, uniforms and bats.

In addition, the Jackets will cover 50 percent of the salary to pay an equipment manager. The Pittsburgh Pirates, Augusta's parent club, will pick up the other half of the tab for the new position.

Currently, there are no plans by the GreenJackets to cushion the blow with a hike in ticket prices, though several SAL general managers say they likely will have no choice but to let the PBA's fallout trickle down to fans.

"We're going to have to come up with new ways to generate revenue to make up for the added expenses," Scheuer said. "Next year, we're going to look at ourselves as an entertainment-type business rather than just a baseball club."

Among the plans for Augusta next season is hosting additional non-baseball events, such as concerts and company picnics.

The Jackets this season brought to Lake Olmstead Stadium two concerts—the Beach Blast during the week of the Masters Tournament, and Hot Country Nights in July. They expect to add two more shows next season.

The club hosts picnics for area businesses, offering softball and volleyball games among other activities. Companies can cater the event themselves or pay an additional cost to have the GreenJackets handle everything.

Bringing high school football to The Lake is another idea the Jackets have thrown around, but Scheuer doesn't anticipate that happening in the immediate future.

Greensboro GM John Frye agreed that entertainment is where the business is headed. He also said that the Bats will "almost definitely" raise ticket prices next season.

"Everyone is going to have to consider this as a major challenge," Frye said. "Most teams have always tried to do as much as they can with the baseball aspect, and now we've got to get into outside promotions. This isn't just about baseball anymore."

"I personally don't like (the PBA); it's going to cost us a lot of money," Frye added. "Losing stability and affiliation never worried me very much."

For the second straight year, attendance is down slightly at The Lake, but the Jackets will make money in 1997, Scheuer said, after two years of operating in the red. The club was hit hard by start-up costs to open the new ballpark in 1995.

Augusta set a franchise attendance record in '95, drawing more than 170,000 fans in The Lake's debut season. They drew 157,000 last season—fourth best in the SAL—and are currently sixth out of 14 SAL clubs this season, having drawn 145,000 fans with two regular-season games remaining, including Saturday night's game.

"The (PBA) is definitely going to make it harder for us financially, but we've been anticipating this for a couple of years now," Scheuer said. "We've been trying to run the ballpark more efficiently, cutting out a bit of the waste here and there. I think we were well prepared for this, and we're going to continue to thrive."

84

Florida Marlins Win World Series in Extra Innings (1997)

SOURCE: *Miami Herald*, October 27, 1997

Wayne Huizenga, the billionaire owner of the Florida Marlins since its 1993 inception, was determined to make a profit on his investment. Huizenga realized that his best option was to rapidly build a championship-quality team through free agency that would attract fans to Pro Player Stadium, which he also owned, even though wealthy owners like George Steinbrenner and Ted Turner, among others, had tried this strategy and failed. However, baseball economics by the late 1990s had changed in Huizenga's favor. Owners and players alike understood the free-agency system better than in previous years, and salaries had escalated to the point where intelligent general managers could target and acquire top players while they were still good enough to merit their eight-figure contracts.

Marlins general manager Dave Dombrowski, following his owner's orders, signed expensive free agents like Bobby Bonilla, Moises Alou, and Miami native Alex Fernandez prior to the 1997 season. In all, Huizenga spent a record $89 million on free-agent contracts, not including the signing of top manager Jim Leyland. To the surprise and dismay of many in baseball, Florida earned a wild-card berth, where it shocked the defending NL champion Atlanta Braves in the NLCS behind the record-setting performance of Cuban rookie pitcher Livan Hernandez. Hernandez matched his playoff performance with a 2-0 mark in the World Series, but the Marlins needed a dramatic ninth-inning comeback in the seventh game of the Series to defeat the favored Cleveland Indians in extra innings.

Immediately after the 1997 season Huizenga capitalized on his Series title by selling nearly every star player to the highest bidder. The Marlins crashed to the cellar of the NL

East with a dismal record of 54-108, losing thirty-eight more games than the previous season, a modern record. But Huizenga made a profit.

Loudest Sports Cheer in Years

Hysterical, Historical Win

Edwin Pope
Sports Editor

It was all amazing, every inch and second of it. Edgar Renteria's single skittering out into the night. Craig Counsell sprinting across the plate. South Florida letting out its breath in the loudest, craziest sports cheer since the Dolphins won the seventh Super Bowl, all the way out in California.

Most amazingly, *no one left*. It was past midnight on a Sunday night and the Florida Marlins had finished one of baseball's unlikeliest journeys ever in a 3–2, 11-inning victory over the Cleveland Indians in Game 7 of the World Series.

And not one of the 67,204 fans seemed to so much as think about leaving for the longest time.

Victory—hysterical, historical victory—held them there. But one Florida Marlin nailed them in their seats early. One player saw to it they stayed, and the Marlins stayed in the biggest baseball game South Florida ever had.

His name was Al Leiter and all he was getting was knocks before going against an Indians batting order that had basically been knocking the heck out of Marlins pitching most of this frantic, controversial tournament.

Honest Al pitched his heart out for six innings. He held his often treacherous control. He held the Indians except for a two-run flurry in the third inning.

"It's a wonderful feeling," he said. "Not just for me. For everybody."

Everybody had a little piece of this.

Bobby Bonilla whacked that 462-foot home run in the seventh inning. Moises Alou, Charles Johnson and Craig Counsell sent the game into extra innings. Robb Nen took over in the most important pinch of his life and struck out the Indians' side in the 10th.

Then came the 11th, dropping that anchor on Indians hearts, with Renteria, the rookie from Colombia, and Counsell, the pickup from the Colorado Rockies, putting the Marlins over the top.

Tough luck for Jaret Wright, a kid three years out of high school, stopping the Marlins for 6 $1/_3$ innings of two-hit ball.

Leiter vs. Wright; great-hearted veteran vs. whiz kid. No-hit pitcher against the son of a no-hit pitcher. Leiter did his no-hitter last season. Wright's father, Clyde, a zany character who did 10 years in the bigs, pitched his no-hitter for the California Angels in 1970.

The only way Leiter could have matched Wright was with a no-hitter in his fine six innings. And guess who got the only hit off Wright until Bonilla busted his 6-for-26 Series slump with that monster shot?

Renteria. But you know that. Of course, you know that. Everybody knows everything about the Marlins this morning. They are overnight legends, truly fashioned in one endlessly emotional Sunday night.

None more this morning than Leiter, unless it is Livan Hernandez, who was named Most Valuable Player but couldn't pitch in the wind-up because the rookie from Cuba had thrown 142 pitches in winning Game 5 two nights before.

"I'm just glad I could give them some good innings out there," Leiter said. "This hasn't been an easy year."

It has actually been crazier for Leiter than any of the Marlins. He didn't have much to celebrate Thursday night when he turned 32. He had mysteriously turned sour in his on-the-road assignments. An eight-year veteran, and he had to be home to win it.

He came home Sunday night, all right. Came home throwing a cut fastball 90 mph, and keeping it inside. After last year's no-hitter against Colorado, victims' Manager Don Baylor said, "We're always waiting for (Atlanta's) Tommy Glavine to throw inside, and now we're still waiting for Leiter to throw outside."

Sixty-five of Leiter's 115 pitches Sunday night went for strikes, a daunting number from a man with Leiter's stuff.

"I felt it early," he said. "I had good location. I was throwing the change."

He was *pitching* again, finally out of the nasty habit of *throwing*.

He was pitching a game he and his wife Lori and their two daughters, Lindsay Brooke, 2, and Carly Jane, will be telling to their children and grandchildren. And we will be telling ours.

"This was for all the guys, and all the fans," Al said.

They all got the hint when Leiter wore a tight little smile as he strode back to the dugout after setting down the first six Indians. Bases-on-balls pitchers trudge. Leiter strode. He deserved that smile. He hadn't walked a single batter.

The crowd came in charged, and Leiter was recharging it. "We will . . . we will . . . rock you!" came the chant, speaking for Leiter.

That chant might be considered small-town stuff some other places, but it's been big here since Miami Hurricanes football crowds of the early 1980s started it.

This was the same thing, except far, far larger. This was another team on the verge of its first title, arguably the most important in all sports. This was all of South Florida going bonkers out there. The franchise may be only 5 years old, but what happened Sunday night has been a long, long time coming.

Henry Flagler brought the railroad in here seven years before the first World Series in 1903. Then we waited until 1993 just for a team. All those years, while baseball was so big in Cleveland and New York and Chicago and Boston and Philadelphia and such bulging canyons of steel and concrete, most of our baseball would be played on patches of dirt carved out of scrub pine.

Al Rosen, later a slugger for the Indians, played at Miami Beach High School in the 1940s when the population was so sparse the only way his team knew it had reached Hollywood was by looking up and seeing the water tower.

A few folks have moved into this megalopolis since then, and they all seemed to be at the ballpark for Game 7 and yelling for Honest Al Leiter.

Then it all changed, in seconds, as baseball does. Changed as suddenly as it had just the night before, when Chad Ogea delivered the first base hit of any Indians pitcher in 25 years of the designated-hitter rule, and knocked in the only two runs his team needed to win Game 6.

This time it was Jim Thome who walked and Marquis Grissom who cracked a Leiter slider to left. After Wright sac-bunted them up, Tony Fernandez's sharp single scored Thome and Grissom.

And that 2–0 Indians lead looked like the whole ballgame for the longest.

Bonilla slammed his bat angrily onto the plate after striking out his second time up and dropping his World Series batting average to .154.

Leiter only gathered strength. Across one patch, he struck out five of eight Indians he faced. He was whiffing his way out of potential disaster early and late. With men on first and third in the fifth, he made David Justice his third whiffee of the inning and bailed himself out again.

You may talk about Miami's vapid baseball crowds, but this one was barbed wire, electrified by Leiter if not by what the Marlins were futilely trying to form in the way of offense.

This was The Pro's answer to The Jake.

When it snowed in Cleveland's Jacobs Field before and during Wednesday's Game 4, legendary broadcaster Vince Scully was waiting for the starting lineups and talking about Marlins baseball. "When I first went to Vero Beach and Dodgertown with the Dodgers 48 years ago," Scully said, "nobody even bothered to think about whether there would ever be a team to the South."

Then, that bitter-cold and snowy night in Cleveland at midweek. Scully turned to New York Daily News baseball columnist Bill Madden and said, "What's taking the starting lineups so long?"

"I think they're waiting for volunteers," Madden said.

Leiter volunteered himself Sunday night, fiercely, confidently, and as it turned out, wonderfully.

85

"El Duque" Makes Major League Debut (1998)

SOURCE: *New York Daily News*, June 4, 1998

The most heralded rookie of 1998 was Orlando "El Duque" Hernandez, a star pitcher whose dramatic escape from Cuba—which had banned him from his Industriales club because they suspected that he was planning to defect—electrified the baseball world. Hernandez, the older brother of Livan Hernandez and the winner of a gold medal in the 1992 Olympics, arranged to claim refugee status in Costa Rica instead of the United States, enabling *him to avoid the player draft and accept a four-year, $6.6 million free-agent contract with the New York Yankees barely three months after fleeing his homeland in a sailboat (not a leaky raft, as Hernandez initially claimed).*

El Duque lived up to his billing in his debut, as described in the following article. He maintained his excellence for the rest of the season with a 12-4 record, helping New York to win an AL-record 114 games in the regular season. In addition, Hernandez earned a reputation as one of the best clutch pitchers in baseball, winning his first eight post-season decisions with the powerhouse Yankees and receiving the MVP for his performance in the 1999 ALCS.

Hernandez's dramatic story is best told in Steve Fainaru and Ray Sanchez, The Duke of Havana: Baseball, Cuba, and the Search for the American Dream *(New York: Villard, 2001).*

EL DUQUE DELIVERS

Dominates Devil Rays in His Debut
By Pete Botte
Daily News Sports Writer

If you're looking to place this magical night into proper perspective, remember that Hideki Irabu also completely wowed New York the first time he set foot on the Yankee Stadium mound last summer.

And remember too, that this night also might go down as the one that landed the Yankees' most important all-around player—Derek Jeter—on the disabled list.

But that doesn't mean you can't wake up today and feel good for the stoic man they call El Duque.

Multiple members of the Yankees brass insisted before the game that it was a clear-cut decision that Orlando Hernandez would be returned to Columbus today with an eye towards a recall later this month regardless of his performance last night.

But Joe Torre not surprisingly was forced to leave that door ajar after the heralded $6.6 million Cuban defector lived up to—if not exceeded—his lofty billing with seven stellar innings of one-run ball as the Yankees clubbed the Devil Rays, 7–1, before 27,291 fans and several Cuban flags at the Stadium.

"He'll be here (today) because there's nothing he can do down there for five days anyway, but he did a helluva job," Torre said before being asked if it was foreseeable that Hernandez might supplant Ramiro Mendoza or someone else in the Yankees' rotation.

"There's always a chance (he'll stay here) if that phone rings and somebody tells me that's the way it's going to be," Torre said. "You have the wrong guy, because I'm not the boss. But as of right now, I don't anticipate that happening."

The Yankees, however, do seem to be revising that thinking, although GM Brian Cashman would not commit either way following the game.

That's because even in Hernandez' or the Yankees' wildest dreams, no one could have envisioned his debut would have resulted in such a staggering line score.

Seven innings, one run (a Fred McGriff homer), five hits, seven strikeouts, two walks, a victory, and the dreamiest of dreams come true that had to make those frightful December days in that flimsy raft seem all worthwhile.

"As to how I feel, I'm very emotional and more than happy," said Hernandez, who fought back tears as he dedicated the game to the family members—including two young daughters—he left behind in Cuba. "It was a long time—years, in fact—since I've had the chance to pitch in front of so many people. My first game as a major-league ballplayer, I will always remember."

Scott Brosius clubbed a pair of two-run doubles—and Jeter notably left the game with a strained abdominal muscle that could land him on the disabled list today—as the Yanks (40-13) won their third straight.

But this day—from start to finish—was about El Duque.

Hernandez, who was 6-0 with a 3.88 ERA at Columbus, initially was summoned to serve as an insurance policy for David Wells' barking left shoulder. But David Cone's well-documented dog-bite on his right index finger served as the remarkable springboard for Hernandez' debut.

Wearing knee-high socks that were accentuated every time he began his eye-high leg kick, El Duque performed as advertised from the start. He worked inside and outside with excellent control among his 117 pitches. He dropped down to different arm angles and mixed speeds brilliantly on his baffling array of breaking pitches.

And as for the Yankees' original plan to shuttle him back to his Columbus post to await his next chance, El Duque did whatever he could to make them consider immediately changing their minds.

"For us, the Columbus club is still a part of the Yankees' organization," Hernandez said. "Wherever I am sent I will do my job."

86

Selig Officially Elected as Commissioner (1998)

SOURCE: *New York Daily News,* July 10, 1998

Ever since the owners forced Fay Vincent to resign as commissioner in September 1992, Milwaukee Brewers owner Bud Selig had been running baseball as the acting commissioner. Selig testified to Congress in 1992 and 1994 that an active search for a permanent commissioner was well under way, to Selig's relief, since he stated that he had no desire to remain in that post. However, the announcement of Selig's election as commissioner surprised no one. It reaffirmed the obvious—the baseball leadership that contributed to the most chaotic decade in the sport's history remained intact and that its philosophy would not change in the near future.

Lords Elect Selig Commissioner

By Bill Madden
Daily News Sports Writer

The coronation of Bud Selig as baseball commissioner, which has been five years, 10 months, a 230-day strike, two expansions and one realignment in the making, became official yesterday by a unanimous 30–0 vote of his fellow owners.

In removing the "acting" from his title and becoming baseball's ninth commissioner, Selig has agreed to place his team, the Milwaukee Brewers, in a trust to remove himself from a conflict-of-interest position.

His daughter, Wendy, who has been running the team while Selig has been acting commissioner, will continue in that role. The only change in the situation is that Selig will move his office from the Brewers' County Stadium to downtown Milwaukee. He will not move to New York, but instead will leave baseball's central office under the direction of MLB president and CEO Paul Beeston.

"I will start spending a significant amount of time (in New York)," Selig said, "but essentially I plan to be wherever there are problems."

Selig's election to a five-year term, at a meeting of the owners in Chicago that lasted little more than an hour, is an affirmation of his fellow lords' faith in his leadership.

Twice in the nearly six years he has served them, search committees for a new commissioner were formed only to come to the same conclusion: Selig, despite his avowed intention not to take the job on a full-time basis, was the only candidate.

Selig said salary terms have not been worked out, but baseball sources said he would be paid $3 million per year.

"I never thought it would come to this," Selig insisted by phone yesterday. "What swayed me to take the job? (Owners urging him to take it) came from everywhere. Basically they said, 'We're on an upswing, you understand the problems of the game and we just can't begin all over again now, no matter how good these candidates are.'

"They cited my knowledge of the game's inner workings and told me my depth of history was invaluable to them. I couldn't argue with them."

Though he already has guided the owners through several momentous events and changes—none more traumatic than the strike that resulted in the cancellation of the 1994 World Series—the 63-year-old Selig acknowledged facing a full plate of problems as he takes the game into the 21st century. The most vexing of them is the continuing disparity between large- and small-market teams which is growing despite the advent of revenue sharing. This year, the Orioles have the highest payroll at $70 million, compared with the Expos at $9 million at the other end of the spectrum.

"All I can say is there will be no surprises," Selig said. "But there's no question we have a serious problem with the disparity of payrolls. The game can't continue to operate with so many teams having so little hope. I had hoped revenue sharing would help resolve the problem, but it may not be enough."

Selig went on to say that having the "acting" removed from his title will enable him to function with more flexibility in regard to the disciplinary part of the job. In that area he will have to address Pete Rose's application for reinstatement and Reds owner Marge Schott's continuing suspension.

Selig took over as acting commissioner when Fay Vincent resigned under fire Sept. 9, 1992, and even in his "interim" capacity, Selig has served longer than four of his recent predecessors—Vincent (three years), Bart Giamatti (four months), Peter Ueberroth (4 ½ years) and William Eckert (three years).

During his term as baseball's acting czar, Selig has presided over more radical change than at any other time in the game's history. Expansions in 1993 and '98 brought four new franchises, Florida, Colorado, Tampa Bay and Arizona. Those expansions, in turn, brought about realignment and a radical change in the post-season format to three divisions and a wild card in each league.

As for the continuing perception that, as one of the owners' own, he can't function as a truly independent commissioner, Selig said: "I understand that, but I consider myself above all a baseball man and everything I do will be what I consider to be in the best interest of the game, not the owners. Thanks to Paul (Beeston) we already have begun building a spirit of cooperation with the (players) union that didn't exist before."

87

Reporter Questions McGwire's Use of Supplements (1998)

SOURCE: *Pocono Record*, August 23, 1998, www.poconorecord.com

Throughout the magical summer of 1998, fans and reporters alike were mesmerized by the race between St. Louis Cardinals first baseman Mark McGwire and Chicago Cubs right fielder Sammy Sosa to break Roger Maris's record of sixty-one home runs in a season. Although many writers had noted McGwire's impressive physique and had asked him about his workout regimen (without getting a clear answer), none had questioned the means by which McGwire attained his level of muscular development until Associated Press reporter Steve Wilstein noticed a distinctive bottle in McGwire's locker. In the following article Wilstein introduced the baseball public to androstenedione and to supplements in general, a subject with which it would become intimately familiar in the near future.

McGwire's Power Aided by "Andro"
By Steve Wilstein
AP Sports Writer

Sitting on the top shelf of Mark McGwire's locker, next to a can of Popeye spinach and packs of sugarless gum, is a brown bottle labeled Androstenedione.

For more than a year, McGwire says, he has been using the testosterone-producing pill, which is perfectly legal in baseball but banned in the NFL, Olympics and the NCAA.

No one suggests that McGwire wouldn't be closing in on Roger Maris' home run record without the over-the-counter drug. After all, he hit 49 homers without it as a rookie in 1987, and more than 50 each of the past two seasons.

But the drug's ability to raise levels of the male hormone, which builds lean muscle mass and promotes recovery after injury, is seen outside baseball as cheating and potentially dangerous.

"Everything I've done is natural. Everybody that I know in the game of baseball uses the same stuff I use," said McGwire, who also takes the popular muscle-builder Creatine, an amino acid powder.

However, many other players insist they do not take Androstenedione (pronounced Andro-steen'-die-own), although the use of other supplements is common.

Sammy Sosa, close to McGwire in the homer chase, uses Creatine after games to keep up his weight and strength. For energy before games he takes the Chinese herb ginseng.

But Sosa says he doesn't use Androstenedione or any other testosterone booster. Nor does Boston slugger Mo Vaughn.

"Anything illegal is definitely wrong," Vaughn said. "But if you get something over the counter and legal, guys in that power-hitting position are going to use them. Strength is the key to maintaining and gaining endurance for 162 games. The pitchers keep getting bigger and stronger."

Andres Galarraga, Atlanta's top home run hitter, said he would be "scared" to take a drug like Androstenedione.

"I do my weight (lifting) and take my vitamins. That's it," he said. "You have to be careful what you take. It could cause secondary problems with your body."

Shot putter Randy Barnes, the 1996 Olympic gold medalist and world record-holder, recently drew a lifetime ban for using Androstenedione. Barnes claimed he wasn't told about the ban until after his out-of-competition drug test on April 1. Barnes is appealing the decision.

Baseball bans only illegal drugs as does the NBA, and the reason in both cases has nothing to do with competitive fairness or health. The players associations and management in both sports simply haven't agreed on ways of dealing with the issue.

"Obviously, if there's more research and it's shown that it's harmful, we'll make people aware," baseball spokesman Rich Levin said of Androstenedione.

Numerous studies suggest there are dangers associated with drugs that raise testosterone levels—even if there isn't much research specifically on Androstenedione.

"It's just a fluke of the law that this is totally unstudied," said Dr. John Lombardo of Ohio State, the NFL's adviser on steroids. "There are no adverse-effects studies. There are no efficacy studies. Because the people who produce it never had to do them, thanks to the (federal) supplement act of 1994. Androstenedione is no different than taking testosterone.

"Androstenedione is a steroid," he said. "It has anabolic qualities. Therefore it is an anabolic steroid."

Anabolic steroids have been associated with potentially fatal side effects, including heart attacks, cancers, liver dysfunction, and severe disorders of mood and mental function.

"You can't even buy testosterone with a regular prescription," said Dr. Gary I. Wadler, an expert in supplement use and assistant professor of medicine at Cornell University Medical College. "You have to get a triplicate prescription. It's a controlled substance by an act of Congress. The schizophrenia of all this is, product A, which is over the counter, becomes product B, which is a controlled substance."

Creatine, which the 34-year-old McGwire believes helps him recover faster from daily weightlifting, is purported to increase muscle energy and mass. Long-term effects of the powder are unknown. It has been known to lead to muscle tears and cramps due to dehydration.

"I've been using Creatine for about four years," said the 6-foot-5, 245-pound McGwire, who played for the U.S. baseball team at the 1984 Olympics. "It's a good thing. It helps strength. It helps recovery.

"I think Creatine is getting a bad rap now because people abuse it," he said. "That's the problem. It says to take one to two scoops a day. People started taking 15 or 20. If you abuse anything you're going to hurt yourself. If you just use common sense, there's absolutely nothing wrong with it. It's a form of eating red meat."

Chicago Cubs trainer David Tumbas said he doesn't recommend Creatine but doesn't tell players not to take it. He asked the players in spring training if they were using it or similar supplements, and about 10 said they were. He added, though, that he believes no one on the Cubs is taking Androstenedione.

The IOC added Androstenedione to its lengthy banned list last December after it found the pills and various steroids being hawked on the Internet by a company called Price's Power International of Newport News, Va. The company, which offered the product for $49.95 a bottle and gave tips on how to avoid detection, claimed Androstenedione helps build lean muscle mass "faster than ever imagined."

But that's hardly the only place where "Andro," as it is popularly called, is available. Great Earth Vitamin stores, a chain of 138 franchises in 23 states, sell the drug over the counter and by mail order. It is bundled with several supplements in a packet called "Andro-Flav Stack."

"It's very popular," said Andrew Fischman, director of marketing for the Hicksville, N.Y.-based chain. "The primary target of it is the 18- to 35-year-old muscle-head.

"If you can support your body's natural ability to produce testosterone and other hormones through diet, exercise and nutritional supplementation, that may lead to increased muscle mass and overall size," he said. "That's where the movement is."

San Diego conditioning coordinator Sam Gannelli said none of the Padres take Androstenedione, and he didn't believe steroids were widely used in baseball.

"Compared to every other sport, there's no time to heal in baseball," he said. "In football, you have six days off after every game. In basketball, it's three or four days. These guys are going every day for six months. Steroids can really get you broken down. They can do a lot of harm in the long run."

88

McGwire Breaks Record with Sixty-second Home Run (1998)

SOURCE: *St. Louis Post-Dispatch*, September 9, 1998

In September 1998 major league baseball was enjoying one of its greatest seasons. The New York Yankees were threatening the all-time record for wins during the regular season (they would "settle" for 114 victories, then continue their dominance in the postseason by sweeping the San Diego Padres in the World Series). Pitcher Kerry Wood, in the fifth start of his career, struck out twenty Houston Astros and permitted only one hit in one of the most dominant mound performances ever. David Wells of the New York Yankees topped Wood by throwing a perfect game. On September 20 Cal Ripken voluntarily ended his untouchable consecutive-games-played streak at 2,632. Other players enjoying spectacular seasons included Juan Gonzalez, Ken Griffey Jr., Alex Rodriguez, and Roger Clemens.

But the unquestioned stars of the 1998 season were Mark McGwire and Sammy Sosa. Together they mesmerized the nation during their assault on one of baseball's most treasured records—Roger Maris's sixty-one home runs in a season. After Sosa caught fire in June, hitting a record twenty home runs in the month, he and McGwire were paired in the public eye as they approached Maris's mark. Frequently when one player edged ahead in the race, the other would homer later that day or the following day. It helped that the ebullient Sosa showed McGwire, normally a quiet player, how to enjoy the spotlight. When McGwire finally hit his sixty-second home run, it seemed especially appropriate that his opponent that day was Sosa's Chicago Cubs.

JUBILATION!

**For Mark McGwire, it was the culmination of a season-long quest.
For the fans of St. Louis, it was the thrill of a lifetime.**
By Mike Eisenbath
Of the Post-Dispatch

Mark McGwire reached baseball immortality Tuesday night with a line-drive home run at Busch Stadium that shone the spotlight on St. Louis and rejuvenated the baseball pastime.

McGwire hit his 62nd home run of the season, breaking Roger Maris' single-season standard of 61 home runs—the most hallowed record in baseball.

Maris' record stood for nearly 37 years until 8:18 p.m. Tuesday, Sept. 8, on a balmy evening graced by a nearly full moon. The Chicago Cubs were up 2–0 in the fourth inning when McGwire lashed Cubs pitcher Steve Trachsel's first pitch on a line to left field. The ball began to sink as it neared the eight-foot fence, making over by less than two feet. It was his shortest home run of the season but touched off the most electric, emotional celebration that possibly could be mustered in the best baseball town in America. The Cardinals went on to beat the Cubs, 6–3.

"Yesterday," McGwire said afterward, "doing what I did for my father, hitting my 61st home run on his 61st birthday, I thought what a perfect way to end the home stand, by hitting my 62nd home run for the city of St. Louis and all the great fans. I really and truly wanted to do it here.

"Thank you, St. Louis."

McGwire trotted around the bases with the glee of a 10-year-old, the deliberate manner of a man wanting to savor each step, the lightness of someone who has just felt a burden lifted from his shoulders.

He had stepped in the batter's box in his trademark manner, relaxed and yet intense. As the flashes of thousands of cameras twinkled around the ballpark, McGwire dug his back foot into the dirt.

The pitch came in low and he sent it on a line over the fence and began a joyous tour of the bases.

"I don't remember anything after that," McGwire said later. "I was numb. I thought, 'I still have to play the game. Oh, my God, I can't believe this.'

"It's such an incredible feeling. I can't believe I did it."

McGwire embraced his first-base coach Dave McKay, his batting-practice coach with the Oakland Athletics and now with the Cardinals. Afterward, McKay reminded McGwire to touch the base before making his turn toward second. On his way, Cubs first baseman Mark Grace slapped hands with McGwire. Second baseman Mickey Morandini and shortstop Jose Hernandez each congratulated him with handshakes.

As McGwire approached third base, he saw former Cardinals buddy and Cubs third baseman Gary Gaetti. McGwire paused momentarily and saluted, then ran to hug Gaetti. He rounded third but, before heading for home, gave third-base coach Rene Lachemann a forearm bash and then pointed to the seats behind the plate, where John and Ginger McGwire were applauding proudly for their son.

An enormous welcoming committee awaited 90 feet ahead. In those few final steps, McGwire pointed to the sky.

He hugged Cubs catcher Scott Servais, dealt his familiar smashing-fists, punch-to-the-stomach greeting to teammate Ray Lankford.

Finally, there was Matthew McGwire, St. Louis' favorite bat boy. Mark picked up his 10-year-old son and held him aloft.

Red-and-white streamers floated gently into the outfield grass, fireworks boomed overhead. McGwire partied with his teammates, one emotional encounter at a time. He hugged manager Tony La Russa, pitching coach Dave Duncan . . . slowly, he worked through the crowd.

He found Matthew once more and wrapped his huge arms around the boy, hoisted him up and planted a kiss smack on his lips.

"I don't know how big the Arch is," McGwire said later, "but the Arch is off my back now."

Moments later, a Cubs player appeared among the sea of Cardinals. Sammy Sosa, who has 58 home runs and has been McGwire's friendly challenger in the chase for Maris' mark all summer, came from his spot in right field.

McGwire hugged Sosa with overwhelming affection.

Soon, McGwire had almost everyone in the place wiping away tears. He ran to the box seats just outside the far end of the Cardinals dugout, climbed over the short wall and engulfed Maris' four sons and a daughter one at a time. Rich and Randy Maris clearly had trouble blinking back their tears.

Their father had never known the kind of adulation McGwire was getting. Many Americans considered Maris unworthy when he broke Babe Ruth's home run record on Oct. 1, 1961. McGwire made sure the Marises knew how much he revered their father.

In a flash, McGwire disappeared into the dugout. He emerged holding a microphone and, with a wave of his arm, quieted the crowd of 49,987.

"I dedicate this home run to the whole city of St. Louis and all the fans here," McGwire said. "Thank you for all your support. It's unbelievable. All my family, everybody, my son, Chicago Cubs, Sammy Sosa—unbelievable."

McGwire paused.

"Class," he finished.

President Bill Clinton telephoned McGwire in the Cardinals clubhouse about 90 minutes after the game ended.

McGwire said Clinton told him: "It was outstanding. America is really enjoying this."

McGwire said he appreciated the call. "A really neat thing is that my son talked to him, too."

The home run will likely be remembered as the greatest moment in St. Louis sports history. The Cardinals' 1926 World Series championship, the first in the franchise's history, triggered a wild celebration in the streets of the city. There were other memorable world championships for the Cardinals, such as 1964 and 1982.

None of those moments and none of the city's most talented athletes ever created so much impact.

This season-long home run chase has been about more than sports for St. Louis. It will go down as one of the top defining moments for the city in this century, one that not only made St. Louis citizens feel a surge of self-esteem but carried the city onto a stage for all the world to admire.

There was the World's Fair of 1904. There was Charles Lindbergh's heroic flight across the Atlantic in "The Spirit of St. Louis" in 1927. There was the completion of the Gateway Arch.

And there is Mark McGwire toppling the most coveted mark in all of sports.

McGwire's summer of power went a long way toward reviving the national pastime, helping to erase bitter memories of the players' strike of 1994 and the cancellation of that year's World Series. Fans who vowed to never again return to a major-league ballpark followed the game again.

"This put baseball back on the map," McGwire said. "It's the sport, America's pastime. Look at the people at the parks now, all the great players in the game.

"People say this has been bringing the country together. If it has, so be it. I'm happy to bring the country together."

All this from a superhero who has 20-500 vision and bad feet. "God doesn't give you everything," McGwire said recently.

He grew up in Claremont, Calif., a suburb of Los Angeles. One of his boyhood friends once described the neighborhood like something from "The Brady Bunch." His dad was a dentist and his little-league coach. His mom volunteered countless hours at the concession stand of the town's park while her five sons played a variety of sports.

It was the All-American childhood for the All-American boy. He was a star at Damien High in Claremont—as a pitcher, drafted in the eighth round by the Montreal Expos. With the signing bonus they offered less than flattering, McGwire chose instead to accept the only scholarship offered him, from the University of Southern California.

He played on the 1984 U.S. Olympic Team and was drafted that year by the Oakland Athletics with the 10th pick overall. Three years later, he spent his first full season in the big leagues and whacked 49 homers, a rookie record.

McGwire had a chance to hit a record-breaking 50th home run that season. Instead, he skipped the last game so he could be on hand for the birth of his son.

On July 31, 1997, with the Oakland Athletics struggling to make money and be competitive, they traded McGwire to St. Louis, where he could play for La Russa once more. He hit 24 home runs the final two months of the season.

In signing a long-term deal with the Cardinals, McGwire also said he would donate $1 million each year to help support facilities in St. Louis and Los Angeles that work with abused children.

Cardinals fans fell in love with McGwire, whose signing gave the Cardinals their greatest power hitter.

Now, he belongs to all of baseball.

"I just hope I didn't act foolish," McGwire said of his performance Tuesday night. "But this is history."

89

Baltimore Defeats Cuban Team in Exhibition Game (1999)

SOURCE: *Miami Herald*, March 29, 1999

After failed attempts by Commissioner Kuhn a quarter century earlier, a major league team finally gained permission from the U.S. State Department to play an exhibition game in Cuba. In spite of the passage of time, the contest was still controversial to many,

especially Cuban exiles in south Florida. On March 28 the Baltimore Orioles interrupt-
ed spring training to play a Cuban all-star team before more than 50,000 raucous fans in
Havana, and barely escaped with a 3–2 win in eleven innings. The Cuban team gained
revenge on May 3, when they routed the Orioles in Baltimore, 12–6.

The best performance was by Cuban pitcher Jose Contreras, who threw eight innings
of shutout relief. Several years later Contreras defected and signed a multimillion-dollar
contract with the New York Yankees.

HISTORY IN HAVANA

Cuban Fans Rock, but Orioles Win, 3–2
Castro, U.S. Dignitaries Join Bedlam
By Rick Jervis and Jordan Levin
Herald Sports Writers

HAVANA—The first wave of the first game between American big-leaguers
and Cuban ballplayers in more than 40 years swelled at 1 p.m. Sunday in the left-
field bleachers of Latinoamericano Stadium, rolled counterclockwise behind home
plate, and moved across the right-field stands with such force that even the blue-
uniformed policemen had to raise their hands.

It would be 12 more minutes before the first pitch was launched in the historic match between the Cuban national team and the Baltimore Orioles. But no one
would wait.

The 50,000-seat stadium was already rocking with singing, cheering, flag-
waving Cubans.

"This has been discussed here for years—are the Cubans good enough to play
Americans?" said Delis Rojas Lopez, a 27-year-old engineer who received an invitation from the government to attend the game. "Now . . . we could finally see."

The game was tight, with the Orioles squeaking by, 3–2, in the 11th inning. Not
that it mattered.

As early as 10 a.m., fans streamed down Calle 20 de Mayo on their way to the
first baseball game involving U.S. major-leaguers in four decades. The Havana lo-
cals came pumped for baseball, their blood still hot from a close victory Saturday
night for their Industriales, the local amateur team, in Game 2 of the national championship series against Santiago.

Sunday's game was criticized for the Cuban government's decision to hand out
invitations to worker unions instead of opening the game to the public.

But in the small park on the north side of the stadium, scalpers sold tickets for
$2 for bleacher seats, $5 for infield seating.

"This is capitalism creeping in, just like China," said Tony Walker, a real estate
developer from Southern California who came to Havana for the game. "I've been
coming here 15 years. There's never been anything like this."

But not everyone was pleased with the setup.

DISAPPOINTED FAN

Reynaldo Biset, a 40-year-old construction worker from Havana, wanted to go to the game but didn't receive an invitation. With the scalping prices too high, he watched the game on a black-and-white TV set at a small bar on Hospital Street, near Havana's Chinatown.

"Five dollars is what I earn in a month," Biset said. "What am I supposed to do? Go to the game and not eat?

"Some of the people inside don't even understand baseball," he said. "It's not fair. They should give everyone a chance to go."

At the stadium, those who could attend came to the game waving blanket-size Cuban flags and carrying conga drums. They had cigars stuffed in their shirt pockets and wore New York Yankees baseball caps. There were a lot of Yankees caps.

Noticeably missing were the rum and Cristal beer usually taken to Cuban ballgames. No alcohol was allowed in the stadium Sunday.

CASTRO SEES THE GAME

President Fidel Castro arrived about 1 p.m. in a caravan of Mercedes-Benzes and walked out to the field soon afterward to boisterous applause. Later, he watched the game from behind home plate, flanked on either side by baseball commissioner Bud Selig and Orioles owner Peter Angelos.

Also present in the stands: U.S. Sens. Patrick Leahy of Vermont and Jack Reed of Rhode Island.

"It's interesting that this all came together haphazardly but purposely," said singer Jimmy Buffett, who attended the game since he was in town for the Music Bridges concert Sunday night.

By the seventh inning, the fans erupted into more waves, shouting "Eso es! Eso es!" (That's it!)

The energy wowed 13-year-old Kevin Kistler, of Baltimore's St. Ignatius Loyola Academy, who was brought to the game with 78 other Little League and inner-city baseball and basketball players.

During the game, Kevin gave a T-shirt to a Cuban boy. He said it was the second one he had given away.

"The people are really nice here," he said. "I don't think the government gives them what they deserve."

90

Umpires' Negotiating Strategy Starts to Backfire (1999)

SOURCE: *Baltimore Sun*, July 16, 1999

Richie Phillips, the combative leader of the Major League Umpires' Association (MLUA), thought he had a sure-fire method of pressuring baseball to renegotiate their collective bargaining agreement. On July 14 he announced that more than fifty umpires had submitted their resignations from the major leagues, effective September 2. At this point the umpires would form a new union—which, Phillips felt, was a necessary step given that the MLUA had agreed not to go on strike. The new union would not only gain another increase in salary but also fight baseball's efforts to standardize the strike zone for all umpires and to rank the umpires in ability.

The following article is an indication that Phillips and his loyal umpires made a grave miscalculation. Not only did the umpires garner no sympathy from the media, fans, or players, but baseball officials announced that they would honor the resignations unless they were rescinded, and started to hire minor league umpires as replacements. By July 26 all but nine AL umpires and thirty-three NL umpires had rescinded their resignations, but the leagues announced that all nine AL umpires, and thirteen of the tardy NL umpires, would lose their jobs come September 2. The MLUA had been crushed. In February 2000 a new organization, the World Umpires Association, was certified to represent major league umpires.

The dispute continued in the courts. In December 2001 a federal judge ruled that baseball had to rehire nine of the twenty-two umpires, and ordered arbitration hearings for three more. Three months later five of the nine had been rehired, and the remaining four were allowed to retire with back pay. Three additional umpires were also rehired, leaving ten umpires without a major league position.

Umpires Spurred by Fear of Lockout

McKean: Union's Threat of Sept. 2 Resignation Is Bid "To Force the Issue"

By Peter Schmuck
Sun Staff

The Major League Baseball Umpires Association picked a strange time to declare labor war—the day after an emotionally charged All-Star celebration cast baseball in an enormously positive light—but veteran umpire Jim McKean defended Wednesday's decision by the union to take the offensive in its strained relationship with baseball ownership.

The umpires announced that they would resign on Sept. 2 if their labor situation is not settled, a huge public relations gamble that could cost them any chance of garnering sympathy from the fans.

McKean, in Baltimore to work the Orioles-Montreal Expos series, said yesterday that the umpires felt that they had to take pre-emptive action to avoid being locked out after their collective bargaining agreement expires Dec. 31.

"We're trying to force the issue," he said. "We don't want to go into the winter and then get locked out. We're trying to get our contract done."

If that was the intent, the announcement by union chief Richie Phillips did not get the desired reaction from Major League Baseball officials. MLB vice president Sandy Alderson's response almost sounded as if the umpires had saved management officials the trouble of playing hardball with them in the off-season.

"That sounds like either a threat to be ignored," Alderson quipped, "or an offer to be accepted."

The umpires are portraying Alderson's cavalier reaction as a prime illustration of a perceived lack of support from management that dates back to the light disciplinary action levied on former Oriole Roberto Alomar for spitting in the face of umpire John Hirschbeck in 1996.

"That reaction typifies the smugness, the arrogance that has led us to where we are, and it exemplifies the lack of appreciation for the umpires," Phillips said yesterday.

McKean discounted rumors of a split in the umpires union, though only 57 of the 68 full-time umpires joined in Wednesday's resignation resolution. There was an attempt in March by a group of umpires to recruit Ron Shapiro to replace Phillips, but McKean said that it was "a dead issue" and indicated that the umpires are solidly behind their present leadership.

The owners have issues, too, and they were preparing to tackle them during the off-season. Management wants to take the supervision of the umpires away from the two league presidents and place all of them under the direction of the commissioner's office. The owners also want more authority to enforce physical requirements and set performance standards.

Though ownership's labor strategy had yet to be revealed, it was widely believed that management would take a very hard line during the upcoming negotiations in an attempt to alter the balance of power in the collective bargaining relationship and wrest major concessions from the union.

If that's true, the umpires may have handed ownership a golden opportunity to replace them without incurring the risk of the kind of labor litigation that helped Major League Baseball Players Association counter management's hard-line strategy during the 1994–95 players strike.

Now, should they be so inclined, the owners could simply give the umpires their severance package and bring in replacements from the college and minor league ranks.

Alderson didn't exactly dismiss that notion when he wondered aloud Wednesday whether it might be the most cost-effective way to solve the umpire problem.

"There is always concern that something like that could happen," McKean said, "but we're a proud group. We feel we do a pretty good job. We think that it will be hard to immediately replace us. I'm not saying that we couldn't be replaced in the long run, but I think that the players still want us to umpire."

Baseball Enters the Twenty-First Century

Baseball entered the twenty-first century when it realized its place in the world. Many Americans gained a greater sense of the importance of baseball—still hailed by many as the United States' "national pastime"—to other countries, most notably Cuba, in the 1990s when Cuban refugees like Livan and Orlando Hernandez escaped and rose to prominence. The refugee community in South Florida protested but could not prevent the Baltimore Orioles from traveling to Havana to play a Cuban all-star team, a trip first attempted a quarter century earlier. However, Cuban expatriates regained their faith in baseball the following year as eleven Hispanic players (including the Hernandez brothers) and a number of coaches made public their political beliefs and cultural loyalties by boycotting the games of April 25, 2000, in protest of the federal government's seizure of another Cuban refugee, a child named Elian Gonzalez. On September 11, 2001, baseball shrank into insignificance, but soon regained its status as a diversion of note in a number of countries across the world.

In the United States, baseball's resumption was marked by the sublime and the ridiculous. The 2001 postseason will be long remembered for Derek Jeter's backhanded toss that helped the New York Yankees survive the ALCS, and for the inspired performance of Arizona Diamondbacks pitchers Randy Johnson and Curt Schilling in their defeat of the Yankees in a thrilling World Series. Commissioner Selig doused the afterglow of the Series just two days later with his announcement that the sport was (once again) doomed and that only by contracting two franchises could it be saved.

Selig was reacting in part to the dire conclusions drawn by a "blue-ribbon panel" chosen and assigned by Selig to analyze economic data supplied by the owners. The panel found that the lack of competitive balance in the major leagues, caused primarily by the lack of effective revenue sharing among the clubs, was a growing threat to the survival of the major leagues and must be reversed as quickly as possible. The union responded by noting that competitive imbalance was actually the norm throughout baseball history and that through intelligent management even less-affluent franchises could compete. The success of the Minnesota Twins and the Florida Marlins (who won the 2003 World Series)—the two teams scheduled to be eliminated—has proved the MLBPA correct, but in the subsequent Basic Agreement they agreed to a window in which the owners could impose contraction without opposition by the union. At the turn of the century the world in which baseball exists was evolving rapidly, but within the game the owners and players proved incapable of learning from their mistakes and helping their profession grow.

91

Eleven Hispanic Players Boycott Games in Support of Elian Gonzalez (2000)

SOURCE: *Miami Herald*, April 26, 2000

Baseball players have seldom been noted for their political activism, either because of their single-minded devotion to the game or their fear of offending sponsors and fans. The events of April 22, however, persuaded eleven Hispanic players (and a number of Hispanic coaches and team employees) to take a stand. They, like millions of Americans, were horrified at the sight of armed federal agents breaking into a Miami home and removing six-year-old Elian Gonzalez to be reunited with his father with the intention of returning the boy to Cuba. Three days later eleven players—including six members of the Florida Marlins, based in Miami—boycotted scheduled games to communicate their outrage at the actions of the government.

Due in part to their acute player shortage, the Marlins lost the game to the San Francisco Giants, 6–4.

Boycott Is Felt All Over Baseball

Canseco, Duque, Others Take Part
By Clark Spencer

There was extra elbow room inside the Marlins' dugout for Tuesday's game against the San Francisco Giants as six players and two coaches stayed home in support of a work stoppage over the Elian Gonzalez controversy.

And the Marlins weren't the only team left short-handed, as several players and coaches from around Major League Baseball joined the one-day demonstration. Most notable among the absentees were Devil Rays designated hitter Jose Canseco; Yankees pitcher Orlando "El Duque" Hernandez; his half-brother, Giants pitcher and former Marlin Livan Hernandez; and Mets shortstop Rey Ordonez.

All of the Marlins' absences were with pay, and the others were believed to be as well. Said Marlins manager John Boles: "There aren't many more important things in life than this [baseball]. But this is more important."

In addition to Alex Fernandez, Mike Lowell and Vladimir Nunez, who announced their decisions Monday, three more Marlins joined the work stoppage Tuesday, leaving the Marlins with just 19 players for the game.

The three—Antonio Alfonseca, Danny Bautista and Jesus Sanchez—are all from the Dominican Republic. Boles said he was informed by each of them Tuesday that they had also decided to show their solidarity.

"I didn't ask them for an explanation, just thanks for telling me," Boles said. "We are not setting world-wide policy here. But I would have been disappointed if our organization wouldn't have [supported] this. If it had been the World Series—and I'm not speaking for the organization—I'd feel the same way."

Other members of the Marlins' organization also stayed home, including vice president of marketing Julio Rebull Jr., third-base coach Fredi Gonzalez, infield coach Tony Taylor, bullpen catcher Luis Perez, assistant equipment manager Javier Castro and a bat boy.

"I support this," said first baseman Kevin Millar, who played Tuesday. "This is definitely bigger than a baseball game."

The Giants were without Hernandez, who defected from Cuba and is scheduled to start this afternoon's game, and catcher Bobby Estalella, who went to high school in Cooper City and lives in South Florida during the off-season.

"We don't know what kind of repercussions would have happened had they played," Giants manager Dusty Baker said. "That supercedes baseball. It's sad politics have to get into baseball. But we're part of the world like everybody else."

Said Giants infielder Felipe Crespo, who would have served as an emergency backup catcher: "There could be harm if they [Hernandez and Estalella] came out. It's based on the security of them and their families."

Ordonez and Mets third-base coach Cookie Rojas—both natives of Cuba who live in South Florida during the off-season—stayed home from Tuesday's game against Cincinnati.

"Baseball should not be a political forum," said Mets general manager Steve Phillips, "but they felt they needed to support the community in which they live, and I support their decision. I realize this sets a precedent. You open yourself up to the next case, but we'll take care of that when we come to it."

Not every player of Cuban descent took part in the protest.

Rafael Palmeiro of Miami Jackson High and the Texas Rangers, who had stated previously that Elian Gonzalez should not be returned to Cuba, played Tuesday against the Red Sox.

"That's a local issue down there and that's the way it should stay," said Palmeiro, adding he felt it was important he play because Boston pitching ace Pedro Martinez was starting against the Rangers.

Reds outfielder Alex Ochoa, whose parents were born in Cuba, decided to play. He said he fully supports the cause but did not want to miss an opportunity to be in the starting lineup.

"It's an easier decision for an everyday player," said Ochoa, who is from Hialeah Miami Lakes High. "I didn't want to let the team down."

92

Owners' "Blue Ribbon Panel" Analyzes Baseball Economics and Competitive Imbalance (2000)

SOURCE: Richard C. Levin, George J. Mitchell, Paul A. Volcker, and George F. Will, *The Report of the Independent Members of the Commissioner's Blue Ribbon Panel on Baseball Economics*, July 2000, 1–10

Throughout the 1990s the owners consistently argued that under baseball's current economic system—especially free agency and salary arbitration—competitive balance was nearly impossible to achieve. Between 1978 and 1992 no team repeated as World Series champion, and "low-revenue" teams like Pittsburgh, Baltimore, Kansas City, Oakland, and Minnesota won the Series. By the mid-1990s, owners maintained, a significant number of teams simply had no chance to reach the postseason, much less the World Series, because they could not afford to acquire enough talented players to compete. In spite of the addition of four expansion teams and numerous new stadiums, owners claimed that very few teams managed to finish the season with a profit. For these reasons Commissioner Selig formed a "Blue Ribbon Panel" to analyze the problem and to suggest a solution.

Critics, from the union to the Wall Street Journal, *noted that not only was the panel appointed by the commissioner but it also used only economic data supplied by the owners. Even though the information had been audited, many felt that it was presented and interpreted in such a way as to favor the owners' position. The* Journal, *citing information from* Forbes *magazine, concluded that most baseball teams made money—a contention vociferously denied by Selig. The arguments concerning competitive balance seemed to have more merit, but others pointed out that throughout most of baseball history certain teams rarely challenged for the pennant, while others regularly advanced to the Series.*

I. Summary of Findings, Conclusions and Recommendations

I.1. OVERALL CONCLUSIONS

The Commissioner's Blue Ribbon Panel on Baseball Economics, representing the interests of baseball fans, was formed to study whether revenue disparities among clubs are seriously damaging competitive balance, and, if so, to recommend structural reforms to ameliorate the problem. After 18 months of extensive investigation, we conclude:

a. *Large and growing revenue disparities exist* and are causing problems of chronic competitive imbalance.

b. *These problems have become substantially worse* during the five complete seasons since the strike-shortened season of 1994, and seem likely to remain severe unless Major League Baseball ("MLB") undertakes remedial actions proportional to the problem.

c. The limited revenue sharing and payroll tax that were approved as part of MLB's 1996 Collective Bargaining Agreement with the Major League Baseball Players Association ("MLBPA") *have produced neither the intended moderating of payroll disparities nor improved competitive balance.* Some low-revenue clubs, believing the amount of their proceeds from revenue sharing insufficient to enable them to become competitive, used those proceeds to become modestly profitable.

d. In a majority of MLB markets, *the cost of clubs trying to be competitive is causing escalation of ticket and concession prices,* jeopardizing MLB's traditional position as the affordable family spectator sport.

I.2. REVENUE DISPARITIES

Measured simply in terms of gross revenues, which almost doubled during the five complete seasons (1995–1999) since 1994, MLB is prospering. But that simple measurement is a highly inadequate gauge of MLB's economic health. Because of anachronistic aspects of MLB's economic arrangements, the prosperity of some clubs is having perverse effects that pose a threat to the game's long-term vitality. Here are a few of the facts about revenue imbalances:

a. What are called local revenues (including gate receipts, local television, radio and cable rights fees, ballpark concessions, advertising and publications, parking, suite rentals, postseason and spring training) are the largest single component of most clubs' annual revenues. The ratio between the highest and lowest club's local revenues has more than doubled in just five years, from 5.5:1 in 1995 to 14.7:1 in 1999. The average ratio between the three clubs with the highest local revenue and the three with the lowest has risen from 4.1:1 to 7:1. . . .

h. Between 1995 and 1999, the difference between the highest and lowest club's total revenues rose from $74 million to $129 million.

i. In 1999, the total revenue of the highest revenue club exceeded by $14 million the combined revenues of the three lowest revenue clubs.

j. In 1999, the sum of the revenues of the top three revenue clubs exceeded the *combined* revenues of *all* the clubs in Quartile IV by $33 million.

I.3. PAYROLL DISPARITIES

Not surprisingly, widening revenue disparities have been accompanied by widening payroll disparities.

a. In 1999, one club had a payroll approximately equal to the sum of the payrolls of the lowest five payroll clubs.

b. In 1999, the combined payrolls of the highest two payroll clubs exceeded the *combined* payrolls of *all* clubs in payroll Quartile IV by $30 million.

c. In 2000, the salary of the game's highest paid player is equal to the entire Opening Day player payroll of one club (Minnesota). . . .

I.4. PAYROLL AND COMPETITIVENESS

Not surprisingly, there is a strong correlation between high payrolls and success on the field. Although a high payroll is not always sufficient to produce a club capable of reaching postseason play—there are instances of competitive failures by high payroll clubs—a high payroll has become an increasingly necessary ingredient of on-field success:

a. From 1995 through 1999, every World Series winner was from payroll Quartile I and no club outside payroll Quartile I won even a single game in the Series. Indeed, the winner each year was among the five clubs with the largest payrolls.

b. With the exception of 1998, even the World Series loser has been from payroll Quartile I. (The 1998 loser, San Diego, was from Quartile II and lost in four games.)

c. No team in payroll Quartiles III or IV won any of the 158 playoff games from 1995 through 1999.

I.5. OTHER FINDINGS AND CONCLUSIONS

Sports leagues do not function as free markets. If they did, the clubs would be clustered in a few large markets. Rather, sports leagues are blends of cooperation and competition— cooperation for the sake of producing satisfactory competitiveness. . . .

In the context of baseball, proper competitive balance should be understood to exist when there are no clubs chronically weak because of MLB's structural features. Proper competitive balance will not exist until every well-run club has a *regularly recurring reasonable hope of reaching postseason play*.

Granted, competitive balance as here defined has been an elusive goal, when it has been a goal at all, throughout MLB's history. However, the fact that baseball's structural flaws are historic is not an argument for continuing acceptance of them. This is particularly so when they are producing revenue disparities with unhealthy consequences for competitive balance.

What has made baseball's recent seasons disturbing, and what makes its current economic structure untenable in the long run, is that, year after year, too many clubs know in spring training that they have no realistic prospect of reaching postseason play. Too many clubs in low-revenue markets can only expect to compete for postseason berths if ownership is willing to incur staggering operating losses to subsidize a competitive player payroll. . . .

1.6. RECOMMENDATIONS

a. Revenue Sharing—*MLB should share at least 40 percent, and perhaps as much as 50 percent, of all member clubs' local revenue, less local ballpark expenses as uniformly defined.*

The limited revenue sharing enacted in recent years has failed to promote competitive balance, as intended. The modest amount of revenue that has been shared in recent years should be increased substantially in recognition of the indispensable role played by the visiting team in generating what historically but misleadingly has been referred to as "local revenue."

b. Competitive Balance Tax—*MLB should levy a 50 percent competitive balance tax on club payrolls that are above a fixed threshold of $84 million and all clubs should be encouraged to have a minimum payroll of $40 million.*

The recommended "fixed threshold" is intended to refine the "luxury tax" adopted in 1996 and to raise the tax rate to promote compliance. We also recommend specific measures to encourage low payroll clubs to spend more on player payroll with the intent that the combination of these measures moves all MLB franchises into a payroll range that encourages competitive balance. The goal would be to constrain club payrolls that are very high and simultaneously raise club payrolls that are very low. The impact of these mechanisms, assuming no taxes were collected (probably an unrealistic assumption) and all clubs complied with the minimum payroll, would be that all clubs' payrolls would be in a zone bounded on the high side by $84 million, and bounded on the low side by $40 million, thus nearly reestablishing the 2:1 payroll ratio between the highest and lowest payroll clubs. In the event that our combined recommendations prove inadequate to reestablish this ratio, further adjustments should be made.

c. Central Fund Distributions—*MLB should use unequal distribution of new Central Fund revenues to improve competitive balance, creating a "Commissioner's Pool" that is allocated to assist low-revenue clubs in improving their competitiveness and in meeting the minimum payroll obligation of $40 million.*

MLB, in January 2000, granted the Commissioner new powers to distribute new Central Fund revenues in unequal amounts. The Commissioner's exercise of this power should be focused on "incremental" Central Fund revenues, beyond the $13 million per club distributed in 1999. The Commissioner should distribute new Central Fund revenues in a way that addresses the core problem of competitive balance: widely disparate local revenues.

Specifically, given the current level of local revenue disparity, a $40 million minimum payroll would sentence a number of clubs to significant and persistent unprofitability. The Commissioner should use the mechanism of disproportionate allocation to address this problem, to encourage revenue enhancing activities such as investments in new ballparks and to reward low-revenue clubs for developing young talent. To encourage compliance with the minimum payroll obligation, the Commissioner should declare any club below the $40 million minimum ineligible for an enhanced distribution.

d. Competitive Balance Draft—*Major League Baseball should conduct an annual "Competitive Balance Draft" of players in which the weakest eight clubs would have a unique opportunity to select non-40-man roster players from the organizations of the eight clubs that qualified for the playoffs.*

The recommendation is intended to promote long-term competitive balance by discouraging high revenue franchises from stockpiling talent in their farm systems that is unavailable to low-revenue franchises. The "Competitive Balance Draft" would distribute player talent more equally among all MLB clubs, but the ability to "protect" the 40-man roster would reward clubs for good baseball management and protect fans in each local community from having an established favorite player drafted by another team.

e. Rule 4 Draft—*Major League Baseball should implement reforms in the Rule 4 draft.*

Among the reforms would be inclusion of international players, elimination of compensation picks, increased opportunity for low-revenue clubs to sign top prospects, allocation of a disproportionate number of picks to chronically uncompetitive clubs, and allowing the trading of draft picks.

f. Franchise Relocations—*Major League Baseball should utilize strategic franchise relocations to address the competitive issues facing the game.*

Franchise relocation should be an available tool to address the competitive issues facing the game. Clubs that have little likelihood of securing a new ballpark or undertaking other revenue enhancing activities should have the option of relocation if better markets can be identified.

93

Baseball Hall of Fame Reconfigures Veterans Committee (2001)

SOURCE: National Baseball Hall of Fame press release, August 6, 2001
http://www.baseballhalloffame.org/whats_new/press_releases/2001/pr2001_08_06htm

By most accounts the weakest link of the Baseball Hall of Fame's system for electing its honorees is the Veterans Committee. Although the rules of the committee have changed over the years, in general its members could elect players, umpires, managers, and executives not selected by the Baseball Writers Association of America (BWAA) who were active for at least ten years and who received a certain minimum number of votes by the BWAA (at least 100 votes in a single year from 1946 to 1991, and between 60 percent and 74 percent of the BWAA vote in a single year from 1992 to 2001). Any objective examination of the HOF members reveals that players elected by the Veterans Committee are among the weakest candidates, but a closer investigation makes clear that many committee members used their influence to select former teammates who otherwise might not have been honored.

After decades of complaints from critics, the HOF finally acted to reform their election policy. The Hall announced that membership in the Veterans Committee would be vastly expanded to include all living HOF members, as well as certain baseball writers and announcers honored previously by the HOF. The new committee would meet every two years to consider players, while candidates who were not players could only be considered every four years. Significantly, the policy of holding special ballots for nineteenth-century players and Negro Leagues players, which existed from 1995 to 1999 and in 2000–01, was abandoned. In the two special elections held since the voting system was changed, no candidate has been selected. However, a special committee elected seventeen Negro Leagues players and executives in 2006.

The best source on the Byzantine history of the Hall of Fame is Bill James, The Politics of Glory: How Baseball's Hall of Fame Really Works (New York: Macmillan, 1994).

Press Release—August 6, 2001

Hall of Fame Board of Directors Restructures Veterans Committee and Its Rules for Election

COOPERSTOWN, NY—The National Baseball Hall of Fame and Museum's Board of Directors this morning voted to restructure the Committee on Baseball Veterans and its procedures for electing long-retired players, managers, umpires and executives. The changes, effective immediately, are designed to make the process much more open and understandable while maintaining the high standards for earning election to the Hall of Fame.

The membership of both the screening committee and the voting body will change dramatically, as will the actual method of voting. In addition, more than 1,700 players who spent 10 or more seasons in the major leagues, but whose names were dropped from consideration for failing to receive a requisite number of votes in past elections have been given new hope.

"The Board believes in keeping the standards very high and continuing to make it very difficult to earn election," said Jane Forbes Clark, the Board's chairman. "These new procedures are simply the next evolution of Hall of Fame voting rules. They open up and streamline the process so every baseball fan has a much easier time understanding and following along," Clark said. "The Board also thought it fair to give the Baseball Writers' Association of America (BWAA) the opportunity to place players its organization has previously not elected back on the ballot for a second chance, given changing historical perspectives."

Highlights of the new Veterans Committee procedures include:

Membership: The current 15-member Veterans Committee is replaced by a group comprised of the living members of the Baseball Hall of Fame (61), the living recipients of the J. G. Taylor Spink Award (12), the living recipients of the Ford C. Frick Award (14) and the current Veterans Committee members whose terms have not yet expired (2). This group of 90 increases the size of the existing committee six-fold.

Frequency of Elections: Beginning in 2003, the Veterans Committee will hold its election of players every other year. Also beginning in 2003, the election of managers, umpires and executives will occur every four years.

Eligible candidates: All players who played in at least 10 major league seasons, including those from the 19th century, who are not on Major League Baseball's ineligible list, and who are not being considered by the BWAA, are eligible for election by the new Veterans Committee. Managers, umpires and executives with 10 or more years in Baseball are eligible. A Hall of Fame–sponsored study of African-American Baseball, 1860–1960, is underway. The Board will appoint a committee to review the results when they are complete. After this review, a recommendation will be made to the Board concerning how to proceed with respect to Negro League candidates.

Screening Committee: Sixty BWAA members—two from each major league city and four from cities with two teams—will identify 25 candidates for the Players Ballot and 15 candidates for the Composite Ballot (managers, umpires and executives). In addition, the Hall of Fame Board of Directors will appoint an independent Screening Committee of six Hall of Fame members to identify five candidates for the Players Ballot. The final ballot will contain 25–30 names, depending on duplicate results. In compiling its list of candidates, the Screening Committee shall call upon resources of organizations such as the Elias Sports Bureau, the official statistician of Major League Baseball since the 1920s, and the National Baseball Hall of Fame Library.

Voting: Voting will continue to be based upon the individual's record, ability, integrity, sportsmanship, character and contribution to the game of Baseball. All candidates receiving votes on at least 75 percent of ballots cast will earn election.

Schedule and Method of Voting: Veterans Committee members will receive ballots and supporting material—prepared by the Hall of Fame—in January prior to induction. The vote will be completed by mail and counted in the presence of Ernst & Young and a Hall of Fame representative. Results will be announced in February.

94

Baseball Returns to New York After September 11

Disaster (2001)

SOURCE: *New York Daily News*, September 22, 2001

In the aftermath of the terrorist attacks on the World Trade Center, the Pentagon, and a plane forced by passengers to crash in a Pennsylvania field, professional sports were an unnecessary extravagance. Baseball commissioner Bud Selig suspended the major league season by a week, as did his NFL counterpart Paul Tagliabue and most college sports administrators. When baseball resumed, New York was given additional time to heal as both the Yankees and the Mets were on the road. On September 21 the Mets—who by winning twenty of the previous twenty-five games had jumped to within five and a half games of the Atlanta Braves in the NL East—returned home to play the Braves in games whose significance had nothing to do with the pennant race.

Shea Stadium was packed with flag-waving, emotionally ravaged fans who were treated to an exciting game. When Mets star Mike Piazza hit a dramatic home run late in the game to give the Mets the lead in a 3–2 victory, he sent a jolt throughout the stadium and provided yet another reminder that the spirit of New York was alive and well.

Piazza Is Glad to Contribute

HR Lights Way for New York, New York
By Roger Rubin
Daily News Sports Writer

With one swing of the bat, Mike Piazza may have helped to pick up the spirits of a devastated city and, on a smaller scale, kept the Mets' miracle September run going.

Piazza's two-run homer in the eighth not only led the Mets to a 3–2 victory over the first-place Braves, it also capped a night in which American flags and patriotism took over Shea in the first baseball game played in New York since last week's attacks.

The whole scene was almost too much for Met manager Bobby Valentine. "We came here and paid tribute to a lot of heroes," he said. "One of the true New York heroes of the sports world put the icing on the cake."

By winning 21 of the last 26 games, the Mets have injected themselves into the thick of a pennant race and have given the people of the city a boost, if not a needed diversion.

The climb the Mets have been making to reach the postseason is beginning to look a lot less formidable. They stand 4 ½ games behind the NL East–leading Braves and four games behind the second-place Phillies. The Mets have five games left against Atlanta.

The Mets had announced they were donating their pay for the night to families of the emergency workers lost in the World Trade Center tragedy. All the Mets have talked about how much they wanted to win this game for the people of New York and it was appropriate that Piazza, who has spoken so emotionally about how the tragedy has affected him, would deliver the win. With one on and one out and the Mets trailing 2–1, he crushed a home run to center field, sending a crowd of 41,235 into celebration. "I felt like we were spectators tonight as everyone saluted fallen brothers and sisters," said Piazza. "I'm very sad for the loss of life but felt good we gave them something to cheer about."

The emotional nature of the game was unavoidable. High on the right center field scoreboard where the neon replica of the skyline straddles the Mets' logo, a red, white and blue ribbon covered the place where the city's twin towers were.

For the "Star-Spangled Banner," the voices of the crowd nearly drowned out vocalist Marc Anthony. Diana Ross sang "God Bless America" in front of a chorus of New Yorkers in the stands waving American flags. And Liza Minnelli's rendition of "New York, New York" during the seventh-inning stretch brought the house down.

The emotion ran on through the final out as winner Armando Benitez, who had given up the go-ahead hit in the eighth, finished the game by getting Keith Lockhart to hit into a 6-3 double play to chants of "USA! USA! USA!" and a standing ovation.

Piazza, wearing an NYPD helmet behind the plate, had figured prominently in the Mets falling behind. In the top of the fourth, he dropped a perfect one-hop throw from Edgardo Alfonzo to the plate from right field. It would have cut down Chipper Jones at the plate, but instead left the Mets down 1–0.

They tied the game in the last of the fourth when Tsuyoshi Shinjo drove in Piazza from third on a sacrifice fly, but the Mets stranded two runners in scoring position later in the inning when Jay Payton grounded out to third.

Atlanta took the lead in the eighth. John Franco had come in to relieve Bruce Chen, who pitched seven innings, allowing only one unearned run. Franco retired the first two batters, but allowed a walk to Julio Franco and a single to Chipper Jones.

Not wanting to let this one slip away, Valentine immediately went to his closer, Benitez. But Andruw Jones drove his first pitch to center for a run-scoring double. Benitez escaped without further damage, but returned to the Mets dugout with the stands quiet.

In the bottom of the inning, Piazza awakened the crowd.

Valentine could not have written a more fitting finale. "The fans got what they deserved. Put it in a bottle and whip it out when you need to get back into never-never land and get away from things."

95

Jeter's Spectacular Play Helps Save Yankees' Season (2001)

source: *San Francisco Chronicle*, October 14, 2001

The New York Yankees were on the verge of elimination in the ALDS. The three-time defending world champions had lost the first two games of the series to the upstart Oakland A's in New York and were faced with the prospect of sweeping the final three games, including two games in Oakland. In the pivotal third game the Yankees were nursing a 1–0 lead in the bottom of the seventh inning when Oakland's Jeremy Giambi, who had singled with two outs, lumbered toward the plate after a Terrence Long double. A terrible throw from Yankees right fielder Shane Spencer seemed to assure Oakland of the tying run, but shortstop Derek Jeter suddenly appeared inside the first-base foul line, intercepted the throw, and acrobatically tossed it behind his back to catcher Jorge Posada, who tagged out a stunned Giambi on a close play. New York held on to win the game 1–0 and proceeded to oust Oakland from the series.

The play was replayed hundreds of times in the weeks to follow. Many commentators questioned why Jeter was in position to make the play, but both Jeter and manager Joe Torre maintained that the shortstop was executing a designed defensive strategy. Also questioned was Giambi's failure to slide, most hilariously by New York Times *columnist George Vescey, whose story on the subject consisted of thirty-three paragraphs, each beginning with the sentence "Slide, Jeremy, slide."*

Jeter's Athletic Play Saves Yankees

Backup Relay Flip to Home Plate Catches Giambi

By Henry Schulman
Chronicle Staff Writer

The Yankees made Derek Jeter the second-highest-paid shortstop in baseball for his bat, his legs and his arm, not because he has the instincts and athleticism of a free safety.

Call it a bonus for the Yankees, who stayed alive in their American League Division Series against Oakland thanks in part to Jeter's imitation of a defensive back during the pivotal play of Game 3 last night.

"No doubt about it. He's the best athlete on the team. That's why he makes the money that he does," said right fielder Shane Spencer, the quarterback who overthrew his two receivers on the play. "He might not put up some of the numbers that other guys do, but he showed tonight why he's the best."

With the Yankees leading 1–0 on Jorge Posada's fifth-inning homer off Barry Zito, Jeremy Giambi singled to right with two out in the seventh. Terrence Long then ripped a double into the right-field corner. With Mike Mussina working on a dominating four-hit shutout, there was little doubt A's third-base coach Ron Washington would send Giambi home.

Two good relays, and Giambi would have been nailed by 20 feet, but Spencer overthrew his first two cutoff men, second baseman Alfonso Soriano and first baseman Tino Martinez, and the ball bounced between first and home with no Yankee seemingly in sight of it. The ball did not have enough juice to get to home plate by itself.

That's when Jeter, the "trailer," emerged from the middle of the infield, grabbed the ball and back-flipped it to catcher Posada as his momentum carried him toward the Yankees dugout. The throw was perfect, and Posada swipe-tagged Giambi's leg just before it was about to touch the plate with the tying run.

The A's never got that run, and the Yankees staved off elimination.

Manager Joe Torre said Jeter actually followed a designed defensive scheme.

"You come to spring training and watch us. That's one of the plays he has to read," Torre said. "He's the backup cutoff man. We overthrew the first cutoff man and he was there and made a sensational play."

Jeter may have practiced cutoffs, but as third baseman Scott Brosius said, "He doesn't practice the old running-toward-the-dugout-and-flipping-back-home play."

Jeter said he could never recall making a backhand flip to a catcher, although he's made many to second base on double plays. Jeter also said pure instinct kicked in after he gloved the wayward throw on one hop.

The play fired up the Yankees, who were already humped up because of the way this game was shaking out. Posada's home run and Spencer's double on the next pitch were the sum of New York's offense. Indeed, Jeter said that after his play, the Yankees were more focused on the runs they still needed more than the one he just saved.

"When you play Oakland, everybody in the lineup is capable of hitting home runs, especially here. Everyone was excited, but the game wasn't over," Jeter said.

The Yankees never did get another run, and when it was over the Yankees were well aware they had scored just once in 18 innings. They were still breathing, though. When they face Cory Lidle this afternoon in another do-or-die game, they would like to score a few more runs for their pitcher, Orlando Hernandez.

"I think the guys in here know that if we can take it back to New York we have a good chance," Brosius said. "We'd like to find some bats in our bag that have some more hits in them. It took a great performance by 'Moose' today. He gave us exactly what we needed."

So did Posada, whose home run on a Zito fastball toward the inside of the plate made Mussina's seven shutout innings stand up.

Torre said Mussina winning a 1–0 game "didn't surprise me. I just wish we could have scored more than one run. He's been pitching like that all year. A couple of games he got whacked around a little bit, but he's a big-game guy."

That's a title that fits Torre's shortstop quite well, too.

96

Arizona Rallies to Beat Rivera, Yankees in World Series (2001)

SOURCE: *Arizona Republic*, November 5, 2001

In the 2001 World Series both the New York Yankees and the Arizona Diamondbacks seemed to have fate on their side. The Yankees had won the last three Series, had won the ALDS only after a miraculous play by Derek Jeter, and were playing for the honor of the thousands of people killed in the World Trade Center six weeks earlier. The Diamondbacks—who like the Florida Marlins four years earlier were an expansion team that won the NL pennant just a few years after their inception—boasted the two most dominant pitchers in baseball, Randy Johnson and Curt Schilling. After falling behind two games to one, the Yankees won consecutive games in similarly astonishing fashion, by hitting last-inning game-winning home runs off Arizona relief ace Byung-Hyun Kim. Johnson won Game 6 in a rout, bringing the Series to the final game with Schilling on his home mound against future Hall of Fame legend Roger Clemens.

Both Clemens and Schilling pitched to form, but New York took a 2–1 lead in the eighth inning on a solo home run by Alfonso Soriano. With two out in the eighth, Arizona rookie manager Bob Brenly brought back the thirty-seven-year-old Johnson—who had thrown 105 pitches the previous day—in relief. New York countered by protecting its lead with Maria-no Rivera, who in recent postseasons had proven to be nearly invincible. After Johnson held the Yankees scoreless, the Diamondbacks strung together three hits, a hit-by-pitch, and an error to score two runs and record a stunning 3–2 win and the World Series title. Johnson became the first pitcher since 1968 to win three games in the Series, and he shared the MVP award with Schilling. The aftermath of this exciting Series is summed up below.

To Yankees fans (and especially George Steinbrenner) this loss marked the end of an extraordinary run of dominance in which New York won four World Series in five years. The best account of this era, and the 2001 Series in particular, is Buster Olney, The Last Night of the Yankee Dynasty: The Game, the Team, and the Cost of Greatness *(New York: HarperCollins, 2004).*

Gonzo's Hit Caps Comeback
By Mark Gonzales
The Arizona Republic

The Diamondbacks saved their best to beat the best Sunday night in grand style.

They conquered baseball's most storied franchise and the most dominant closer in postseason history by scoring two runs with one out in the bottom of the ninth inning. Luis Gonzalez hit a 150-foot single over a drawn-in infield to cap a two-run rally and beat the New York Yankees 3–2 in the seventh and deciding game of the World Series.

"I've passed the bar three times, but this is the first time I've done this, and this is better," general manager Joe Garagiola Jr. said during a mass celebration on the Bank One Ballpark field as nearly all of the 49,589 fans roared for their heroes during a steady drizzle.

In ending the Yankees' three-year Series reign, the D-Backs became the first expansion team to win a World Series in its first four years and brought the first major professional sports championship to the Valley.

They also beat Mariano Rivera, who saw his streak of 23 consecutive saves in postseason play end in an amazing manner.

"We saw Rivera come in the game in the eighth, and everyone in the dugout believed we'd worked too hard to let him do it again," center fielder Steve Finley said.

This also marked the first major sports championship for managing general partner Jerry Colangelo, who failed twice in previous attempts with the Suns in the NBA Finals.

But Colangelo and Garagiola sought high-profile free agents after the 1998 season, then fortified the roster with seasoned veterans seeking a world title that eluded them throughout their careers.

Bob Brenly became the fourth rookie manager to win a Series, and he did it his way by maximizing his roster.

"Bob made this a 25-man team, not just Randy (Johnson) and Curt (Schilling)," second baseman Craig Counsell said.

But Schilling and Johnson brought the D-Backs as far as they could in the biggest game of their storied careers. Schilling, working on three days' rest for the second consecutive time, pitched six innings of one-hit ball before allowing a tying run in the seventh and a solo homer to Alfonso Soriano to start the eighth.

Johnson, who threw 105 pitches Saturday to win Game 6, stopped the Yankees' rally by pitching 1 1/3 scoreless innings of relief and finished with a 3-0 record and 1.04 ERA in three games.

Johnson became the first pitcher to win on consecutive days as a starter and reliever.

The D-Backs' offense, which failed to hit with runners in scoring position against starter Roger Clemens, came through in a manner that typified the team's will to win throughout the season.

Brenly elected to start Danny Bautista over Reggie Sanders in right field because of Bautista's ability to lay off Clemens' high fastball. Bautista proved Brenly right when he ripped a double to left center to score Finley for a 1–0 lead in the sixth.

But one of Brenly's bigger moves was starting veteran Mark Grace over Erubiel Durazo because of Grace's experience and Brenly's hunch that Grace would deliver a big hit.

Grace capped his three-hit game by hitting a single up the middle against Rivera to start the ninth. Damian Miller attempted a sacrifice bunt, but Rivera's throw to second was wide and allowed pinch runner David Dellucci to reach second.

Jay Bell hit into a force play, but National League Division Series hero Tony

Womack came through by pulling a game-tying double down the right field line, scoring pinch runner Midre Cummings and moving Bell to third.

Counsell was struck in the hand by a Rivera pitch to load the bases for Gonzalez, who led the D-Backs with 57 home runs during the regular season but had been nagged during the Series with wrist and hamstring injuries.

"Going to the plate, I'm thinking this is a childhood dream," Gonzalez said. "You have a chance to be the hero that wins this game."

Gonzalez poked a pitch that would have been a routine popup had the infield not been drawn in. Nevertheless, it did drop and Gonzalez leaped high as the crowd roared.

"Running to first base, my legs went numb," Gonzalez said.

Bell crossed home plate and was met immediately by Matt Williams, who suffered 97 losses along with Bell in the Diamondbacks expansion season of 1998.

"If I was going to score the winning run, Matty had to be the first guy there," Bell said.

After the game, Yankees general manager Brian Cashman visited the D-Backs' clubhouse to congratulate Brenly.

Four of the games were decided by one run, and this marked the third time in Series history the home team won every game.

"I'd like to thank Jerry Colangelo for bringing me in here," Grace said. "I wasn't good enough for the Chicago Cubs but I was good enough to play for the World Champion Arizona Diamondbacks."

97

Commentary on Announcement of Baseball's Decision to Contract Two Teams (2001)

SOURCE: Doug Pappas, *Doug Pappas's Business of Baseball Pages*, MLB Labor and Contraction Coverage, Feature Articles, http://roadsidephotos.com/baseball/index.htm

Just two days after one of the most dramatic World Series ever played helped excite a nation still reeling from the September 11 disaster, Commissioner Selig announced that major league baseball was in such dire straits that during the off-season two teams would be contracted. Although Selig did not mention the teams to be contracted, it was soon revealed that the two candidates were the Minnesota Twins—whose billionaire owner, Carl Pohlad, was a friend of Selig's and had loaned Selig money before he became commissioner—and the Montreal Expos. Complicating the issue was the recent purchase of the Florida Marlins by Jeffrey Loria, previously the owner of the Expos, which would now be run by major league baseball. Both Loria and Pohlad would receive generous buyouts from baseball in exchange for allowing their clubs to be contracted.

Predictably, there was a public uproar, especially in the affected states, where the attorneys general threatened to file federal lawsuits. The House Committee of the Judiciary

held a hearing on December 6 in which Selig, colorful Minnesota governor Jesse Ventura, and several others testified on the pros and cons of contraction. Selig never publicly retracted his position that contraction was necessary, but in the new Basic Agreement he and the owners committed themselves to maintaining thirty teams through the 2006 season.

One of the many critics of the contraction scheme was the late Doug Pappas, a lawyer and an expert on the business of baseball. The following column, originally published in SABR's "Business of Baseball" newsletter, was posted on his Web site on December 6, the same day as the congressional hearing.

Contraction Follies

On November 4, fans thrilled to the ninth-inning, seventh-game conclusion of the most exciting World Series in years. Two days later, Major League Baseball's owners, led by Commissioner-for-Life Bud Selig, destroyed all the goodwill the Series had produced by declaring that two of MLB's thirty teams would be eliminated during the off-season.

When contraction was first proposed, a major obstacle was the shortage of owners willing to get out of baseball. Disney was looking to sell the Angels, but only to someone who would keep the club in Anaheim. Montreal was the most obvious target, but Jeffrey Loria was determined to operate a baseball team. So was John Henry in Florida. The Tampa Bay Devil Rays were locked into a long-term lease and played in a state whose Attorney General had vowed to stop any attempt to move or fold the team, and whose courts had already held MLB's antitrust exemption inapplicable to issues of franchise movement.

Then Carl Pohlad came to Selig's rescue. Pohlad, MLB's wealthiest non-corporate owner, was frustrated that Minnesotans wouldn't build him a nearly-free stadium after he had pocketed tens of millions of revenue-sharing dollars without reinvesting them in the club. If Selig needed another team to contract, he could have the Twins—for a sizeable premium over their market value, of course.

Never mind that the Twins are an original American League franchise with 40 years of history in Minnesota. Never mind that the Twins had won two World Series since 1987, and almost won their division this year. Never mind that the Twins outdrew the Yankees from 1987 through 1994, or that attendance had risen 68% in 2001. Never mind that Minneapolis–St. Paul is larger than Cleveland, St. Louis or Denver, or that local investors (including Clark Griffith, son of the man who sold the Twins to Pohlad) are willing to buy the team. The Twins were the missing piece in Commissioner Bud's master plan, so they had to go.

But Pohlad had forgotten two things. First, on September 26, Twins president Jerry Bell had notified the Metropolitan Sports Facilities Commission, owner of the Metrodome, that the team was exercising its option to play at the Metrodome in 2002. Second, the Twins' lease at the Metrodome provided: *"If the Team ceases to play major league professional baseball games for any reason, the Team shall have breached this Agreement and will be liable for such remedies as may be available to the commission at law or in equity, including, but not limited to injunctive relief, and orders for specific performance requiring the Team to play its Home Games at the Stadium during the Term hereof."*

Relying on this provision, a local judge enjoined MLB and the Twins from contracting the team or playing home games anywhere but the Metrodome in 2002. The Minnesota Supreme Court rejected MLB's emergency appeal, leaving the injunction in place and directing the intermediate appellate court to expedite consideration of the case. Even on an expedited basis, though, the appeal won't be decided until 2002—too late for the Twins to be contracted over this off-season.

Another major roadblock is, not surprisingly, the MLBPA. While the owners recognized that they would have to negotiate the effects of contraction with the union, they took the position that the decision to eliminate teams did not have to be bargained. The MLBPA's grievance will not be heard until mid-December—and even if MLB wins, it is unlikely to be able to negotiate the details in time to contract for the 2002 season. MLB wants to allocate players from the affected organizations through a dispersal draft, while the MLBPA would insist on free agency for all affected players.

One man who thinks the players are likely to win their grievance is former Commissioner Fay Vincent, who told ESPN Radio, "I would put my money on Donald [Fehr]'s legal opinion over the owners because Donald is always right and the owners never are." Terming contraction "a public-relations fiasco delivered by the owners," Vincent asked pointedly, "If baseball is suffering financially as much as they say they are, then where are they going to get the money to buy these teams out?"

Contraction also met with swift legal opposition. Minnesota Senator Paul Wellstone and Michigan Representative John Conyers introduced bills to strip MLB of its antitrust exemption with respect to franchise matters. Conyers explained, "Any time 30 of the wealthiest and most influential individuals get together behind closed doors and agree to reduce output, that cannot be a good thing for anyone but the monopolists." Conyers has asked MLB to produce a host of financial and other documents—notably including studies on contraction or relocation, and any studies on territorial rights to San Jose, New Jersey and Washington, D.C. The attorneys general of Minnesota and Florida have vowed to sue if clubs in their states are contracted; as a pre-emptive move, Florida's Bob Butterworth has subpoenaed financial records and all contraction-related documents from MLB, the Marlins and Devil Rays.

Bud Selig will testify before Congress on December 6. At that time he promises to show that even though MLB's gross revenues have risen from $2.1 billion to $3.5 billion since 1997, this year 25 clubs lost money and MLB posted a collective loss of over $500 million. He can expect to be asked why clubs that are supposedly hemorrhaging money would (a) pay a nine-figure premium to buy and fold two teams, or (b) award a three-year contract extension to the man who led them into such desperate straits.

Whatever Selig tells Congress is unlikely to undo the damage to MLB's reputation, and his own, caused by the contraction announcement. If MLB was truly determined to eliminate two teams, it could have simply bought them, proclaimed their dissolution, and presented the MLBPA and local officials with a *fait accompli*. Selig's announcement that two *unnamed* teams would be contracted was widely viewed as a bluff to force the MLBPA into givebacks, and to pressure governments in Montreal, Minnesota, Miami and Oakland into subsidizing new stadia. Such tactics are resented in ordinary times; when used even as the aftermath of the September 11 bombing wreaked havoc on state and local government budgets across North America, they're despised. Selig compounded the public relations debacle by telling Minnesotans to "look in the mirror" when looking for someone to blame for the prospective loss of the Twins, suggesting that any city unwilling to subsidize its local team didn't deserve one.

And Selig's justifications for contraction ranged from the disingenuous to the ludicrous. In MLB's official press release announcing the contraction vote, Selig stated: "The problems facing the potentially affected teams will not be resolved by either changing ownership or changing location. Merely transferring existing problems to another ownership group or another city would only exacerbate the problem, not resolve it." In other words, MLB already had the best possible owners, located in the best possible cities: Washington, D.C. was a worse baseball market than Montreal, and no one could run the Twins better than Carl Pohlad. When critics noted that Selig's own Brewers stood to gain from the elimination of the Twins, Selig called the suggestion of a conflict of interest "childish" and "inane." Selig's assertion to the *Milwaukee Journal-Sentinel* that "St. Louis is closer to Minneapolis than Milwaukee is" should also surprise anyone with a map.

In that same press release, Selig declared, "This action, though difficult, should not surprise anyone who is familiar with the economics of the game. Our industry has significant financial problems that we are trying to address in a myriad of ways. Contraction is one step toward addressing the industry's problems." Yet barely a year before, MLB's own hand-picked "Blue Ribbon Economic Panel" had unequivocally concluded, "If the recommendations outlined in this report are implemented, there should be no immediate need for contraction." MLB implemented *none* of these recommendations before voting to kill two clubs.

On November 7, Selig told mlb.com, "I honestly believe that we can get this done by the end of November." Not quite. At the end of November, MLB still had thirty teams. It also had a lawsuit in Minnesota; a grievance filed by the Players' Association; an investigation by the Florida Attorney General; and a Congressional effort to revoke its antitrust exemption . . . not to mention an expired labor agreement which could produce another work stoppage before or during the 2002 season. MLB had consistently misplayed its hand, alienating fans, angering commentators and infuriating elected officials while moving no closer to either its stated goal of contraction or its implicit goal of new stadia and concessions from the MLBPA. And Bud Selig had a raise and a new three-year contract extension.

98

Selig Stops All-Star Game After Eleven-Inning Tie (2002)

SOURCE: *Milwaukee Journal Sentinel*, July 11, 2002

Baseball commissioner Bud Selig had reason to eagerly anticipate the events of July 9. On that night the All-Star Game would be played in his hometown of Milwaukee, in the new ballpark he was instrumental in getting financed and built. After being criticized in the press for his advocacy of contraction, Selig could finally bask in the applause of appreciative fans.

Initially he did. The game featured several exciting plays, most notably a tremendous over-the-wall catch by Torii Hunter of a Barry Bonds fly ball (after which Bonds playfully pretended to tackle Hunter at the end of the inning). All-Star Game managers Bob Brenly and Joe Torre followed recent precedent and made sure every player, with the exception of one pitcher reserved in case of extra innings, got into the game. Sure enough, those pitchers were pressed into duty when the ninth inning ended with the AL and the NL tied 7–7.

At this point an unexpected problem occurred. NL pitcher Vicente Padilla informed Brenly after pitching the top of the eleventh inning that he could not continue because his arm was tight. The managers conferred with the umpires and Selig, who hoped that the NL would solve the dilemma by scoring off Freddy Garcia in the bottom of the inning. When Garcia held the NL squad scoreless, Selig was forced to declare the All-Star Game a tie and end the game—a decision that drew a chorus of boos from his fellow Milwaukeeans.

Selig was not to blame for the outcome, but he received the majority of the blame from outraged fans who by now were accustomed to public relations gaffes by the commissioner. Selig called for changes to the All-Star Game format (including a proposal that would reward the winning league with the home-field advantage in that year's World Series), but no solution could remove the sting of Selig's latest perceived failure.

73RD ALL-STAR GAME: ALL KNOTTED UP

Selig Defends All-Star Ending
Commissioner Calls for Change in Managing Style
By Drew Olson
of the Journal Sentinel staff

Major League Baseball, a sport that revels in its history like no other, again will look to its past in an effort to avoid a repeat of the controversial 7–7 deadlock that left fans jeering the inconclusive finish of the 73rd All-Star Game Tuesday night at Miller Park.

After watching managers Bob Brenly of the National League and Joe Torre of the American League plow through all 19 available pitchers in the first 10 innings, baseball Commissioner Bud Selig agreed with Brenly's assessment that Vicente Padilla's creaky right arm wouldn't permit the Philadelphia right-hander to continue into the top of the 12th.

Selig declared the game a tie, touching off a national controversy and leaving a huge smudge on Milwaukee's five-day all-star party. An event that was one run away from being a solid success is being viewed by many as a travesty that underscores the sport's problems.

"Nobody wanted to play more than I did," said Selig, who said he spent "a very lonely, sad evening" at home on what could have been a triumphant night. "I know how long I was looking forward to this. I know how hard everybody in baseball worked on this. It was a great, great five days, but for a couple minutes."

Speaking at a news conference Wednesday at his downtown Milwaukee office, Selig defended his decision and vowed to avoid a repeat.

"While this is a horribly painful and heartbreaking lesson, we'll learn from this, and this will never happen again," Selig said.

To avoid a tie in the future, Selig must overhaul the culture surrounding the All-Star Game, which has evolved from a prestigious and competitive summer event to an "everyone must play" affair that many star players view as an inconvenience.

Consider the key moments of three famous all-star leftfielders:

In the 1941 game at Detroit's Briggs Stadium, Boston Red Sox great Ted Williams came to the plate with two out in the bottom of the ninth inning and belted a three-run homer to give his team a 7–5 victory. Williams, who died Friday and was honored during the pregame ceremony Tuesday night, called the shot one of the highlights of his career.

In the 1955 game, St. Louis leftfielder Stan Musial, one of the bigger stars at the time, belted a game-winning homer in the bottom of the 12th inning to cap an electrifying 6–5 National League victory.

Tuesday night, the best leftfielder of the modern era, San Francisco's Barry Bonds, was robbed of a home run by Minnesota's Torii Hunter in the first inning and belted a two-run blast in the third. Shortly after circling the bases and accepting congratulations from teammates, Bonds went to the clubhouse, showered, left the park and took a private plane to Los Angeles, where he attended ESPN's ESPY Awards on Wednesday night.

GAME HAS CHANGED

"We have to evaluate the whole all-star process," Selig said. "Managers manage the All-Star Game differently than they did 10, 15, 20 or 30 years ago. The solutions are not difficult. We need to maybe take the game back where it was two or three decades ago."

From 1970-'77, his first eight seasons as president of the Milwaukee Brewers, Selig saw his club send a total of 11 players to the All-Star Game. Six of them did not play, leaving the Brewers unrepresented in four of the eight seasons.

"It always killed me when our guys didn't get in the game," Selig said. "All the years I've watched and gone to All-Star Games, the starters would play longer. Pitchers always used to pitch a minimum of three innings."

The tenor of the game began to change during the 1990s, thanks to what Selig called "The Mussina Syndrome."

At the 1993 All-Star Game in Baltimore, fans became enraged when American League manager Cito Gaston of Toronto did not use Orioles right-hander Mike Mussina, the only healthy representative from the hometown team.

Gaston took an enormous amount of heat from fans that night and was booed lustily on subsequent visits to Oriole Park at Camden Yards. As a result, all-star managers made it a priority to get every player in the game.

To do that, managers began to follow a strict blueprint for using players. The starters, who were voted in by fans, generally would get two at-bats and play three or four innings before hitting the showers. Starting pitchers would throw two innings, no more. Relievers would throw an inning apiece, with some of them splitting an inning based on left-handed and right-handed matchups. Managers generally saved one pitcher for possible extra-inning duty.

It was this substitution pattern that prompted the fiasco on Tuesday night.

Beyond managing philosophy, Selig offered no immediate solutions aimed at avoiding another tie.

PADILLA'S ARM A PROBLEM

After the bottom of the 11th inning, Selig, who had been watching the game from a seat adjacent to the first-base dugout, was approached by Sandy Alderson, baseball's executive vice-president of baseball operations, who informed him of a problem.

Padilla, the 10th and final pitcher on the National League roster, had just completed his second inning of duty and was having trouble getting loose. Brenly did not think Padilla would be available for a third inning.

Brenly spoke with Selig, and they were quickly joined by Torre, who was down to his final pitcher, Seattle's Freddy Garcia. Neither Torre nor Brenly wanted the game to continue.

"They came with very strong feelings," Selig said. "They both said, 'We're done.' I said, 'Well, wait a minute. We have to think about that.'

"Calling the game off up to that moment had not even entered my mind. I was faced with having to make an immediate decision based on the facts on hand: There were no position players left; no pitchers left. The National League pitcher (Padilla) was really struggling."

Selig quickly considered his options. He could tell both managers, "You made your bed, lie in it," and force play to continue. "That kind of answer I would consider flippant," he said. "The fact of the matter is, I (would then) have to figure out what their options are."

Selig could have ordered Brenly to send a non-pitcher to the mound—a move used in desperation by managers several times each regular season.

"If you want to create another travesty, that would be it," Selig said. "Yes, of course teams do it during the season when they are hopelessly behind and don't want to waste anybody in the bullpen. The fact of the matter is that's a very, very unattractive option."

Selig feared that using a player who is not used to being on the mound presents an injury risk for both pitcher and hitter. Imagine if Los Angeles rightfielder Shawn Green came in to pitch and injured his shoulder. Or, say Green threw a pitch that hit Boston's Johnny Damon on the hand, breaking a finger and putting Damon on the injured list.

Putting a non-pitcher on the mound also creates the potential for numerous walks and multi-run innings that could have turned a close game into a blowout.

SAFETY CONSIDERED

Selig also considered allowing a pitcher who had worked earlier in the game to re-enter, a move that is not even allowed during spring training exhibition games. Because most of the pitchers had already undergone post-game treatment and showered, it would have taken several minutes for one of them to warm up and get ready to pitch. Selig dismissed the idea.

"You don't want to put anybody at risk," he said. "I think it was Bob Brenly who said, 'These clubs entrust us with their players.' For me to see a pitcher walk off the mound holding his arm or his shoulder, I didn't want that."

Brenly suggested holding an impromptu home-run derby to decide the winner, much like the penalty-kick approach used in soccer and the shootout used in hockey. "I can't really find any support for that," Selig said. "Even in retrospect, the fact is you don't want to pile one gimmick on another gimmick. That's not the way to solve the problem. We've never done that before."

With his head swimming, his body quivering and the time of the game delay approaching 10 minutes, Selig decided to begin the bottom of the 11th inning and—if the National League failed to score—declare the game a tie.

"As I quickly reviewed my options, I came to the very painful and extremely difficult conclusion that given the Philadelphia pitcher's physical condition, that I had no choice," he said.

"I have to balance the concern and hopes of the fans against the welfare of the players and the game. Every so often, you get caught. Many people have reminded me from time to time, this is why they have a commissioner. Somebody had to make those decisions."

LAST CHANCE

Selig made his decision, but almost got a reprieve. With two out, the National League advanced Florida third baseman Mike Lowell to second, but San Francisco catcher Benito Santiago struck out on a sweeping curveball to end the game.

"If Benito Santiago got the (game-winning) hit, I'd have been on the field and hugged him and carried him off on my own shoulders," Selig said.

Of course, a game-ending hit by Santiago might have sparked accusations that

Garcia had "grooved" a pitch to ensure a happy ending. Baseball faced similar charges in the 2001 All-Star Game in Seattle, when Baltimore star Cal Ripken Jr., playing in his final Midsummer Classic, hammered a thigh-high pitch from Los Angeles' Chan Ho Park for a home run.

"When you look at the options, you also get into a lot of other things that get to be very unpleasant," Selig said. "This is something that people have different opinions on. I understand that.

"I don't like to say it was a no-win situation, but I think the options eliminated themselves rather quickly."

99

Basic Agreement Signed by All Clubs Except Yankees (2002)

SOURCE: 2003–2006 Basic Agreement, 50–51, 146, http://roadsidephotos.com/baseball/BasicAgreement.pdf

In the Blue Ribbon Panel Report of 2000 one of the suggestions advanced by the authors was an expansion of revenue sharing calculated not only to redistribute money to small-market teams, but to compel these teams to use the proceeds to increase salary as a means toward improving their clubs and thus reducing competitive imbalance. The collective bargaining agreement (CBA) signed by every team except the New York Yankees (which, not coincidentally, would return far more money to a central fund for redistribution than any other club) took a small step in that direction, but did not dictate how any shared revenue was to be spent.

The excerpt here from the 2003–2006 Basic Agreement (retroactive to 2002) briefly describes the compromise reached on the contraction issue. The owners promised to maintain thirty major league teams through the duration of the agreement, but retained the right, under certain conditions, to contract two teams after the 2006 season. Economists such as Roger Noll and Andrew Zimbalist have argued that revenue sharing, as envisioned in the Blue Ribbon Panel report and in the new CBA, not only would have little impact on competitive balance, but would actually make contraction a more attractive option than it would have been otherwise because it would improve the level of talent to be redistributed to the surviving clubs. The excerpted clauses are taken from Article XV, "Miscellaneous," and a related document in the appendix.

G. FUTURE EXPANSION

During the term of this Agreement, the Clubs have the right to expand the number of Major League Clubs by adding up to two (2) new Expansion Clubs. Notice of a decision to expand by two Clubs shall promptly be given to the Association and the Association may reopen this Agreement with reference solely to the effect upon the Players of such expansion, upon the giving of 10 days' written notice.

The Office of the Commissioner and/or the Clubs shall not undertake any centralized effort to reduce the number of Major League Clubs effective for a season covered by this Agreement. The Clubs shall, however, have the right, subject to the terms and conditions set forth in this Article XV (H), to reduce by as many as two (2) the number of Major League Clubs effective for the 2007 championship season.

(1) *Procedure*

(a) The Clubs may not take a vote relating to contraction effective for the 2007 season prior to April 1, 2006. The Clubs shall notify the Association of any decision to contract effective for the 2007 championship season no later than July 1, 2006 and, on or before that date, shall supply to the Association a tentative championship schedule for the 2007 championship season reflecting such decision.

(b) Any decision to contract effective for the 2007 championship season shall be subject to effects bargaining and such bargaining shall commence no later than July 15, 2006.

(2) *Covenants of the Clubs and the Association*

(a) The Association, on behalf of itself and the Major League Players, shall not bring in any forum any contractual or NLRA challenge to the decision to contract (but not the effects thereof). Moreover, the Association shall not pursue, encourage, finance or assist any antitrust challenge to such decision to contract; and

(b) The Clubs shall not contend, in any litigation related to a decision to contract effective for the 2007 championship season, that the decision to contract is a mandatory subject of bargaining under the NLRA. Notwithstanding subparagraph (a) above, the Association may intervene in any such litigation to enforce the covenant set out in this subparagraph (b).

(3) *Exclusion*

This Article XV (H) shall not preclude the owner or owners of an individual Club from taking action (*e.g.*, bankruptcy) that would result in the elimination of such Club.

(4) *Survival of the Basic Agreement*

The Clubs and the Association expressly acknowledge and agree that this Article XV (H) shall, in all events, survive the expiration of the Basic Agreement. (See Attachment 8.)

ATTACHMENT 8

Eugene D. Orza, Esquire
Associate General Counsel
Major League Baseball Players Association
12 East 49th Street
New York, NY 10017
Dear Gene:

The Players Association has consistently maintained that a centralized effort by the Office of the Commissioner and/or the Clubs to reduce the number of Major

League Clubs is a mandatory subject of bargaining under the National Labor Relations Act ("NLRA"). The Clubs, on the other hand, have consistently taken the position that such action is a permissive subject of bargaining under the NLRA. Without resolving this difference of opinion, the Parties have reached certain agreements on this topic during the negotiations over a successor Basic Agreement. Those agreements are reflected in Article XV (H) (Future Contraction) of the new Basic Agreement. The Parties agree, by this letter, that their agreement on this topic and the bargaining that preceded it shall not be used by either party as evidence that the topic is or is not a mandatory subject of bargaining in any subsequent litigation, including any grievance or NLRB proceeding.

Very truly yours,

Robert D. Manfred, Jr.

AGREED: Major League Baseball Players Association

100

Summary of BALCO Steroid Probe and Barry Bonds (2003)

SOURCE: *San Francisco Chronicle*, December 21, 2003

Ever since a vial of androstenedione was found in the locker of Mark McGwire during his record-setting 1998 season, the suspicion among many baseball fans that players were inflating their bodies and statistics with the help of steroids and other substances increased. Knowledgeable fans already were aware that for decades players had taken drugs such as "greenies" to improve performance (as detailed in Jim Bouton's book Ball Four*) and that a number of Olympic athletes had been caught through mandatory drug testing. However, these tests were widely believed to be inadequate because athletes and their chemists were always several steps ahead of the testers—and baseball had no policy regarding performance-enhancing drugs. Baseball players, for all intents and purposes, were free to use whatever substances they could without fear of exposure. The extraordinary explosion in offensive statistics during the 1990s was assumed to be in part the result of steroid use, but no one could prove it.*

On September 3, 2003, federal and local officials raided the headquarters of the Bay Area Laboratory Co-Operative (BALCO) during an investigation of the production and distribution of a previously unknown steroid, tetrahydroestrinone (THG). Two days later the home of Greg Anderson, a local trainer best known for his work with his longtime friend Barry Bonds, was raided. Subsequent investigations revealed that many athletes in addition to Bonds—most notably track star Marion Jones and baseball players Jason Giambi and Gary Sheffield—were also involved with BALCO and received subpoenas to testify before a grand jury investigating BALCO's president and founder, Victor Conte.

This investigation has fueled the controversy over baseball and its almost nonexistent policy against steroids (weakened at the insistence of the MLBPA, whose leaders—though

*not many of the players—saw drug testing as incriminatory and illegal if without cause),
but has also clouded the reputation of stars like Giambi (who admitted in leaked grand
jury testimony that he knowingly took performance-enhancing drugs) and Bonds. As
Bonds approached the home run records of Babe Ruth and Hank Aaron, discussion raged
over the ethics of steroid use, the legitimacy of baseball statistics, and the never-ending
battle for power between the players and major league baseball. On January 13, 2005,
baseball and the MLBPA announced a new policy under which players will be random-
ly tested throughout the year and be subject to immediate penalties for positive tests for
steroids, human growth hormone, and other illegal substances. The policy was soon attacked by several members of Congress, who held hearings on the issue (see Document
102 later in this chapter).*

The article below is one of many written for the Chronicle *by Mark Fainaru-Wada
and Lance Williams, who have followed the story from the beginning and who have published classified grand jury testimony and other documents. Their findings are detailed in*
Game of Shadows: Barry Bonds, BALCO, and the Steroids Scandal That Rocked Professional Sports *(New York: Gotham Books, 2006).*

SPORTS AND DRUGS

How the Doping Scandal Unfolded
Fallout from BALCO Probe Could Taint Olympics, Pro Sports
Mark Fainaru-Wada, Lance Williams, Chronicle Staff Writers

Barry Bonds hit a career-high 49 home runs during the 2000 season, but within days of the last game, he set his sights on 2001. A contract year lay ahead for the
aging left fielder, a chance to regain the status of baseball's highest paid player.

Bonds already was doing weight training with Greg Anderson, his boyhood friend.
Anderson took him to see Victor Conte, a self-taught scientist who boasted he could
propel top-level athletes to peak performance through an unconventional mix of
blood analysis and nutritional supplements.

The outfielder returned the next season bigger and stronger. The results are etched
in baseball's record books—and, perhaps, in a transcript of the secret proceedings
of a federal grand jury convened in San Francisco this fall.

For while Bonds' alliance with the weight trainer and the nutritionist may have
helped him hit 73 home runs in 2001—breaking baseball's most storied record and
persuading the Giants to offer him a $90 million contract—it also involved him in
what may be the worst sports doping scandal of a generation.

It is a scandal involving high-tech designer steroids and masking agents, human
growth hormone and suspected money laundering, drugs with code names like "the
cream" and "the clear," and a mystery chemist who concocted a new performance-
enhancing drug called THG.

Already the scandal has roiled both the upcoming 2004 Olympic Games in Athens
and American professional sports, calling into question whether some of the world's
greatest athletic achievements have been attained by deliberate cheating.

And with the new year comes the possibility of indictments—and the prospect of elite athletes turning government witness and seeing their achievements discredited at a public trial.

At the center of the scandal are Conte and Anderson—targets of the federal grand jury investigation—as well as some of the biggest names in the National Football League, Major League Baseball and Olympic track and field, who have been summoned to testify. But the biggest name of all is Bonds, who after an offseason with Conte and Anderson emerged, according to the team media guide, 18 pounds heavier, solid as a rock—and a better hitter than he had been in his entire life.

The 39-year-old Bonds has denied using performance-enhancing drugs and attributed his bulk and success to nutrition and weight training. But his relationship with Conte and Anderson has underscored speculation that his late-career assault on the home run record was steroid-fueled.

FLAUNTING ELITE CLIENTELE

Conte was an odd mixture of sports guru and sports fan. His Burlingame Bay Area Laboratory Co-Operative (BALCO) sold sophisticated blood and urine testing services to athletes, and a subsidiary offered an array of supplements, including the popular zinc and magnesium product, ZMA.

Conte sometimes flaunted his clientele.

"I don't just hang out with elite athletes, they pay me large sums of money to advise them," he wrote once on an Internet message board. Another time, he wrote: "... elite athletes like Marion Jones and Barry Bonds routinely pay me for my services in cashier's checks."

The walls of BALCO were a shrine to Conte's clients—from Bonds to the entire Miami Dolphins football team—covered with autographed photos, jerseys and other memorabilia.

It was an unusual second career. After growing up in Fresno, where he ran track in junior college, Conte spent more than a decade working as a musician. His high point was a brief stint playing bass for the Oakland funk band Tower of Power.

Making a go of it in the fiercely competitive nutritional supplements business wasn't easy, but Conte was smart and charismatic. He seemed to have a photographic memory, and he was a master networker.

Soon, he was connecting with Olympic hopefuls and other athletes who wanted to be bigger, stronger and faster.

In 1988, Conte provided free testing and supplements for a group he called "BALCO Olympians," then joined them at the Summer Games in Seoul.

"All the athletes wanted to deal with the guy," said Gregg Tafralis, a former internationally ranked shot putter and one of Conte's original BALCO Olympians. "The guy is the smartest son of a bitch I've ever met in my life."

Conte's client list also included top-level bodybuilders. It was an odd mix of customers: mainstream athletes whose sports banned the use of performance-enhancing drugs, and musclemen, whose very success was predicated on steroid use.

Conte's first major breakthrough into the world of professional sports came thanks to Randy Huntington, coach to Olympic athletes, early advocate of nutritional supplements and personal trainer for linebacker Bill Romanowski. Huntington recalls sending Romanowski to BALCO in the summer of 1996.

Romanowski seemed the perfect Conte client: a high-profile athlete who believed in the notion of exploring all things related to improving his body.

Romanowski received more than testing and supplements from Conte, according to reports by investigators for the U.S. Drug Enforcement Administration and the Douglas County, Colo., sheriff's office. In 1999, while the linebacker was under investigation for prescription-drug fraud, his wife, Julie, told the investigators that Romanowski obtained human growth hormone from BALCO, investigative records show.

The drug's benefits are said to include increased muscle mass, improved vision and higher energy. There is no test to detect its use, and it's legal only if prescribed by a doctor.

Romanowski was acquitted in the prescription-drug case, and no one was prosecuted in connection with the growth hormone. Conte has denied he gave the linebacker the substance. Romanowski did not respond to requests for comment, but his lawyer, Harvey Steinberg, said the investigators' account of their interview with Julie Romanowski was not believable.

Through Romanowski, Conte generated business with more pro football players, including many members of the Denver Broncos and the Dolphins. Romanowski also steered athletes from other sports to Conte—people like six-time Olympic gold medalist Amy Van Dyken, who once described herself as "the Bill Romanowski of the swimming world," and 1996 Olympic gold medal–winning sprinter Chryste Gaines of San Leandro, a Stanford graduate.

Romanowski also brought together Conte with Remi Korchemny of Castro Valley, a Russian-born spring coach who has coached three Olympic medalists over the years. Korchemny exposed Conte to Olympic runners, which led to relationships with people like Kelli White, the Union City sprinter, and Dwain Chambers, Britain's fastest man.

Conte and Korchemny eventually formed the ZMA Track Club, which served as a marketing tool and claimed among its athletes Marion Jones and Tim Montgomery, the American sprinters who at one time were the fastest man and woman in the world.

But as big as those clients were, Bonds' arrival in 2000 signaled even greater opportunities.

ANDERSON, CONTE MEET

Conte ran his business out of a nondescript building off Highway 101 in Burlingame. Just around the corner was the gym where Greg Anderson worked out Bonds, his boyhood buddy.

It was a heavy-duty gym, a place for serious bodybuilders, a place that led to Anderson meeting Conte.

Bonds and Anderson had grown up together on the Peninsula, hanging out with the same friends and playing in the San Carlos Little League.

Anderson had dreamed of playing professional baseball, but he never made it farther than a luckless team at Fort Hays State University in western Kansas. When a coach told the stocky second baseman he'd never make a living at baseball, he turned his focus to weight training.

It became his passion, and occupation. He started a personal training business called Get Big Productions and worked with clients ranging from high school athletes to adult bodybuilders. In about 1998, he began working with Bonds—and his business opportunities soared.

Anderson gained access to the Giants' clubhouse, and that led to connections with Benito Santiago, Bobby Estalella, and Armando Rios, among others. Bonds once took Anderson on a winter tour of Japan by several major leaguers, a trip that created business relationships with Yankees slugger Jason Giambi and Minnesota Twins catcher A. J. Pierzynski, recently acquired by the Giants.

After Anderson introduced Bonds to Conte, the slugger began a year-round training and supplement plan. He told Muscle & Fitness magazine he visited BALCO every few months to have his blood tested for deficiencies, and Conte said Bonds' nutritional regimen included a long list of items taken at different points of the day, including three capsules of ZMA before bedtime.

"Barry takes ZMA every night without fail," Conte boasted on an Internet message board. "He loves getting a deep and restful sleep each night. He says it also helps his recovery as well as his concentration and focus."

THE CONTRACT SEASON

The 2001 season was Bonds' contract year, a time when outstanding performance could lead to big money.

Bonds began his contract drive with a 423-foot home run on Opening Day at Pacific Bell Park. From that point on, he produced a torrent of homers, a power surge during which he went more than four team games between home runs only six times the entire year.

With Bonds bombing away and the team vying for a playoff spot, there was no attendance drop-off from Pac Bell's inaugural season, when the team drew 3.3 million fans. People came to see Bonds crush the ball, and they streamed for the exits when it was clear he had batted for the final time of a game.

When the Giants visited other ballparks, attendance spiked. This was good not only for the Giants but for all of baseball.

"He's doing things he's not supposed to do at 37 years old," teammate Shawon Dunston marveled to reporters.

Dunston made that comment the night Bonds hit his 70th home run of the season, a monstrous shot in Houston that traveled 454 feet. People around the Giants were commenting about Bonds; how much harder he was hitting the ball, how much farther it was traveling and how much more muscular his body had become.

When Bonds entered the league in 1986, he was a wiry phenom listed at 6-foot-1, 185 pounds. In the 2001 season, he was 6-2 and pushing 230—a linebacker in a baseball uniform.

On Oct. 5, 2001, Bonds broke the single-season home run record that had been set just three years earlier by Mark McGwire. Speaking to a crowd of 41,730 people that night at Pac Bell Park, the Giants' slugger thanked several people, including Anderson. Bonds finished the season with 73 home runs, and the Giants re-signed him to a five-year, $90 million deal—a significant advance over the three-year, $22.9 million deal under which he had been working.

When McGwire broke the home run record that had stood for nearly 40 years, there were news reports about his use of androstenedione (Andro), an over-the-counter supplement that performed like a steroid and was banned in some sports, but not baseball.

By the start of the 2002 season, there were growing questions among those who follow baseball about what Bonds might be doing to enhance his performance.

After he hit a two-run homer to lift the Giants past San Diego in the fourth game of the year, he was asked about steroids.

"You can test me and solve that problem real quick," Bonds answered. " . . . To me, in baseball it really doesn't matter what you do; you still have to hit that baseball. If you're incapable of hitting it, it doesn't matter what you take. You have to have eye-hand coordination to be able to produce. I think (steroid use) is really irrelevant to the game of baseball."

Two months later, a June 3 Sports Illustrated article quoted former Houston Astro and San Diego Padre Ken Caminiti saying he used steroids during the 1996 season, when he won the National League Most Valuable Player Award. Caminiti said drug use was widespread.

"It's no secret what's going on in baseball," he said. "At least half the guys are using steroids."

Former Oakland A's slugger Jose Canseco told the magazine he thought the problem was bigger, estimating about 80 percent of the players were on the juice.

And then-Arizona pitcher Curt Schilling told the Washington Post: "Steroids are incredibly prominent in the game, I don't think there's any question about that . . . It has enhanced numbers into the stratosphere."

At the time—in contrast to virtually all other sports—there was no testing program for major leaguers. The players had the strongest union in sports, and it had steadfastly resisted testing.

All that talk of steroids during the 2002 season, though, put pressure on Major League Baseball and the players' union. In the end, management and the players agreed to limited drug testing.

Under the plan, a player could test positive for steroid use five times before receiving a one-year suspension—and even then the language gave the league an option to fine a player rather than suspend him. In the Olympic world, an athlete caught once was banned two years.

The baseball policy was mocked and lambasted, called everything from "a joke" to "worse than terrible."

And the balls just kept sailing out of ballparks.

NEW DRUG IS DETECTED

On Aug. 31, a few months after the steroid allegations shook baseball, an Olympic cyclist named Tammy Thomas was banned from her sport. A steroid used in only a few clinical studies three decades earlier had been found in her urine samples.

The drug was norbolethone, and its discovery in an athlete's system prompted an investigation not only by the U.S. Anti-Doping Agency (USADA), an independent organization that oversees drug-testing of Olympic sports, but also by federal authorities.

Norbolethone had never been marketed for public use, which made it helpful to athletes seeking an undetectable edge. The substance, also known as Genabol, became popular among Olympic athletes during the 2000 Sydney Games, according to track coach Charlie Francis—the man who coached Ben Johnson when the Canadian sprinter tested positive for steroids at the 1988 Summer Games.

"Another unmodified drug that became widely used up to and during the Sydney Olympics was Genabol," Francis wrote in the Oct. 26, 2001 issue of Testosterone Magazine.

" . . . By the time a test was developed, the word was out and the athletes moved on to newer products."

The scientist who uncovered the mystery drug was Dr. Don Catlin, who runs the Olympic drug-testing lab at UCLA. He had seen something suspicious in an Aug. 2001 urine sample from Thomas and ultimately unmasked it as norbolethone.

Officials at the doping agency told the Washington Post they believed the norbolethone was connected to Patrick Arnold, an Illinois chemist and noted supplement maker most famous for bringing Andro to the U.S. market. The agency sent its files on the matter to the U.S. Justice Department. Arnold was never charged with wrongdoing, though, and he denied a link between himself and Thomas.

He did have a link, though, to Victor Conte, the Bay Area nutritionist and supplement maker. Arnold and Conte were online acquaintances, Internet postings show, engaging in regular exchanges on a message board for weight lifters.

A little more than a year after norbolethone's discovery was made public, sources familiar with the current investigation say, authorities came to believe Conte and Arnold were connected by Catlin's latest find: a new designer steroid.

In June, the anti-doping agency said, it received an anonymous phone call from a man who said he was a "high-profile track and field coach." He named athletes he believed were using an undetectable steroid, cited Conte as the source of the drug and offered as evidence a used syringe with the substance in it.

The tipster sent the syringe by overnight delivery. Catlin performed what was described as "reverse engineering" on the substance in the syringe, and he had himself another hit.

The new drug, which Catlin named tetrahydrogestrinone, or THG, was closely related to the steroids gestrinone and trenbolone, but it was altered slightly to avoid detection. Catlin created a test to detect the drug.

Hundreds of urine samples from athletes inside and outside track and field were retested, and the agency also sent word about THG to international sports agencies and U.S. professional leagues. So far, five track and field competitors and four Oakland Raiders, including Romanowski, reportedly have tested positive for the drug.

The organization also notified federal authorities.

On Sept. 3, about 20 officials from agencies representing the Internal Revenue Service, the U.S. Food and Drug Administration, the San Mateo Narcotics Task Force and the anti-doping agency raided BALCO. They knew going in what they were looking for: illegal performance-enhancing drugs, including THG. They thought they knew the name of the chemist who had created this new drug: Patrick Arnold. And they thought they knew two men who were getting paid to supply it to elite athletes: Conte and Anderson.

That day, Conte led authorities to an off-site storage facility, according to an official familiar with the results of the raid. There, authorities discovered suspected human growth hormone and various anabolic steroids, including testosterone.

In the BALCO offices, documents were discovered bearing the names of some of Conte's athlete clients. They, too, became evidence in the case that would be presented to the grand jury.

At one point during the BALCO raid, some agents went to the nearby gym where Anderson worked and pulled him out for questioning. Two days later, authorities knocked down the door of the rented Burlingame condominium where he lived with his girlfriend.

Suspected anabolic steroids and $60,000 in cash were taken from the condo, according to sources familiar with the results of the raid. Also taken was information—some stored in computer files, the rest in a manila envelope—with the names of athletes, along with types of drugs and the schedule on which they were allegedly administered, sources said.

A month-and-a-half later, the anti-doping agency announced a major doping scandal. Terry Madden, head of the organization, told reporters about the anonymous tipster and the designer steroid, and he named Conte and BALCO as the source of the drug.

Madden said "several" athletes had tested positive for THG, and he characterized the events as the largest drug bust in sports history. Madden described a "conspiracy" of coaches, chemists and athletes that represent "intentional doping of the worst sort."

In e-mails to The Chronicle, Conte denied being the source of THG, questioned whether it was really a banned substance and said he was the victim of jealous and hypocritical track and field coaches.

Names of athletes who tested positive for THG began to leak out. When it was reported that British sprinter Dwain Chambers was among them, the story drew huge attention in Europe, where a track and field doping scandal makes for big news.

And, in San Francisco, some of the world's greatest athletes began appearing before the grand jury in a room on the 17th floor of the Phillip A. Burton Federal Building.

The testimony was secret, but sources familiar with the proceedings said some of these elite athletes were reluctant participants until offered immunity for any truthful testimony.

Then, many admitted knowing they had been getting illicit drugs from Conte. Some said he called their drugs "the clear" and "the cream." The clear was THG, taken orally, and the cream was a testosterone lotion rubbed onto the body.

On Dec. 4, Bonds strode into the federal building wearing a gray sport coat, tie and dark slacks. He spent five hours behind closed doors, though only testifying for about half that time.

What he said inside the grand-jury room is unknown.

Indictments, already predicted by one defense lawyer, could come early in the year. Conte and Anderson are targets of the investigation, suspected of laundering funds generated through the sale and distribution of controlled substances. But prosecutors also have asked witnesses about supplement maker Arnold, who declined to comment for this story.

If the investigation proceeds to criminal prosecution, the testimony of the sports stars could become public. Some could find themselves testifying about drug use, in open court.

Conte's attorney, Robert Holley, has predicted the doping scandal could become "bigger than the Kobe Bryant case (in which the basketball star faces a rape charge in Colorado) when you talk about the way sports are looked at in the United States."

Athletes and the nations they represent could pay a price when the Olympics open in Athens next August. Chambers, the British sprinter, faces a two-year suspension for using THG, and that would keep him from competing in the Olympics. The same is true for four potential U.S. Olympians.

But baseball is where the scandal may cut deepest. The sport recently announced that 5 to 7 percent of its 1,200 players tested positive for steroids this year despite advance warning of the testing. Baseball will begin enforcing its much-criticized steroid policy next season, but the fans will impose their own judgment.

"I think the public will put its own asterisk (on all the records), even if baseball doesn't," said former baseball Commissioner Fay Vincent. "I think the sadness for McGwire . . . and maybe even Bonds is that people will not look at them the way they did before all these drug allegations.

"I think it's bad all the way around. Nobody comes out a plus in all this."

101

Boston Ends "The Curse," Wins World Series (2004)

SOURCE: *Boston Globe*, October 31, 2004, *www.boston.com*

The Boston Red Sox found the most dramatic way imaginable to end its 86-year World Series championship drought. They fell behind their hated rivals, the New York Yankees, three games to none in the ALCS, and then became the only club in baseball history to overcome such a deficit in a postseason series. Their first two wins in the ALCS were achieved in extra innings, and in both they scored the tying run in the bottom of the ninth inning off invincible reliever Mariano Rivera. After the ALCS triumph, the Series itself was almost (but not quite) an anticlimax, as Boston continued its winning streak by sweeping the St. Louis Cardinals.

Nineteen years earlier, the Red Sox were on the verge of winning the World Series against the New York Mets when Bill Buckner made his infamous error that lead to a Mets comeback in the sixth game. After the Sox completed their collapse and lost the Series, Boston Globe *columnist Leigh Montville brilliantly captured the pathos and black humor implicit in the defeat (see Document 51). After the Red Sox finally exorcised their demons, Montville returned to express the emotions he and other Sox fans had never experienced in their lifetimes.*

Joy Knows No Bounds

Sox Triumph Leads to a Flight of Fancy
By Leigh Montville
October 31, 2004

I learned how to fly a few minutes before midnight on Oct. 27, 2004. I always thought I could fly, watching those seagulls gracefully drop out of the sky to spear yet another French fry from the MDC trash cans across from Kelly's Roast Beef in Revere, but I never had given it a shot. The Boston Red Sox gave me strength.

"If the Red Sox can win the World Series," I said, stepping from the house just moments after reliever Keith Foulke fielded a ground ball and flipped it to first baseman Doug Mientkiewicz for the final out and the 4–0 sweep of the St. Louis Cardinals, "then I surely can fly."

I flapped my arms as fast as I could, jumped into the air and was off. Simple as that. I soon was soaring across Boston Harbor and then downtown and then directly over the celebrating crowds in Kenmore Square. I buzzed a couple of Northeastern University kids climbing a lamppost, startled a TPF trooper into dropping his truncheon, took a hard left at the Prudential Building, and glided back home.

"I can fly!" I exclaimed to my cocker spaniel, Slugger, the only one still awake in the house.

"Sacre bleu!" he replied.

I always thought Slugger could talk. He would stare at me with those brown eyes and that little panting sound and I knew conversation was possible. Now he could. In French. And I could understand him. I always thought I could understand French, three years in high school, just wishing the people would slow down when they talked, and now I had no problem.

"Tres bien, beau chien," I said.

I slept my best sleep in ages—a delightful dream in the middle involving New York Yankees owner George Steinbrenner, chained to a post in the lowest circle of hell—and made breakfast for the family in the morning. I always knew I could make perfect Eggs Benedict. I sang while I served, exactly like Frank Sinatra. I moved exactly like Fred Astaire. I always knew I could tap dance.

I felt an energy I hadn't felt in years. I felt as strong as David Ortiz. I felt as fast as Dave Roberts, as happy as Manny Ramirez, as focused as Curt Schilling, as solid as Jason Varitek, as smart as Theo Epstein. I whistled "Sweet Caroline" (uh-uh-ohh), typed out a 500-page novel that I always knew I had inside me, took care of some plumbing and electrical work around the house that I always knew I could do if I just tried, yodeled goodbye (I always knew I could yodel) and hit the streets.

What next? I ran from Hopkinton to Boston, just for the heck of it. I walked on my hands. I juggled a Ted Williams baseball card, a copy of the Baseball Encyclopedia and an apple. Didn't drop a one. I swam with the L Street Brownies. I dunked a basketball. Backward. After jumping over a Toyota. I drove the length of Massachusetts Avenue and all the lights were green. Every one of them.

I found a parking space. I found an honest politician. I tried broccoli and liked it. Every now and then a picture would pop into my head. Ortiz, clapping his hands, grabbing the bat, swinging as hard as he could, the baseball flying into the night. Schilling, the dollop of blood on his white sock. Derek Jeter looking befuddled. Every office I called, a real person answered the phone. I signed to appear in a feature film. (Leading man.) I was computer literate. I baked a cake. I changed my own oil. Fast as a cat, I multiplied large numbers in my head.

All items were on sale everywhere. All stocks were up. The pictures just kept coming. All those people that the Fox network showed biting their nails, crossing their fingers and their toes during the first three games against the Yankees. Where were they now? What were they doing? Derek Lowe on the mound. Talking to himself. Mark Bellhorn. Saying nothing. I played the piano, discovered I had a strong left hand. Went to the post office and found no lines. Roller bladed. Rode a motorcycle. Never fell down. I always knew I could do that. I booked a trip to the Dominican Republic. I joined a gym, started a diet, bought a new suit of clothes. Something funky.

The Charles River—it appeared to me, at least—had been turned into buttermilk. The John Hancock building now was made out of chocolate. The strings on the Zakim Bridge played a melody when the wind hit them just right. The hospitals all were empty. The churches were all full. A heart seemed to beat in the middle of Fenway Park, right under the mound.

I had always wondered what it would be like when the Red Sox won the Series. I suppose everyone under the age of 86 in New England had wondered. The Red Sox story had gone along for so many years with its annual disappointments that the pain had become an almost masochistic delight. Sort of like record snowstorms in winter. Sort of like the daily bad cup of coffee from the company cafeteria. Sort of like a mole on the tip of your nose. Endurance and acceptance had become virtues. Life had to be lived within limitations.

What would it be like without those limitations?

I suppose I'm not much different from anyone else around here. I thought about departed friends and long-ago moments. I heard from people I hadn't heard from in years. I told my wife I loved her. I told my kids I loved them. I drank a little champagne. I flew through the air. I talked to my dog in French and he talked back. I smiled a lot.

I say so far so good.

102

Congress Pressures Baseball to Strengthen Steroid Testing Policy (2005)

SOURCE: Letter from Congressmen Tom Davis and Henry Waxman to Bud Selig and Donald Fehr, March 16, 2005, http://reform.house.gov

Shortly after the owners and the MLBPA jointly announced the drafting of a new policy to test players for steroids and other performance-enhancing drugs (PEDS), critics attacked it as too weak. Of particular concern were the penalties for positive tests. Baseball's plan called for suspensions for the first four positive results, with the fourth positive test resulting in a one-year expulsion. This was considered by many to be too lenient, but when Congressmen Tom Davis (the Republican from Virginia) and Henry Waxman (the Democrat from California) subpoenaed a copy of the policy (which in fact had not yet been finalized or officially approved) and learned that fines could be substituted for even the mild suspensions, they were enraged.

Given their reaction to baseball's policy, it was hardly surprising that the March 17, 2005, hearing on PEDS held by the House Committee on Government Reform turned out to be a nightmare for baseball. Viewers of the nationally televised hearing saw distraught parents testify about the deaths of their sons from steroids, befuddled baseball officials try in vain to defend their new testing policy, and several star players unconvincingly claim that steroids were not a major problem (in direct contrast to published comments made by several of them). Worst of all was the testimony of former star slugger Mark McGwire (whose use of androstenedione during his record-setting season of 1998 was well documented), who refused to confirm or deny his, or any other player's, use of PEDS. After this public relations disaster, baseball again claimed that it would soon tighten its testing policy, but the damage was done.

Printed here is the March 16, 2005, letter from Davis and Waxman to Commissioner

Bud Selig and MLBPA *executive director Donald Fehr in which the congressmen make clear their displeasure with the original testing plan of major league baseball. The footnotes accompanying this letter have been deleted.*

Dear Commissioner Selig and Mr. Fehr:

On January 13, 2005, Major League Baseball and the Players' Association announced a new policy on performance-enhancing drugs. In meetings with us, senior baseball officials represented this policy as the "gold standard" for drug testing. In public statements, Commissioner Selig stated, "My job is to protect the integrity of the sport and solve a problem. And I think we've done that." He has also said, "Do I believe the new program . . . will work? I really do . . . We will eradicate steroid use." Relying on Major League Baseball's assurances, observers have called the new policy "very strict," "finally . . . the right thing," and "one strike—you're out."

On Monday, Major League Baseball provided the Committee with a copy of its new policy, which was noted to be "still in draft form." Our preliminary review raises questions about whether the new policy is as comprehensive and effective as you have claimed. For example, we have questions about:

The Penalties for Violations. In public statements, Major League Baseball representatives have emphasized that players who violate the new policy will be publicly identified and suspended from baseball for ten days. In fact, the details of the new policy reveal that the penalty for a first offense can be either a suspension or a fine of $10,000 or less; that there is no public identification of players who are fined instead of suspended; and that even if players are suspended, the public disclosure is limited to the fact of their suspensions with no official confirmation that the player tested positive for steroids. In contrast, the Olympic policy calls for a two-year suspension for a first offense.

The Scope of the Ban. The new Major League Baseball policy appears to differ markedly from the Olympic policy in the scope of the drugs covered. At least four anabolic steroids banned by the Olympics are excluded from Major League Baseball's ban, as are novel "designer" steroids that the Olympics prohibit because they have a "similar chemical structure or similar biological effect." Unlike the Olympic policy, the Major League Baseball policy does not include tests for human growth hormone or amphetamines.

The Makeup of the Supervisory Committee. Under the new Major League Baseball policy, many key implementation decisions, such as how to conduct off-season testing and whether to prohibit additional substances, are to be made by a four-person committee that includes Robert D. Manfred, Jr., Major League Baseball's Executive Vice President, Labor and Human Resources, and Gene Orza, the Chief Operating Officer and Associate General Counsel of the Major League Players Association. According to the policy, some of these decisions must be made unanimously, giving both Major League Baseball management and the players union a veto. The Olympic drug testing policy takes a different approach, giving an independent expert agency, the World Anti-Doping Agency, the authority to make important scientific judgments.

The Anti-Oversight Clause. An unusual provision in the new Major League Baseball policy provides that the new policy "will be suspended immediately" if there is an independent government investigation into drug use in baseball.

There are other significant differences between Major League Baseball's new policy and the more stringent Olympic policy. For example, while the Olympics require continuous monitoring of the athlete from the notification of the test until its completion, Major League Baseball appears to permit players to leave in the middle of a drug test.

In these areas and others, we have a number of questions about the discrepancies between Major League Baseball's public presentation of its new drug testing effort and the language of the new policy. We hope you will come prepared to address these questions at tomorrow's hearing.

THE PENALTIES FOR VIOLATIONS

In announcing its new policy in January, Major League Baseball described a set of specific penalties to the public. Robert D. Manfred, Jr., Executive Vice President, Labor and Human Resources, stated:

> For the first time, we will have discipline for first-time offenders under the drug program. Such offenders will be suspended for 10 days. All of the suspensions under this program are without pay. For the second offense, a 30-day suspension will be imposed. Third offense, a 60-day suspension. And fourth offense, the suspension will be for one year.

Referring to the penalty for a first offense, Commissioner Selig has stated: "People have said that policy is weak . . . I strongly disagree. A player making the average salary would lose $140,000 for a first offense."

Major League Baseball officials have also indicated that the names of players who test positive for steroids will be disclosed to the public. Commissioner Selig has stated, "The fact that it is announced and everybody in America will know who it is, that's a huge deterrent . . . No player wants that."

These descriptions of the policy, however, appear to contradict its text. The policy states that after testing positive for steroids, a player faces *either* "a 10-day suspension *or* up to a $10,000 fine." The second violation may be settled by *either* "a 30-day suspension *or* up to a $25,000 fine." The third violation may be settled by *either* "a 60-day suspension *or* up to a $50,000 fine." The fourth violation may be punished by *either* "a one-year suspension *or* up to a $100,000 fine." One hundred thousand dollars is less money than some players earn in one game. The penalty for a fifth violation is at the discretion of the Commissioner.

In addition, contrary to public statements by Major League Baseball, the policy does not require public disclosure of positive steroid tests. In fact, the policy appears to prohibit such disclosure. The policy states that "the results of any Prohibited

Substance testing . . . shall remain strictly confidential." In the case of a fine, the policy also states that "any disciplinary fines imposed upon the Player by the Commissioner shall remain strictly confidential." Under the policy, there appears to be public disclosure only in the case of a suspension, and even then the disclosure appears to be limited. The policy states that "the only public comment from the Club or the Office of the Commissioner shall be that the Player was suspended for a specific number of days for a violation of this Program."

The testing program covers ephedra, ecstacy, and a variety of other drugs. Consequently, a public announcement that a player has been suspended for a violation of the program would not reveal whether the drug involved is a performance-enhancing steroid.

By comparison, the first violation in Olympic sports carries a two-year suspension, and the second requires a lifetime ban. All disciplinary actions are made public.

THE SCOPE OF THE BAN

A central element of Major League Baseball's new drug testing policy is the list of substances that are (1) prohibited and (2) subject to testing so that the ban can be enforced. In key areas, however, the baseball list appears limited, especially when compared to the more comprehensive Olympic standards.

First, the new policy does not ban all anabolic steroids. It appears that at least four anabolic steroids recognized by the World Anti-Doping Agency and prohibited for Olympic athletes are still permitted for major league ballplayers. These include boldione, danazol, quinbolone, and dihydroepiandrostone.

The policy does not explain the rationale for exempting these substances, all of which can enhance performance. One of the substances, boldione, is marketed on the web as "Boldione for Muscle Mass!" and "the most potent anabolic prohormone ever developed." After boldione was detected in the urine sample of a swimmer, she was barred from Olympic competition for two years. Yet boldione and the other anabolic steroids listed above are not included on either of the two lists that, according to Major League Baseball officials, are the basis of Major League Baseball's steroid testing regimen.

Major League Baseball's new policy also fails to ban novel or "designer" steroids. These are drugs created in the lab to evade laboratory detection and marketed directly to sport's top stars. In contrast, the Olympic ban broadly includes all substances that have "a similar chemical structure or similar biological effect(s)" to existing anabolic steroids. The Olympics enforces this ban by conducting tests on stored samples from athletes as novel drugs are identified.

The failure of Major League Baseball to cover designer steroids would appear to be a significant omission. According to experts, hundreds of potential "designer" steroids already exist. Major League Baseball is still confronting a major scandal caused by the designer steroid tetrahydragestrinone (THG). According to leaked grand jury testimony, several baseball stars may have used THG for years before its detection by authorities and its addition to the list of federal controlled substances.

Yet under the new Major League Baseball policy, the use of the next THG would appear to be permissible in baseball.

Another apparent gap is the policy's failure to test for human growth hormone, a substance with similar effects to anabolic steroids. Major League Baseball officials have assured the public that "human growth hormone will be banned under the program." Yet the new policy fails to enforce this ban. Testing of major league ballplayers is limited to urine samples, and all available tests for human growth hormone require analysis of blood.

When asked about the omission of testing for human growth hormone, Major League Baseball officials have responded that there is no reliable blood test for the substance. Publicly, Major League Baseball's officials have expressed optimism about the availability of a urine test "in the relatively short term," perhaps as early as next season. Yet independent experts have raised doubts about Major League Baseball's approach. In April 2004, the U.S. Anti-Doping Agency convened a meeting of the world's leading researchers and concluded that all promising approaches for measuring human growth hormone "use blood for measurement, as opposed to the traditional use of urine in doping control." According to Dr. Gary Wadler, who serves on the Prohibited Lists and Methods Committee of the World Anti-Doping Agency, a validated blood test for human growth hormone was employed at the Olympic games in Athens. Blood testing for human growth hormone is now standard for Olympic athletes.

Major League Baseball's policy also fails to ban other substances that have similar effects to anabolic steroids, including insulin, human chorionic gonadotropin, and IGF-1. These substances are all banned for Olympic athletes.

In addition, Major League Baseball's new policy apparently fails to ban amphetamines and most other stimulants. Experts believe this omission makes no sense. Dr. Wadler has stated, "The most classic of all studies ever done in doping was on amphetamines . . . It clearly is performance-enhancing." At the Olympic level, athletes are prohibited from using a wide range of amphetamines and other stimulants.

THE MAKEUP OF THE HEALTH POLICY ADVISORY COMMITTEE

According to the new policy, Major League Baseball's drug program will be run by a four-member Health Policy Advisory Committee. This committee determines many key elements of the program's implementation including (1) how to conduct off-season testing; (2) whether to prohibit the use of additional substances; (3) whether a player's challenge to a testing result has a "reasonable basis"; and (4) whether a player has good cause to refuse to submit a sample.

According to Major League Baseball, one member of the Health Policy Advisory Committee is Robert D. Manfred, Jr., Major League Baseball's Executive Vice President, Labor and Human Resources. Another member is Gene Orza, the Chief Operating Officer and Associate General Counsel of the Major League Baseball Players Association. For many years, these two men have led collective bargaining efforts for management and the players' union, respectively. The two other members are physicians, one appointed by Major League Baseball and the other by the Players' Association.

The staffing of the Health Policy Advisory Committee raises serious questions about the credibility of the drug testing policy. For example, the Players Association has long resisted a random testing program for anabolic steroids. Under the new policy, either Mr. Orza or the physician appointed by the Players Association has a veto over adding any new steroid to the existing program. The policy also permits any single member of the committee to deem that a player's objection to a positive result has a "reasonable basis," triggering automatic arbitration.

The Olympics takes a markedly different approach to oversight of its testing program. To assure integrity, the Olympics has handed control over drug testing to an independent expert agency, the World Anti-Doping Agency.

THE ANTI-OVERSIGHT CLAUSE

The new policy contains an extraordinary provision that in the event of a "governmental investigation" relating to drug testing of players, "all testing . . . shall be suspended immediately." The suspension will remain in effect until the government investigation is withdrawn, the league and players' union "have successfully resisted an investigation at the trial court level," or both sides agree to resume testing. If testing is suspended for a year, then the entire drug program is subject to renegotiation.

We have serious questions about this provision. By requiring the indefinite suspension of the testing program when government officials, including elected representatives, ask basic questions about drug use in baseball, this provision appears designed to discourage responsible independent oversight.

OTHER QUESTIONS

We have questions about other significant differences between testing for Olympic athletes and the new Major League Baseball policy.

One question relates to the integrity of the testing process. For Olympic athletes, the World Anti-Doping Agency requires uninterrupted monitoring from the "first moment of in-person notification until the completion of the sample collection procedure." We understand that the goal of such monitoring is to keep athletes from having opportunities to cheat. In addition, the Olympic rules do not permit an athlete to evade testing by only providing a partial specimen. If an Olympic athlete provides less than the required amount of urine, the sample is not discarded. Instead, he or she must drink liquids under supervision until the remainder of the sample is provided.

By contrast, under the new policy, when a major league player fails to provide the required amount of urine, his sample must be discarded. He may then leave the testing site unmonitored and return in an hour. This extended break could provide an opportunity to cheat or develop an excuse to postpone the testing altogether.

This provision for interrupting drug testing is a departure from the previous Major League Baseball policy on testing, which did not permit players to leave in the middle of a drug test. The 2002 collective bargaining agreement stipulated that "players may not leave the place of testing without giving a specimen unless authorized to do so." We intend to ask why Major League Baseball's approach was weakened and why it falls so far short of the Olympic standard.

We also plan to ask you about several important issues that are not specified in the new policy. For example, Major League Baseball officials have stated: "We're using only Olympic-certified labs . . . these are the best labs in the world, the gold standard of laboratories." However, the new policy apparently does not require Major League Baseball to continue using a certified lab. The policy only states that analyses be done "pursuant to a scientifically-validated urine test."

CONCLUSION

Despite the public assurances of Major League Baseball officials, we have questions about the effectiveness of its new drug policy. There appear to be major differences between Major League Baseball's new policy and the independent, widely respected testing program of the Olympics. The Olympic policy appears comprehensive, strict, independent, and transparent. Major League Baseball's program appears to raise questions on all four counts.

We hope to explore these and other questions with you at the Committee's hearing tomorrow.

Sincerely,

Tom Davis, Chairman
Henry A. Waxman, Ranking Minority Member

103

Bonds Hits 756th Home Run Amidst Controversy (2007)

SOURCE: *San Francisco Chronicle*, August 8, 2007, http://sfgate.com/cgi-bin/article.cgi?f= .c/a/2007/08/08/SP8LREVAT3.DTL

Ever since the earliest revelations about the BALCO scandal, many baseball fans (and baseball writers) waited in disgust for the inevitable to occur: the breaking of Hank Aaron's career home run total of 755 by San Francisco Giants superstar Barry Bonds. As Bonds approached the record, prominent columnists like Mike Lupica, Mitch Albom, Richard Justice, and Terence Moore (a personal friend of Aaron's) attacked Bonds on a regular basis, and fans outside San Francisco showered Bonds with boos and hostile signs (and on one occasion, an empty syringe) declaring him a cheat and a fraud.

Bonds concluded the season with 762 home runs. On November 15, 2007, Bonds was served with federal indictments on four counts of perjury and one count of obstruction

of justice. By the end of 2007 former Senator George Mitchell released the report of his investigation into steroid and other PED *use in baseball, in which Bonds was be prominently mentioned.*

NEW KING OF SWING
Like It or Not, You'll Just Have to Deal with It
By Scott Ostler

It's been a long, hard road to glory, but in the end, Barry Bonds made it look easy.

He dug into the batter's box at 8:49 p.m. Tuesday night against Washington Nationals lefty Mike Bacsik, worked the count to 3-2 and blasted a million-dollar souvenir into the bleachers in center, where it landed like a raw steak in a den of starving lions.

Love him or loathe him, Barry Bonds is your new all-time home run king.

Like so many of Bonds' homers, No. 756 went to a place where most humans cannot send a baseball—an estimated 435 feet from the launching pad. Bonds, ever the drama king, wasn't going to take Hank Aaron's record away with a cheapie.

It wasn't a splash hit, unless it landed in someone's beer, but it was a majestic high blast, an arc de triumph.

Even Hammerin' Hank was impressed, or he seemed to be in the prerecorded video shown on the ballpark screen just after the historic homer. In the end, despite Aaron's seeming boycott of Bonds and the chase, Hank gave it up for Barry, passing the torch like a true champion.

Maybe the guy they called Bad Henry realized that being a sports hero is about a lot more than numbers. Aaron didn't disappear in a puff of smoke when Bonds hit his homer, nor did the memory of Babe Ruth. Their legends and legacies are still fully intact, probably even strengthened by all the controversy and discussion.

Bonds' legacy is still up in the air. The free world will forever be divided along the love-Barry/hate-Barry line. To many, Bonds' achievement is like a bad movie, "Honey, I Shrunk the Home Run Record."

But to Bonds' fans, including seemingly every last person in the packed house at the Giants' ballpark Tuesday night, the new record is the real deal.

The fans rose to their feet as one every time Bonds came to bat, beginning the previous night. The controversy over the legitimacy of Bonds' record, which rages even within San Francisco city limits, has caused the hard-core Bonds backers to bond more tightly, determined not to let carpers and critics dim their love for Bonds or their joy in his record.

"Scorn this, world," the fans seemed to say, as Bonds circled the bases.

Whether you consider Bonds' record a messy bit of baseball bookkeeping, or a towering achievement, it's etched in stone now, so deal with it.

Along with elation, the historic homer set off a massive sigh of relief, and not just from the 400 or so media people who have jumped on the Bondswagon over the last couple of weeks, and were wondering if they would ever get off.

Bonds unintentionally stretched out the final drive for Aaron's record. For the media, for Bonds' teammates, for fans and probably for Barry himself, who endured such anxiety-type side effects as a rash on his head, the record chase has sometimes been as painful as frontier dental work.

The chase has been fun, too, and it stimulated a lot of national debate, but it also brought out the worst in a lot of people.

The world was polarized into Barry-cherishers and Barry-haters. And sadly, a lot of the split was along racial lines. Sixty years after Jackie Robinson, many of us are still looking at the world in black and white.

Commissioner Bud Selig cemented his place as baseball's all-time waffle. After grudgingly, almost painfully deciding to honor Bonds with his presence, Selig saluted No. 755 with his hands in his pockets, possibly reaching for his cell phone to text his fond wishes to Bonds. Selig was not in the house Tuesday, although he did send along a mattress-tag statement calling Bonds' record "noteworthy," but later phoned Bonds. Years from now when fans are talking about where they were when Bonds set the record, they'll also wonder where Bud was.

Bonds and Bob Costas indulged in a mini mudslinging match, one of them (the tall one) calling the other a midget. However tawdry the exchange, it was the only time Bonds seemed to show any public anger toward his critics. His human side.

Opposing managers and pitchers were afflicted with mass cowardice. Like Selig, they didn't realize how the wimpy, fainthearted approach plays with the public, and how it will look when history examines the chase.

Give the Nationals and manager Manny Acta credit for having sufficient chest hair to throw the ball over the plate to a guy who came into the game hitting .175 since the All-Star Game.

Bonds' historic homer momentarily put aside concern among Giants fans that Bonds, who recently turned 43, might have lost it. Too often he seemed awkward, off-balance and lost at the plate he once owned.

Maybe it was the pressure, and now Bonds will reestablish command of his domain. Maybe not.

Either way, No. 756 is in the bank and in the books. Bonds hit it a mile and it's never coming back.

The Radio Call

Jon Miller's radio call of No. 756, with ellipses indicating pauses.

"Everybody standing here at 24 Willie Mays Plaza. An armada of nautical craft gathered in McCovey Cove beyond the right-field wall. Bonds one home run away from history, and he swings and there's a long one. Deep into right-center field. Way back there. It's gone! A home run! . . . Into the center-field bleachers to the left of the 421-foot marker. An extraordinary shot to the deepest part of the yard. . . . And Barry Bonds with 756 home runs. He has hit more home runs than anyone who has ever played the game. . . . Henry Aaron, the home run king, 755. He hit his last one 31 years ago. And now tonight in downtown San Francisco, Barry Bonds hits number 756, one more than Aaron."

104

The "Process of the Investigation" of "The Mitchell Report" (2007)

SOURCE: George J. Mitchell, *Report to the Commissioner of Baseball of an Independent Investigation into the Illegal Use of Steroids and Other Performance Enhancing Substances by Players in Major League Baseball*, December 13, 2007, www.mlb.com, B1–B10

After years of ignoring the use of various performance-enhancing drugs by players, baseball was finally forced to confront the issue under the threat of congressional action—at least to an extent. The owners proposed a testing policy, which though considered weak by many, was only approved by the MLBPA with great reluctance. In the spring of 2006 Commissioner Selig appointed former U.S. Senator George J. Mitchell (a coauthor of Selig's "Blue Ribbon Panel" in 2000) to write an official account of baseball's "Steroid Era." Selig noted that Mitchell would have complete access to major league officials and records and was acting independently of MLB, but union officials openly warned its members not to cooperate with Mitchell.

The persistent conflict between players and owners made Mitchell's task more difficult. Many commentators agreed with the MLBPA that Mitchell's objectivity was in doubt, given his longtime association with baseball ownership, and suggested that a truly independent investigation was preferable. However, these doubts were trumped by the utter refusal of the union to look beyond the present to the long-term health of the players and the game.

Below, Mitchell describes the process that guided his investigation. Following are a letter to the MLBPA asking for cooperation and a reply from the union.

Process of the Investigation

On March 30, 2006, Commissioner Selig announced this independent investigation into the illegal use of performance enhancing substances in Major League Baseball. As discussed earlier in this report, he asked me "to attempt to determine, as a factual matter, whether any Major League players associated with BALCO or otherwise used steroids or other illegal performance enhancing substances at any point after" the 2002 Basic Agreement was entered into. In his announcement, Commissioner Selig also recognized that "[i]t may be helpful in reaching the necessary factual determinations," and he therefore authorized me to follow the evidence wherever it may lead.

The Commissioner agreed that I would have "all of the investigatory powers available to the Commissioner" for the purposes of the investigation and that I would have "full discretion with respect to the means and manner of carrying out this investigation."

The Commissioner and the thirty major league clubs are subject to the provisions of the Basic Agreement with the Players Association. This imposes certain limitations upon actions that the Commissioner can take with respect to current players, and to the disclosure of information arising out of the Major League Baseball Joint Drug Prevention and Treatment Program. The Commissioner retained the authority to determine whether particular activities in the course of this investigation might violate his obligations. I agreed to be bound by his decisions, but I retained the right to state in my report if I disagreed with any such decisions.

I also agreed that the Commissioner's Office would have the right to review my report three business days in advance of its release to the public to make certain that I did not improperly include in it any information that is required to be kept confidential. I retained, however, "unhindered discretion to include in . . . [the] report whatever information [I] deemed appropriate" subject only to the Commissioner's right to instruct me not to include information that the Commissioner concluded he was under a legal duty to keep confidential. The Commissioner's Office reviewed this report before it was released. No material changes were made to the report as a result of that review. . . .

DOCUMENTS REVIEWED

This investigation was an independent inquiry on behalf of a private entity. As a result, I had no subpoena power or any other method of compelling cooperation. I made a number of requests for the production of documents from the Commissioner's Office and each of the thirty clubs. I received over 115,000 pages of documents from the Commissioner's Office and the thirty clubs. I also received over 20,000 electronic records retrieved from the computer systems of the Commissioner's Office and some of the clubs. Each of the thirty clubs certified that it had provided all responsive non-privileged documents that I requested.

I also requested the Players Association to provide documents based on essentially identical requests. It declined to do so.

I also obtained documents from a variety of third parties and from public sources.

INTERVIEWS

We interviewed more than 700 witnesses in the United States, Canada, and the Dominican Republic.

The Commissioner required the clubs to make their non-playing personnel available for interviews, and the clubs complied. In all, we conducted interviews of over 550 individuals who are current or former club officials, managers or coaches, team physicians, athletic trainers, or resident security agents.

We also interviewed 16 persons from the Commissioner's Office, including Commissioner Selig, president and chief operating officer Robert DuPuy, senior vice president for security and facility management Kevin Hallinan and executive vice president for labor relations Robert D. Manfred, Jr., who was interviewed formally on three separate occasions. During the investigation, we also had some meetings and telephone calls with Rob Manfred, Bob DuPuy, and on a few occasions with Commissioner Selig that, while not formal interviews, often included some discussion of the relevant issues.

Under the Basic Agreement, any request for an interview with a current player must be made through his representative, the Players Association. Through the Players Association, I asked to interview more than 50 players who were at the time on the 40-man roster of a major league club. Almost without exception, those players declined to meet with me.

In addition, I prepared a memorandum to all current players that was distributed to them at my request by the Commissioner's Office. In it, I invited any player to speak with me who had relevant information or who otherwise wanted to do so. The Players Association also prepared a memorandum that was distributed to players at the same time. Copies of both memoranda are included at the end of this Appendix. No player responded to my memorandum.

We spoke with a number of former players, some of whom were forthcoming about the prevalence of performance enhancing substances in Major League Baseball, and also about their own use. We attempted to contact almost 500 former players and conducted substantive interviews of over 70 of them.

I asked to interview Donald Fehr, the executive director of the Players Association, and Gene Orza, its chief operating officer. Mr. Fehr agreed to an interview; Mr. Orza did not.

We also received significant cooperation from individuals who are no longer employed in Major League Baseball, including executives, managers, coaches, athletic trainers, doctors, and clubhouse personnel. We interviewed over 100 former club employees and other individuals with relevant knowledge.

We interviewed or consulted with many others whose views and information were very helpful, including: former Commissioners of Baseball Peter V. Ueberroth and Francis T. ("Fay") Vincent; numerous law enforcement and other officials; experts from the United States Anti-Doping Agency, the World Anti-Doping Agency and the Australian Sports Anti-Doping Authority; John Dowd, who conducted the Pete Rose investigation; Don Hooton, chairman of The Taylor Hooton Foundation; Dr. Gary Green; Dr. Jay Hoffman; Frank Thomas of the Toronto Blue Jays; and many others.

Many persons declined our requests for an interview, including many former players who are alleged to have used banned substances; central figures in the BALCO investigation; and, as noted earlier, over fifty current players from whom we sought interviews. The persons we did interview were not under oath.

Although I was not able to obtain every relevant fact, I did receive enough information to be able to describe the history and current status of the illegal use of performance enhancing substances in Major League Baseball.

To: ALL MAJOR LEAGUE BASEBALL PLAYERS
From: Senator George J. Mitchell
Date: September 6, 2007
Subject: Independent Investigation of Performance Enhancing Substance Use

I have been retained by the Commissioner of Baseball to conduct an independent investigation into the alleged illegal use of performance enhancing substances in Major League Baseball. I have pledged to conduct an investigation and to complete a report that is independent, thorough, and fair. I believe it's in your interest to help me achieve those objectives.

The illegal use of performance enhancing substances is a serious violation of the rules of Major League Baseball which directly affects the integrity of the game. The principal victims are the majority of players who don't use such substances.

That reality is too often overlooked in discussions about steroids. Much has been said and written about the adverse effect on the integrity of the game, on the fans, and on the general public. All are important. But those who are most harmed, those whose careers and livelihoods are put at risk, are the players who don't use such substances. They rely on their talent, skill, and hard work, as should all players. And a younger generation of aspiring major league players is affected as well, as young players may be led to believe that, even though Baseball currently has a tough drug policy, they cannot succeed without violating that policy and the law.

No one has a stronger interest in dealing with this issue than major league players. Accordingly, I am inviting all current Major League Baseball players who believe they may have relevant information, or who for any reason wish to speak to me or to a senior member of my team, to contact me.

If you wish to provide information on a confidential basis, I assure you that I will fully honor your request for confidentiality in my report.

As has been announced publicly, Kirk Radomski has agreed to cooperate with my investigation at the direction of the United States Attorneys Office for the Northern District of California ("USAO"). Under our agreement with the USAO, neither I nor my staff are required to supply any information to that Office. The USAO has not made any request that we supply them with information nor do we anticipate receiving any such request. I previously served as a United States Attorney and can confirm from direct personal experience that the USAO has at its disposal a vast array of investigative tools—subpoena power, search warrants, the use of agents from several federal agencies, to name just a few—which eliminate any need on their part for my assistance.

So any allegation that the USAO is using me or my investigation to do their work for them, or to obtain information from me, is simply untrue.

The Players Association understandably has expressed concern about possible criminal prosecutions of players for the illegal use of steroids. As you evaluate that concern please keep in mind that through the 2006 season 221 professional baseball players (14 major leaguers and 207 minor leaguers) have been suspended after testing positive for steroids or other performance enhancing substances, including stimulants, but not one of them was ever convicted in a criminal prosecution. I asked the Players Association and the Commissioner's office to provide me with the name of any player who has been prosecuted and convicted for the illegal use or possession of steroids. Both said that they are not aware of that ever happening. This is because prosecuting authorities generally follow practices like those of the U.S. Department of Justice which pursues prosecution of the manufacturers and distributors of such substances, not the athletes who use them.

You or your representative may reach me at 212-XXX-XXXX or Charlie Scheeler of my staff (XXX-XXX-XXXX or [email address]) and we will arrange a meeting at a time and place convenient for you. Of course, if you choose to so volunteer, you will have the right to bring representatives to the meeting, including your personal counsel and/or a representative of the Major League Baseball Players Association. Under the Basic Agreement, the Players Association also has the right to receive prior notice of any interview that we conduct with a major league player.

To: All Players
From: Donald Fehr & Michael Weiner
Date: 6 September 2007
Re: *Mitchell Investigation*

As you know, in early 2006, shortly after the players had agreed to the new Joint Drug Agreement, Commissioner Selig hired former Senator George Mitchell and his law firm (DLA Piper) to conduct an investigation into the use of steroids and other illegal performance-enhancing drugs in baseball. We write today regarding a memo Senator Mitchell is sending to all players, in which he encourages players to meet with his investigative team.

Any player who wishes to speak to Senator Mitchell in response to this request has the right to do so. Any such player has the right to be represented by the MLBPA and his own lawyer in arranging any such meeting and during the meeting itself. Given the serious legal issues which may be involved here, both inside and outside of baseball, *we strongly encourage you to seek the advice of MLBPA counsel and a qualified private attorney before proceeding.*

Commissioner Selig has not ruled out disciplining (suspending and/or fining) players as a result of information gathered by the Mitchell investigation. Therefore, you should be aware that any information provided could lead to discipline of you and/or others. (Any discipline imposed could be challenged by grievance.) Remember also that there are a number of ongoing federal and state criminal investigations in this area, and any information gathered by Senator Mitchell in player interviews is not legally privileged. What this means is that while Senator Mitchell pledges in his memo that he will honor any player request for confidentiality *in his report,* he does not pledge, because he cannot pledge, that any information you provide will actually remain confidential and not be disclosed without your consent. For example, Senator Mitchell cannot promise that information you disclose will not be given to a federal or state prosecutor, a Congressional committee, or even turned over in a private lawsuit in response to a request or a subpoena (a legally enforceable order).

Senator Mitchell points out that no player has yet been prosecuted for illegal use of steroids and that prosecutors "generally follow practices" of pursuing manufacturers and distributors, not users. Be aware, though, that a federal prosecutor recently stated in court that the nationwide federal criminal investigation of steroids in sports is ongoing and clearly indicated that the investigation could lead to prosecution of individual athletes for use.

Senator Mitchell mentions his agreement with the United States Attorney's Office in California (USAO), and states that his agreement with the USAO does not require him to provide information to the prosecutor. (Senator Mitchell has refused to provide us with a copy of this agreement, which we asked for so that we can understand the relationship of his investigation to the US Attorney's Office.) But Senator Mitchell does not promise, because, again, he cannot promise, that he will not disclose the information to the USAO (or another prosecutor, Congressional committee, or other governmental entity) in response to a request or subpoena.

Finally, as you know, the owners and the players have bargained long and hard over the subject of performance-enhancing drugs several times over the past five years. The positions adopted by the union in those talks reflect a consensus among all players after numerous meetings, discussions and conference calls. Any comments made to Senator Mitchell—Commissioner Selig's lawyer—by an individual player regarding the operation of the Program might well be used by the owners in future bargaining with the union.

It is in light of these considerations that we recommend that you first consult with MLBPA counsel and your own private counsel before responding to Senator Mitchell.

If you have any questions, please call Michael or another MLBPA lawyer at XXX-XXX-XXXX.

105

Congressmen Question Truthfulness of Roger Clemens's Testimony (2008)

SOURCE: Memorandum from Majority Staff, Committee on Oversight and Government Reform, House of Representatives, to Chairman Henry A. Waxman, February 26, 2008, http://reform.house.gov

The most notable revelation of the "Mitchell Report" on the usage of performance-enhancing drugs in baseball was that star pitcher Roger Clemens had used human growth

hormone (HGH) on numerous occasions. Clemens publicly proclaimed his innocence in a press conference, a nationally televised interview on 60 Minutes, and through his pugnacious attorney, Rusty Hardin. Clemens argued that his primary accuser, personal trainer Brian McNamee, was a serial liar and drug dealer who implicated Clemens and teammate Andy Pettitte in order to appease federal prosecutors. At the insistence of Clemens and Hardin, Congressman Henry Waxman, who had chaired several hearings on the issue of PEDs in sports, agreed to hold another hearing featuring Clemens and McNamee to try to determine the truth.

Neither principal fared particularly well in the televised hearings. McNamee admitted to lying to investigators years earlier on another matter and conceded that he had distributed drugs illegally. Clemens took advantage of friendly questioning by Republican committee members and so vigorously asserted his innocence that at one point Chairman Waxman had to silence him. However, Clemens's testimony was undermined not only by his own inconsistency, but by the deposition of his friend and training partner Pettitte, who admitted that he had used HGH and that Clemens had mentioned his own HGH use to Pettitte several times.

After the dust had cleared, Waxman and his Republican counterpart on the committee, Tom Davis, concluded that Clemens's testimony was questionable enough to warrant a further investigation by the FBI into possible perjury charges against Clemens. The staff memorandum to Waxman outlining the case against Clemens is reprinted here.

You asked for an analysis of the credibility of the testimony of Roger Clemens in his February 5, 2008, deposition and his February 13, 2008, appearance before the House Oversight and Government Reform Committee. In response to your request, this memorandum summarizes seven sets of assertions made by Mr. Clemens in his testimony that appear to be contradicted by other evidence before the Committee or implausible.

I. MR. CLEMENS'S TESTIMONY THAT HE HAS "NEVER TAKEN STEROIDS OR HGH"

In his deposition and at the Committee's hearing, Mr. Clemens repeatedly denied that he has taken steroids or human growth hormone. During his deposition on February 5, 2008, Mr. Clemens testified that "I have not used steroids or growth hormone"; "I am just making it as possibly as clear as I can. I haven't done steroids or growth hormone"; and "I never used steroids. Never performance-enhancing steroids" or "human growth hormone." Mr. Clemens also testified during his deposition that he had never "possessed" or "seen" anabolic steroids or human growth hormone. During his testimony at the Committee's hearing on February 13, 2008, Mr. Clemens made similar statements, including the following: "Let me be clear. I have never taken steroids or HGH"; "Brian McNamee has never given me growth hormone or steroids"; and "this man [Mr. McNamee] has never given me HGH or growth hormone or steroids of any kind."

The Committee received three pieces of evidence that call Mr. Clemens's testimony

into question: (1) the testimony of Mr. Clemens's former strength and conditioning coach, Brian McNamee; (2) the testimony and affidavit of Mr. Clemens's former teammate, Andrew Pettitte, and the affidavit of Mr. Pettitte's wife, Laura Pettitte; and (3) Mr. Clemens's medical records.

A. *The Testimony of Brian McNamee*

In his deposition and in the Committee's hearing, Mr. McNamee testified that he
personally injected Mr. Clemens with steroids and human growth hormone on several occasions in 1998, 2000, and 2001. During his deposition on February 7, 2008,
Mr. McNamee testified that he injected Mr. Clemens with the steroid Winstrol "maybe 16 to 20" times in 1998, with testosterone "more than six and less than 10" times
and HGH "eight to 12 or eight to 20" times in 2000, and with testosterone and nan-
drolone "8 to 14" times in 2001.

Additionally, Mr. McNamee testified at the Committee's hearing on February 13
that "[d]uring the time that I worked with Roger Clemens, I injected him on numerous occasions with steroids and human growth hormone." Mr. McNamee also
made this statement at the hearing:

> [M]ake no mistake, when I told Senator Mitchell that I injected Roger Clemens
> with performance-enhancing drugs, I told the truth. I told the truth about ste-
> roids and human growth hormone. I injected those drugs into the body of Rog-
> er Clemens at his direction.

Mr. McNamee has a history of misleading investigators. He admitted to the Committee that he lied to the police in a criminal investigation in Florida in 2001. He also
admitted that he withheld evidence from federal prosecutors investigating steroid
use by professional baseball players. According to Mr. McNamee, he took those actions to protect others.

In this case, however, Mr. McNamee's testimony is bolstered by the deposition
testimony of Andrew Pettitte and the transcribed interview of Chuck Knoblauch,
another former teammate of Mr. Clemens. Mr. McNamee testified that he injected
both Mr. Pettitte and Mr. Knoblauch with human growth hormone. Both Mr. Pettitte and Mr. Knoblauch confirmed Mr. McNamee's testimony that he injected them
with human growth hormone. There is little reason to believe that Mr. McNamee
would provide truthful testimony about Mr. Pettitte and Mr. Knoblauch, but false
testimony about Mr. Clemens.

There is also other evidence that lends corroboration to Mr. McNamee's testimony.
In his deposition with Committee staff, Mr. McNamee testified about a conversation
he had with one of Mr. Clemens's agents, Jim Murray, in 2003 or 2004. This conversation occurred after Major League Baseball had conducted what were supposed to
be anonymous drug tests of baseball players, including Mr. Clemens. Mr. McNamee
testified that after learning of news reports that the test results could become public,
he met with Mr. Murray because he "feared that he [Mr. Clemens] might test positive." Mr. McNamee described calling Mr. Murray to set up this meeting, described

the Starbucks in Manhattan where it occurred, and described how Mr. Murray "took note after note and asked question after question about Roger's steroid use."

On January 31, 2008, Committee staff conducted an interview of Mr. Murray, in which Mr. Murray confirmed many details of this meeting. Although Mr. Murray could not remember certain details, he stated that he remembered Mr. McNamee calling to set up the meeting, remembered that it occurred in a coffee shop in New York, and remembered Mr. McNamee "saying something about drug test results, having knowledge of the drug test results."

In addition, the Committee obtained a copy of an e-mail sent by Mr. McNamee to Mr. Murray on January 3, 2007, in which Mr. McNamee described a conversation he had with "Jeff Novitki [sic], the FBI/IRS agent," who is investigating steroid use by athletes. In this e-mail, Mr. McNamee asked Mr. Murray to assure Mr. Clemens and Mr. Pettitte that "I WAS NOT OFFICIALLY TALKED TO AND WILL NEVER BE, I WILL NEVER BETRAY MY CLIENTS AND I WANT THEM NOT TO WORRY ABOUT BEING AROUND ME."

B. *The Testimony and Affidavit of Andy Pettitte and Affidavit of Laura Pettitte*

In his deposition with the Committee, Mr. Pettitte testified that Mr. McNamee injected him with HGH in 2002 and that Mr. Pettitte injected himself with HGH in 2004. Mr. Pettitte also testified in his deposition that he remembered a conversation in 1999 or 2000 in which Mr. Clemens admitted using human growth hormone. . . .

According to Mr. Pettitte, his first conversation with Mr. Clemens occurred in 1999 or 2000. Both Mr. Clemens and Mr. McNamee stated to the Committee that Mr. Clemens's wife did use HGH, but did not do so until 2002 or 2003. This timeline would appear to rule out the possibility that Mr. Clemens could have been referring to his wife's use of HGH in the first conversation with Mr. Pettitte. Furthermore, Mr. Pettitte testified that prior to the 2005 conversation, Mr. Clemens never told him that his wife had used HGH.

During his deposition, Mr. Pettitte told the Committee that he told his wife, Laura Pettitte, about his conversations with Mr. Clemens. His wife also submitted an affidavit to the Committee. This affidavit confirmed that Mr. Pettitte told Mrs. Pettitte about both his conversations with Mr. Clemens. . . .

Mr. Pettitte also recalled two conversations with Mr. McNamee in which Mr. McNamee confirmed that Mr. Clemens used HGH and told Mr. Pettitte that Mr. Clemens used steroids. According to Mr. Pettitte's affidavit, shortly after the 1999 or 2000 conversation with Mr. Clemens about HGH:

> I spoke with Brian McNamee. Only he and I were parties to the conversation. I asked Brian about HGH and told him that Roger said he had used it. Brian McNamee became angry. He told me that Roger should not have told me about his use of HGH because it was supposed to be confidential.

The other conversation took place in Mr. Pettitte's home in 2003 or 2004. In this conversation, Mr. McNamee told Mr. Pettitte that "he had gotten steroids for

Roger." Mr. Pettitte was asked whether he had "any reason to think" that Mr. Mc-Namee "wasn't being straight with you about that." He replied: "No . . . I had no reason to think that."

In his deposition, Mr. McNamee independently confirmed two conversations with Mr. Pettitte that appear to be the same conversations described by Mr. Pettitte. Mr. McNamee testified that he recalled a conversation in Mr. Clemens's gym in which Mr. Pettitte told Mr. McNamee that Mr. Clemens had admitted using human growth hormone. Mr. McNamee was unsure of the exact date, but said this conversation could have occurred in 2000.

Mr. McNamee also described a second conversation with Mr. Pettitte that occurred in 2004 during a workout with Mr. Pettitte. According to Mr. McNamee, he believed that Mr. Pettitte was aware of steroid use by Mr. Clemens. Mr. McNamee told the Committee: "I had a conversation with Andy in 2004 . . . [Mr. Pettitte] knew that Roger was taking steroids and growth hormones."

C. The Medical Evidence

On December 12, 2007, investigators working for Mr. Clemens secretly taped an interview of Mr. McNamee. During this interview, Mr. McNamee asserted that "Roger got an abscess through shooting steroids." In his deposition, Mr. McNamee provided a similar account. He told the Committee that after he injected Mr. Clemens with the steroid Winstrol in 1998, Mr. Clemens developed an abscess on his buttocks from the steroid injections. Mr. McNamee again confirmed this account in his testimony before the Committee.

The Committee asked for medical records to confirm whether Mr. Clemens had developed such an injury in 1998. A July 28, 1998, medical record from the Blue Jays states that Mr. Clemens "started complaining of right buttocks soreness" and that the "diagnosis was a small collection of blood below the surface of the skin." The July 28 record also stated: "Roger received a B-12 injection approximately 7-10 days ago into his right buttocks from Dr. Taylor at the Skydome." A July 30 record described Mr. Clemens's injury as a "palpable mass." A second medical record from August 4 indicates that Mr. Clemens also had a palpable mass on his left buttocks.

In a transcribed interview, Dr. Ron Taylor, the Toronto Blue Jays team doctor, remembered giving Mr. Clemens a vitamin B-12 injection, but he did not remember when he administered it. There is no direct documentation of this vitamin B-12 injection in the medication and medical visit records kept by the physicians who provide injections.

In his deposition, Mr. Clemens said "I don't know what caused" the palpable mass. He said that it was probably due to the vitamin B-12 injection or physical damage to the muscle, caused when he "strained my glute."

The medical records provided to the Committee indicated that Mr. Clemens was sent for an MRI on July 30, 1998. The Committee made repeated requests starting on February 5, 2008, for the MRI and its results. Mr. Clemens's lawyers did not produce the MRI results to the Committee until February 11, 2008, just two days before the hearing. . . .

The Committee asked Dr. Taylor, and the Blue Jays team trainers, Tommy Craig and Scott Shannon, whether they thought a vitamin B-12 injection could have caused the mass on Mr. Clemens's buttocks. Dr. Taylor told the Committee that this was unlikely. He stated that he had given close to 1,000 vitamin B-12 injections in his medical career and that he had never seen a complication like Mr. Clemens's. Mr. Craig told the Committee that he had never seen a side effect like Mr. Clemens's from a vitamin B-12 injection in almost 30 years as a trainer. The assistant trainer, Scott Shannon, in a career of almost 20 years, also said he had never seen a vitamin B-12 injection cause this kind of reaction.

II. MR. CLEMENS'S TESTIMONY THAT MR. MCNAMEE INJECTED HIM WITH LIDOCAINE

In his deposition with Committee staff, Mr. Clemens stated that Mr. McNamee injected him with lidocaine, an anesthetic, in an "open area" in the team's weight training room. According to Mr. Clemens: Mr. McNamee "gave me lidocaine once," and "it gave me some comfort for about 2 days. It was a numbing effect, and it was in my . . . lower back." During the Committee hearing, Mr. Clemens confirmed this account, stating that Mr. McNamee "gave me one shot of lidocaine in my lower back, and that happened in Toronto." According to Mr. Clemens, this injection occurred "after [the] All Star break," which was in July 1998.

Mr. McNamee denied that these injections occurred, stating that "I never injected Roger Clemens or anyone else with lidocaine. . . ."

Dr. Ronald Taylor, the team doctor, was asked in his interview: "Does it make sense to you that an athletic trainer like Mr. McNamee would have been performing lidocaine injections for lower back pain?" He responded: "No, definitely not, it does not make sense." He further stated: "It doesn't make sense to me because it borders on—well, it's malpractice." According to Dr. Taylor, because "[y]ou're dealing with nerves there in the spinal cord," it would have been "very dangerous" for Mr. McNamee to perform this procedure. Because of the risks and complications involved with injecting lidocaine in the lower back, Dr. Taylor stated that he would not perform the procedure himself, but would refer such a case to an orthopedic specialist. He also said that no one on the training staff was allowed to give players any injections.

Tommy Craig, the Blue Jays head medical trainer, told the Committee that he was "baffled" when he heard the claim that Mr. McNamee gave Mr. Clemens a lidocaine injection because "there is an array of things that could go wrong" and "[i]t doesn't make any sense." Scott Shannon, the Blue Jays assistant trainer, told the Committee that lidocaine "was something that the doctors always took care of" and "it was never anything that a trainer would go near."

Committee staff reviewed Mr. Clemens's medical records from the Blue Jays, and there was no evidence that he ever received a lidocaine injection. Dr. Taylor told the

Committee that he was not aware of Mr. Clemens receiving any lidocaine injections, and Mr. Craig and Mr. Shannon agreed. Mr. Clemens did receive a lidocaine injection in his lower back on October 26, 2005, when he was playing for the Houston Astros. The circumstances of that injection contrast markedly with the injection that Mr. Clemens says Mr. McNamee gave him in the Blue Jays weight room in July 1998. When Mr. Clemens received his October 2005 injection, he was under anesthesia, and the injection was administered by a specialist using X-ray fluoroscopy....

III. MR. CLEMENS'S TESTIMONY THAT
TEAM TRAINERS GAVE HIM PAIN INJECTIONS

In his deposition with Committee staff, Mr. Clemens stated that "all trainers have given me shots." He specifically indicated that trainers from all four of his Major League teams—the Red Sox, Blue Jays, Yankees, and Astros—provided him with pain injections ....

These statements by Mr. Clemens are contradicted by numerous team trainers and medical officials. The Committee staff conducted interviews of both medical trainers with the Toronto Blue Jays, Tommy Craig and Scott Shannon. Each stated that they never gave Mr. Clemens a single injection, and that it was team policy that only doctors could give injections. Mr. Craig said that this was something that every player should have known, because it "would be just common sense."

Both of Mr. Clemens's trainers with the Astros, Dave LaBossiere and Rex Jones, also denied ever giving Mr. Clemens an injection. Mr. LaBossiere stated that he gave an injection to only one person in the last five years and "[i]t's not Mr. Clemens."

Committee staff also interviewed Dr. Arthur Pappas, the Medical Director of the Red Sox during Mr. Clemens's time with the team. He stated that it was against team policy for trainers to provide injections, and that "[t]rainers did nothing with needles."

The one exception among Mr. Clemens's four teams was the Yankees, who did allow trainers to provide injections. In a transcribed interview with the Committee, Mr. Eugene Monahan, the team's head trainer during Mr. Clemens's tenure with the team, indicated that he had provided Mr. Clemens with one injection. This injection contained "a light dose of Toradol," a pain medication....

V. MR. CLEMENS'S TESTIMONY THAT HE
NEVER DISCUSSED HGH WITH MR. McNAMEE

In his deposition, Mr. Clemens was asked repeatedly whether he had spoken with Mr. McNamee about human growth hormone. He denied talking with Mr. McNamee about HGH ...

Mr. Clemens was also asked: "Do you recall a specific instance where you did speak with Mr. McNamee about HGH?" He answered:

I don't remember. The only thing I remember about the topic was, there was an article or show about some elderly men ... one guy ... had a curve in his spine

... and then later on in the show he was able to play golf. . . . [T]hat's basically ... the conversation that we had.

These answers were not truthful. Near the end of the deposition, Mr. Clemens was asked whether any family member had used HGH. He said that Mr. McNamee had injected Mr. Clemens's wife, Debbie Clemens, with HGH in 2003 without Mr. Clemens's knowledge. According to Mr. Clemens, his wife had an adverse reaction to the HGH. Mr. Clemens told the Committee in his deposition: "I was not present at the time. I found out later that evening. And the reason I found out . . . she was telling me that something was going on with her circulation, and this concerned me." At the hearing, Mr. Clemens testified that after the injection, Mrs. Clemens also experienced "itching and she had some type of circulation problem."

Mr. Clemens told the Committee that after he learned of his wife's adverse reaction, he had two specific conversations with Mr. McNamee about HGH. The first conversation happened the night Mrs. Clemens was injected. Mr. Clemens said: "We had a pretty heated discussion about it, that I don't know enough about it, and that we don't know enough about it."

The second conversation occurred the next day. In his deposition, Mr. Clemens testified: "I also called him the next day, because she was still not feeling comfortable . . . something about her circulation . . . I wasn't happy about it. I said . . . we don't know anything about this. He says it's legal. There's no laws against it." Mr. Clemens told the Committee that he also searched Mr. McNamee's luggage, which Mr. McNamee had stored at his home, for evidence of HGH. . . .

Mr. Clemens testified that he had no conversations with Mr. McNamee about HGH in the same proceeding in which he later described two specific conversations with Mr. McNamee. As a legal matter, this may affect whether the statements meet the legal definition of perjury or false statement. They are evidence, however, that Mr. Clemens affirmatively sought to mislead the Committee. If the Committee staff had not asked Mr. Clemens whether a family member had used HGH, the Committee would never have known about Mr. Clemens's conversations with Mr. McNamee.

Another aspect of Mr. Clemens's account seems implausible. At the hearing, Mr. Clemens testified that he never called the doctor after his wife began to suffer adverse reactions from the HGH injection. In his deposition, he also testified that he "never researched" HGH and said, "I couldn't tell you the first thing about it." Most individuals in Mr. Clemens's position would have reacted differently. It is unusual that Mr. Clemens neither called the doctor nor investigated the effects of HGH after learning that his wife was experiencing circulation and other problems from the injection.

In his deposition to the Committee, Mr. McNamee confirmed that he gave Mrs. Clemens an HGH injection in 2004 but gave a different account of the circumstances. According to Mr. McNamee, Mr. Clemens asked Mr. McNamee to inject Mrs. Clemens with HGH because "he said his wife wanted to do it. He had it and he wanted me to teach her how to do it. . . ."

VII. MR. CLEMENS'S TESTIMONY THAT HE WAS "NEVER TOLD" ABOUT SENATOR MITCHELL'S REQUEST

When Mr. Clemens appeared on *60 Minutes* on January 6, 2008, he was asked the following question by Mike Wallace: "Why didn't you speak to George Mitchell's investigators?" In response, Mr. Clemens stated: "I listened to my counsel. I was advised not to. A lot of the players didn't go down and talk to him."

In his deposition before the Committee, Mr. Clemens gave a different and contradictory explanation, stating at least six times under oath that he had no idea that Senator Mitchell was seeking to interview him. For example, during his deposition, Mr. Clemens was asked: "[W]ere you aware that Senator Mitchell was seeking to interview you?" He answered: "I was not."

Mr. Clemens gave the same testimony at the Committee's hearing on February 13, 2008, stating: [T]he fact of the matter was I was never told by my baseball agent/attorney that we were asked to come down and see Senator Mitchell" and "I was never told by my baseball agent or the Players Association that Mr. Mitchell requested to see me. Those letters or phone calls never came to me."

Mr. Clemens was also asked the following question at the hearing: "[W]ould you say then that your agents did you a terrible disservice by not bringing this information to you that you had an opportunity to talk before the report came out?" Mr. Clemens answered: "I would say so." According to Mr. Clemens, however, he did not terminate his relationship with his agents or take other steps to reprimand them.

Charles Scheeler, who served as the lead counsel for Senator Mitchell's investigation, testified that Mr. Clemens did receive notice and declined to speak with Senator Mitchell:

> [I]n the summer of 2007, Senator Mitchell sent a letter to the Major League Baseball Players Association in which he requested the interviews of Roger Clemens and a number of others and in which Senator Mitchell stated that we had evidence that Mr. Clemens had used performance enhancing substances . . . during the period of 1998 through 2001. We received a letter back on August 8, 2007, from the players association in which they stated, the following players have asked us to inform you that they respectfully decline your request for an interview at this time. Roger Clemens and several others. . . . Senator Mitchell sent another letter to the players association on October 22 in which he stated, to be clear, I have been and remain willing to meet with any player about whom allegations of performance enhancing substance use has been made in order to provide those players with an opportunity to respond to those allegations. . . . Five weeks later Senator Mitchell received another letter from the players association, indicating that the players . . . continue to respectfully decline your request.

Andy Pettitte, who has the same agent as Mr. Clemens, Randy Hendricks, indicated in his deposition with the Committee that he had been informed by Mr. Hendricks that Senator Mitchell wished to interview him regarding allegations of Mr. Pettitte's use of human growth hormone.

The evidence before the Committee does not establish conclusively that Mr. Clemens received notice of Senator Mitchell's inquiry. It seems unlikely, however, that on a matter as significant as Senator Mitchell's inquiry, Mr. Clemens's agents would have declined Senator Mitchell's request to meet with Mr. Clemens without conferring with Mr. Clemens.

Bibliographic Essay

The compilation of documentary histories has changed dramatically since the publication of my previous book, *Late Innings*, in 2002. For that book I depended almost entirely on visits to archives and research libraries, and on my ever-growing book collection. I only utilized the Internet to double-check statistical information. Increasingly, however, historical newspapers are becoming available online, and important documents such as congressional testimony and Basic Agreements are being distributed primarily if not exclusively through the Internet. Fortunately, valuable books on baseball are still being published, and future documentarians will have an abundance of sources, both print and electronic, to consult.

The most recent general history of baseball is George Vescey, *Baseball: A History of America's Favorite Game* (New York: Modern Library, 2006), which briefly summarizes this rich subject. Benjamin G. Rader, *Baseball: A History of America's Game*, 2nd ed. (Urbana: University of Illinois Press, 2002), is an able accounting of baseball history by a leading sports historian. Jules Tygiel, another prominent sports historian, addresses many intriguing issues in his essay collection *Past Time: Baseball as History* (New York: Oxford University Press, 2000). Veteran sportswriter Leonard Koppett, in *Koppett's Concise History of Major League Baseball* (Philadelphia: Temple University Press, 1998), offers a unique perspective on his favorite sport. Another choice is John Rossi, *The National Game: Baseball and American Culture* (Chicago: Ivan R. Dee, 2000). Noted baseball biographer Charles Alexander, *Our Game: An American Baseball History* (New York: Henry Holt, 1991), is succinct but still worthwhile. Those seeking wonderful pictures accompanying historical text can choose from Geoffrey C. Ward and Ken Burns, *Baseball: An Illustrated History* (New York: Knopf, 1994); Daniel Okrent and Harris Lewine, eds., *The Ultimate Baseball Book* (Boston: Houghton Mifflin, 1979); or Lawrence Ritter and Donald Honig, *The Image of Their Greatness: An Illustrated History of Baseball from 1900 to the Present* (New York: Crown, 1979). One of baseball's foremost historians, David Voigt, concluded his multipart history of baseball with *American Baseball: From Postwar Expansion to the Electronic Age* (University Park: Pennsylvania State University Press, 1983). Finally, an extraordinary two-volume collection from Peter Morris, *A Game of Inches: The Stories Behind the Innovations That Shaped Baseball: The Game on the Field* (Chicago: Ivan R. Dee, 2006) and *A Game of Inches: The Stories Behind the Innovations That Shaped Baseball: The Game Behind the Scenes* (Chicago: Ivan R. Dee, 2006), focuses on baseball's earliest history but also offers valuable information on more recent events.

One of the most prevalent formats for baseball books is the seasonal study, an intense focus on one particular season or era, often on one club. Tom Adelman, *The Long Ball: The Summer of '75—Spaceman, Catfish, Charlie Hustle, and the Greatest World Series Ever Played* (New York: Little Brown and Co., 2003), is one of several books chronicling that memorable season. Jonathan Mahler, in *Ladies and Gentlemen, The Bronx Is Burning: 1977, Baseball,*

Politics, and the Battle for the Soul of a City (New York: Farrar, Straus and Girioux, 2005), integrates baseball into a study of New York City. Legendary New York–based sportswriter Roger Kahn examines one of baseball's most outlandish teams in *October Men: Reggie Jackson, George Steinbrenner, Billy Martin, and the Yankees' Miraculous Finish in 1978* (New York: Harvest, 2004). Two other biographies of Steinbrenner are Dick Schaap, *Steinbrenner!* (New York: G. P. Putnam's Sons, 1982); and Maury Allen, *All Roads Lead to October: Boss Steinbrenner's 25-Year Reign Over the New York Yankees* (New York: St. Martin's Press, 2000). As prelude to these books I recommend Philip Baste, *Dog Days: The New York Yankees' Fall from Grace and Return to Glory, 1964–1976* (New York: Random House, 1994); and Phil Pepe, *Talkin' Baseball: An Oral History of Baseball in the 1970s* (New York: Ballantine Books, 1998).

The period between the mid-1970s and mid-1980s are described by one of baseball's best journalists, Peter Gammons, in *Beyond the Sixth Game: What's Happened to Baseball Since the Greatest Game in World Series History* (Boston: Houghton Mifflin, 1985). The tumultuous 1986 season was encapsulated in two books, Mike Sowell, *One Pitch Away: The Players' Stories of the 1986 League Championships and World Series* (New York: Macmillan, 1995); and Jeff Pearlman, *The Bad Guys Won! A Season of Brawling, Boozing, Bimbo Chasing, and Championship Baseball with Straw, Doc, Mookie, Nails, The Kid, and the Rest of the 1986 Mets, The Rowdiest Team Ever to Put on a New York Uniform, and Maybe the Best* (New York: HarperCollins, 2004). The aftermath of the Mets' one shining season is covered by Bob Klapisch and John Harper, *The Worst Team Money Could Buy: The Collapse of the New York Mets* (New York: Random House, 1993). Political columnist and celebrated baseball fan George F. Will turned his eye on four notable 1980s baseball figures—Cal Ripken Jr., Tony Gwynn, Tony LaRussa, and Orel Hershiser—in *Men at Work: The Craft of Baseball* (New York: Macmillan, 1990).

Two of baseball's best writers, Roger Angell and Thomas Boswell, each published several collections of their erudite baseball writings in the 1970s and 1980s. Angell assembled his best baseball writings from the *New Yorker* in *Five Seasons: A Baseball Companion* (New York: Popular Library, 1978); *Late Innings: A Baseball Companion* (New York: Simon and Schuster, 1982); and *Season Ticket: A Baseball Companion* (Boston: Houghton Mifflin, 1988). His writings were also anthologized in *Once More Around the Park: A Baseball Reader* (New York: Ballantine Books, 1991) and *Game Time: A Baseball Companion* (Orlando FL: Harcourt, 2003). Boswell's columns from the *Washington Post* appeared in *How Life Imitates the World Series* (New York: Penguin, 1982); *Why Time Begins on Opening Day* (Garden City NY: Doubleday, 1984); *The Heart of the Order* (New York: Doubleday, 1984); and *Cracking the Order* (New York: Doubleday, 1989). Other top baseball writers of this era also published anthologies of their best work. These include Dave Kindred, *Glove Stories: The Collected Baseball Writings of Dave Kindred* (St. Louis: Sporting News, 2002); and Bill Conlin, *Batting Cleanup: Bill Conlin, ed. Kevin Kerrane* (Philadelphia: Temple University Press), 1997.

The most influential writer of the period is unquestionably Bill James. After working for several years to develop statistical methods to answer his questions about how baseball was played, his first *Bill James Baseball Abstract* was published in 1982 (New York: Ballantine, 1982–88), earning him a growing audience among fans (though not baseball executives). He resumed his seasonal analyses with *The Baseball Book* (New York: Villard, 1990–92) and *The Bill James Player Rating Book* (New York: Collier, 1993–94; New York: Fireside, 1995). James also participated in annual books published by STATS, a baseball statistical publishing company he cofounded. Perhaps the most interesting of these was the STATS *Major League Handbook 1995* (Skokie IL: STATS, 1995), which included James's projections of an imaginary 162-game

1994 season (abbreviated to 144 games due to owner/labor strife). James (with John Dewan, Neil Munro, and Don Zminda) issued a massive two-volume baseball encyclopedia based on sabermetric statistics, the best of which was *Bill James Presents* STATS *Inc. All-Time Baseball Sourcebook* (Skokie IL: STATS, 1998).

Bill James was much more than a number-cruncher. He clearly explained the thought process behind his formulas and was perfectly capable of writing persuasively without statistics, as his essay collection *This Time Let's Not Eat the Bones: Bill James Without the Numbers* (New York: Villard, 1989) demonstrates. More often he expertly mixed statistics with historical analysis, as in *The Bill James Guide to Baseball Managers: From 1870 to Today* (New York: Scribner, 1997); *The Politics of Glory: How Baseball's Hall of Fame Really Works* (New York: Macmillan, 1994); and the reissued *The New Bill James Historical Baseball Abstract* (New York: Free Press, 2001). Throughout this period James and his colleague Jim Henzler were perfecting a new statistical measure to rate and rank baseball players, which they released in the influential book *Win Shares* (Morton Grove IL: STATS, 2002). James's career is analyzed by Scott Gray in *The Mind of Bill James: How a Complete Outsider Changed Baseball* (New York: Doubleday, 2006); and by Gregory F. Augustine Pierce, ed., *How Bill James Changed Our View of Baseball* (Skokie IL: Acta Sports, 2007).

The revival of the New York Yankees in the mid-1990s, in particular their extraordinary 1998 season, inspired a number of baseball books. Joel Sherman, *Birth of a Dynasty: Behind the Pinstripes with the 1996 Yankees* (New York: Rodale, 2006), explains how the rebirth took place. The story was continued in Buster Olney, *The Last Night of the Yankee Dynasty: The Game, the Team, and the Cost of Greatness* (New York: HarperCollins, 2004). Dean Chadwick takes a much more cynical look at the Yankees in *Those Damn Yankees: The Secret Life of America's Greatest Franchise* (New York: Verso, 1999). The historic 1998 season, dominated by the Yankees, generated a number of celebratory books, the best known of which were by sportswriter Mike Lupica, *Summer of '98: When Homers Flew, Records Fell, and Baseball Reclaimed America* (New York: G. P. Putnam's Sons, 1999); and by sportscaster Tim McCarver with Danny Peary, *The Perfect Season: Why 1998 Was Baseball's Greatest Year* (New York: Villard, 1999). Former star and current broadcaster Joe Morgan (with Richard Lally) made suggestions for continuing baseball's success in *Long Balls, No Strikes: What Baseball Must Do to Keep the Good Times Rolling* (New York: Crown, 1999). Between 1996 and 2001 the Yankees only failed to win the American League pennant once, and the surprising World Series triumph of the Florida Marlins in 1997 is chronicled by Dave Rosenbaum, *If They Don't Win It's a Shame: The Year the Marlins Bought the World Series* (Tampa: McGregor, 1998). In 2004 New York was finally beaten by their old rivals, the Boston Red Sox, who staged an unforgettable comeback in the ALCS and proceeded to win their first World Series since 1918. Their wild ride to the top was best captured by Dan Shaughnessy, both in *Reversing the Curse: Inside the 2004 Boston Red Sox* (Boston: Houghton Mifflin, 2005), and in an updated version of *The Curse of the Bambino* (New York: Penguin, 2004).

One of the defining characteristics of the modern era of baseball is the ascendancy of the MLBPA, led by Marvin Miller, and its subsequent battles with the baseball establishment. Miller forcefully expresses his interpretation of the baseball wars in *A Whole Different Ball Game: The Sport and Business of Baseball* (New York: Birch Lane Press, 1991). Miller's papers, an invaluable source for baseball historians, are maintained at the Robert F. Wagner Labor Archives, Taminent Library, at New York University. Miller's opponent for much of his career was Bowie Kuhn, who defended his reign as commissioner in *Hardball: The Education of a Baseball Commissioner* (1987; reprint, Lincoln: University of Nebraska Press, 1997). Howard Cosell (with Peter Bonventre) offers a strong endorsement of Kuhn in a chapter of *I Never Played the Game* (New York: William Morrow, 1985). The best treatment of the labor conflicts of the 1970s is Charles P. Korr, *The End of Baseball as We Knew It: The Players' Union, 1960–81* (Urbana: University of Illinois Press, 2002).

Although Bart Giamatti was a prolific writer, he died before having the opportunity to apply his elegant prose to his term in office. Books that examine the most important event in Giamatti's career include James Reston Jr., *Collision at Home Plate: The Lives of Pete Rose and Bart Giamatti* (New York: HarperCollins, 1991); and Michael Y. Sokolove, *Hustle: The Myth, Life and Lies of Pete Rose* (New York: Simon and Schuster, 1990). Perhaps the best testament to his legacy is John M. Dowd's *Report to the Commissioner: In the Matter of Peter Edward Rose, Manager, Cincinnati Reds Baseball Club*, which is available on Dowd's own Web site (http://dowdreport.com) as well as on www.bizofbaseball.com. The only other commissioner to write a book on his experience in baseball is Fay Vincent, who alternates analysis with commentary on the game in *The Last Commissioner: A Baseball Valentine* (New York: Simon and Schuster, 2002). Howard Cosell, a fan of Bowie Kuhn, did not approve of Vincent's actions in the George Steinbrenner/Howard Spira case, as he (with Shelby Whitfield) makes clear in *What's Wrong with Sports* (New York: Simon and Schuster, 1991).

After Vincent was forced from office, he was replaced by Milwaukee Brewers owner Bud Selig. Selig's actions as commissioner were attacked in the online columns of the late Doug Pappas, which can be found at www.roadsidephotos.com. Economist Andrew Zimbalist examines Selig's impact in *In the Best Interests of Baseball: The Revolutionary Reign of Bud Selig* (Hoboken NJ: Wiley, 2006). Throughout the 1990s Selig maintained that baseball was in serious financial trouble due to the competitive imbalance in baseball resulting, in large part, from free agency. He formed a commission to study and confirm this belief, and this report—Richard C. Levin, George J. Mitchell, Paul A. Volcker, and George F. Will, *The Report of the Independent Members of the Commissioner's Blue Ribbon Panel on Baseball Economics, July 2000* (available at www.mlb.com)—achieved this goal. The report was widely criticized, including by Michael K. Ozanian and Kurt Badenhausen, "Baseball Going Broke? Don't Believe It," *Wall Street Journal*, July 27, 2000. Selig's claim that competitive imbalance was at an all-time high in the 1990s is rejected by Robert Cull in *Rumors of Baseball's Demise: How the Balance of Competition Swung and the Critics Missed* (Jefferson NC: McFarland, 2006). For a study of all of baseball's commissioners, see Larry Moffi, *The Conscience of the Game: Baseball's Commissioners from Landis to Selig* (Lincoln: University of Nebraska Press, 2006).

As baseball fans became increasingly confronted by economic and labor issues they had previously not concerned themselves with, their representatives in Congress were quick to hold hearings on these subjects. Controversies over television contracts with baseball were aired in House of Representatives, Hearings Before the Subcommittee on Communications of the Committee on Interstate and Foreign Commerce, *Sports Broadcasting Act of 1975*, 94th Cong., 1st sess., October 31, 1975; and Senate Subcommittee on Antitrust, Monopolies and Business Rights, *Sports Programming and Cable Television*, 101st Cong., 1st sess., 1989. The extended battle between the MLBPA and the owners that culminated in the cancellation of the 1994 World Series generated numerous hearings in which union leader Donald Fehr and Commissioner Selig often faced off against each other and skeptical congressmen. These include Senate Subcommittee on Antitrust, Monopolies and Business Rights, *The Validity of Major League Baseball's Exception from the Antitrust Laws*, 102nd Cong., 2nd sess., December

10, 1992; Senate Subcommittee on Antitrust, Monopolies and Business Rights, *Profession-al Baseball Teams and the Antitrust Laws*, 103rd Cong., 2nd sess., March 21, 1994, St. Peters-burg FL; Senate Subcommittee on Antitrust, Business Rights and Competition, *The Court-Imposed Major League Baseball Antitrust Exemption*, 104th Cong., 1st sess., February 15, 1995; and Senate Committee on the Judiciary, *Major League Baseball Antitrust Reform*, 105th Cong., 1st sess., 1997.

Many books have been written on the economics of baseball. The most noted of these is Michael Lewis, *Moneyball: The Art of Winning an Unfair Game* (New York: W. W. Norton, 2003), which explained the statistical basis behind the decisions of Oakland A's general man-ager Billy Beane. Other books on the economic and business practices on particular teams include Henry D. Fetter, *Taking On the Yankees: Winning and Losing in the Business of Base-ball, 1903–2003* (New York: W. W. Norton, 2003); and Seth Mnookin's look behind the suc-cess of the Boston Red Sox, *Feeding the Monster: How Money, Smarts, and Nerve Took a Team to the Top* (New York: Simon and Schuster, 2006). Other books have addressed the phenom-enon of new stadiums and expansion teams. Among the best of these are David Whitford, *Playing Hardball: The High-Stakes Battle for Baseball's New Franchises* (New York: Double-day, 1993); Peter Richmond, *Ballpark: Camden Yards and the Building of an American Dream* (New York: Simon and Schuster, 1993); Thom Loverro, *Home of the Game: The Story of Cam-den Yards* (Dallas: Taylor, 1999); Bob Andelman, *Stadium for Rent: Tampa Bay's Quest for Ma-jor League Baseball* (Jefferson NC: McFarland, 1993); and Barry Svrluga, *National Pastime: Sports, Politics, and the Return of Baseball to Washington, D.C.* (New York: Doubleday, 2006). A Web site that collects significant documents and other statistical information on baseball business and economics is www.bizofbaseball.com.

Ever since the publication of Jim Bouton's *Ball Four* in 1970, fans have been generally aware that baseball players took drugs of various kinds. The concept of performance-enhancing drugs (PEDs) was not addressed until the late 1980s, when rumors of steroid use surrounded Oak-land A's star Jose Canseco. It took another decade before the revelation that one of Canseco's former teammates, Mark McGwire, used a PED called androstenedione during his record-setting 1998 season, alerted the public that baseball might have a serious problem. Canseco's controversial book *Juiced: Wild Times, Rampant 'Roids, Smash Hits, and How Baseball Got Big* (New York: HarperCollins, 2005), loud and brash as it was, shed much light on the subject. A more serious account can be found in Howard Bryant, *Juicing the Game: Drugs, Power, and the Fight for the Soul of Major League Baseball* (New York: Viking, 2005).

In the mid-2000s a pair of *San Francisco Chronicle* reporters, Mark Fainaru-Wada and Lance Williams, started investigating a local company, BALCO, which had been found to be actively involved in the production and distribution of PEDs to elite athletes. Their articles can be accessed at www.sfgate.com. In their influential book *Game of Shadows: Barry Bonds, BALCO, and the Steroids Scandal That Rocked Professional Sports* (New York: Gotham Books, 2006), they summarize their devastating case against the game's top slugger. Bonds's volatile personality is exposed in Jeff Pearlman, *Love Me, Hate Me: Barry Bonds and the Making of an Antihero* (New York: HarperCollins, 2006). Investigative efforts such as these inspired Con-gress to hold hearings in 2005 in which they threatened both Commissioner Selig and MLBPA executive director Don Fehr to make a serious effort to eliminate PEDs from baseball. Docu-ments from these hearings can be found at http://reform.house.gov. This pressure drove Se-lig to appoint former U.S. Senator George J. Mitchell to conduct an investigation into the is-sue. His findings were released in *Report to the Commissioner of Baseball of an Independent*

Investigation into the Illegal Use of Steroids and Other Performance Enhancing Substances by Players in Major League Baseball, December 13, 2007, which can be found at www.mlb.com.

Racism is a more prevalent problem than drugs. Advances, like the hiring of Frank Robinson as the first African American manager, were countered with racist comments a decade later on national television by Al Campanis. Two excellent books that deal with the specter of race in major league organizations are Cecil Harris, *Call the Yankees My Daddy: Reflections on Baseball, Race, and Family* (Guilford CT: The Lyons Press, 2006); and Howard Bryant's superb *Shut Out: A Story of Race and Baseball in Boston* (New York: Routledge, 2002). Other authors have started to examine the impact of the rapidly growing number of Hispanic major leaguers and the prejudice they still face. The best history of Hispanics in baseball remains Samuel O. Regalado, *Viva Baseball! Latin Major Leaguers and Their Special Hunger* (Urbana: University of Illinois Press, 1998). Other histories include Tim Wendel, *The New Face of Baseball: The One-Hundred-Year Rise and Triumph of Latinos in America's Favorite Sport* (New York: HarperCollins, 2003); and Adrian Burgos Jr., *Playing America's Game: Baseball, Latinos, and the Color Line* (Berkeley: University of California Press, 2007). Also of interest are John Krich, *El Beisbol: Travels Through the Pan-American Pastime* (New York: Atlantic Monthly Press, 1989); and Marcos Breton and Jose Luis Villegas, *Away Games: The Life and Times of a Latin Player* (New York: Simon and Schuster, 1999).

The lifeblood of baseball is statistics. Aside from the works of Bill James, other writers and publishers have contributed to increasing our understanding of baseball through numbers. The foremost encyclopedia of baseball, edited by John Thorn, Phil Birnbaum, and Bill Deane, remains *Total Baseball: The Ultimate Baseball Encyclopedia,* 8th ed. (Wilmington DE: Sport Classic Books, 2004). Filling the void until the next edition of *Total Baseball* is Gary Gillette and Pete Palmer, eds., *The ESPN Baseball Encyclopedia,* 5th ed. (New York: Sterling, 2008). Print encyclopedias have been supplemented (hopefully not replaced) by Web sites. The best source for tracing the game-by-game records of almost any team is www.retrosheet.org, which has become an invaluable resource for fans and baseball writers alike. Outstanding sites for player statistics are www.baseball1.com and www.baseball-reference.com.

James's *Abstracts* were not the only annual statistical examinations of baseball. Baseball's official statisticians, the Elias Sports Bureau, led by Seymour Siwoff and Steve, Tom, and Peter Hirdt, started publishing their *Elias Baseball Analyst* (New York: Collier Books, 1985–89; New York: Fireside, 1991–93), which, as James acidly noted, were pale copies of his own books. Much better are the annual *Baseball Prospectus* volumes (New York: Workman, 2004–6; New York: Plume Books, 2007–8). *Prospectus* editor Jonah Keri also led a team writing *Baseball Between the Numbers: Why Everything You Know About the Game Is Wrong* (New York: Basic Books, 2006), in which they reach out beyond hard-core statisticians to the average fan. Rob Neyer, a former employee of James, has written several entertaining books using statistics to explain baseball, including (with Eddie Epstein) *Baseball Dynasties: The Greatest Teams of All Time* (New York: W. W. Norton, 2000) and *Rob Neyer's Big Book of Baseball Blunders: A Complete Guide to the Worst Decisions and Stupidest Moments in Baseball History* (New York: Fireside, 2006). David Vincent, in *Home Run: The Definitive History of Baseball's Ultimate Weapon* (Washington DC: Potomac Books, 2007), uses statistics not only to chronicle baseball history but also to bolster his contention that PEDs were not responsible for the explosion of home runs in the 1990s. His views echo those of Russell Wright in *Crossing the Plate: The Upswing in Runs Scored by Major League Teams, 1993–1997* (Jefferson NC: McFarland, 1998). The best history of the development of baseball statistics is Alan Schwartz, *The Numbers Game: Baseball's Lifelong Fascination with Statistics* (New York: St. Martin's Press, 2004).

Statistics can only say so much about the greatest players and officials. Skilled biographers can fill that void. Some of the best works on the stars of the 1970s include David Maraniss, *Clemente: The Passion and Grace of Baseball's Last Hero* (New York: Simon and Schuster, 2006); and Tom Stanton, *Hank Aaron and the Home Run That Changed America* (New York: HarperCollins, 2004). The lives of the two most explosive New York Yankees are unveiled in Dick Schaap, *Steinbrenner!* (New York: G. P. Putnam's Sons, 1982); Maury Allen, *All Roads Lead to October: Boss Steinbrenner's 25-Year Reign Over the New York Yankees* (New York: St. Martin's Press, 2000); and Peter Golenbock, *Wild, High and Tight: The Life and Death of Billy Martin* (New York: St. Martin's Press, 1994). Perhaps the best book on a current baseball personality is Buzz Bissinger, *3 Nights in August: Strategy, Heartbreak, and Joy Inside the Mind of a Manager* (Boston: Houghton Mifflin, 2005), which closely examines the mind of Tony La Russa. Books that collect information on many players include Bob McCullough, ed., *My Greatest Day in Baseball 1946–1997: Baseball's Legends Recount Their Epic Moments* (Dallas: Taylor, 1998); and David Pietrusza, Matthew Silverman, and Michael Gershman, eds., *Baseball: The Biographical Encyclopedia* (New York: Total/Sports Illustrated, 2000).

Acknowledgments

1. THE PLAYERS DISCOVER THEIR FREEDOM

1. "Marvin J. Miller, Lawyer for Association of Professional Ball Players of America at Littnaur Center, Harvard University, April 27, 1972," Marvin Miller Papers, Robert F. Wagner Archives, Tamiment Library, New York University.

2. "Letter from Marvin J. Miller to E. J. 'Buzzie' Bavasi," Marvin Miller Papers, Robert F. Wagner Archives, Tamiment Library, New York University.

3. "The Scoreboard: Pirates Go Out with Their Heads High," Copyright *Pittsburgh Post Gazette*, 2005, all rights reserved. Reprinted with permission.

4. "Joe Rudi's Moment in the Sun," Wells Twombly/*San Francisco Examiner*.

5. "CBS Sells Yanks to Burke, 11 Others: Group Pays $10 Million—MacPhail, Houk Stay," *New York Daily News* L.P., reprinted with permission.

6. "Explanation of Designated Hitter Rule as Adopted by the American League for the 1973 Championship Season," National Baseball Hall of Fame, Cooperstown NY.

7. "Article V—Salaries," Peter Seitz Papers, Kheel Center for Labor Management Documentation and Archives, Cornell University.

8. "Harris Survey: 3 Strikes but Still in Game," National Baseball Hall of Fame, Cooperstown NY.

9. "'Andrews On (Finley's) Disabled List,'" *San Jose Mercury News*.

10. "Footnotes to Baseball Salary Arbitration," Peter Seitz Papers, Kheel Center for Labor Management Documentation and Archives, Cornell University.

11. "Stadium Beer Night Fans Riot; Ending Indians' Rally in Forfeit," © 1974 *The Plain Dealer*. All rights reserved. Reprinted with permission.

12. "Hal Asks . . .: Robbie . . . His Time Has Come," © 1974 *The Plain Dealer*. All rights reserved. Reprinted with permission.

13. "Statement from MLBPA," Peter Seitz Papers, Kheel Center for Labor Management Documentation and Archives, Cornell University.

2. THE SEITZ ERA

14. "Department of State telegram from Assistant Secretary of State William D. Rogers," February 15, 1975, Freedom of Information Act Request No. 199903253.

15. "Commemoration Planned of Baseball's 1-Millionth Run," Congressional record.

16. "Joe Garagiola/Bazooka BIG LEAGUE BUBBLE GUM BLOWING CHAMPIONSHIP," National Baseball Hall of Fame Library, Cooperstown NY, and Old Time Candy Company.

17. "Gullett to Face Sox' Lee: Fisk's Homer Beats Reds in 12th; Finale Tonight," Bob Hertzel/*Cincinatti Enquirer*.

18. "Hearings Before the Subcommittee on Communications of the Committee on Interstate

and Foreign Commerce, *Sports Broadcasting Act of 1975*," House of Representatives, October 31, 1975.

19. "*NOTICE OF GRIEVANCE*," Marvin Miller Papers, Robert F. Wagner Archives, Tamiment Library, New York University.

20. "Letter from John J. Gaherin to Peter Seitz," Peter Seitz Papers, Kheel Center for Labor Management Documentation and Archives, Cornell University.

21. "Kuhn Opens Doors to Spring Training Camps," Stan Isle/*The Sporting News.*

22. "Letter from Commissioner Bowie Kuhn to Charles O. Finley, George Steinbrenner, and Richard O'Connell," Harold and Dorothy Seymour Papers, #4809, Box 1, Folder 13, division of Rare and Manuscript Collections, Cornell University Library.

23. "Kuhn Describes New Basic Agreement," House Select Committee on Professional Sports.

24. "Press release from the Office of the Commissioner," "Economics—Free Agency 1976" file, National Baseball Hall of Fame, Cooperstown NY.

3. THE DAWN OF FREE AGENCY

25. "Ohio Gal Breaks Somers Ump Barrier," Brad Wilson/*The Sporting News.*

26. "The Sports Collector by Bill Madden: Live, Die with SABR," Bill Madden/*The Sporting News.*

27. "Martin, Reggie Erupt . . . So Do Sox, 10–4," Bob Ryan/*The Boston Globe.*

28. "News release from the National Baseball Hall of Fame Museum," "Hall of Fame" file, National Baseball Hall of Fame Library, Cooperstown NY.

29. "Jax's 3 Homers Rip L.A.: Reggie a Record-Setter in 8–4 Win," © *New York Daily News*, L.P., reprinted with permission.

30. "Yankees Reach the Top: New York Sweeps, 7–4, Ties Red Sox for First," Peter Gammons/*Boston Globe.*

31. "So What? We're Used to Waiting," Leigh Montville/*Boston Globe.*

32. "Letter from Marvin Miller to MLBPA player representatives," Marvin Miller Papers, Robert F. Wagner Archives, Tamiment Library, New York University.

33. "Various press releases from the Player Relations Committee," National Baseball Hall of Fame Library, Cooperstown NY.

34. "Phils Come Up with a Surprise Ending in Wild and Crazy 5–3 Win over Astros: 5th-Game Shootout Tonight," Used with permission of the *Philadelphia Inquirer.* © All rights reserved.

35. "So, What's Kuhn Doing about It?: His Powers Limited, He Still Spends Hours Advising Both Sides in Strike," Peter Gammons/*Boston Globe.*

36. "Tempers Stay Hot Although Strike's Over," © *New York Daily News*, L.P., reprinted with permission.

37. "Baseball's Best Record Gets Reds Armchair Seat," Tim Sullivan/*Cincinnati Enquirer*

38. "Letter from Marvin Miller to A. Bartlett Giamatti," Marvin Miller Papers, Robert F. Wagner Archives, Tamiment Library, New York University.

4. A LULL IN THE STORM

39. "Introduction," Copyright © 1982 Bill James. Used courtesy of Darhansoff, Verrill, Feldman Literary Agents.

40. "Letter from Peter Seitz to Bowie Kuhn," Peter Seitz Papers, Kheel Center for Labor Management Documentation and Archives, Cornell University.

41. "Mick's Dollar and Sense Decision," © *New York Daily News*, L.P., reprinted with permission.

42. "Memorandum from Marvin Miller to MLBPA Executive Board," Marvin Miller Papers, Robert F. Wagner Archives, Tamiment Library, New York University.

43. "Joint Drug Program & Discipline," Marvin Miller Papers, Robert F. Wagner Archives, Tamiment Library, New York University.

44. "Baseball," U.S. Olympic Committee Official Reports.

45. "Letter from Peter Ueberroth to Andrew McKenna," National Baseball Hall of Fame Library, Cooperstown NY.

46. "Strike Ends; Play Resumes Today," Kent Baker/*Baltimore Sun*.

47. "Players Blame Cocaine Addiction on Lonely Road Trips and Money," Copyright *Pittsburgh Post Gazette*, 2005, all rights reserved. Reprinted with permission.

48. "Numbers Don't Tell Full Story," Tim Sullivan/*Cincinnati Enquirer*.

49. "Clemens Fans a Record 20: Sox Pitcher Baffles Mariners, 3–1," Dan Shaughnessy / *Boston Globe*.

50. "Mets Get Off Scott Free: N.Y. Wins in 16 to Sidestep Date with Astros' Ace," Copyright 1986 *Houston Post*. Reprinted with permission. All rights reserved.

51. "Mets Steal Win from Sox, 6–5, in 10th: Error by Buckner Allows Knight to Score Winning Run; Boyd to Pitch 7th," Leigh Montville/*Boston Globe*.

52. "Transcript of *Nightline*, episode #1530," ABCNews.com, *Nightline*. Reprinted with permission.

5. ROSE, GIAMATTI, AND COLLUSION

53. "Major League Baseball Arbitration Panel," Marvin Miller Papers, Robert F. Wagner Archives, Tamiment Library, New York University.

54. "Collusion: Owners Are Batting .000," Murray Chass/*The Sporting News*.

55. "Just Trying to Do 'Best We Can': Gibson, Hershiser Carry Dodgers to Stunning 2–0 Start in World Series," Paul Attner/*The Sporting News*.

56. "No Place Like Dome: Fans Greet SkyDome Opener Warmly," Gary Loewenn/*Toronto Globe and Mail*.

57. "Agreement and Resolution," www.baseball1.com/bb-data/rose/agreement.html.

58. "For Giamatti, It Ended at Head of the Class," Shirley Povich/*Washington Post*.

59. "Vincent's Priorities Are in the Right Place," Art Spander/*The Sporting News*.

60. "Sports Programming and Cable Television," Senate Subcommittee on Antitrust, Monopolies and Business Rights.

61. "Ah, Spring: 4-Year Pact Opens Camps: 17 Pct. Solution on Arbitration Brings End to 32-Day Lockout," Murray Chass/*The Sporting News*.

62. "Owners Guilty of Collusion Once Again," Ken Gurnick/*National Sports Daily*.

63. "Decision of the Commissioner," Marvin Miller Papers, Robert F. Wagner Archives, Tamiment Library, New York University.

64. "On Top of the World: Morris and Larkin Key Another Magic Carpet Ride," Copyright 1991 *Star Tribune*. Republished with permission of *Star Tribune*, Minneapolis MN. No further republication or redistribution is permitted without the consent of *Star Tribune*.

6. SELIG, FEHR, AND THE STRIKE

65. "A Shift in Power: Realignment Has Brought on Big Changes for Fay Vincent and the NL East," Peter Pascarelli/*The Sporting News*.

66. "Selig an Easy Choice, Other Owners Declare: Werner, Bush Praise His Love for the Game, Ability to Mediate Problems," Bob Berghaus/*Milwaukee Journal*.

67. "Baseball Winter Meetings: Owners Reopen Labor Agreement; Lockout Possible," © *The Courier Journal*.

68. "Statement by Former Commissioner Fay Vincent," Senate Subcommittee on Antitrust, Monopolies, and Business Rights.

69. "Baseball: 'Appropriate Remedy and Punishment,'" *Cincinnati Inquirer*.

70. "A Wild, Wacky Ride as Phils Make It Their Kind of Game: Bad Pitching, Lots of Hitting, Unbelievable Statistics," Used with permission of the *Philadelphia Inquirer*. © All rights reserved.

71. "Revenue Deal OK'd by Owners: Selig Calls 28–0 Vote 'Remarkable, Historic,'" Peter Schmuck/*Baltimore Sun*.

72. "Professional Baseball Teams and the Antitrust Laws," Senate Subcommittee on Antitrust, Monopolies and Business Rights.

73. "With Baseball's Last Out, a Strike: Players Walk Off Job After Failing to Agree with Owners," Richard Justice/*Washington Post*.

74. "Baseball as a Metaphor for America: Ken Burns' New Series Goes for a Grand Slam" Diane Holloway/*American Statesman*.

75. "This One's for You, Bud," Dave Kindred/*The Sporting News*.

76. "Potential Solutions to the Alleged Market Failure," Senate Subcommittee on Antitrust, Monopolies, and Business Rights.

77. "Setting the Baseball Record Straight," Senate Subcommittee on Antitrust, Monopolies, and Business Rights.

78. "Order," U.S. District Court, Southern District of New York.

7. BASEBALL STARTS TO HEAL

79. "Baseball Rewrites Its Official Record Book," Stefan Fatsis/*Wall Street Journal*.

80. "Immortal Cal: He Touches Home with Victory Lap," Ken Rosenthal/*Baltimore Sun*.

81. "Players' Ratification Brings Baseball Peace," Larry Whiteside/*Boston Globe*.

82. "Prepared Statement of Donald A. Fehr," Major League Baseball Trust Reform, 105th Congress, 1st session.

83. "Jackets Will Feel Effects of New Agreement in '98," Courtesy of *Augusta Chronicle*.

84. "Loudest Sports Cheer in Years: Hysterical, Historical Win," Edwin Pope/*Miami Herald*.

85. "El Duque Delivers: Dominates Devil Rays in His Debut," Peter Botte/*New York Daily News*, L.P., reprinted with permission.

86. "Lords Elect Selig Commissioner," *New York Daily News*, L.P., reprinted with permission.

87. "McGwire's Power Aided by 'Andro,'" Used with permission of the Associated Press. Copyright 2007. All Rights Reserved.

88. "Jubilation!" Mike Eisenbath/*Post-Dispatch*.

89. "History in Havana," Rick Jervis/Jordan Levin/*Miami Herald*.

90. "Umpires Spurred by Fear of Lockout: McKean: Union's Threat of Sept. 2 Resignation Is Bid 'To Force the Issue,'" Peter Schmuck/*Baltimore Sun.*

8. BASEBALL ENTERS THE TWENTY-FIRST CENTURY

91. "Boycott Is Felt All Over Baseball: Canseco, Duque, Others Take Part," Clark Spencer/*Miami Herald.*

92. "Summary of Findings, Conclusions and Recommendations," The Report of the Independent Members of the Commissioner's Blue Ribbon Panel.

93. "Hall of Fame Board of Directors Restructures Veterans Committee and Its Rules for Election," National Baseball Hall of Fame Library, Cooperstown, NY.

94. "Piazza Is Glad to Contribute: HR Lights Way for New York, New York," *New York Daily News*, L.P., reprinted with permission.

95. "Jeter's Athletic Play Saves Yankees: Backup Relay Flip to Home Plate Catches Giambi," Henry Schulman/*San Francisco Chronicle.*

96. "Gonzo's Hit Caps Comeback," © *Arizona Republic*. November 5, 2001. Mark Gonzales. Used with Permission. Permission does not imply endorsement.

97. "Contraction Follies," Doug Pappas.

98. "73rd All-Star Game: All Knotted Up," Drew Olsen/*Milwaukee Journal Sentinel.*

99. "2003–2006 Basic Agreement," www.roadsidephotos.com.

100. "Sports and Drugs: How the Doping Scandal Unfolded," Mark Fainaru-Wada/Lance Williams/*San Francisco Chronicle.*

101. "Joy Knows No Bounds: Sox Triumph Leads to a Flight of Fancy," Leigh Montville/*Boston Globe.*

102. "Letter from Congressmen Tom Davis and Henry Waxman to Bud Selig and Donald Fehr," http://reform.house.gov.

103. "New King of Swing: Like It or Not, You'll Just Have to Deal with It," Scott Ostler/*San Francisco Chronicle.*

104. "Process of the Investigation," George J. Mitchell, www.mlb.com.

105. "Memorandum from Majority Staff, Committee on Oversight and Government Reform, House of Representatives, to Chairman Henry A. Waxman," http://reform.house.gov.

Index